**Evening Star**

Wine
Guide 1997

ESB

Andrew Jefford

For my parents

First published in Great Britain in 1995 by
Pavilion Books Limited
26 Upper Ground, London SE1 9PD

This fully revised and expanded edition published in 1996 by
EVENING STANDARD BOOKS
Northcliffe House,
2 Derry Street, London W8 5EE

Publishing Manager Joanne Bowlby
Editorial Manager Charlotte Coleman-Smith
Production Manager Roger Hall

Designed by Nick Cave
Typesetting by Sally Blackmore

Illustrations by Clive Goodyer
Index by Isabel McClean

A CIP catalogue record for this book is available from the British Library

ISBN 1 900625 30 X

Printed and bound in Great Britain by Redwood Books Ltd, Trowbridge, Wilts.

This book may be ordered direct from the publisher
but please try your bookshop first.
Corporate editions and personal subscriptions of the *Evening Standard Wine
Guide* are available. Call us for details. Tel: 0171 938 6774.

Also published by Evening Standard Books:
Evening Standard London Restaurant Guide by Fay Maschler
Evening Standard London Pub Guide by Angus McGill

Contents

Acknowledgments

Every word of this guide has been written by the author,
who is therefore responsible for all its errors and omissions;
comments and corrections are gratefully received. The author wishes
to thank all those from whom he has received help and guidance
in the preparation of this guide, particularly Vicky Bishop, Jo Bowlby,
Charlotte Coleman-Smith, Jane Hunt M.W., Wink Lorch,
Lisa McGovern, Sue Prike, Steve Pryer and Stephen Skelton.

Introduction

Foreword

Wine guides, customarily, fall into one of two types. The first type attempts to circumnavigate the entire wine world in a dense and reductive style: such guides leave you theoretically wiser but bereft of ready, practical shopping tips. The second type steers you around what's available in the shops at the moment of publication: such guides are of immense practical value for a short period and useless thereafter. The ideal wine guide, it seems to me, should do both. This is what The Evening Standard Wine Guide attempts to do. Following this Introduction, you will find 'Dispatches' – an aperitif of gingery paragraphs designed to whet the appetite and provide a partisan view of some of the key wine issues in the autumn of 1996. The Eros Wine Pantheon, a collection of Eros Award-winning Wines of the Year, follows.

Chapter Two tells you, simply and succinctly, what wine is, and suggests some of the ways to maximise your enjoyment of it. It contains a guide to the most important grape varieties, and explains some of the terms you'll see on the back labels of wine bottles or used by wine writers.

Chapter Three, the heart of the book, is a country-by-country guide to the wines of the world. The entries in this section, thoroughly updated and revised every year, are designed to provide useful references as you explore the world of wine for yourself; introductions attempt to provide a readable overview of each country's role in our drinking. An innovation for this year is the incorporation of features concerning individual wine producers, adapted from articles originally appearing in the Tuesday wine column in the *Evening Standard.*

Chapter Four begins with a guide to all the merchants, off-licence chains and supermarkets who sell us our wine. Each entry includes a list of wines worth trying; another innovation for this year is the incorporation of scores out of 25 for recommended wines from all of the major retailers. For my view of scores in general, see page 14; readers, however, like scores and find them useful, and the guide-book writer's task is to serve the reader.

Next comes a full descriptive listing of London wine bars, including the Eros Award-winning Wine Bar of the Year, which this year goes to Albertine in Shepherd's Bush. Each wine-bar entry contains a list of suggested wines to try.

Last year, 1995, was an unexpectedly black year for the British wine drinker — a combination of poor harvests in Europe from 1991 onwards, short harvests in parts of the Southern Hemisphere, a weak pound and supermarket price wars meant that the standard of wine in our shops (and particularly our supermarkets) dropped markedly. This year, 1996, has been much better, though looming wine shortages are putting prices under pressure: make the most of what's on offer with this book. If you have any criticisms, suggestions or tips of your own, I'd be delighted to hear from you, and to incorporate them in next year's Guide.

Andrew Jefford, Drink Correspondent,
Evening Standard, Northcliffe House, 2 Derry St, London W8 5EE.

Dispatches

In this section, the author takes an alphabetical tour of the wine world in 1996, looking with an unpeeled eye at issues consequential, inconsequential and frivolous, and climbing on a soap box whenever he gets the chance.

A is for Appellation

Appellations (see page 60) provide the regulatory, organising force in European winemaking. Elsewhere in the world the idea of specifying which varieties should be grown in which soils, how much fruit a vine should produce, what sort of oak-ageing a wine should receive and how it should taste is regarded with amusement or incredulity. Since appellations fail to guarantee quality, they are now generally regarded by British critics as a bureaucratic anachronism, stifling creativity and perpetuating the vices of the past.

Nonsense. At their best (in France, where the system was born) they have succeeded in preserving the essence of wine's beauty: rich regional diversity. They enable individual growers to prosper, and act as a useful check on the dominance by large companies which the fallible free market would otherwise solicit. They fail to guarantee quality because nothing, save the integrity of the individual producer, can ever guarantee quality. The value of an appellation system, albeit more loosely defined than in Europe, is beginning to be recognised around the wine world; appellations are instituted whenever a clear regional style emerges.

And yet ... take a look at Bordeaux in 1996. This, the most classically French of French wine regions, has been undergoing a slow change over the last 15 years towards what can only be described as a kind of `Show Wine' system. Le Pin haunts the proprietors: the rewards for becoming a contemporary Bordeaux superstar are dazzling. Few nowadays aim to make appellation wines; the aim is a wine of maximum impact and individuality. Depth of flavour, suppleness of texture, wealth of fruit, richness of oak: heard this before somewhere? Somewhere like ... Adelaide?

The truth seems to be that appellations are an evolutionary stage through which all wine cultures must pass. A chaos of effort gets the whole process going, then time reveals the range of expression of each locality. Once that is explored and defined through an appellation system, the emphasis then passes back to the individual to, as it were, surpass the soil. See also **Mad Cow, Wine Law.**

A is also for Acid

and Australians – sometimes a dangerous combination. Australia is hot. Hot climates can produce flabby wines. The antidote to flabbiness is acidity, in powdered form, by the bucketful. Yet this technique only succeeds if practised with great subtlety, and subtlety is not necessarily an Australian virtue. I like the Australia's finest wines as much as anyone, yet far too many of Australia's average wines are rendered coarse and crude by an overdose of added acid. The

Australian influence, via the flying winemaker, stretches around the world, and automatic, unthinking acid-adjustment spoils many flying winemakers' wines, too. The tell-tale symptom (for me) that excess acid has been added to a wine is when I begin to sweat lightly under the eyes after half a glass or so. See also **Digestibility**.

A is also for Afterbreath

When you're tasting wine, check your afterbreath: the first exhalation following the swallow. The better the wine, the finer the scents and flavours triggered by the afterbreath. This goes for beer and spirits, too; most of the pleasure I take in Cognac, indeed, is connected with the superbly stony, floral afterbreath it fetches up from my appreciative throat.

A is also for Argentina

which, during 1996, was much discussed as a promising new wine supplier. Its potential impresses everyone, though it is realised very patchily as yet (try the Midweight Red Wine of the Year, page 202, for a taste of the best of Argentina).

B is for Bad Wine

A thing of the past? Not at all. There have been plenty of bad wines swimming about supermarket shelves during 1995 and 1996: poor vintages, a limp pound and the curse of the price point have combined to destructive effect. Don't put up with them: complain, follow trustworthy newspaper recommendations, spend a bit more. The pleasure a good wine can bring is akin to a glimpse of heaven; a bad wine is tawdry tedium. Since it seems to me to be as useful to steer people away from a bad wine as recommend a good wine, I am drawing readers attention to what I consider bad wines in the main Section Four entries in this book. See also **Cheap Wine, Philosophy, Value**.

C is for Cheap Wine

Don't misunderstand me: I'm not against cheap wine as such, nor am I claiming that all cheap wine is bad wine. What is incontrovertibly true is that we pay much less for wine than we once did; and that many of the world's best wines now circumnavigate Britain altogether. Britain is ceasing to be, as it once was, the crossroads of the wine world; instead it is becoming a highly competitive clearing house for wines produced by the economically weak or those at the early stages of building an international reputation. Perhaps, as Britain slowly slips down the world economic ladder, this is inevitable; it is still sad. I am haunted by the possibility that it is also needless — that our bondage to the supermarket ideal has made us more penny-pinching about wine than we need be. The cheap-wine movement has opened up the pleasures of wine to many of those who might not otherwise have tasted them, and that is a great thing; taken to extremes, though, it is a kind of philistinism, narrowing our horizons and stunting our palates. See also **Junk, Supermarket, Uniformity, Value**.

D is for Digestibility

which, I realised during 1996, is a rarely discussed yet critically important quality of wine. Many highly flavoured wines — the kind of wines which win tasting competitions and impress jaded critics' palates — are in fact indigestible; their flavour burns the mouth, pickles the oesophagus, and strafes the stomach. Other wines, wines like the Château Haut-Bailly 1981 I drank as a second bottle at lunch with two friends just before Christmas 1995 at the Tate Gallery Restaurant, slip down as softly and comfortably as mother's milk. Claret, Rioja, some burgundies and some Eastern European wines all show high levels of digestibility; this should be something Chile and Argentina are able to achieve before long, too, provided that their winemakers can learn the lessons, genuinely important, of understatement, delicacy and restraint.

D is also for Deals

You might assume that quality (the best wine at the best price) is the reason why a particular bottle sits on a shop shelf. Perhaps. About half the bottles, say. The rest of the bottles sit on the shop shelf because the deal was right. During the last year I've sat with wine producers and wine agents on two or three nocturnal occasions and heard them unburden themselves, bitterly and feelingly, about the injustices of the deals imposed on them by retailers; often, too, about the impossibility of competing fairly with the large multinational companies and groupings which control so much drink distribution. You can only make a sale, of course, if you're on the shelf in the first place. The retailer might respond by saying (with partial truth only) that he uses the thumbscrews on producers in order to get the best deal for consumers. I'm not sure what the multinational company's argument would be; they might refer to the law of the jungle and the survival of the

fittest. The point in mentioning these things is to draw your attention to the fact that, when you see A's wine in B's supermarket or C's off-licence chain at a bargain price, it is generally B or C who is making a fat profit on it, while A or his agent is financing the deal under duress because he knows that failing to do so might jeopardise his listing. (What he doesn't know is that he's going to lose it next year anyway because the supermarket will find a cheaper source for similar wine.) The higher prices charged by independent retailers may leave you disgruntled, but they often mean a fairer deal for the producer – which in turn is likely to increase the quality of his wine. See also e**X**ploitation.

E is for En Primeur

Buying wine en primeur means buying wine 'pre-arrival', before it has actually been bottled. What is the point? For wines in great demand, this is when they are actually cheapest. Indeed for some wines, it is the only way to purchase them at anything which resembles a reasonable price. By contrast there is no point whatsoever in buying inexpensive wines in this way, since they almost invariably arrive on the market eighteen months later at exactly the same price, and you have given the merchant the interest you would otherwise have earned on your money. The most significant development for en primeur sales during 1996 was that, for certain key 1995 Bordeaux wines (such as L'Eglise-Clinet, Clinet, Angélus, Trotanoy and others), demand outstripped supply hugely. Some wines (Le Pin, Pétrus) are simply unavailable to anyone who doesn't know Someone. In the future, therefore, favoured customers will be faithful customers; Just as the merchant has to justify his allocation from producer or negociant by buying consistently, so customers will have to stick with one merchant and buy regularly in order to merit the favour of being allowed to purchase the most sought-after wines. Purchasing promiscuity will no longer be possible. The game is scarcely a game any more.

F is for Free Wine

I can tell you how to get hold of free wine, though paradoxically one is only able to obtain fine wine in this way; the scam, if scam it is, doesn't work for cheap wine. You'll also need capital of one or two thousand pounds and, as with all of these market-playing schemes, it comes with the proviso that what's worked in the past may not always work in the future. Here's what you do. Pick a good Bordeaux vintage (like 1995; it also works with older vintages if you have more capital available). Using your capital, and following the form given in papers, magazines and books (and especially the form given by Robert Parker, the Great Tipster), invest your capital in small quantities of the best clarets anybody will sell you. Over the following five years, the value of the wine you have bought is, on past performance, liable to double or more. You then sell half your wine, recouping your capital; the rest of the wine is free. You don't necessarily have to buy at the earliest stage of sale (in other words en primeur); the only essential requirement is to buy the best, since it is only the best which will improve in price to such an extent as to make the scheme work. An example: in November 1994, I buy four cases of Château Pichon-Baron 1990 (95 points from Robert Parker) at £270 per case: total outlay £1,080. In May 1996, the price stands at £550 per case. I can then sell two cases back to the merchant from whom I bought them (merchants with a broking department are generally happy to buy good stock back) at the list price minus 10%. The other two cases at the moment cost £45 each; they will be free within six months.

G is for Gender

French wine producers often speak of their wines in gender terms ("Zis Volnay is a beaudiful woman wearing zee silk stuckings, no?") and it usually makes British journalists groan. Yet gender is the single animal distinction in life with which we are most familiar, which brings us the most pleasure, and which is most easily communicated. When thinking about the wines of Bordeaux's Médoc, for example, it is hard to avoid considering Margaux feminine in comparison with Pauillac or St Estèphe. So why not?

H is for History

Wine is a number of things, and liquid history is one of them. In its flavour lies the history of a season's weather, and the history of millions of years of geological activity. More simply and straightforwardly, it is also a mute liquid witness to all the events, global and personal, which happened in a particular year. No other food or drink has the same commemorative value. How can we not treasure it? See also **Philosophy**.

I is for Imagination

There is, I would argue, such a thing as the drinking imagination. It is this which enables you to remember hillside herbs and sun-warmed stones in a glass of Corbières, to remember fresh sea air in a glass of Muscadet, to remember frost in Eiswein and yellow autumn in Sauternes. Cultivate the drinking imagination; wine is much more enjoyable when imagined as well as simply drunk.

J is for Junk

We're all familiar with the concept of junk food; we would do well to familiarise ourselves with the concept of junk wine. I would define it thus: wine produced on an industrial or semi-industrial scale whose flavour is predominantly created by technological interventions or chemical adjustments. It includes Liebfraumilch from Germany, plonk from France, and cheap wines from most of the New World but particularly from Australia and California. Like junk food, it salves appetites temporarily and unsatisfactorily, is possibly unhealthy, and leaves the soul undernourished.

K is for Knowledge

Most pleasures are intensified by knowledge; the pleasure of wine certainly is. It is easy enough to learn about wine by reading about it and tasting it; if you want the additional stimulation of a class or course, see page 29.

L is for Label

And specifically the label of Château Mouton-Rothschild 1993. Ever since 1945, this famous Bordeaux château has commissioned designs from leading artists for its labels: Dali contributed the 1958, Picasso the 1973, Francis Bacon the 1990 — and a Swiss artist called Balthus the 1993. Balthus's design shows a young girl reclining, naked, her arms above her head and legs askew; it doesn't seem to me to be a particularly successful drawing, but it has a kind of pretty and innocent charm. Not in America. There it is regarded as evil and dangerous; there the authorities can be certain that it will corrupt wine drinkers (a group of adults, no doubt, already depraved enough); so there the label is banned, and no picture adorns the label of the 1993 vintage of Château Mouton-Rothschild. It is not merely beauty which lies in the eye of the beholder.

M is for Mad Cow

No, I'm not referring to gelatine or ox-blood finings, but to the cost-cutting industrialization of agricultural processes. This is what has led to the BSE crisis; this is what has led to the major wine scandals of the past. If Britain had possessed an appellation system for its best beef, and if the appellation regulations had specified (as they surely ought to) natural feeds in place of ground-up, diseased sheep, then at least some producers and consumers might have been spared the disasters of the last year. The lesson of mad cow disease for the wine drinker is to beware of cheap, industrially produced wine and to favour, where possible, wine produced by organic or biodynamic means.

N is for Nose

Our most undervalued organ. Learning to use your nose through the discipline of wine tasting can pay huge dividends of pleasure in other areas of life, too. You can, for example, learn to smell people (the appealingly odorous, not merely the unappealingly malodorous), sea, rain, woods, rooms, dust ... the list is as long and as delightful as life.

O is for Old Burgundy

Beautiful wine, if it was good to start with, but often fragile. Open it only when you're ready to drink it, then enjoy its rapid evolution in the glass.

P is for Philosophy

To speak of a philosophy of wine is pretentious and inaccurate; nonetheless a plain understanding of what wine represents will help us to value it and appreciate it. We may buy it in a supermarket, but it's far from being just another grocery item like breakfast cereal or cheese. It is the most subtly flavoured comestible in existence. Its flavours reflect geographical origin to a far greater extent than any other item of food or drink. Unlike food, it is not necessary to life; it is therefore a recreational luxury. Yet it contains the most familiar of all mood-altering drugs (ethanol) at perfect sipping concentrations: this gives it the power to enhance our state of mind greatly, as well as the power (if abused) to kill us. Unlike most other alcholic drinks, wine is generally taken with food, at mealtimes: its mood-altering effect aids digestion, and its flavour profile complements most foods. These factors, in combination with the chemical effects of wine's other components (and especially those of red wine), make it the most health-giving of alcoholic beverages. Psychologically, its close association with food and mealtimes adds to its aura of restorative warmth. Culturally, it is an extremely powerful artefact, thanks both to its absolute antiquity (wine is much drunk in Homer's works and in *The Bible*) and

to the symbolic force it is given (wine is connected with escape, relaxation and triumph in *The Odyssey*, and its symbolic value in Jewish and Christian scripture is complex and redemptive). When we drink wine, in sum, we restore mind and soul, just as the food we eat restores the body; we drink the world, thanks to wine's ability to help us taste places on earth; we renew our links with the distant past; and we unlock imaginative and symbolic forces which help reconcile us with time, with light and with darkness.

P is also for Price Point

Ah, the wretched price points! Those £2.99, £3.99 and £4.99 price tags are such a bad habit: they stifle our enjoyment of wine and cut us off from intense pleasures we might otherwise experience. The damn things don't even save us money; canny retailers are just as likely to round up the real cost of a passably good wine from £3.63 to £3.99 as they are to peel it back from £4.25 to £3.99. I can't go so far as to suggest that all the best wines cost £3.10, £4.15 or £5.20, but temperamentally I'm strongly predisposed towards favouring them.

Q is for Quest

We all need quests and imperatives; modern life, that great multiple-choice exam, provides few. I met a man last year who had just completed his conquest, as he put it, of every Bordeaux classed growth; the bottles lined the walls. As quests go, there are worse.

R is for Rolland

It is interesting to see how, despite the widespread grass-roots influence of Australian and New Zealand winemakers, the one undisputed superstar among present-day winemaking consultants comes from Bordeaux. His name is Michel Rolland, and his back yard, significantly, is Pomerol. He is so much in demand not only for his innate understanding of the Merlot grape variety, but also for his ability to shape and fashion other red grapes towards suppleness, unctuousness and richness – without, I might add, ever losing the balance of acids and tannins required to make red wines drink well. Among the estates advised by Rolland whose wines I have enjoyed enormously in the last year are Dominio di Valdepusa in Spain and Casa Lapostolle in Chile.

S is for Supermarkets

Which for a short period this year sold baked beans at three pence a tin; customers were limited to four tins each. Why is it that we feel it so necessary to scrimp pence on the food and drink we buy, whereas we are prepared to squander, with irrational abandon, vastly larger sums on items for which we have no real need, like expensive cars, superfluous clothes, technological detritus and no-win lottery gambles? In part, it is because supermarkets sell us food and drink in that penny-pinching way; cars, clothes, gadgets and lottery tickets, by contrast, are sold to us by appealing to our emotions, dreams and aspirations. Who could doubt that Britain would be a saner, healthier society if we were to spend more of our income on food and drink of purity and quality, and less on over-sized, over-powerful, over-expensive, road-choking motor vehicles? Profit-dizzy supermarkets owe it to us to take a lead with nutritional and gastronomic

evangelism; instead we get four tins of sugary baked beans for 12p.

S is also for Scores

I have argued elsewhere against the scoring of wines; yet this book (particularly the supermarket and chain entries in Section Four) contains scores for wines. Why? Simple: you, the readers, asked for them, and the author's role is to serve the reader. Readers, it seems, like scores: they are a swift way to gauge the strength of a recommendation. They are, of course, only the opinion of one palate at one moment in time, so they shouldn't be taken too seriously. I hope at least some of you disagree with my scores: tastes differ, wine is subjectively appreciated, and if I have an overriding aim in this book it is to enable you, the reader, to cultivate and trust your own tastes in wine. Use the scores as a starting point, therefore, not as lapidary verdicts. All scores are out of 25, and are for absolute quality qualified (unsystematically but, I hope, fairly) by price. I do not give cheap wines extravagant scores simply because they are drinkable. As a rough guide, scores of 13-16 signify a good wine at its price, 17-20 an excellent wine at its price, and 21-25 an exceptional wine at its price. The same scores are used in the 'Drink' recommendation slot in *ES* magazine on Fridays and, where relevant, in my Tuesday Drink column in the *Evening Standard*.

T is for Treatments

The best winemakers do the least work. The perfect wine is made by gently collecting a small crop of healthy grapes, then letting it get on with what it wants to do anyway once it has been crushed or pressed: fermentation in clean containers. Yet perfection, as we all know, is rare, and many wines have a large list of substances which are added to them to make less-than-perfect fruit taste 'right' as a wine; they are also treated brutally so that their stability (or sterility) can be assured once they are in bottle. Finings, a series of filtrations and tartrate stabilization (by giving the wine a day or two at Arctic temperatures): all of these remove flavour and life from a wine. The first step towards getting wine producers to ease up on these treatments is for us to accept the presence of sediment in wine, even cheap wine, as wholesome and natural.

U is for Uniformity

You might think that we are offered greater diversity and choice every year by our wine retailers, yet uniformity lurks behind the teeming multitudes of bottles. Some wine brands are now in almost every outlet: there is no major retailer which does not stock Rosemount Chardonnay in some form or other, for example. Over the last three or four years, agents and retailers have got very creative with wine names, usually involving entirely fictitious ridges, hills, mountains, cliffs or creeks of various colours (blue, yellow and red are all popular): this enables the same 'winemaker' wines to be sold over and over again in different guises. Finally, there is the great stylistic consensus about What We Want: same grapes, same technical parameters, same bright fruity flavours, no matter what or where the origin. The only way to fight this hidden, creeping uniformity is to make the effort, at least, to try the stranger, more singular wines when they reach us.

V is for Value

Often assumed to be an absolute; in fact hugely relative. Value can only be defined in relation to your own income and tastes. There is a good case for saying expensive wine is always bad value, since a £30 bottle is never six times as good as a £5 bottle; yet the pursuit of beauty has little to do with applied mathematics, and there are a surprising number of people for whom £30 is a trifling sum. Cheap wine is often bad value, since it is foolish to exchange even small amounts of money for something which smells and tastes nasty and leaves you with a moping head. Look for value, by all means, but keep an open mind about how and when you find it.

W is for Wine Law

Wine law has, in general, done far more good than harm, but all laws have a tendency to sclerosis and need revision from time to time. Additionally, some wine laws (such as those of Germany and Italy) have been written under political pressure from large producers, and are thus bad laws; many of France's generally admirable laws are badly policed. Yet in situations like that of the wine world where the consumer is far removed from the producer, and has no innate understanding of the processes of production, good regulatory laws are essential. Wine laws should guarantee safety and authenticity; they can never guarantee quality, though they should provide a framework within which quality is readily achievable by the conscientious.

X is (almost) for eXploitation

There is an exploitative aspect to the British wine trade, and we may, in the long run, find ourselves suffering for this. Our obsession with finding sound, cheap wines means that we are forever roaming the world looking for regions or producers who have not exported before, and who are therefore prepared to sell to us at a profitless price in order to establish themselves in our market. When these producers raise their price in order to make a decent living, they get dropped, and our buyers are off looking for the next gullible victim. As a result, many of the world's best wines now by-pass Britain altogether; these exploitative tactics mean that assiduous wine producers may spurn us in the future.

Y is for Yeast

Wine's *sine qua non*, and the most helpful of beasts. But should the yeasts be cultured (added from a bottle or a packet) or wild (riding in on grape skins and in the air)? Many of the world's most complex wines are fermented with wild yeasts. Industrially produced wines always use the safer option of cultured yeasts.

Z is for Zzzzz

A moderate dose of good wine and good food puts you to sleep, and sleep is one of the sweetest and healthiest pleasures in life. You can use wine for many things: it has no more noble role than as a nourishing soporific.

Enjoying Wine

Enjoying Wine

What is wine?

Wine is fermented grape juice. Consider that for a moment. It means that the contents of every bottle of wine in the showiest superstore in Britain, in the most sumptuously stocked private cellar, in Christie's warehouses, in Le Gavroche or Le Manoir aux Quat'Saisons — bottles able to command the reverence of the subtlest minds of All Souls, to empty the pockets of the wealthy, to still conversation on the gravest matters and restore faith in life's warmth to those from whom tragedy, disappointment or failure have torn it — all of these contain nothing more than fermented fruit juice. The fruit of a season, sucked from the earth by a lungful of roots.

There is no other agricultural product with similar powers. Potatoes are good, bad and indifferent, but rarely sublime. There is a limit to what millionaires will pay for mushrooms, even wild ones. Savoy cabbage alone seldom rekindles hope when bad days have lasted for months. Wine is special.

But where does wine's specialness lie? Not in its alcohol content, for sure. Vodka and coke can provide exactly the same alcoholic fix, but the synthetic triviality of the soft drink and the raw, oily taste of the alcohol make an ugly, empty combination. It is the taste of wine, both appealing and complex, which is so special.

Beer (particularly England's great cask-conditioned ales) can taste appealingly complex too; so can whisky. Is wine any different?

It is, and for one reason alone: variety. The vine does not differ greatly in appearance from Australia to Germany, from Chile to Canada; nor do bunches of grapes. School those grapes into wine, though, and the tutorial human hand unlocks a labyrinth of differences. A white wine from the Mosel is as delicate and intricate as a watch mechanism. Its fruit flavours dance in the mouth like sunlight on wind-ruffled water; its low alcohol level leaves palate refreshed and unbefuddled. A Barossa Valley Shiraz, by contrast, glowers in the glass blackly. It smells of crushed blackberries, of hot windless nights, of the burnt earth of an old baked land. It rolls on to the tongue like a carpet tumbling downstairs, felt-heavy, salty, mineral-saturated, yet voluptuously fruity. Between these poles lies a spectrum of cultured complexity.

Wine is a soft agricultural prism by which soil, light, the seasons and human endeavour can be captured and expressed in aromatic, flavoury liquids. Wine, indeed, is the only agricultural product which is capable of reflecting, in sensually palpable form, a little of the diversity of the world and of humanity. It is for this that we love it, admire it, desire it.

Making wine: the naked leap

Grapes are small, intricate, juice-filled sponges wrapped in skin. Squeeze the sponge, break its intricate honeycomb of cells, and the juice which trickles out will almost always be colourless, regardless of whether the skin is black, red or white.

This is the first fact of winemaking. If you want to create white wines, you separate juice from grape skins; if you want to make red wines, you must soak the skins in the juice. All of the colour and rough-textured tannin of red wine comes from materials contained in red grape skins.

Fermentation involves the conversion, by yeast, of the sugars in grape juice into equal quantities of alcohol (ethanol) and carbon dioxide. It's a natural process: yeasts ride the air, and the bloom on grape skins constitutes a larder of yeast nutrients. Each grape, therefore, is a sort of mini-winemaking kit, an intoxication waiting to surprise.

In the case of white wines, the juice is chilled, settled and clarified. Nearly every stage of winemaking is capable of variation and refinement, and this is no exception: skin maceration is sometimes used to add aroma; deliberately solid-rich juices are sometimes used to give fuller-bodied wines, and very clear juices for pure fruit flavours; sometimes juice is deliberately oxidised to prevent this process happening later and spoiling the wine. In general, the more lightly pressed the grapes, the finer the quality of wine.

Cultured strains of yeast are widely used, since their action (and the flavours they provide) are certain and predictable. Wild yeasts, however, are capable of giving more complex flavours, as well as intensifying the effect of *terroir* (see page 21), since they are the product of the local environment. Using them, however, is not risk-free: they can also create unpleasant flavours.

Most white-wine fermentations nowadays are temperature-controlled; the cooler the temperature, the lighter and crisper will be the wine. Richer, more expressive white wines are often fermented in barrels of new or nearly new oak: this provides different, subtler oak flavours than merely ageing the wine in oak, once it has finished fermentation, does.

You may sometimes read references to something called secondary or malolactic fermentation. This is not, in fact, a true fermentation, but a bacteriological conversion of malic acid to lactic acid. It is something all red wines, and some white wines (or a part of some white wines) undergo after alcoholic fermentation. Its effect is to soften out the edges of a white wine. Those, thus, designed to be drunk young, crisp and fresh generally do not undergo malolactic fermentation, while those of richer flavour or greater ageing potential do.

Red-wine fermentation may be preceded by a period of skin maceration, or it may be followed by a period of skin maceration. The former is designed to liberate fresh fruit flavours and perfumes; the latter to consolidate vinous flavours and extract colour and tannin. Fermentation itself always takes place wholly or partly in contact with the skins. In the past, grape stalks were sometimes included in the fermentation, but they tend to produce astringent wines, and so are rarely included nowadays. In contrast to white wines, barrel fermentation is uncommon for red wines (though Pinot Noir sometimes benefits from this). It is much easier to vinify and macerate wine (which occasionally means jumping into it, stark naked, feet first) in a larger container than in a small barrel. Those red wines which benefit from oak ageing flavours are put into oak casks after fermentation is complete. Malolactic fermentation in cask is an increasingly widely practiced technique (particularly for Merlot): it provides lushness and suppleness.

The main variant on this process is called carbonic maceration or whole-berry fermentation. Grapes are put in unbroken bunches into a sealed fermentation vat, and fermentation takes place inside each berry. That's the theory, anyway — in fact there's always some juice at the bottom of the vat, and some broken berries; as fermentation proceeds, too, the grapes' structure is disrupted. This method produces very fresh, fruity, supple red wines, best drunk (sometimes lightly chilled) as soon as possible after bottling.

Sparkling wine: foamy liberation

How do you sow bubbles in wine? The easiest way is the fizzy drink method — carbonation. Fizzy drinks quickly lose their sparkle once poured, and so do fizzy wines. The bubbles are fat and coarse: toads' eyes. This method is only used for the cheapest sparkling wines. All the other methods involve a second fermentation in a sealed container. Sugar and yeast are added to new wine which ferments, producing alcohol and carbon dioxide. The gas has nowhere to go, so it dissolves in the wine. Its foamy liberation comes when you open the bottle. The problem is that the second fermentation also produces a yeasty deposit: how do you separate this from the wine without losing the dissolved sparkle?

If the wine has carried out its second fermentation in a tank (the Charmat, *cuve close* or tank method), it is simply pumped to another tank under pressure through a filter. More finesse, though, can be obtained by carrying out the second fermentation in bottle. The transfer method involves decanting the contents of one bottle to another through a filter, again under pressure. Best of all is the champagne method, now often described as the traditional method. The second fermentation takes place in bottle. Once finished, the bottle is gradually inverted so that the sediment slides like fine mud down into the bottle's neck. The inverted bottle is then whisked through a sub-zero brine bath in order to freeze the sediment into a solid plug. The bottle is reinverted to its normal position and opened; out shoots the sedimentary plug. The wine is topped up and the bottle corked.

The best sparkling wines are those produced with high-acid but ripely fruity base wines. The problem with many New World sparkling wines is that the required high-acid profile can only be achieved by picking the grapes before they are fully ripe and thus fully expressive, whereas in Champagne itself even the ripest grapes will always have high acidity. The flavours given to the wine by the yeast deposits produced during the second fermentation (sometimes called autolytic flavours) are important, too, so good-quality sparkling wine takes three or more years to produce. During this period, the wine itself seems to ripen, its piercing flavours becoming balanced by a bready, biscuity or creamy fullness.

Fortified wine: velvet liaisons

Fortified wines are those to which alcohol has been added. They are usually, though not invariably, sweet wines: the purpose of the alcohol is to prevent or arrest fermentation, leaving unfermented sugars in a stable condition in the wine. Sometimes no fermentation takes place at all: this fortified grape juice is known as mistelle, and sold (in France) as Vin de Liqueur. Pineau des Charentes, the honeyed and velvety liaison of Cognac and grape juice, is a well-aged mistelle.

On other occasions, wines are allowed to ferment partially before fortification: this is the case for port, as well as for French Vins Doux Naturels such as Muscat de Beaumes de Venise. Sherry is an example of a wine which is fully fermented before fortification. All sherry, consequently, begins life dry; sweeter sherries are made by adding small amounts of very sweet wine to the dry base sherries.

Flavour creation: the philosophies of wine

The basic flavour of wine, and where it comes from, is a controversial matter. Is it created by the grape variety or varieties from which a wine is made? Or does it, rather, come from the soils and climate in which and under which a vine works its way towards fruition?

There are, as so often with wine, human analogies. Is your personality a consequence of your nature or your nurture? Is it your genes which have made you what you are, or your upbringing and experiences? The honest answer is that you are the creation of both. Indissolubly so.

Thus with wine. Grape varieties provide the basic pattern of a flavour; a wine's origins (and we should include under this heading local winemaking practices) modify, shape and colour that pattern. The less expensive a wine, the plainer and clearer grape variety flavours are likely to be; the more expensive a wine, the more conspicuous the flavour contributions of a vine's environment will be.

Wines sold under the name of their contributory grape variety or varieties are known as varietal wines. The key 'nurture' word, by contrast, is *terroir*. This French word is best translated by an English neologism: 'placeness'. It embraces everything, in other words, which distinguishes one place from another. Soil, climate and topography are particularly important, but there is at least one French winegrower (Nicolas Joly of la Coulée de Serrant in Savennières) who extends the notion of placeness, not illogically, to the flora and fauna of his immediate environment. He has even saved a local breed of cows from bovine eclipse in order to use their manure in his vineyards, thereby reinforcing and strengthening his *terroir*.

The French system of *appellations d'origin contrôlée* (see page 60) codifies the country's *terroirs*; other systems of geographical origin imitate that of France to a greater or lesser extent.

Both approaches to flavour creation are capable of dangerous perversions. There is no doubt that the production of simple varietal wines throughout the world, including the production of 'international' varietals in countries with a long winemaking tradition (and indigenous varieties) of their own, has led for the time being to monotony, speciously dressed as multiplicity. Nothing, indeed, could be more perverse than this, since wine's defining beauty, and its joy, lies in its variety. On the other hand, 'placeness' will not do as an excuse for sloppy, unimaginative and inarticulate winemaking. Wine must at all times give pleasure, or it is worthless.

Varietal wines are fashionable at the moment thanks to their simple, fresh fruit flavours and the fact that they are easy to understand. Section Two of this book is, in large part, a guide to those wines whose flavours reflect their place of origin; here is a short guide to major grape varieties and their flavours.

Grape varieties: White grapes

Chardonnay

Origin: France.

Scents and flavours: vary from light and lemony to fat, smoky, nutty and buttery.

Key wines: white burgundy (including Chablis); all New World regions. Undisputed grape champion of the world thanks to its general amenability, unfailingly pleasant style, wide expressive range and ability to reflect vineyard and winery endeavour in palpable intensity of flavour.

Chenin Blanc

Origin: France.

Scents and flavours: wax, honey, damp straw, apples.

Key wines: Savennières, Vouvray and other Loire valley whites. South African versions are pleasant, but (apart from a few 'bush-vine' versions) have little of Chenin's noble traits to them; potentially good in New Zealand, though handicapped by unfashionability.

Gewürztraminer

Origin: Italian Tyrol.

Scents and flavours: flowers, overt spice.

Key wines: Heady, rich, fat-textured Alsace versions are still far better than those from other areas.

Marsanne

Origin: France.

Scents and flavours: almond blossom, fresh bread, mangoes.

Key wines: white Hermitage, Goulburn valley Marsanne (Australia). Look out for new Southern French and Californian versions. Blends well with livelier Roussanne to create wines which can rival the finest white burgundies.

Muscat

Origin: Middle East.

Scents and flavours: grapes, flowers, spices, honey, oranges, raisins.

Key wines: strong, sweet vins doux naturels and vins de liqueur in France; low-alcohol sweet sparkling wines in Italy; sweet wines in all countries; increasingly spicy dry wines in new regions (and traditionally in Alsace). A family, not a single variety.

Pinot Blanc (Pinot Bianco)

Origin: France

Scents and flavours: grapes, apples and pears.

Key wines: Alsace, Northern Italy; a good all-purpose white elsewhere. A good fall-back choice.

Pinot Gris (Pinot Grigio)

Origin: France.

Scents and flavours: smoke, honey, ripe fruits.

Key wines: Alsace, Northern Italy (though only the more expensive wines from lower yields are good); Hungary; Oregon. In cooler climates (i.e. where Viognier doesn't perform well), this is becoming the grape of choice for ABC (Anything But Chardonnay) producers, and it nearly always seems more serious, chewy and richly flavoured than Pinot Blanc.

Riesling

Origin: Germany.

Scents and flavours: when young: fresh fruits, citrus zests and minerals; when aged: kerosene, honey.

Key wines: fine German wine, Alsace, Australia, New Zealand. Considered the greatest white grape in the world by some of wine's thinking drinkers (like Jancis Robinson and Simon Loftus). Slowly regaining fashionability; the best, though, is yet to come.

Roussanne
Origin: France.
Scents and flavours: ripe apricots, peaches; honey; white flowers.
Key wines: white Rhône wines; a few Savoie whites (as Bergeron); increasingly widely planted in Languedoc. Blends well with heavier Marsanne to create wines which can rival the finest white burgundies.

Sauvignon Blanc
Origin: France.
Scents and flavours: fresh green leaves, cut grass, gooseberry, asparagus.
Key wines: Sancerre and Pouilly-Fumé, dry white Bordeaux, Sauternes (sweet), everywhere in New Zealand, but especially in Marlborough; increasingly impressive in South Africa and Chile (Casablanca). Much South American 'Sauvignon Blanc' is in fact Sauvignonasse (also known as Tocai Friuliano). When good, makes sensationally appealing wines; when less than good, can be acidulous, sharp and simple.

Sémillon
Origin: France.
Scents and flavours: dry: lemon, citrus peel, toast, cheese; sweet: butter, lanolin, heavy honey, butterscotch.
Key wines: Sauternes (sweet), dry white Bordeaux, Australian Semillon (especially Hunter Valley). Takes well to oak, but is best blended with other varieties (especially Sauvignon Blanc); can be heavy and tedious (though aromatically fascinating) on its own.

Silvaner
Origin: Austria.
Scents and flavours: vanilla, earth.
Key wines: Alsace wines, dry German wines (especially in Franconia). Not a characterful variety, but makes good all-purpose white wines for food.

Vermentino
Origin: France.
Scents and flavours: fennel, aniseed.
Key wines: some pleasant, subtle wines from the Mediterranean basin (Languedoc, Corsica, Sardinia).

Viognier
Origin: France
Scents and flavours: flowers, peaches, apricots. A powerfully scented wine.
Key wines: Condrieu, plus 'new wave' alternatives to Chardonnay in southern France and (more successfully) in California. Still getting established in Australia, and scarcely present at all yet in South Africa and Chile, but a coming grape.

Grape varieties: Red grapes

Barbera
Origin: Italy.
Scents and flavours: currants, raspberries, sharp plums; very brightly flavoured, sometimes aggressive.
Key wines: Barbera d'Alba. Increasingly widely planted elsewhere: Californian versions are softer.

Cabernet Franc
Origin: France
Scents and flavours: raspberries, redcurrants, sometimes bitter chocolate and iron.
Key wines: St Emilion, Pomerol, Fronsac, Chinon, Bourgueil. Some good examples from South Africa, too. Finding its feet globally, but a worthy alternative to Cabernet Sauvignon.

Cabernet Sauvignon
Origin: France.
Scents and flavours: blackcurrant or other currants, cedarwood; sometimes austere, lead pencils; sometimes rich chocolate.

23

Key wines: claret, Spain, Italy, Eastern Europe, all New World regions. Traditionally the champion red variety globally, but increasingly challenged by Syrah/Shiraz, Merlot and even Grenache. Can be tough and unlovely when unblended.

Grenache (Garnacha)
Origin: Spain.
Scents and flavours: raisins, sweet red fruits.
Key wines: Châteauneuf-du-Pape (in part or in whole), most Spanish regions, Languedoc-Roussillon, Australia. The softest of all great red grape varieties.

Malbec (Côte Auxerrois)
Origin: France.
Scents and flavours: earth, minerals, sloes, blackberries.
Key wines: South America, especially Argentina; a small but vital contribution to red Bordeaux; also much of South West France (especially Cahors) and, in the Loire, a rosé grape. The sturdy reds of Argentina and Chile show the variety at its best.

Merlot
Origin: France.
Scents and flavours: Plums and cream.
Key wines: St Emilion, Pomerol; increasingly planted in New World (Californian versions tend to be tougher than French originals), South America and Eastern Europe. When well-made, this provides the most hedonistic of all red wines. The global influence of the Pomerol consultant Michel Rolland carries Merlot with it.

Mourvèdre (Mataro)
Origin: Spain.
Scents and flavours: tea leaves, roast meat, blackberries.

Key wines: wines from Provence (especially Bandol) and Languedoc; Australian reds, often as a blending component. An enigmatic variety: promises much, yet ungracious.

Nebbiolo (Spanna)
Origin: Italy.
Scents and flavours: tar, roses, violets, black fruits, leather, truffles.
Key wines: Barolo, Barbaresco. Italy's grandee, but needs careful handling to keep fruit levels unblemished by the deluge of tannins.

Negroamaro
Origin: Italy
Scents and flavours: tends to be sweet-scented (raisins and toffee) yet dry-flavoured (young plums).
Key wines: a rising star, thanks to the success of Puglian reds (like Salice Salentino) over the last year or two. Seems likely to pack its bags and hit the road before long.

Pinot Noir
Origin: France.
Scents and flavours: when young: cherries, strawberries, raspberries, plums; when aged: game, decaying vegetation, undergrowth.
Key wines: Burgundy, and varietal wines from Germany, Eastern Europe, California, Oregon, Yarra Valley (Australia), New Zealand. An irregular performer, but when good produces the world's most soaringly lyrical wines.

Sangiovese
Origin: Italy.
Scents and flavours: green coffee, fresh and dried cherries, apples.
Key wines: Chianti, Brunello di Montalcino, Vino Nobile di Montalcino. New World examples are still finding their feet.

Syrah (Shiraz)

Origin: France.

Scents and flavours: smoke, hot rubber, flowers (violets), dark plums, earth, pepper.

Key wines: Hermitage, Crozes-Hermitage, Cornas, Côte-Rôtie, Barossa Valley Shiraz (Australia). This is a great grape which can rival Cabernet for depth and complexity, and Pinot Noir for lyricism. Looks set to provide the basis for Languedoc's greatest wines.

Tempranillo (Cencibel, Tinta Roriz)

Origin: Spain.

Scents and flavours: strawberries, often lacquered with the vanillins of American oak.

Key wines: Rioja, Valdepeñas, Navarra, Ribera del Duero. Can be flimsy, but when treated seriously rivals Grenache for sweet, soothing accessibility.

Zinfandel

Origin: Italy (Primitivo).

Scents and flavours: blackberries and other squashy red/black fruits.

Key wines: Californian Zinfandel can reach very great heights, but don't bother ageing them. Even the most dense and tannic examples lose their way in time: drink young for the excitement factor. White Zinfandel is junk wine.

Tasting & drinking wine

This, you might reasonably argue, is an idle passage. Who needs to be taught how to drink wine? Just tip it in your mouth, sluice it over your tongue and swallow.

Well, yes; to a point. You have, though, paid a lot more for a glass of wine than you would for a glass of cola or milk, and the reason isn't simply the Chancellor's avarice. Wine is capable of sensually summarising geography, just as poems or songs can summarise emotional experiences. If you want to understand wine's message, you need to learn its language. As learning goes, this is a hugely enjoyable experience, but it is irrefutably true that the more thoughtfully you taste, the more you will enjoy the wine you have bought.

Equipment first. The best wine glasses are relatively simple vessels: plain glass, tulip-shaped. Large glasses are much better than smaller ones, since a wine glass should never be filled more than half-full. Why not? Aroma, in a word.

Scent is the Cinderella sense. Once upon a time, we smelled everything before we ate it; our lives depended on it. Today we have betrayed the sense of smell to such an extent that we eat things (like fast-food hamburgers) which by common agreement smell repulsive. We live in an age of wilful aromatic amnesia.

Scent may not comprise half the pleasure of wine, but it furnishes at least one third, and no wine can ever be called 'good' unless it smells appealing. The scents of the finest wines (occasionally but not invariably expensive) are aromatic constructions of extraordinary complexity and beauty, pulling you into the wine by a process for which 'seduction' is not too extravagant a word. Fill a wine glass to its brim, and you squander something you have paid for. Fill a wine glass half full, swirl the wine in the glass, and you allow it to express itself; you bathe in an uncommon pleasure.

There is no great secret to appreciating the scent of a wine. You don't have to 'get' blackcurrants, cut grass, mangoes, dusty attics, plimsolls or damped-down bonfires; all you have to do is decide whether you like it or not. Those terms are just analogical shorthand for saying why we like a wine. They are necessary because there is a paucity of words for the plenitude of scents with which our world is filled; the only way we can describe them, thus, is by referring to objects whose own scents are in turn commonly recognised.

Wines can smell bad. There are many causes: too much sulphur, poor storage, inadequate aeration of the wine, cork taint. If a wine smells bad to you, then it probably is bad; only old Pinot Noir occupies a strange shadowland where its aromas become half-appealing, half-repellent. You might try decanting a wine which smells bad; if the wine is reductive – in other words has been inadequately exposed to oxygen – this may help. Otherwise don't buy it again.

What about tasting? The only essential requirement is to make sure that you give wine a chance to reach every part of your tongue. Certain zones are sensitive to specific taste stimuli, so the complete 'portrait' of a wine can only be painted by the whole tongue, rather than its central runnel alone. You may find that some wines taste best on specific sites on the tongue; German Riesling seems to taste most exciting at the tip of the tongue; white burgundy, by contrast, asserts its grandeur most forcefully as it washes around the root and heart of the tongue.

The second reason for giving wine maximum tongue exposure is to warm it up and allow its volatile parts to ascend the retronasal passage into the nasal chamber. This process occurs with all food and drink, which is why most of what we 'taste' is really smell (hence the loss of 'taste' when our noses are blocked by colds). Aromas released by a wine in the mouth are known as retronasal aromas. You may find that some wines (like whites from the Rhône or Portugal) have little scent when sniffed but become excitingly aromatic in the mouth, as you taste.

And so to swallowing – easiest of all. The flavour of a little wine fades rapidly; the flavour of a grand wine lingers.

By now, you will have a clear idea of whether you like a wine a lot, a little, or not at all, and most choose to leave it at that. If you want to analyse why you like a wine, though, the best way to do this is to think about each of its component parts in turn. The main components of white wines are aroma, acidity and sweetness; red wines add the element of texture (tannin) to the picture. Both red and white wines can be rich (glycerous or extractive) without being sweet, and both red and white wines may have varying degrees of fruitiness. Another useful concept for analysing wines is 'vinosity' – literally 'wininess', the distinctive structuring sensation which fermentation leaves in its wake. Vinosity provides wines with the skeleton on which its flesh and its fruit are draped. Vanillic or toasty scents and flavours usually indicate that a wine has been aged in oak barrels – or has had oak chips added to it during fermentation.

So much for tasting. Drinking is your affair; if you want to drink red wine as an aperitif, sweet white with a pork chop, or champagne as a nightcap, go ahead. For what it's worth, here are a few of my own drinking principles (at present).

The best aperitifs and drink-alone wines are sherry, good German wine and champagne; the best all-purpose wine for food is chilled fino sherry; the most easily enjoyable white wine is Alsace Gewürztraminer; the most well-structured white wines are white burgundies; the silkiest white wines are expensive California Chardonnays; the most profound white wines are well-aged whites from the Northern Rhône and from Savennières; the dullest white wines in the world come from Italy. If you like good Sauvignon Blanc, don't neglect white Bordeaux (especially from '94): it can be much subtler than either Sancerre/Pouilly-Fumé or New Zealand examples, as well as offering better value.

The most satisfyingly gutsy red wine is Barossa Shiraz; the best balanced, most digestible and most civilized red wines are clarets from good vintages; the easiest drinking inexpensive reds come from Bulgaria and Romania; the most underrated, subtly flavoured red wines come from Portugal; the most deliciously fruited red wines come from Chile; the most unpredictable red wines in the world (for better and worse) are red burgundies; and the most exciting, inspiring red wines in the world come from the Northern Rhône, Piedmont and Languedoc. Port is the world's most generous and warming wine; the best (vintage) madeira is the world's most intensely flavoured wine.

It seems to me to be almost impossible to say anything certain about matching wine with food, other than that the classic rules (dry whites with fish and so on) are useful starting points. But only that – red wines are bad partners for most cheeses, for example, which really taste best with sweet wines. Again, there is no substitute for personal experiment, though several good books are now available on this subject (see page 30) to get you started on your own research programme.

Serving wine is done best with little fuss. Don't over-chill white wines (a refrigerator temperature of 4°C is too cold for most fuller dry whites, and richly flavoured dry whites like expensive white burgundy are best cool – around 12°C – rather than chilled). Likewise, don't let red wines get too warm: 18°C to 20°C is ideal, yet many houses are routinely heated to 21°C or 22°C in winter, and summer or fireside temperatures of 25°C or more will ruin red wines. Lights reds are pleasant chilled. Young red wines of good quality (especially from northern Italy) are often improved by the oxygenation which pouring a wine into a decanter achieves. Merely removing the cork is of little other than ceremonial use.

Storing wine & building a cellar

Most wines are meant to be drunk today; if not today, then for tomorrow lunch. They'll taste worse in two months than they will in a week; worse still in six months; dead and gone in 18. There are few sadder moments for folk like myself than being summoned to view a lovingly treasured rackful of moribund bottles, proffered with shy pride for 'expert' opinion. If in doubt, drink it up.

Indeed, even those wines which do need age before they taste at their best, like good claret and vintage port, are often drunk too old. If you buy wine by the case for cellaring, check its progress every two years or so, and if it tastes wonderful to you, plough into it. I have drunk most of my 1982 clarets with unalloyed pleasure, for example, and have no compunction about dipping into 1985 vintage ports. I prefer good red wine while it still has fire in its loins, and I actively dislike the weedy, reedy old claret and burgundy eulogised by some. The one red grape variety which always seems to swallow the passing years gratefully is the Nebbiolo; many of the best old wines I have drunk have been Nebbiolo-based.

Certain white wines, by contrast, are often drunk too young. Fine white burgundy is often mute when young, and tastes mealy and mechanical. Give it ten years, by contrast, and you can see why poems have been written about it: its expressivity has increased tenfold. The same is true of the best white Rhône and Chenin-based Loire wines. Fine German wines are delicious young and old; the difference is stylistic. Age other dry white wines on an experimental basis only.

Wine is best stored in darkness and tranquillity. A steady, low temperature is ideal; if you can't manage this, then a steady moderate temperature won't do much harm. What wine hates is light, especially sunlight; vibrations; and fluctuating temperatures. If you don't have a cellar, the best place in the house for wine is generally towards its centre; under-stairs cupboards are often good, though lag any heating pipes which may run through them. Humidity is less clear-cut an issue: from the wine's point of view, a moist temperature is ideal; from the label's point of view, a relatively dry atmosphere is better. Absolute dryness is at all times undesirable.

A cellar of wonderful wines is a most agreeable luxury, so assuming you have the space to fill and the money to fill it, what should you buy? Obviously you should only buy wines which will improve with age, which rules out almost all supermarket wines and the vast majority of wines sold by everybody else. Some good-quality wines are sold ready-aged, like most Rioja, so there's no point in cellaring those. Prime candidates for cellaring are young, top-quality clarets and Rhône wines, white burgundy, Sauternes and the best white Chenin Blanc-based wines, especially sweet ones. Other wines you might like to cellar include top red burgundy (though not everyone agrees that red burgundy improves with age) and fine German whites. Many Californian reds are certainly tough enough and dense enough to seem to need age, as are the best Australian reds (particularly Coonawarra Cabernets). No one yet knows just how well they will age. My own view, based on limited tastings of older Australian wines, is that they are best drunk whenever they are drinkable – in other words when the tannic portcullis has softened adequately to encourage entry and exploration.

Those who have trouble spending a night under the same roof as an unopened bottle of wine may find this hard to believe, but it is easy to overstock a cellar. Enthusiasts get carried away by enthusiasm; tastes evolve. It's particularly easy to buy too much claret, since so much is offered for sale from new vintages on a pre-arrival or 'en primeur' basis. There's nothing wrong with buying too much, if it is going to increase in value and can be sold later at a profit. This applies, however, to a tiny collection of wines – specifically the best clarets from the best years, a few prestige burgundies and a very few prestige Italian wines. My advice to anyone wishing to build a cellar is to stick to single-bottle purchases until you have discovered the wines which you find truly thrilling – and then buy a case or two of those from time to time. If possible, taste before you buy – then at least you have no one to blame but yourself if the wine proves a disappointment later.

Further education

Learning a little about wine will increase the pleasure it brings you to a disproportionate degree. It's easy enough to teach yourself, by reading some of the many books and magazines available about wine (see below); there are, though, for the lazy or the sociable, enjoyable wine courses on offer. These have the advantage of a built-in tasting component (for which, of course, you pay). Wine courses are run by local authorities (for details, buy a copy of *Floodlight*, published each year in early autumn and widely available from bookshops and newsagents) as well as by the following:

The Association of Wine Educators: contact Wink Lorch, 15 Pymers Mead, London SE21 8NQ. Tel: 0181 670 6885

Christie's: 63 Old Brompton Road, London SW7 3JS. Tel: 0171 581 3933

Leith's School of Food and Wine: 21 St Albans Grove, London W8 5BP. Tel: 0171 229 0177

The Scala School of Wine: 24 Scala St, London W1P 1LU. Tel: 0171 637 9077

Sotheby's: 34 New Bond St, London W1A 2AA. Tel: 0171 493 8080

The Wine and Spirit Education Trust: Five Kings House, 1 Queen St Place, London EC4R 1QS. Tel: 0171 236 3551

The Wine Education Service: 76 St Margaret's Road, London N17 6TY. Tel: 0181 801 2229

Winewise: 107 Culford Road, London N1 4HL. Tel: 0171 254 9734. (First-class small group tuition led by the calm, scholarly and enthusiastic Michael Schuster MW.)

Many merchants (such as La Réserve or Bibendum) also offer a tasting programme which, if followed regularly, would provide a specialised but immensely enjoyable wine education.

Further reading

There are two leading British wine magazines: *WINE* and *Decanter*. Both have improved over the last year under new editors. In general, I find *WINE* a more entertaining read, with wider scope and greater critical independence than *Decanter*. *Decanter*, however, contains more of interest for those who enjoy fine, classic wines. Anyone interested in buying fine wine is likely to find a subscription to *The Wine Advocate*, a newsletter written and published by the American wine critic Robert M. Parker, Jr, well worth while (contact P.O.Box 311, Monkton, MD 21111, USA, phone 001 410 329 6477, fax 001 410 357 4504, for latest subscription rates). Parker tastes widely, thoroughly and reliably, and often spots exciting new developments and trends (such as the Priorato renaissance in Spain or the St Emilion renaissance in Bordeaux) well before anyone, journalist or merchant, in Britain. His campaigning on matters like filtration and acid adjustment has improved the quality of wine around the world.

Books

A basic wine library should contain the following four books:

The World Atlas of Wine, Hugh Johnson (Mitchell Beazley)
The Story of Wine, Hugh Johnson (Mitchell Beazley)
The Wine Buyer's Guide, Robert Parker (Dorling Kindersley)
The Oxford Companion to Wine, ed. Jancis Robinson (OUP).

Other books which I find very useful, or for which I have a high regard, include those listed below. As is the way with wine books, some will soon need, or already need, updating; others are out of print, but can be found by the persistent in second-hand bookshops.

The Wine Atlas of Italy, Burton Anderson (Mitchell Beazley)
Drink, Andrew Barr (Bantam Press)
The Great Vintage Wine Book II, Michael Broadbent (Mitchell Beazley/Christie's)
Oz Clarke's New Classic Wines (Webster's/Mitchell Beazley)
Oz Clarke's Wine Atlas (Little, Brown)
The Wines of Italy, David Gleave (Salamander)
The Art and Science of Wine, James Halliday and Hugh Johnson (Mitchell Beazley)
Burgundy, Anthony Hanson (Faber & Faber)
*The Mitchell Beazley Pocket Guide to German
Wines,* Ian Jamieson (Mitchell Beazley)
Port Wine Quintas of the Douro, Alex Liddell and Janet Price (Sotheby's)
The Wines of the Rhône, John Livingstone-Learmonth (Faber & Faber)
Anatomy of the Wine Trade, Simon Loftus (Sidgwick & Jackson)
A Pike in the Basement, Simon Loftus (Century)
Puligny-Montrachet: Journal of a Village in Burgundy, Simon Loftus (Penguin)
Portugal's Wines and Winemakers, Richard Mayson (Ebury Press)
The Wines of Spain and Portugal, Kathryn McWhirter and Charles Metcalfe
(Salamander)
Sainsbury's Pocket Wine and Food Guide, Kathryn McWhirter and Charles
Metcalfe (Sainsbury)
Rhône Renaissance, Remington Norman (Mitchell Beazley)
The Wine Atlas of Germany, Stuart Pigott (Mitchell Beazley)
John Platter's South African Wine Guide (Mitchell Beazley)
The Demon Drink, Jancis Robinson (Mandarin)
Jancis Robinson's Wine Course, Jancis Robinson (BBC Books)
Vines, Grapes and Wines, Jancis Robinson (Mitchell Beazley)
The Wines of Alsace, Tom Stevenson (Faber & Faber)
Champagne, Tom Stevenson (Sotheby's)
Wines of South-West France, Paul Strang (Kyle Cathie)
Vintage Port, James Suckling (Wine Spectator Press)
Buying Wine in France, Hilary Wright (Mitchell Beazley)

Wines of the World

Algeria

In search of lost wine

Algeria has, thanks to its French colonial past, a prodigious expanse of vines (around 100,000 hectares), though this is much reduced since independence in 1962. In deference to the strictures of Islam and economic reality, around half the country's vineyards are now used for table grapes rather than wine. The best wine-growing regions are in the west of the country: Coteaux de Tlemcen and Coteaux de Mascara. Old vines and generous sunshine provide deep, salty flavours and the natural structure so appreciated by French table-wine blenders (and their Burgundian chums) until the 1970s. Winemaking techniques remain unsophisticated.

Will we see an upswing in production in North Africa? Climatically, this region could be Europe's Australia or Chile, a sunny wine-factory, with Algeria the best placed of all to add vinous zest to its export figures. Yet the desire to make wine, and make wine well, matters more than any felicity of climate; and this desire appears not to be growing but to be diminishing.

Argentina

The giant stirs

It would be splendid to be able to report that during 1996 Argentina has finally fastened its belt, zipped up its leather jacket, laced up its seven-league boots and come speeding across the waters with the generously flavoured and more-than-occasionally profound wines it has the potential to make. Alas, the truth is that despite a bigger spectrum of Argentinian wines on our shelves, quality is as patchy as ever. There have been excitements – like Norton's chewy '94 Malbec and lyrical '93 Merlot, and Weinert's generally fine reds – but there have also been some exceptionally dreary supermarket wines, their only use being to exemplify the fact that wines from high-yielding vines taste weak and feeble.

The fact is that Argentina's enormous production (it's the world's sixth largest wine-making nation) is mostly mediocre in quality, vinified from indifferent varieties which, thanks to limitless Andean snow-melt irrigation, romp off towards monstrous yields of sometimes 500 hectolitres per hectare or more. It is, though, a wine-loving, wine-drinking, wine-cultured country, and one where the Italian influence is of more consequence than that of Spain, California or Australia. Argentina's best wines are its reds, often based on the Malbec grape which produces a rumpled wine of unpredictably savoury flavour; Cabernet Sauvignon grows well, too, and Merlot has already produced some classically creamy reds from Weinert and others. Among white wines, it is the Torrontés – spicy Muscat-like scents and a dry, firm, neutral-to-gingery flavour – which provides most interest. Occasionally, modern winemaking produces clean, scented and tasty whites even from unpromising (pink) Criolla and Cereza varieties, yet many whites remain heavy and plodding.

Mendoza has traditionally been the key growing area, sited on the Andean foothills at about the same latitude as Chile's central wine-growing regions, but Patagonia's cooler Rio Negro promises much for white and sparkling wines, and there are other quality regions further north, such as Salta. The best producers are the Californian-style Catena (including Alamos Ridge, La Rural and Libertad), Norton (now Austrian-owned) and Weinert; other good producers include La Agricola (sold in the UK under the Picajuan Peak, Santa Julia and Viejo Surco labels), Flichman, Navarro Correas, Santa Anna (now owned by Chile's Santa Carolina), Trapiche (owned by the country's largest producer, Peñaflor) and Pascual Toso. Michel Rolland, the omnipotent Pomerol-based consultant, is working with El Recreo. Good wines available in the UK include the Trapiche Oak Cask Reserves stocked by M&S and Waitrose's heavyweight Santa Julia Chardonnay from La Agricola; the Picajuan Peak wines from La Agricola, too, were sound buys amongst Tesco's generally dismal spring Wine Festival selection. Argentina has some 2,000 wineries, so there must be plenty of good things still out there for the unearthing; the disincentive is that prices within Argentina are relatively high, reducing its competitivity.

Australia

Cold front from the warm south

The last twelve months have seen Australian wine workers beaming. The harvest problems of eighteen months ago have eased, and more wine is sluicing into the system. Export volumes may be down, but value is up. So, too, is acclaim: French winegrowers no longer laugh indulgently and joke about kangaroos. They think, instead, of a serious challenge to their own livelihood and agricultural philosophy.

Paradoxically, these developments may herald a cold spell for British drinkers. The most significant figures from our point of view over the last year were the fact that Australia's exports to Switzerland rose by 84 per cent, and to America by 22 per cent. As any French grower will confirm, if the Swiss or the Americans take a fancy to a wine, they will buy it more or less regardless of price. We are parsimonious; we won't. We're the discount raiders of the wine world. If we persist in shopping for wine at £2.99, £3.99 and £4.99, then we will increasingly see the best from Australia go elsewhere. Already many of the Australian wines in our supermarkets are dull: crudely flavoured, a clear testament to second-class fruit, bolstered by artificial adjuncts and winemaking stratagems (added acids to give 'edge' and 'balance', residual sugars to 'round out', oak flavourings for 'richness' and 'mouthfeel'). They could become the junk food of the wine world.

Even the thunderball reds we've grown to love at £6.49 or £6.99, pounding Shiraz or Cabernets from try-harder medium-sized producers in Victoria or the Barossa, are now showing up at £8.99 or £9.99, and the really good wines are available to us in smaller quantities than in the past. It's an hour of reckoning.

Australia, you see, is beginning to take its place in the world. It may still wear shorts and a tee-shirt, but it's edging into the sort of position of power and influence previously reserved for the besuited aristocrats of Europe and the wine barons of America. Its footsoldier winemakers are more sought-after, more influential, than those of any other country; its wine styles, too, are the most unapologetically unEuropean – leaders of the Southern Hemisphere alternative.

The achievement

What Australia has given us so far are technically adept and innovative wines based on sunshine-charged fruit: flavours as bright and brassy as a day's production at the Royal Mint.

Exploration further away from Cab, Shiraz and Chard into the silent, beckoning glades of varietal non-conformism, by contrast, has been timid. Australians, like all New World producers, don't have traditions; they have markets. If the market wants Cab and Chard, that's what it gets. There are signs, though, that drinkers are beginning to look for other varietals: Riesling, Semillon and Marsanne among whites, and Grenache and Mourvèdre among reds seem to perform most memorably.

The greatest challenge facing Australian winemakers at present is to admit the truth which all European viticulture is predicated on: that the final arbiter of flavour in a wine is not the professorial viticulturalist trimming vine canopies into double lyres, nor the wine maker blending a series of cleverly differentiated vats into a technically impeccable but finally passionless whole, but earth, stones, sky, air and water. The most exciting development at present in Australian wine-making is the way that its regional styles are rising up out of the earth like a three-dimensional relief map taking form. "What can our land give us? What secret potential is inscribed in our soil? How can we honour our place on earth?" These, finally, are the great agricultural questions, and no one is likely to get a more exciting or inspiring answer than winegrowers. The bold drama of Australian wine has come in part from its pragmatic winemaking approaches – but it has more enduringly come from the Australian earth and the Australian sky. That is where the future lies, whether we in Britain can afford it or not.

New South Wales
Tropic of Semillon

New South Wales, and specifically the Hunter Valley north of Sydney, was where Australian wine growing passed its infancy. As the growers there cheerfully admit, the Hunter is not ideal vine-growing country: owing to its sub-tropical latitude it suffers a depressing quantity of summer rain. Yet the Hunter has its classics: gentle, animal Shiraz and, especially, Semillons which are dull and plain in youth but which as time passes acquire extraordinarily lemony, cheesy, honky aromas and dry, hard, lime-zesty, broad-bean-like flavours. Chardonnay is a more recent arrival, but is charging towards classic status with some of the fattest, creamiest, toastiest renditions you will find anywhere. Cooler Mudgee lies nearby, while bulk-producing Murrumbidgee is much further flung. Cowra, a recently developed Chardonnay hotspot, lies roughly half way between Sydney and Murrumbidgee. Throughout Australia, producers draw fruit from a multitude of sources, in state and out of state; this is particularly true of the larger New South Wales producers.

Allandale, Hunter Chardonnay over-sweet; Hilltops Cab Sauv mineral-charged.

Barramundi see Cranswick.

Botobolar, Mudgee Organic producer: characterful reds.

Brokenwood, Hunter Exemplary Semillon and Graveyard Vineyard Shiraz.

Cranswick, Griffith Straightforward, unsubtle. Cranswick Oak-Aged Marsanne more interesting than most of the range, and Barossa Shiraz has lots of salty regional style. The Barramundi wines are well-labelled but coarse in flavour.

Lindemans An Australia-wide company, now owned by Southcorp (Penfolds), with its roots in the Hunter Valley though its chief base is now in Karadoc (Victoria). Its Hunter Valley Semillon, Chardonnay and Shiraz are all of benchmark standard, while its trio of Coonawarra wines (fine-grained St George Cabernet, the beefier Limestone Ridge Shiraz-Cabernet and complex, multi-variety Pyrus) make fascinating drinking, though expensive. Bin 65, by contrast, its flagship Chardonnay, has struck me as sweet and simple in the past, though '95 seems a little dryer and more grown-up. Padthaway Chardonnay is serious, vinous, almost fiery. The Bin 45 Cab Sauv and Bin 50 Shiraz wines are satisfying and gutsy.

McWilliams, HUNTER McWilliams' Elizabeth, sold with six years' bottle age but ready for more, is a classic Hunter Semillon: the aroma is splendidly yielding and butter-rich, but the flavour often disappointingly hollow. A chaos of brand names includes other good wines (fortifieds included).

Rosemount, UPPER HUNTER This highly professional, successful wine business draws fruit from many sources. Its rise to the top has been Chardonnay-powered, and all its Chardonnays, from supermarket own-label versions to the top-of-the-line Show Reserve and Roxburgh (via Honey Tree and Orange Vineyard), are creamy and sumptuous, with a honeyed vanillic burr. If you like Chardonnay, Rosemount is a beacon. Other wines vary from the impressive (most of the Shiraz wines and the Coonawarra Cabernet Sauvignon – friendlier than most) to range-fillers (like the sparkling wine, the Sauvignon Blanc and some of the double varietal blends). Ryecroft is a McLaren Vale-based operation. The resonant Balmoral Syrah (sic, though it tastes like Shiraz to me) also comes from McLaren Vale.

Rothbury Estate, HUNTER AND COWRA Typically full, creamy Hunter Valley Chardonnay and plumper, buttery Cowra Chardonnay. The Semillon is classic and unyielding at first; the Shiraz fruity and oaky rather than earthy. Now with its own Marlborough operation in New Zealand, as well as Baileys and St Huberts in Victoria.

Trentham, HUNTER Grape suppliers-turned-winemakers with lively Shiraz.
Tyrrell, HUNTER Long Flat Red and White are comfortable quaffing wines; toasty Semillon (Vat 1), big-bellied Shiraz (Vats 5 and the leathery, iron-clad Vat 9), surprisingly delicate Pinot Noir (Vat 6) and lusciously limey Chardonnay (Vat 47) are all worth trying, though the value for money does not seem to me to be what it once was.

Wyndham Estate, HUNTER AND MUDGEE Large, Orlando-owned producer of wines whose simple, overdrawn and sometimes repellent flavour are pet dislikes of mine.

Vintages
1996 ★★★; 1995 ★★; 1994 ★★★; 1993 ★★★; 1992 ★★★; 1991 ★★★★; 1990 ★★;
1989 ★★; 1988 ★★★; 1987 ★★★★; 1986 ★★★★; 1985 ★★★★.

Specialist retailers
Australian wines are widely stocked but Oddbins remains outstanding. Also The Australian Wine Centre (mail order), Fullers, the London Wine Emporium and Philglas and Swiggot.

Victoria

The native idiom

Victoria has a richer history of viticulture than any other state in Australia; yet phylloxera, which to this day has spared South Australia, obliterated much of Victoria's early endeavours. Today it consists of a mosaic of contrasting sub-regions and specialities. It shares what is known as Riverland with South Australia: this is a necklace of flat, hot, factory vineyards found alongside (and watered by) the Murray river as it meanders towards Adelaide from its source in the Australian Alps. Mildura, Swan Hill and Rutherglen are Victoria's three main Murray vineyard areas; of the three, it is Rutherglen which has most of interest to offer. This is where some of Australia's greatest fortified wines, the super-stickies, are made: liqueur Muscats (from Muscat de Frontignan), Tokays (from Muscadelle) and ports (from a blend of red grape varieties). Fortified wines, too, remain a speciality of Glenrowan and Milawa to the south of Rutherglen, though the larger producers in this region offer a wide range of table wines too.

To the west of the state, Drumborg and Great Western both have sparkling-wine traditions: Drumborg as a source of cool climate fruit, and Great Western as an area where sparkling wines are made, though its Shiraz and Riesling can be good, too.

The Pyrenees, a former gold-mining area, is hotter. Its best wines are muscular reds from Cabernet and Shiraz. The Goulburn Valley is where one of Australia's oldest wine producers, Château Tahbilk, is sited, near to Mitchelton, one of the most determinedly forward-looking. Extravagantly flavoured Marsanne is a speciality.

Near to Melbourne, finally, lies the Yarra Valley, Geelong and the Mornington Peninsula, all relatively cool areas sustaining high-endeavour, boutique-style wineries which produce some of the country's most thought-provoking wines.

Bailey's, Glenrowan Massive, flavour-stuffed reds and fine stickies.

Best's, Great Western Shiraz and Dolcetto worth a look, but don't really justify their prices. Cabernet deeper and better.

De Bortoli, Yarra Valley Generous, peppery Yarra Shiraz.

Brown Brothers, Milawa Sound rather than exciting. Light, raspberryish Tarrango seems now to have lost its early charm; good Rieslings, though.

Campbells of Rutherglen Good value stickies with fresher style than some.

Chambers' Rosewood, Rutherglen Commendably backward-looking, caramel-rich fortified wines; even the labels are stuck in a delicious time warp.

Château Tahbilk, Goulburn Valley Sometimes superb Cabernet and Shiraz, with Private Bin versions from centenarian vines, full of earthy savour (new oak is shunned). The basic varietals, though, can seem dry and slim. Marsanne is aromatically haunting — buttered scone, peach and honeysuckle scents — if heavy.

Coldstream Hills, Yarra Valley Chardonnay and Pinot Noir of pure, tapered though over-controlled fruit from a gifted and hyper-active wine critic for whom criticism (admirably) is not enough: James Halliday. Southcorp (Penfolds) owns.

Domaine Chandon, Yarra Valley Green Point (the export label) is, for me, the most consistently satisfying and complex of all Australia's sparkling wines: the '92 was complex, tight and expressive, while the '94 is full-flavoured though nervier. Still Chardonnay and Pinot Noir are good, though austere by Aussie standards.

Delatite, MANSFIELD High-sited vineyards producing perfumed and intense Riesling, crisper than most, to lead an incisive range. Dead Man's Hill Gewürztraminer is one of the few half-decent Australian versions.

Dromana, MORNINGTON PENINSULA Elegant, limpid Pinot Noir, Chardonnay and Cabernet-Merlot. Second label Schinus Molle offers fair-value alternatives.

Green Point see Domaine Chandon

Longleat, GOULBURN VALLEY Tahbilk-Merrill operation producing lush Marsanne.

Lindemans see New South Wales

Mitchelton, GOULBURN VALLEY Lime-charged Riesling; mallowy, sometimes over-weight, Marsanne; and three-grape blends provide most interest.

Mick Morris, RUTHERGLEN Great fortifieds (especially unctuous, perfumed-garden Muscat); even the table-wine Durif is port-like.

Mount Langi Ghiran, GREAT WESTERN Fine, lean-line Shiraz has attracted Rhône interest, supported by mineral-charged Riesling and high-definition Cabernet. See feature.

Red Cliffs, MILDURA Pleasant but anodyne range.

Great Western see South Australia

Schinus Molle see Dromana

Stanton and Killeen, RUTHERGLEN Complex, Muscat of ravishing depth.

Taltarni, PYRENEES Dominique Portet, brother of Bernard (see Napa Valley, Clos du Val) has produced some titanic, mouth-shattering Shiraz and Cabernet, though these have softened of late. Sauvignon and sparkling wine less successful. See also Tasmania (Clover Hill).

Tarrawarra, YARRA VALLEY Limpid Pinot Noir.

Water Wheel, BENDIGO Excellent purity and complexity across the range, peaking with the grand '94 Shiraz.

Yarra Ridge, YARRA VALLEY Intense, grassy Sauvignon and melony Chardonnay both good; Cabernet clean and refreshing. The subtlest branch of Mildara Blass.

Yarra Yering, YARRA VALLEY Bailey Carrodus, a quiet botanist, takes a hobbyist's approach — and produces some of Australia's greatest reds as he does so: the porcelain-fine Underhill Shiraz and Dry Red No.2, close-grained Cabernet for Dry Red No.1, unintimidating Pinot and evolving Chardonnay.

Vintages
1996 ★★; 1995 ★★; 1994 ★★★; 1993 ★★★; 1992 ★★★; 1991 ★★★★;
1990 ★★★★; 1989 ★★★; 1988 ★★★; 1987 ★★; 1986 ★★★★; 1985 ★★★.

Specialist retailers
see New South Wales.

In bed with Trevor

Trevor Mast has grown up with the Australian wine industry. Indeed this pale, laconic winemaker (he looks like Harpo Marx after a night on the tiles) has succeeded, by luck as much as planning, in staying on the surf side of every new antipodean wine wave over the last quarter century. He's there again now. "All the big boys are desperate to get into bed with us," he says, shaking his head, horrified at the prospect of being a viticultural catamite. "We're not interested."

Let's start at the beginning. When Trevor began work in 1969, as a lab assistant to distillers Gilbey IDV in Melbourne, blokes drank beer. "Drinking red wine was a pretty abnormal thing to do back then," he remembers. Yet his work with spirits revealed he had a very good palate, and this in turn led him to wine, initially through Gilbey's estate purchases.

Trevor decided to quit and to train as a winemaker. He went where the technology at that time was hottest (or, to be more accurate, coolest): Geisenheim in Germany. Before he'd even begun the course, he had 11 job offers in his pocket for later. His studies were complemented by holiday work both locally and in France, Portugal, Hungary ("jeez, their viticulture was good") – and Harlow, tasting wine alongside Gilbey's Masters of Wine. His only complaint about the Geisenheim course was that red winemaking was covered in 20 minutes. This was partly why the first job he accepted was in South Africa for Nederburg. "'I found myself with a huge staff, half of whom were better qualified than I was – but I was white so I was boss." After a year, though, his wife decided she couldn't handle South Africa any longer.

Trevor's first Aussie job was dealing with the barely ripe, rain-sodden fruit Seppelts was bringing up from its Drumborg vineyards southeast of Coonawarra. "I only stayed there a year. There were a lot of political problems." But the future winked at him during those months: he remembers seeing a parcel of fruit from a vineyard called Mount Langi Ghiran arrive at Seppelts and be treated with royal and secretive reverence.

Three years on, the owners of Mount Langi Ghiran approached him; they wanted to begin producing and selling their own wine. Would Trevor make it? "I thought beaut. Let's give it a go."

And it went. Went so well, in fact, that when the owning family decided they wanted to sell the vineyard in 1987, Trevor found a financial partner and bought it himself.

What's so special about Mount Langi Ghiran? The answer is that it has a highly distinctive regional style, especially clear to see in its elegant, polished, limpid Shiraz. Regional styles are now regarded as being the key to future developments in Australia. Just being Australian, in other words – ripe, fruity, generous – won't be enough; future wine drinkers are going to want to tell with a sip whether they're drinking a Barossa Shiraz (Dumpty-fat, blackberry-sodden and salt-oozing) or a Grampians Shiraz like Mount Langi Ghiran (racehorse-lean, blackcurrant-crisp, buffed to a polish with spice).

I've tried three vintages of the Shiraz recently (1992, 1990 and 1986) and each time, behind the distinctive Australian 'fruit-first' approach, there was a hint of the shapely elegance of, say, Côte-Rôtie. Sure enough, Trevor admitted, a leading Rhône valley wine producer was also very keen to make Shiraz with Mount Langi Ghiran. He wouldn't tell me who it was, but my guess would be the many-horizoned Chapoutier brothers. Watch this wave.

South Australia
The big one

When I think of the best of non-European wine-growing, I think of Australia. When I think of the best of Australia, I think of the Barossa Valley, northeast of Adelaide. When I think of the best of the Barossa Valley, I think of its massive, inky yet soft-bellied Shiraz wines, made from the fruit of old, twisted vines. These might have been drilled from the centre of the earth rather than merely farmed: black, drenched in salts and minerals, dense as medicine balls, they seem a delicious yet complicated, ghost-honouring expression of this old continent's long, sun-charred geological history. A sense of *terroir* (see page 21) surges from them. Australia will, one day, have its Bordeaux, an area where quality combines with quantity; Barossa Valley will be a leading contender.

The importance of South Australia is that it has half a dozen regions very nearly as distinctive as this, as well as the bulk of Riverland and with it the bulk of Australian wine. Coonawarra is the Barossa's chief rival: a long tongue of red earth over limestone, lying a giant's throw out and away southeast of Adelaide on the cooler marches of Victoria. It is Coonawarra — a precise nine mile by one mile zone with half a metre of perfectly drained red soil over a metre and a half of pure limestone — that is providing the blueprint for regional definition in Australia. Even here, the process has been controversial, yet anyone who tastes an authentic Coonawarra wine will quickly understand the point of the exercise. While Barossa's greatest wines are made from Shiraz, Coonawarra's are made from Cabernet Sauvignon, which acquires a driving depth of flavour there, a peppery concentration and a curranty purity achieved nowhere else in Australia. When young, however, Coonwarra reds can be unpalatably aggressive, and some of the more ambitious Cabernets look set to frighten the unwary for years.

Clare, Watervale and the Polish Hill River lie north of Barossa; Langhorne Creek and the Southern Vales are further south, with the Vales (which include McLaren Vale) lying on the outskirts of Adelaide. Clare produces a slightly harder, punchier style of wine than lush Barossa; while the Southern Vales' booming Shiraz and Cabernets of tradition are now balanced by successful whites from higher, hill sites. Langhorne Creek continues the boom. Padthaway, finally, lies two-thirds of the way to Coonawarra, and was developed as a Coonawarra-growalike. In the event, it has been Chardonnay which has outperformed all other varieties there.

Tim Adams, CLARE Fine though now expensive Semillon and Shiraz (including brooding old-vine Aberfeldy) lead the range. Rhône-style Fergus worth trying (though '94 is light). Riesling has good citrus-pith style.

Angas see Yalumba

Angove's Nanya, RIVERLAND Inexpensive and unsubtle wines.

Jim Barry, CLARE Ambitious family winery with flavoury Riesling and powerful though expensive Armagh Shiraz, full of artless honesty.

Basedow, BAROSSA Gutsy, salty wines.

Berri–Renmano, RIVERLAND Unsubtle; often good value.

Wolf Blass, BAROSSA Popular, oaky, obvious wines include Ribena-like Cabernet Sauvignon. Riesling's my favourite, and the Wolf Blass Brut sparkler is better than it is given credit for.

Blaxland, BAROSSA Spicy '94 Mourvèdre-Grenache a great Rhônealike.

Buckley's, BAROSSA Fine pencilly '95 Clare Valley Malbec and surprisingly dense, grippy '94 Barossa Grenache.

Breakaway see Geoff Merrill.

Grant Burge, BAROSSA Big Barossa landholdings promise wines of increasing excitement. Look out for Black Monster Shiraz and the controlled power of the Cameron Vale Cabernet Sauvignon.

Bridgwater Mill, ADELAIDE HILLS Reliable second-label to Petaluma.

Chapel Hill, MCLAREN VALE Tight, fine-crafted wines, especially dark, brooding Cabernet (includes Coonawarra component) and sweet, lush, pure McLaren Vale Shiraz. Eden Valley Riesling is zestily definitive, one of Australia's best, and unwooded Chardonnay cleanly drinkable.

Château Reynella, MCLAREN VALE Hardy-owned, and among the best wines in the group. The Basket Pressed Shiraz is a thunderer, and superb value; the Cabernet-Merlot hardly less good; '94 Chardonnay has fine intensity and a zingier style than many.

Croser Technically impeccable but rather hard, cold, ungiving sparkling wine. See also **Petaluma.**

D'Arenberg, SOUTHERN VALES Old-established favourite producing dark, almost sombre wines from old vines.

Eden Ridge see Mountadam.

Hardy's, SOUTHERN VALES Large company now merged with Riverland giant Berri-Renmano, and including the reliable Nottage Hill (good '95 Chardonnay), Leasingham and Château Reynella labels. Eileen Hardy range peaks with the earthy Shiraz; Bird Series offers pretty labels and reliability. Bankside Shiraz very solid for its price. The 1991 Thomas Hardy Coonawarra Cabernet Sauvignon is wonderfully deep and peppery, and basic Hardy's '93 Coonawarra Cabernet Sauvignon offers great depth and value for money.

Heggies, ADELAIDE HILLS Owned by Yalumba. Citrus-zesty Riesling in straight and botrytised versions worth seeking out.

Henschke, BAROSSA One of the regional thoroughbreds and – phew! – rarely overoaked. Pure, expressive Hill of Grace Shiraz is most sought-after, but Mount Edelstone can be just as lingering and still more generous; Cyril Henschke is the top Cabernet. Riesling (including the generous Julius and citrussy Greens' Hill) and Semillon lead the whites for me, but everything's worth trying.

Heritage, BAROSSA Whites lack focus, but reds (especially gritty '94 Cabernet-Malbec) exciting.

Hill-Smith Estate, ADELAIDE HILLS Good value, especially Yalumba Chardonnay.

Hollick, COONAWARRA Classy regional range led by dense, almost violent Ravenswood Cabernet. Terra Red offers good value.

Katnook Estate, COONAWARRA   Powerful Chardonnay (including sumptuous though unbalanced botrytis version) and mid-weight Merlot supported by elegant yet deep Cabernet; Sauvignon Blanc least successful. Riddoch Estate second label (includes good tangy burnt-earth Riesling).

Tim Knappstein, CLARE   Clare clarity throughout the range, led by delicious Riesling and limpid Cabernet. The '93 Lenswood Pinot Noir is magnificently burgundian. Petaluma-owned.

Leasingham, CLARE   Hardy-owned estate producing authentically cindery Shiraz among other varietals. Consistent quality.

Peter Lehmann, BAROSSA   Soft, fat Barossa character aplenty in Lehmann's Shiraz and Chardonnay; unoaked Semillon has a nice waxy nose, but lacks palate interest. '90 Cabernet-Malbec 'Cellar Collection' is still huge.

Lindemans see New South Wales.

Maglieri, McLAREN VALE   Deliciously slushy Shiraz.

Charles Melton, BAROSSA   Nine Popes, a smooth, deep Grenache-Syrah blend from old vines, has swiftly established itself as a Barossa classic. Good rosé too, and who else would blend Pinot and Shiraz?

Geoff Merrill, SOUTHERN VALES   Geoff Merrill label offers fair value only; Mount Hurtle range full-flavoured but heavy handed. Breakaway a second label. Generally good big-bellied rosé wines.

Moculta, BAROSSA   Cooperative-produced wines: impressive '94 Cab-Merlot.

Mountadam, ADELAIDE HILLS   A European, vineyard-led approach furnishes fine, complex Chardonnay and Pinot, plus characterful Riesling. David Wynn range varies from the superb ('90 Shiraz) to the dull; Eden Ridge organics are sound rather than exciting.

Mount Bold, McLAREN VALE   Full-throttle Cabernet, Shiraz and Chardonnay.

Mount Hurtle see Geoff Merrill

Nottage Hill see Hardy

Orlando, BAROSSA   Jacob's Creek now too big a brand for regional identity, but reliable. I like Riesling the best of the four.

Oxford Landing see Yalumba

Parker Estate, COONAWARRA   Severe, pricy Cabernet for long ageing.

Penfolds, BAROSSA and elsewhere   The best range of red wines in the world. Bin 28 Kalimna Shiraz has seen a price rise or two, but remains the value-for-money star; Bin 707 Cabernet is hard to beat for down-the-line, pure, curranty quality. Grange richly deserves its 'King of Australia' billing and Bin 389 ('Baby Grange') is thunderous, too; the Koonunga Hills Shiraz-Cabernet and Chardonnay provide good value, as does Bin 2 Shiraz-Mourvèdre. The organic wines are a welcome addition, and improve with each vintage. Rawson's Retreat red (Cabernet-Shiraz) much better than unsubtle white. Riesling attractive and keenly priced.

Penley Estate, COONAWARRA   Ambitious new boy whose first Cabernets and Chardonnays are promising if aggressive.

Petaluma, ADELAIDE HILLS   Distinctively labelled wines of great purity of flavour, consistency, drinkability and fidelity to regional style.

Pewsey Vale, ADELAIDE HILLS   Fine Riesling from another Yalumba scion.

Pikes, CLARE   Wines of shattering intensity, especially Chardonnay.

Pirramimma, ADELAIDE HILLS   Soft, minty style.

Primo Estate, ADELAIDE PLAINS   Oddball excellence from Joe Grilli, including intriguing Colombard; rich, four-square Shiraz (also salty) and dark, slow-evolving Amarone-style Cabernet-Merlot. Sparkler lacks depth and a final 'cut'.

Riddoch Estate see Katnook Estate.

Rockford, BAROSSA   The '*vigneron*' approach (old vines, old equipment, long discussions and a fine beard) produces deliciously lazy yet powerful wines, led by soft tannin Basket Press Shiraz, Dry Country Grenache and low-aroma, weighty Riesling.

Rouge Homme, COONAWARRA   Lindeman's owned: the economy end of Coonawarra, yet fair value throughout.

Ryecroft, McLAREN VALE   Rosemount-owned; fair quality.

St Hallett, BAROSSA   Old Block Shiraz is a wonderful stormy-weather wine, increasingly looking like one of Australia's *grands crus*. The full, salty Chardonnay and Semillon-Sauvignon are reliable regional realisations of their varieties, while Poacher's Blend and Gamekeeper's Reserve offer fine value. The Bordeaux-blend is hardly claretty, but makes a lyrically balanced Australian wine. Straight Shiraz has been fine, but the '93 seemed over-hard.

Samuels Bay, ADELAIDE HILLS   Wynn-owned (see **Mountadam**); the whites don't do much for me, but the '94 Malbec was generously flavoured.

Seaview, SOUTHERN VALES   Penfolds-owned: fine value sparklers. The '92 Vintage Reserve Pinot Noir-Chardonnay Brut was yeasty, rich and ripe.

Seppelts, BAROSSA   Sparkling wine supremo with base in Victoria (Great Western) as well as South Australia. Good standard Great Western up to top-flight Salinger. Sparkling Shiraz improbable and exciting, and reliable table wines. Also superb heavy Fino.

Shaw & Smith, SOUTHERN VALES   As good as Sauvignon gets in Australia, plus a fine-grained Chardonnay (oaked and unoaked).

Tollana, BAROSSA   Used in the UK as a Thresher brand name from Penfolds. Decent though unexciting.

Geoff Weaver, BAROSSA   Fine '92 Riesling with tongue-rousing mango-and-papaya flavours.

Wirra-Wirra, SOUTHERN VALES   Rich Chardonnay, asparagussy Sauvignon Blanc and mid-weight Shiraz 'The Angelus' won't disappoint. WW label offers value.

Woolshed, COONAWARRA   Decent taste of Coonawarra without breaking the bank.

David Wynn see **Mountadam**

Wynns, Coonawarra The regional pioneers, now in Penfolds' hands. Most of the range is consistent and accessible, with typically pure, curranty Coonawarra Cabernet and burnt, earthy Chardonnay. The basic Riesling offers some of the best value in Australia, and even ages well. Top of the range Michael Hermitage and, especially, John Riddoch Cabernet are power-hammer wines for salting away in your cellar.

Yalumba, Barossa One of Australia's most consistent all-rounders. Angas Brut sparklers and Oxford Landing wines are the big sellers, but there's key quality, too – in the powerful Signature Barossa wines; in the soft, sweet Bush-Vine Grenache and saltier, more *terroir*-inspired Reserve Grenache Whitmore Old Vineyard; and in the fine-grained Pinot-Chardonnay and Yalumba D sparklers. Ozzophiles should track down the disarmingly claretty Sparkling Cabernet Sauvignon. The Antipodean, though, seems to me largely an exercise in packaging; perhaps it will improve as the Viognier vines age. See also **Heggies, Hill-Smith** and **Pewsey Vale.**

Vintages
1996 ★★★; 1995 ★★; 1994 ★★★; 1993 ★★★; 1992 ★★; 1991 ★★★★;
1990 ★★★; 1989 ★★; 1988 ★★★; 1987 ★★★; 1986 ★★★★; 1985 ★★★.

Specialist retailers
see New South Wales.

Western Australia

Let's get intense

Western Australia's winegrowing began in the furnace of the Swan Valley, north of Perth, and it has been moving towards the cooler but more remote south ever since. Margaret River – the pig's snout which lies at the continent's south-western tip – has been the most consistently explored area, but even there the possibilities remain expansive; Great Southern, an area which might encompass the rest but is in practice centred around Mount Barker, has barely begun. At their best, Western Australia's wines have remarkable definition, intensity and longevity. The fact that winemaking here has been pioneered as much by cultured or wealthy amateurs as by the big guns of Australian wine business has left a legacy of high prices and inconsistent quality; the region's remoteness ensures that this is changing only slowly. Yet there are benefits, too: the complexity of European models has left a deeper mark here than elsewhere, and the state's best bottles provoke thought as well as grunts of gustative satisfaction. Western Australia produces Aussie wines for French wine lovers.

Cape Mentelle, Margaret River The most consistent of all WA producers, David Hohnen's Cape Mentelle (now co-owned by Veuve Clicquot) manages to turn out a never-less-than-characterful range year after year. The '93 Shiraz is salty, punchy, bitter-edged yet fresh, too, while the '93 Cabernet-Merlot is clean-fruited, gutsy, with lots of green-edged depth; straight Cabernet and Zinfandel are also very good. Tasteful, creamy Chardonnay and zingy Semillon-Sauvignon complete the picture. Second-label Ironstone (not just Margaret River fruit) off to a storming start with salty Cabernet-Shiraz and grassy-zesty '94 Semillon-Chardonnay; the '95 isn't so good.

Capel Vale, BUSSELTON Intense, penetrating whites.

Cullens, MARGARET RIVER Great, age-worthy Cabernet, though not every year, as well as achingly powerful Chardonnay, deep orchestral Sauvignon Blanc and impressive Cab-Merlot.

Devil's Lair, MARGARET RIVER Fine, mouthfilling Chardonnay in exuberant Margaret River style. '93 Pinot Noir a bit hot and dry.

Evans & Tate, SWAN VALLEY Tropical-fruit whites offer better value than generally dryish reds, though the chunky Margaret River Cabernet can be good.

Goundrey, GREAT SOUTHERN Balanced, drinkable wines at a reasonable price. Chardonnay and Cabernet better than Shiraz.

Houghton, SWAN VALLEY Generally big but unsubtle wines. Moondah Brook (north of Perth, but cooler) Chenin Blanc and Verdelho take tropical-fruit flavours almost as far as they can go. HWB is subtler and merits its classic status with fresh acidity and delicate oak. Hardy-owned.

Ironstone see Cape Mentelle

Leeuwin, MARGARET RIVER Tight-grained, rich, finely detailed Chardonnay at white burgundy prices leads the range by a mile. Cabernet to watch and wait on; Riesling to enjoy now.

Moss Wood, MARGARET RIVER A more straightforward approach than some, yet Margaret River complexity marbles the fruit. Semillon (oaked and unoaked) and Pinot are the most individual offerings; full-blooded Chardonnay and mid-weight Cabernet compete seriously.

Plantagenet, GREAT SOUTHERN Perfumed, intense range; '93 Chardonnay has impressive nutty complexity.

Willespie, MARGARET RIVER Interesting, vivid range includes mallowy Verdelho and tangy Sauvignon.

Vintages
1996 ★★★; 1995 ★★; 1994 ★★★★; 1993 ★★; 1992 ★★★; 1991 ★★★;
1990 ★★★★; 1989 ★★; 1988 ★★★; 1987 ★★★; 1986 ★★★; 1985 ★★★★.

Specialist retailers
see New South Wales.

Tasmania
Australia in mittens

Green Tasmania, a crumb of Australia floating off towards Antarctica, provides the last word in cool-climate Antipodean viticulture. Acidity quivers like a saw in every one of its wines. In theory, the slow growing season and coolness combined with southern-hemisphere luminosity should provide superb results; it may yet. For the time being, many of its wines teeter on a raw, thin edge and offer poor value for money. The best are limpid, elegant Chardonnay, Pinot and Riesling from Piper's Brook (second label Tasmania Wine Company/Ninth Island). Sparklers should be good, but Clover Hill (Taltarni's Tasmanian venture) and Jansz from Heemskerk have yet to prove Tasmania's case with wines in which acidity is balanced by vinosity and the grainy counterweight of yeastiness. Early releases are sour.

Austria

The great experiment

I went to dinner with a wine-writing friend last autumn and, as generally happens on these occasions, the guests were asked to guess what the wines we were being served were. The fattest Chardonnay and the richest Cabernet turned out to be — nobody guessed — from Austria. Typical, perhaps, of British ignorance of what the Austrians have been up to over the last few years, and typical, too, of Austria itself, a country whose wine growers are prepared to try any experiment, to disprove any theory, to upset any preconception, so long as it produces a tasty glass of wine for dinner.

The country has renovated its viticulture to exciting effect over the last decade. A spirit of unTeutonic adventurousness has met with an enthusiastic consumer response — so enthusiastic, indeed, that Austria's best wines are generally beyond the reach of British wallets. What we can afford, and what Austria can afford to send us, are inexpensive and luscious, honey-thick dessert wines from Burgenland; and fresh yet rounded dry wines from Riesling, Pinot Blanc (Weissburgunder), Pinot Gris (Ruländer) and Austria's own sappy, peppery Grüner Veltliner grape variety. Red wines (based on Pinot Noir/Blauburgunder, St Laurent, Limberger, Blauer Portugieser, Blauer Zweigelt and Blaufränkisch) tend to be shocking and raspberry-fresh in flavour, though in Burgenland they fatten out impressively enough to mimic the best of France and Italy.

Vienna, Austria's eccentric capital, lies in Danubian fat lands. Vineyards are drawn like skirts around the city, perched on the sunny hills which glide towards Slovakia, the Czech Republic and Slovenia, and tapered into the reedbeds of the Neusiedlersee, an enormous puddle which Austria shares with Hungary. The rest of modern Austria stretches away mountainously and vinelessly to the west.

Most terms on Austrian wine labels are similar to those found on German labels; uniquely Austrian words you may see include Steinfeder, Federspiel and Smaragd (Wachau terms approximately equivalent to Kabinett, Spätlese and Auslese) and Ausbruch (a term used to signify sweet wines made by a Tokaji-like process of mixing sweet botrytised and unbotrytised grapes).

Bründlmayer, Kamptal Concentrated, peppery Grüner Veltliner and delicate Riesling from low yields.

Feiler-Artinger, Burgenland Offers fine dessert wines as well as a range of good reds. Solitaire is a Blaufränkisch-Merlot-Cabernet blend, while 999 is predominantly Merlot.

Freie Weingärtener, WACHAU   Grüner Veltliners have lots of white-pepper style; Riesling is patchier, but the best have good chewy substance.

Hirtzberger, WACHAU   Impressive, fruit-saturated range, with especially succulent Grau and Weissburgunder blend.

Kracher, NEUSIEDLERSEE   Like his cousin Willi Opitz (see below), Kracher produces a huge range of sumptuous dessert wines from different grape varieties.

Krutzler, BURGENLAND   Rich Blaufränkisch. Perwolff includes 15 per cent Cabernet Sauvignon.

Moser, WIENVIERTEL   Leading Austrian producer-merchant. The organically produced estate wines from the Knights of Malta and Siegendorf estates are more interesting than the dry, vinous merchant wines. See also **Servus.**

Opitz, NEUSIEDLERSEE   A huge range of ferociously innovative dry and sweet wines (from both botrytised and raisined grapes). Tiny quantities mean high prices, but Opitz's sweet wines are often thrilling.

Pichler, WACHAU   Dense, clean-edged wines from very low yields from a producer whose philosophy mirrors Müller-Catoir's in Rheinpfalz.

Pöckl, BURGENLAND   Red-wine specialist with a passion for Zweigelt (Admiral mixes it with a little Cabernet Sauvignon and Merlot).

Prager, WACHAU   Great if expensive Grüner Veltliner stuffed with doughy fruit, plus rich, alcoholic Rieslings.

Salomon/Undhof, KREMS   Best for spicy, smoky, extract-laden Riesling from one of Austria's finest sites, the Steiner Hund.

Seewinkler Impressionen, NEUSIEDLERSEE   Good value dessert wines, better balanced than most.

Servus, BURGENLAND   Curious co-venture between Lenz Moser (see above) and the Burgenland regional authorities: large but rather nondescript blend of Grüner Veltliner, Welschriesling and Pinot Blanc, designed to compete with New World whites.

Stiegelmar, BURGENLAND   Wide range, including oaked wines; unoaked varietal dry whites have quivering depth of fruit and fine extract.

Umathum, BURGENLAND   Like Pöckl (q.v.), a red-wine specialist majoring with gutsy Zweigelt.

Wieninger, VIENNA   Impressive, hugely expressive Chardonnay Grand Select '93 shows what Austria can manage – at a price.

Winzer Krems, KREMS   Reliable cooperative producing a range of well-differentiated wines.

Winzerhaus   Austrian Wine Export Centre brand name for wines selected from Lower Austrian cooperatives. UK cuvées are well chosen and appealingly packaged by the British agents, giving some of the best value white and red varietals from Austria. '94 Grüner Veltliner shows the influence of a trip to NZ for winemaker Reinhard Arocker in its fresh, clean, crisp style.

Bosnia-Hercegovina

Out of the ruins

Bosnia-Hercegovina has had more pressing matters than wine production
to think about since independence, and the fluid state of its borders means
that even a provisional verdict on its future potential as a wine nation must wait.
Nevertheless weighty, linden-scented Zilavka from Mostar was always thought to
be one of the best wines produced in this part of the Balkans; let's hope it will
become so again. Both Croatia and Serbia snatched vinelands from Bosnia during
the years of the Yugoslavian conflict; these seem unlikely to be returned.

Brazil

Humid airs

Brazil has a large wine production, but much of it is based on hybrid varieties,
chiefly Isabella, which are able to cope with the generally humid, sub-
tropical conditions. Most Brazilian wine-growing is found in Rio Grande do Sul,
in the far south of the country, and increasingly in Frontera, on the Uruguayan
border. High rainfall and humidity means that the vines are heavily treated with
anti-fungal agents, and good wines are uncommon. I have yet to taste one. Even
John Worontschak, holidaying from Thames Valley (see **England**) for Tesco,
hasn't pulled it off yet.

Bulgaria

Getting sorted

Bulgarian viticulture was, prior to 1989, one of the few state enterprises in
Eastern Europe which worked with anything resembling efficiency. The
country succeeded in modernising its wine industry functionally enough to take
full advantage of its no-hassle growing conditions and low-wage labour. The
unpolished but competently made, cheap varietal wines which resulted were
gratefully poured on most days of the week, winter and summer, in suburban
homes the length and breadth of Northern Europe.

Now the cards have been shuffled and dealt again. Unlike its Hungarian neighbour, Bulgaria has no fine-wine tradition to attract international investment. For a while, the quality of Bulgarian exports became hugely variable as newly privatised wineries sold off questionable stocks at 'bargain' prices to generate some sort of income, but quality has steadied again over the last 18 months. It seems likely that the best wineries (see below) will improve the consistency with which they turn out enjoyably drinkable red wine and clean, spicy whites. Indeed foreign winemakers led by Kym Milne MW have been producing some exceptionally attractive wines – characterised by clean, fresh fruit, natural balance and impressive depth of flavour – over the last year in Bulgaria, and the Bulgarian Vintners Company (BVC) has a major consultancy programme with Australian David Wollan in hand to upgrade fruit quality. Whether they can do more than this, whether fine wines or single-site wines will emerge to deepen our primitive understanding of Bulgaria's regionality, remains to be seen. The potential is unquestionably there – many of the country's vineyards are on the same latitude as Tuscany – but the vineyards, Milne and others report, are in a poor state, and the slow pace of privatisation and lack of foreign investment means that they will get more dilapidated still before improvements begin.

There are six loose categories of Bulgarian wine. 'Quality' is the lowest – a misnomer, as in Germany. 'Country wines' are made from a blend of two varieties: they vary from the mediocre to the simply enjoyable. Straight varietals provide bread-and-butter wines; they can be fruity and good. 'Reserve' and 'Special Reserve' wines are higher quality varietals aged for two (white) or three (red) years in oak (sometimes new or newish). 'Controliran' indicates wine from named varieties grown in a region of controlled origin; such wines supposedly have some regional typicity though this is as yet generally hard to discern.

Most Bulgarian wines are produced from recognised grape varieties, but among Bulgaria's own grape varieties you will find Gamza, a light strawberryish red (the same variety as Hungary's Kadarka); Mavrud, a deeper, fuller-bodied red; Melnik, the only Bulgarian red capable of toughness; Pamid, a soft, quaffing red; Dimiat, a fresh-to-neutral white; Misket, a spicier white (a Dimiat-Riesling cross); and Rkatziteli, the strong-sour white of the East in general.

Assenovgrad, SOUTHERN REGION Soft reds, led by deep, plummy Mavrud.

Domaine Boyar Not a single property, but merchant and agent for a number of privatised wineries.

Burgas, EASTERN REGION Some good-value country wines including tobacco-like Cabernet-Merlot.

Damianitza, SOUTH-WESTERN REGION Look out for purposeful reds from the Melnik grape.

Dve Mogli, NORTHERN REGION Good '91 Cabernet Sauvignon from Rousse unearthed by BVC's consultant Aussie David Wollan. 'Twin Peaks' is the literal and fortuitous translation of Dve Mogli.

Haskovo, SOUTHERN REGION Soft, full-bodied reds, especially Merlot.

Iambol, SOUTHERN REGION Some minty, sapid Cabernet Sauvignon, like the '90, '91 and '92 Special Reserve. In process of management buy-out.

Khan Krum, EASTERN REGION Fresh whites, including oaky Chardonnay ('93 in softer style than previously).

Lyaskovets, NORTHERN REGION Good 'Bear Ridge' wines made with Kym Milne.

Novi Pazar, EASTERN REGION Decent Chardonnay and Sauvignon Blanc.

Lovico Suhindol, NORTHERN REGION The winery which taught us all how to say 'Cabernet Sauvignon'. After a patchy year or two, back on form again, and increasingly good for Merlot. '91 Gamza Reserve a classically soothing, easy-drinking red.

Oriachovitza, SOUTHERN REGION Choice, flavoury Cabernet-Merlot blends, and good straight Cabernet, too.

Preslav, EASTERN REGION Try-harder winery barrel-fermenting some of its Chardonnay. '94 Chardonnay-Sauvignon Blanc Country Wine was brilliant value.

Rousse, NORTHERN REGION Winery up on the Romanian border with an impressive recent turn of speed, especially for fresh-flavoured reds. Some of Bulgaria's rare hill-sited vineyards lie in its catchment area. Good Chardonnay (e.g. '93) coming through now, its fresh acidity comparing favourably with Midi whites, as well as excellent spicy '94 Riesling (sold under Yantra Valley label) – better than Aussies at £2 or £3 more.

Sakar, SOUTHERN REGION Top Merlot, some of Bulgaria's best, leads the range.

Sliven, SUB-BALKAN REGION Monster winery churning out large quantities of everything. Cabernet and Misket can be good.

Stambolovo, SOUTHERN REGION Easy-going reds, especially mid-weight Merlot with pleasant claretty balance.

Svishtov, NORTHERN REGION Good fresh-flavoured Cabernets from this winery on the brown Danube.

Targovischte, NORTHERN REGION Clean Chardonnay, both flowery and vinous, offers excellent value.

Twin Peaks see Dve Mogli.

Varna, EASTERN REGION Whites from this winery on the Black Sea have more aroma and fresher acidity than most.

Yantra Valley see Rousse.

Canada

World leader ... in icewine

Four of Canada's provinces grow wine (Ontario, British Columbia, Quebec and Nova Scotia). The country's ferocious winters mean that most of this has traditionally been from hardy non-vinifera or hybrid varieties; recently, however, producers have been experimenting with classic 'international' varieties such as

Chardonnay and Pinot Noir. Canada's greatest successes have been, unsurprisingly, with its icewines (dessert wines made from juice pressed from frozen berries) based on Riesling and, above all, the hybrid Vidal which gives massive mouthfuls of excruciating intensity; the country is now in volume terms the world's major producer of this normally rare speciality. Chardonnay can be slenderly plausible, though it is often overoaked; un-iced Riesling suffers from stylistic uncertainty, though it ought eventually to give interesting results. Canada's reds have yet to show they belong in the world, though generous vintages may yield worthwhile Pinot Noir. Leading producers include Cave Spring Cellars, Château des Charmes, Henry of Pelham, Hillebrand, Inniskillin and Vineland, all in Ontario; and Gray Monk, Mission Hill and Sumac Ridge in British Columbia.

Chile

Keeping its promises

Wine journalists never get to drink what they want; they drink what other people want them to try. I'm not asking for sympathy, merely explaining why every third bottle through my kitchen last year wasn't an inexpensive Chilean red – which it probably would have been had I been choosing for myself. Chile, I wrote here last year, has played the talented but irresolute adolescent for many years. It began to take life more seriously in the early '90s, and delivered substantially on its promises during 1995 and 1996 with vivid, lushly fruited red wines and creamy, clean, high-definition whites. Chile, in short, offered some of the best value on British wine shelves last year.

Every wine-literate visitor leaves enraptured by the country's phylloxera-free vineyards, its mediterranean climate of heartbeat regularity, its perfect sub-Andean sites. Wine culture here has long antecedents (over four centuries of fermentation); and the country's best wines, such as those of Cousiño Macul, have proved themselves perennially fine, supple and long-lived. Yet most of Chile's large, family-run wine-producing companies doddered and dandered their way through the 1970s and 1980s in a spirit of resounding commercial and qualitative unadventurousness. The trembling purity and comeliness of the typical young Chilean red was squandered in tired old tuns; white wines were pudgy, mealy, as up-to-date as a bakelite wireless. The domestic market drank anything it was given; indeed it still does.

The renovatory process, of course, still has some way to run: yields need to come down further; there is still over-processing in wineries; too many vineyards remain on highly fertile, heavily irrigated valley-floor sites. But the new-found sense of identity and purpose bodes well. Political fresh air has encouraged imaginative outside investors to take the plunge, and a network of small estates with high ambitions looks set to galvanise the elephants of the Chilean wine scene further. The arrival of several of Bordeaux's big guns – Bruno Prats and Paul Pontallier at Viña Aquitania, and Michel Rolland as consultant for Casa Lapostolle – confirms Chile's appeal and potential.

Varieties are the internationally familiar ones, with the exception of the Pais, little if any of which is used in export wines. The only snare is that the vast majority of the wine labelled 'Sauvignon Blanc' is for the time being still made from Sauvignonasse, its cousin. When very young, Sauvignonasse can have a specious appeal; however it fades quickly into triviality, especially when produced from high-yielding vines.

Chile's new system of regional appellations marks a first step rather than a final destination in coming to terms with the geographical potential of its vineyard areas. The planting of the Casablanca valley has been the key regional development of the last decade, since this near-coastal site northwest of Santiago has given the country its first truly fresh, varietally pungent white wines; its fresh-fruited reds promise much, too. The effect has been not only to initiate a search for 'the next Casablanca', but also to prompt a reassessment of existing areas such as Maipo.

Andes Peak see Santa Emiliana

Balbi Lively, plummy Malbec from this Allied Domecq operation.

Paul Bruno see Viña Aquitania.

Bisquertt Dull, dry Cabernet; '95 Merlot, though, is pungent and exciting.

Caliterra Formerly Errazuriz-owned winery with solid, well-priced range; now an Errazuriz-Mondavi joint venture. Reserve Chardonnay and Reserve Cabernets are particularly good. Winemaker Irène Paiva now working with masterly Ed Flaherty, formerly of Cono Sur.

Canepa Big supplier of own-label wines to supermarkets, often (e.g. Sainsbury's Chilean Merlot, Asda's Chilean Cabernet-Merlot) of high standard. Also Vinicola Montealegre (Peteroa, Rowan Brook). Top Cabernet Magnificum deep but overpriced.

Carmen Rapid strides being made under young winemaker Alvaro Espinoza. Reserve Merlot, Cabernet and Chardonnay all very good, combining depth of fruit with understated oak, and will be superb if Espinoza is allowed (by owner Santa Rita) to ease up on filtrations, reduce yields, and pursue his interest in organic viticulture. The '95 Casablanca Sauvignon Blanc Reserve sold by M&S is a good benchmark, and the soft, honeyed Oak-Aged Chardonnay Semillon from M&S offers good value. See feature.

Casablanca Despite its name, does not only produce wines from the Casablanca valley (white-labelled wines may be from other areas; grey-labelled wines are from Casablanca). Fresh, high-impact style from winemaker Ignacio Recabarren, with citrussy whites from the Santa Isabel estate among the best from the Casablanca region; very good '94 Casablanca Cabernet Sauvignon, too. Worthy Gewürztraminer. Owned by Santa Carolina.

Casa Lapostolle Refined, Bordeaux-style Sauvignon Blanc; salty, vinous Chardonnay; supple Merlot and sumptuous Merlot Cuvée Alexandre from this new Rapel winery under consultant Michel Rolland make a promising debut.

Casa Leona Sound wines from this grower-turned-producer include a good Chardonnay in the plump, silky Californian style.

Casa Porta see Viña Porta.

Concha y Toro Huge company with a variable range, but better quality reds are increasingly exciting: top-of-the-line Don Melchior is one of Chile's best Cabernet Sauvignons, and more modestly priced than the top wines from Canepa, Santa Rita and Carmen. Lush Concha y Toro Merlot and Marques de Casa Concha Merlot worth a try, while Casillero del Diablo Cabernet Sauvignon is more claretty than most from Chile. Whites have been rather commercial and sweet in style, but moving towards a tighter, crisper profile (good '94 Casillero Chardonnay). New Trio wines, red and white, reaching market as I write with deep-fruited Chardonnay, lush Merlot and spicy Cabernet Sauvignon.

Cono Sur Dynamic little American-run outfit producing sweet fruited Pinot, deep chocolatey Cabernet and decent whites (the '95 Chardonnay was like a mini-Mâcon at £2 less). Tocornal (Malbec offers good value) and Isla Negra are second labels; top-of-the-range Pinot is on the way. Owned by Concha y Toro.

Cousiño Macul The traditional grandee of the Chilean wine scene, but a generally fine range, and Antiguas Reservas Cabernet Sauvignon reds, despite early accessibility, tend to age superbly (the Château Musar of Chile). Chardonnay is floral, subtle, understated; Bordeaux blend Finis Terrae is pure and long.

Echeverria Carefully made wines with presence and depth, yet a lack of fresh-fruit excitement.

Errazuriz Some good-value wines, but some dullards, too, and even Don Maximiano Cabernet Sauvignon (made from old-vine fruit) hasn't been as expressive of late as it should be. Ed Flaherty, formerly of Cono Sur, has replaced New Zealander Brian Bicknell as winemaker.

Franciscan New player who pinched talented Gaetane Carron from Concha y Toro during 1995: to watch.

Isla Negra Brilliant drinking red at Oddbins under this Tocornal label.

Montes A chaotically labelled range, but the best Merlot and Cabernet Sauvignon wines are softly impressive, and Malbec makes a generous glass, too. Some wines spend too long in wood here, though.

Mont Gras Rich Cabernet and Merlot promise much.

Domaine Oriental Lively Cabernet-Merlot and deep Clos Centenaire Cabernet Sauvignon both worth trying.

Rowan Brook see Canepa.

San Pedro Large producer whose range is in mid-renovation under guidance of Jacques Lurton and New Zealander Brett Jackson. Still some way to go, though the '94 Cabernet is good, considering its yield, and '94 Lontue Chardonnay from M&S has nice guava-like style. Los Fundos red for Fullers is a fine quaffer at its price.

Santa Carolina A major investment programme, and winemaking from Recabarren, has made Santa Carolina one of the most consistent of Chilean producers. Particularly good Maipo Chardonnay Gran Reserva and Cabernet Sauvignon Gran Reserva. Malbec shows raw promise, but needs softer handling.

Santa Emiliana Concha y Toro-owned producer. Consistent range, part-sold in UK as Andes Peak (soft, minty '95 Merlot a good buy).

Santa Monica Competent but unexceptional range. '94 Riesling one of Chile's better examples of this variety.

Santa Rita Generally solid rather than exciting, though Medalla Real Chardonnay has svelte, slick appeal, and there have been some welcome unfiltered wines at Oddbins. Medalla Real Cabernet is deliciously blackcurrant but expensive. Santa Rita now has a shareholding in Los Vascos.

Tarapacá Unimpressive as yet.

Terra Noble Fledgling operation bringing together Chilean personnel with the Loire Valley's Henry Marionnet. Fresh Sauvignon (from purchased fruit) fragrant and good; peppery reds.

Tocornal see **Cono Sur.**

Miguel Torres Early overseas pioneer in Chile, though only the Manso de Valasco Cabernet Sauvignon remains on the pace today.

Undurraga One of the slowest of Chile's wineries to wake up to modern challenges, but beginning to stir with freshened-up '95 Chardonnay and Sauvignon Blanc.

Valdivieso Large, sparkling-wine company (Mitjans) which has recently put on a turn of speed with smooth, creamy, oak-softened Chardonnay and Pinot Noir. Reserve Cabernet-Merlot is deep, sweet and satisfying, and up-market Stonelake series in preparation, too, to begin with '95 Cabernet Franc. 'Casa' is economy range; Cavallo Loco a non-vintage, multi-variety thunderer. Winemaker Philippe de Brus (ex Kendall Jackson) works with consultant Paul Hobbs.

Los Vascos Winery now fully owned by the Lafites of Lafite-Rothschild. Poor-quality whites, but Cabernet Sauvignon can be refined, elegant and lingering.

Thierry Villard Marketeer Villard runs this label in conjunction with Santa Emiliana and Pablo Morande. Herbacious Sauvignon (Sauvignonasse) from Casablanca leads a disparate but lively range. Meaty '95 Merlot looks good.

Viña Aquitania New venture from Bruno Prats and Paul Pontallier, who have planted vineyards close to Cousiño Macul's estate on the outskirts of Santiago; wines are sold as Domaine Paul Bruno. Aromatic, balanced, supple Cabernet Sauvignon expensive, but worth a look.

Viña Porta Chardonnay and Cabernet made in subtle, fine-grained style; Casa Porta wines offer good value.

Vintages

The Casablanca valley is the only region of Chile subject to major vintage variation consequent on spring frosts, and this generally regulates size of crop rather than quality. Chilean vintages are remarkably consistent.

Specialist retailers

Most supermarkets and high-street chains have a good range of Chilean wines; Oddbins and Marks and Spencer take the country more seriously than most.

Notes for success

Mulberry Farm, it was called. The house had a tin roof, and walls of wood; the children were playing with the dogs on the beaten earth outside. Half a dozen horses stood like statues in the long grass of a neighbouring field while the early evening sun, edging down behind the coastal mountains, lacquered their pelts with the rich iridescence of freshly husked conkers. Not that there was time to enjoy any of that: Alvaro Espinoza had been working in the Carmen winery all day, and he had to be at the wine fair in Santiago that evening. He had a quick shower, and we talked for some time, drinking water, drinking tea. Energetically.

Chilean wines have needed the energetic input of a younger generation for at least a generation, and that's exactly what the last few years have brought. Much youthful European and North American talent has been grafted into Chilean soil, but Alvaro represents the home-grown strain. Indeed he looks almost Indian, with his rounded features, golden skin and mahogany eyes.

His father, Mario Espinoza, was also a winemaker – and a professor at Santiago's Catholic University. "He was my teacher and best friend. When I was a boy, I used to go to the winery every weekend with him. Many people in Chile made wines without loving them; from my father I learnt that you have to love wine to make something good."

Ignacio Recabarren, another of Chile's key winemakers, cites his time in New Zealand and Australia as his most formative years; for Alvaro, the influences were different. Bordeaux, first of all, where he studied after his Chilean degree. He set off in 1987 with his wife Marina; they had only met three months earlier. Neither spoke French.

"We had some very hard times. For the first six months, we wanted to come home. I would return after classes to Marina and we'd cry together: I understood nothing. So from seven at night I'd work until one in the morning, trying to understand the notes I'd taken, using the dictionary. It was lucky I had a good basic education – and that the exams were all at the end."

What he relished about Bordeaux was the tasting opportunities his time there provided, and the exposure to French wine culture. "In Chile, there was a lot of contempt and casualness about wine. It was just part of the fruit industry. In Bordeaux, everything is geared to wine culture. So when I came back to Chile, I wanted to work with young people without experience, so that we could create a culture."

After a spell setting up Domaine Oriental's winery in Talca, Alvaro was head-hunted to revitalise Viña Carmen, an old brand belonging to Santa Rita. This brought him into contact with Brown Forman, Carmen's American distributors – and owners of the Californian wine producer and organic pioneer Fetzer. Through his contacts with Fetzer, a nascent interest in organic wine-growing has blossomed. He is moving Carmen towards organic cultivation as fast as its owners will permit (not very: the idea is a new one in Chile); and beginning to run his father's old vineyard organically.

Alvaro's bargaining hand is likely to be strengthened by the success his first wines for Carmen have enjoyed. What marks them out from the crowd is that the lush Chilean fruit is handled in an unshowy, vinous French style. This gives them great drinkability – that all-important virtue sometimes lost sight of in New World winemaking. "I am very optimistic," Alvaro says. "I think we are just beginning the revolution. It was only five years ago we began planting the right grapes in the right places. At the moment we all tend to make our wines in a similar way, but that will change too. You will see. We will make some great wines here. You'll see."

China

Cloud of unknowing

The 'wine' which plays such an important role in Chinese poetry, culture and cooking is, as often as not, not true wine at all, rather a strong, cereal-based beer like the generally delicious sake. Many of China's true, grape-based wines are made from hardy, non-vinifera varieties, and are dark, sweet and repellent. A number of joint-venture wineries (Sino-French Corporative, Huadong, Beijing Friendship, Marco Polo, Summer Palace) and Chinese state wineries grow vinifera varieties – Huadong, for example, has over 50 hectares of Chardonnay. The Shangdong peninsula is the most promising viticultural region, though even here summer humidity is problematic. Wines produced by Chinese state wineries are nearly always sweet and often fault-ridden; the standard from the joint-venture wineries is better, though I have yet to taste a Chinese wine worth buying other than for its novelty value. Nonetheless, multinational involvement underlines the potential market value. Rémy-Martin's brand is Dynasty, Pernod-Ricard's is Dragon Seal and Seagram's is Summer Palace.

Cyprus

Dionysus dozes

Cyprus was, by all accounts, the Coonawarra of the third century BC: Ancient Greek literature and the ubiquity of wine-related mosaics on the island testify to the excellence of its wines. By medieval times, Cypriot wine had become a luxury item in northwestern Europe, thanks to its strength and sweetness. Its modern reputation is less lofty.

Cyprus, in fact, is in a viticultural mess. Much of its huge production used to go to Eastern Europe: prices were low, but the customers didn't care about the quality and they paid promptly. This trade has declined steeply. The rest of production was simmered down into grape-juice concentrate (much of it for 'British wine' and 'British sherry'), shipped off to be turned into vermouth or glühwein, made into Cyprus sherry, or bottled up as communion wine. All of these products, too, are in decline. So Cyprus is desperately trying to create a quality wine industry for itself – with great difficulty.

Even its one wine of excellence, Commanderia, the direct descendant of the Nama of the Ancient World, struggles to make any headway, since it is brown and treacly, and the market for brown, treacly wines is in constant regression. (It's good value, by the way, if you like brown, treacly wine – cleanest and best balanced are the Grand Commanderia and St Nicholas Commanderia from Etko, while Keo's Commanderia St John is rich, full and lingering.)

I have yet to taste a good dry white wine from Cyprus; reds, though, are a bit better: the earthy, full Afames from Sodap is excellent value, and Keo's Domaine d'Ahera is worth seeking out, too. In general, however, Cyprus badly needs a parachute drop of itinerant Australian winemakers.

Czech Republic

Gearing up

The Czech Republic's generally confident approach to the challenges of the post-Communist world is reflected in its wine industry: a new wine law has been passed, and subsidies of up to 60 per cent are available for replanting vineyards. Wise; since eventual EC membership is likely to put a break on any extension of vineyard plantings. The divorce between the Czech Republic and Slovakia left Slovakia with the larger portion of Czechoslovakia's vineyards. There is a little winegrowing around Melnik in Bohemia, but most of the Czech Republic's vineyards lie in Moravia, around the Slovakian and Austrian borders. Moravian whites are aromatic, but surprisingly dry, full and sappy in taste; look out for good Pinot Blanc. The reds tend to be over-sharp.

England

The struggle continues

English wine (a very different creature from British wine, which is an industrial product made with grape-juice concentrate) has a long history, and commercial vineyards were widespread during the period of warm summers between the eleventh and fourteenth century. Modern winegrowing in England, though, dates from the 1950s, and it is only during the last decade that it has changed from being predominantly a hobbyist's activity to a professional one – and one of exceptional difficulty. Spring frosts and cool, late flowering can obliterate the prospect of a crop. Grape ripening can never be taken for granted, and must often be chased into the murky back-end of October or even November, by which time rot may be rampant. Sugar levels are low; acidity is high.

Nevertheless it has been possible to produce good English wines when meteorological fortunes and steady nerves allow. The 1995 harvest was typical, in the best and worst senses. An unusually hot, dry summer contributed to well-advanced ripeness, but a murky, moist September then seemed to betray the hopes of growers. Many picked then, cutting anticipated losses. Those who waited until October were rewarded with more balmy weather and made the best wines – including, in one or two cases, the most luscious botrytis examples ever made in England.

In general, England's wines combine incision and grace. A sense of place is palpable in their aromas, which can evoke the heady perfumes of a blossom-strewn May hedgerow; their whistle-clean fruit, clear as frosty air, can set the tongue jangling deliciously. They benefit from, and indeed often need, a little bottle age. A number of English growers have been playing with oak recently – a mistake, in my view, blunting the wines' fine edge, muddling their flavours and foiling, to no obvious advantage, their fruity acidity. English red wines taste, more often than not, misguided.

Far more promising are current attempts to produce successful sparkling wines, particularly from chalk downland vineyards: these soils are identical to

Champagne's, while the climate is only marginally cooler and moister. If England is ever to produce wine of the global renown of English ale or Scotch whisky, then it seems likely to be sparkling wine of impeccably crisp style.

Adgestone, ISLE OF WIGHT Well-structured wines.

Barkham Manor, EAST SUSSEX Assiduous producer with good range, especially Bacchus and Schönburger.

Battle Estate, KENT Winemaker David Sax working on some good wines after a spell in NZ with Villa Maria. Formerly called Leeford and Saxon Valley.

Bearstead, KENT Small; tasty dry Bacchus in Sauvignon Blanc style is particu larly good.

Beaulieu, HAMPSHIRE see Harvest Wine Group.

Beenleigh Manor, DEVON Leading producer of red wines made from Cabernet and Merlot grown under polythene, and made at Sharpham.

Biddenden, KENT Long-established producer, but I prefer the cider to the wine. Ortega soft and exotic.

Boze Down, OXFORDSHIRE See Harvest Wine Group.

Breaky Bottom, SUSSEX Some of England's best and (with age) creamiest dry varietal whites from Seyval Blanc and Müller-Thurgau made in beautiful down-land setting. Recent gentle oaking adds little. Impressive sparkling wine should reach the market during the life of this book.

Carr Taylor, EAST SUSSEX Variable range.

Chapel Down Winemaker (David Cowderoy) putting together one of Britain's most professionally made ranges from a wide range of fruit sources: sparkling wines are crisply promising; Flint Dry *sur lie* makes an interestingly incisive vari-ation on the Muscadet theme; and the '94 Bacchus turned unpromising raw mate-rials into something almost New Zealand-like. Now working with Tenterden (q.v.).

Chiddingstone, KENT Carefully made wines of some originality, including a white Pinot Noir (served by the Queen to Mitterand in '92) and a Sauvignon-like Seyval/Kerner blend. 'Sevenoaks' is an off-dry blend and 'Tunbridge Wells' a varietal Chasselas.

Denbies, SURREY The elephant of the English wine-growing scene, with 100 hectacres of fine rolling chalk vineyard and pleasant visitor centre. Rapidly improving wines. '92 Bacchus is excellent, and '95 Pinot Blanc remarkably ripe.

English Wine Growers A 20-grower cooperative. Low profile as yet.

Harvest Wine Group Grouping of wineries employing Australian John Worontschak (see Valley Vineyards) as consultant, including Beaulieu, Boze Down, Hidden Spring, Moorlynch, Northbrook Springs and Sharpham. Occasion-ally outstanding and always competent, these are technically accomplished and well-balanced wines.

Hidden Spring, EAST SUSSEX See Harvest Wine Group. Good sparkling wine, oaked white and rounded, soft-fruited rosé made and marketed with infectious enthusiasm and a great sense of fun. Medium white 'Decadence' is pretty and best drunk, apparently, in the bath. Red wine also fine, when nature allows.

High Ridge see Lamberhurst.

Lamberhurst, KENT Large, commercially astute winery whose ownership has recently changed. Vineyards now much reduced in size, but major marketing operation with Manchester United in hand. Wines now sold as High Ridge.

Moorlynch, SOMERSET See Harvest Wine Group.

Northbrook Springs, HAMPSHIRE See Harvest Wine Group. The '93 Oak Barrel Matured Bacchus/Reichensteiner was a dead ringer for subtly oaked Marlborough Sauvignon Blanc.

Nutbourne Manor, SUSSEX A good track record with aromatic German varieties, especially Bacchus. Some fruit now vinified and sold by Chapel Down.

Nyetimber, WEST SUSSEX Large, American-owned property specialising in sparkling wine. Not yet released, but rumoured to be good.

Penshurst, KENT Fair wines; nice day out in pretty village.

Rock Lodge, SUSSEX Impresario is one of England's leading sparkling wines; time may give its boisterous depths the finesse they need.

Saxon Valley see Leeford.

Sharpham, DEVON Part of Harvest Wine Group; also makes wines for Beenleigh Manor. Excellent potential site: Estate Reserve '92 was a fine, Loire-style wine.

Staple St James, KENT This near-coastal site has fine potential, witnessed by the magnificent '89 Huxelrebe; Müller-Thurgau also good. Vineyard size now, sadly, reduced.

Tenterden, KENT One of Britain's most consistent ranges, including excellent Seyval, Bacchus and Schönburger, with winemaking from the talented Stephen Skelton (a former owner and now co-owner). Working with Chapel Down.

Three Choirs, GLOUCESTERSHIRE Good, often excellent, wines from large vineyard marketed with commendable commercial acumen. Shiveringly zingy 'New Release' wine, timed to reach the drinker (as Beaujolais Nouveau does) on the third Thursday of November, is often better than Beaujolais itself.

Valley Vineyards, BERKSHIRE Scrupulous viticulture and Australian-influenced winemaking produce a wide range of soundly made, often exciting wines. Use of oak (for the Fumé) is as good as it gets in England here, but my preference is for the unoaked Regatta. Sparkling Ascot Brut and Heritage promise much. Red Ruscombe '93, though, was sour – a struggle to drink.

Wootton, SOMERSET Consistent varietal wines and unaged brandy.

Wyken, SUFFOLK Perfumed Bacchus, spicy Sonata and impressive Red.

Vintages
1995 ★★★; 1994 ★★; 1993 ★★; 1992 ★★; 1991 ★★; 1990 ★★★★;
1989 ★★★★; 1988 ★; 1987 ★; 1986 ★★.

France

A change of weather

Something has changed. The light is greyer; there's a moist weight in the air; clouds are coming up behind the hill. French wine may not be facing a crisis, but some fundamental challenges lie ahead.

The aristocrats are untroubled by this. French fine wines are, if anything, better made and more sought-after than they have ever been in the past. Fastidious viticulture and scrupulous, watchful, technically adept winemaking have brought great advances to the best from Bordeaux, Burgundy and the Rhône. Prices are high, chiefly because fine wine is now a commodity of limited supply facing unprecedented global demand, and France has the finest of all.

The workers, too, are thriving. French wines below the *appellation contrôlée* belt have the flexibility to respond to whatever changes the market wants – like British buyers commissioning wannabe Australian wine made in the Midi.

It is the middle class of French wine which is feeling increasingly uncomfortable. There is a huge range of AOC wine which will never enjoy the renown of France's fine-wine stars, and which would love to have some of the freedom enjoyed by *vins de pays* producers. The AOC system is philosophically beautiful and has achieved a practical economic purpose with remarkable success (see below) – but the fact that it is strictly legislative is beginning to hinder French wine production as much as help it. Few of us shop for appellations. Names like Saussignac, Coteaux de l'Aubance, Vinsobres or Saint-Péray are never going to mean much to most wine consumers, and to deny wine producers in those areas the opportunity of labelling their wines with names which might mean something (like Sémillon, Chenin Blanc, Grenache or Marsanne) is misguided. What France's wine authorities should try to do is reformulate appellation regulations so that they continue to enshrine and protect the valuable ideal of *terroir* (see page 21), but permit the growers within those areas greater flexibility to create the wines which consumers want today.

The laboratory of the senses

France may not be wine's birthplace, but it is its home. France provides the drinker with a greater choice of wine than does any other nation. France's best wines furnish the wine world with its role-models; France's grape varieties, not wholly coincidentally, are those most in demand on the shelves of the global wine shop.

There are geographical and historical reasons why this should be so; yet Italy, with its vast library of grape varieties and the opportunity to grow vines anywhere within its rumpled mass, might have been expected to do as well. The difference lies in the temper of its people. Italians accept and celebrate what the earth surrenders; the French, by contrast, tease, provoke, question and refine earth's gifts. Sensual delights are as proper to the great French laboratory of thought and discussion as mathematical theorems and microbial colonies. Excellence is not allowed to rest in France without analysis pouncing on it and dismembering it, the better to create it anew next time.

French wine as we know it in Britain today comes to us ordered by the system of *Appellations d'Origine Contrôlée,* or 'names of controlled origin'. The theory is as follows: the taste of a wine is created by certain grape varieties growing in certain soils under certain climates. Tradition (once defined by Professor Emile Peynaud of Bordeaux as 'an experiment which has succeeded') is assumed to have delivered, over the centuries, the right grape varieties to the right sites; the AOC system gives these the sanction of law. The wines of an appellation are the expression, in aroma and flavour, of a *terroir* (see page 21).

The French AOC system has been enormously successful in consolidating the excellence of former times in the modern world. It is a system of beautiful complexity, dressing French geography with haute-couture allure. Because each appellation functions as a sort of brand name, it has protected small growers from the fire-storms of capitalism. France's strength is that its wine production lies in tens of thousands of hands rather than the clumsy paws of a few gigantic, Gallo-like companies; without the AOC system, this diversity would have withered.

Yet, as outlined above, the system has its failings. Greater flexibility is needed; so too is greater qualitative rigour: AOCs should not be used to shield poor wine-makers. The lust for simplicity – both conceptual simplicity and simplicity of flavour – favours Vins de Pays (and especially the varietal wines among them) over AOCs. Vins de Pays, or 'country wines', are the fruit of apprentice *terroirs*, less hedged about with regulations. (Between the two lie the increasingly uncommon VDQS wines – Vins Delimités de Qualité Supérieure.)

Yet if France stands for one quality alone among wine-producing nations, that quality is complexity. Its finest wines, and even some of its simpler wines, have a grain to them, a profundity, a rhythm of detail best measured over the distance of a bottle. This is why one in every three glasses of wine we drink is French.

Alsace

Hocks away

Alsace is France's Rhineland. White wines predominate, and with them luscious, summer-fruit aromas and flavours (the oaked white remains mercifully hard to find in Colmar or Strasbourg). It is the only AOC region of France where grape varieties routinely appear as part of the appellation formula – on labels affixed to stork-slender bottles. France's German wines, then?

Far from it. Few wines are so thoroughly French in their approach as these. The French love alcohol and the Germans despise it; Alsace wines are high in alcohol. The French prefer restrained acidity whereas the Germans solicit piercing acids; Alsace wines have tempered, subdued acids. The French reverence for the individual site (a reverence mocked by German wine law) has been sanctified in the Alsace Grand Cru system (available for certain varieties planted in the best vineyards). The fruit flavours of Alsace wines rarely have the sheer, quivering intensity of German wines, but tend to be ample, round, rich and spicy. German wine is at its best before or after food; Alsace wine is for sitting down at table with, while you tuck your napkin into your collar, grasp your knife and fork in the fist of each hand, and stab deep into the gristly recesses of a ham hock marooned atop a mountain of steaming cabbage.

Alsace's most notable grape variety is Gewürztraminer, that dry spice bomb fused into a golden wine never stronger or headier than here; Pinot Blanc (fresh and grapey) and Pinot Gris (rich and smoky) can both be spicy too. Muscat is fragrant, surprisingly crisp. Riesling is the hard man of Alsace, but deep and profound if given age; Sylvaner, by contrast, is open, earthy, accessible and best drunk young. Auxerrois is generally blended with Pinot Blanc, but can be lush and strawberryish on its own. Alsace does produce red wine from Pinot Noir; it is generally too expensive, but quality can be exciting provided you remain open-minded about its lightweight, counter-tenor style. The Grand Cru appellation is for Gewürztraminer, Riesling, Pinot Gris and Muscat. Late-harvest wines (Vendange Tardive) and botrytised wines (Séléction des Grains Nobles) are made in good years.

Alsace's failings are a tendency to over-chaptalize, resulting in clumsy, top-heavy wines of threadbare fruit; high yields, which give wines of low concentration for the £4.99 base price; and an infuriating refusal to tell consumers how sweet a wine is going to be. Vendange Tardive and Séléction des Grains Nobles wines are likely to be sweet (the latter always are and the former may be), but even Vieilles Vignes (old vines) or Réserve cuvées of 'ordinary' Alsace wines may turn out to be sweet. I have had a number of restaurant meals spoiled by the treachery of sweet Alsace wine masquerading as dry (Pinot Gris seems to be especially vulnerable to this). Do not assume Grand Cru wines will necessarily be better than ordinary Alsace wines; the producer's name is, as ever, a surer guide.

Adam, AMMERSCHWIHR Fair standard, with particularly good Vendange Tardive.

Beyer, EGUISHEIM Wines in a dryer style with good ageing potential.

Boxler, NIEDERMORSCHWIHR Dense yet succulent Riesling and Pinot Gris lead.

Blanck, KIENTZHEIM Sometimes four-square and straightforward, but generally good, especially Riesling.

Burn, GUEBERSCHWIHR Small production of high-definition wines, especially fine from the Clos St Imer.

Théo Cattin, VOEGTLINSHOFFEN '92 Gewürztraminer Bollenberg is fine, fragrant, long and delicious.

Cave Coopérative de Ribeauvillé Another of Alsace's well-run cooperatives offering clearly defined, reasonably priced varietals and high-quality specialities (like the Clos du Zahnacker, a blend of Pinot Gris, Riesling and Gewürztraminer). Andante is a Muscat-Gewürztraminer blend, slimmer and lighter than Gewürz on its own.

Cave Vinicole de Pfaffenheim–Gueberschwihr Clean, well-made wines, including expressive Grand Cru Gewürztraminer from Goldert.

Cave Vinicole de Turckheim Alsace's best cooperative, with fine Grand Cru wines from Brand and Hengst and reliable basic varietals (such as Gewürztraminer). I aged a bottle of Turckheim's basic Pinot Gris '86 and drank it this year: it was smoky, fat and fine.

Deiss, BERGHEIM Fine, expressive wines, rarely unbalanced or over-weighty, right through the range, with fascinating vineyard differentiation. All benefit from age; the Rieslings demand it.

Dopff & Irion, RIQUEWIHR Sound wines in an understated style.

Dopff au Moulin, RIQUEWIHR Sparkling-wine specialists (Crémant d'Alsace); still wines from well-sited vineyards (such as Schoenenbourg Riesling) worth trying.

Frick, PFAFFENHEIM Well-made biodynamic range.

Hugel, RIQUEWIHR The dominant Alsace merchant. Expensive wines are, relatively speaking, better value than basics; sweet wines very luscious and intense.

JosMeyer, WINTZENHEIM Wines of intensity and finesse with clear vineyard differentiation. Dry wines particularly good; more age-worthy than most.

Kreydenweiss, ANDLAU Innovative, thoughtful and (since '91) biodynamic wines. Dense Moenchburg Pinot Gris especially good, and Pinot Blanc has plenty of character, too.

Kuentz-Bas, HUSSEREN-LES-CHÂTEAUX Rich, succulent wines with drinkability.

Lorentz, BERGHEIM Inconsistent range, but best wines worthwhile (such as cleanly spicy Gewürztraminer).

Mann, WETTOLSHEIM Lush, full, rounded wines with remarkable concentration from very low yields. Exceptional '94s.

Julien Meyer, NOTHALTEN Accessible, well-defined, good-value wines.

Muré, ROUFFACH Big, chewy, sometimes clumsy. Muré Clos St-Landelin lies within the Grand Cru of Vorbourg.

Ostertag, EPFIG Low-yield, unfiltered wines from mainly organically grown grapes give exciting flavours, though Ostertag's use of new oak can be disconcerting. Sylvaner Vieilles Vignes, Riesling (especially Riesling Vieilles Vignes) and Pinot Gris all piercing and intense.

Rolly-Gassmann, RORSCHWIHR One of my favourite growers. No Grands Crus, but a wide range of full, soft, stylish, generous wines, including petrolly Muscat Moenchreben and an Auxerrois which resembles white chocolate when aged.

Schleret, TURCKHEIM Rich yet clean, vivid wines. Pinot Gris especially impressive and chewy.

Schlumberger, GUEBWILLER Exceptional vineyard holdings provide the backbone for a range of keenly differentiated wines. Gewürztraminer (especially special cuvées) a rich, heady benchmark.

Schoffit, COLMAR Increasingly impressive wines, especially Gewürztraminer (look for Harth Cuvée Caroline) and Pinot Gris from Clos St Théobald (with Grand Cru of Rangen). Chasselas Vieilles Vignes is worthwhile. Good '93s and '94s.

Sipp, LOUIS, RIBEAUVILLÉ Keenly balanced wines sometimes lack richness.

Trimbach, RIBEAUVILLÉ My favourite among Alsace's merchant houses. Elegant, intense, fresh-flavoured wines led by Riesling Cuvée Frédéric-Emile and expensive but deep, mineral-charged Clos Ste-Hune.

Weinbach, KAYSERBERG   Intense, almost searing wines. Chaotic profusion of cuvées, but no matter – everything is worth trying, Riesling and Gewürztraminer particularly so. Structured successes from '94, unlike many.

Willm, see Wolfberger.

Wolfberger, EGUISHEIM   Large cooperative, also owning Domaine Jux and the merchant house Willm. Variable standards: best to stick to generally sound Grand Cru wines.

Zind-Humbrecht, WINTZENHEIM   Fine vineyard holdings, low yields and painstaking winemaking from Olivier Zind-Humbrecht MW have created a superb range of wines, especially richer Pinot Gris and Gewürztraminer.

Vintages
1995 ★★★; 1994 ★★★; 1993 ★; 1992 ★★★; 1991 ★★; 1990 ★★★★; 1989 ★★★★; 1988 ★★★; 1987 ★; 1986 ★.

Specialist retailers
Wine Rack is the leading specialist: it follows the wines of the Turckheim cooperative and Zind-Humbrecht closely as well as docking other good wines from Alsace. Other retailers with a good Alsace range include Bibendum, O.W.Loeb, Morris & Verdin, Oddbins, La Réserve and La Vigneronne. Supermarket Alsace purchases are often weakly flavoured and disappointing.

Beaujolais
King of the country wines

Know it? Of course you do. As fruit-scented as a strawberry picker's fingers, then cool and refreshing on the tongue, packed with soft, squashy, berry flavours and burnished once in a while with a tarry note, Beaujolais is the great gulping, guzzling, gorging wine. Gamay is its grape; carbonic maceration (see page 20) is the method of acquiring such fruitiness with so little astringency. It can be light or deep, but will never be tough. Welcome to French wine's light entertainment division.

And to the Beaujolais complex. Its confidence fuelled by the global success of Beaujolais Nouveau (new wine sold from the third Thursday in November), the region is forever trying to establish its fine-wine credentials, and to push the price of its best wines up towards the £10 mark. It won't wash. Even the sturdiest wines of the Beaujolais *crus* (the ten villages whose wines are sold under the village name only – see below) remain, at heart, robust quaffing wines; its cheapest wines, meanwhile, are often thin and mean-spirited, produced from over-cropped vines by mechanically-minded cooperatives. Everything from this region sells at its price limit at present. Bargains there are none.

At its best, of course, it's still wonderful. No other wine inspires the same bacchanalian abandon in its drinker; few other wines are capable of delivering the same charge of fun. This wine is close to the core of wine's appeal to humanity – as a remedy for the cold, remorseless intractability of the world.

Beaujolais Nouveau

A wonderful wheeze, eh? It's good for producers (giving them the cash-flow that most wine producers only dream of) and good for consumers (transfusing the jolliest of wine harvests into cold, dark, northern cities at the year's low ebb). Or is it?

Beaujolais Nouveau is never the best Beaujolais; often, it's the worst. Yet it's what the region is best known for. This spells problems for Beaujolais producers, since all their wines become associated with the worst of what the region produces. You could call it the Liebfraumilch syndrome. Liebfraumilch has been enormously successful for a few big operators while destroying the market for good-quality German wine to the detriment of thousands of smaller producers. Beaujolais is now economically reliant on the Nouveau fix, just as German wine exporters to Britain are reliant on Lieb. Nothing could improve the image and taste of Beaujolais more than abandoning Nouveau. But it won't happen.

The Beaujolais crus

Brouilly (rounded, soft, variable); Chénas (mid-weight, occasionally deep); Chiroubles (scented, fresh); Côte de Brouilly (concentrated, mid-weight); Fleurie (soft, gulpable); Juliénas (poised, firm, warm); Morgon (chunky, cherryish); Moulin-à-Vent (concentrated, meaty, deep, age-worthy); Régnié (light to mid-weight, variable); St Amour (soft, smooth, supple). Beaujolais-Villages is wine from the better parts of the overall Beaujolais appellation.

Beaujolais Producers

You could be forgiven for thinking there is only one producer in Beaujolais: Georges Duboeuf. Duboeuf dominates the region, and in the past he has done (for a dominator) a reasonably good job; many of the domain wines he has bottled have been among the best in the region, and his own merchant range has usually been reliable, though often less than exciting. Duboeuf also bottles fair Rhône wines. Many of the Duboeuf selections I have tasted in the last year, however, have been disappointing. Has the company grown too large to maintain high quality standards? Here are a list of other producers (some of whose wines may be bottled by Duboeuf, Aujoux, the Eventail des Vignerons Producteurs or others) whose wines are worth trying: Noël Aucoeur, Aujas, Cellier des Samsons, Château de la Chaize, Chauvet, Domaine du Clos Verdy, Jean Descombes, Sylvain Fessy, Gutty, Jacky Janodet, Domaine Jenny, Claude et Michelle Joubert, René Monnet, J.B. Patissier, Domaine des Quatre Vents, Domaine de Terres Dorées (J.P. Brun; also good Chardonnay), Domaine de la Tour de Bief, Château des Tours, Georges Trichard, Jacques Trichard, Domaine du Vissoux (Pierre Charmette). In general, avoid Beaujolais from Burgundy houses like Jaffelin, Moillard and Mommessin, especially at Nouveau time.

Vintages
1995 ★★★; 1994 ★★; 1993 ★★; 1992 ★; 1991 ★★★; 1990 ★★★; 1989 ★★★★; 1988 ★★★; 1987 ★★; 1986 ★★.

Specialist retailers
Roger Harris (mail-order); Le Nez Rouge (for the Duboeuf range).

Bordeaux

The classical ideal

Bordeaux's best bottles provide wine drinkers with what Shakespeare's plays give those seated in dark auditoria or Dickens' novels offer the curled-up-in-bed: perennial, referential profundity. There is much else beyond them, of course; they vary startlingly in quality from year to year; their urbane, refined flavours can be outperfumed, outpowered and outfruited by other wines from other regions on a regular basis. Yet good claret (the term simply means red Bordeaux) is the most satisfyingly companionable of wines. Its natural balance and whole-some, well-ordered taste are of universal appeal; the themes and variations in flavour offered by its different sub-regions make for endlessly rewarding experiment; it ages well; it is, finally, abundant. The best claret, unlike the best burgundy, is produced in large quantities.

So is the worst claret. Bordeaux is France's largest AOC vineyard area by far, and the vast majority of claret is at best simple wine for everyday drinking. Bordeaux's Atlantic coastline, moreover, means that the vineyards are subject to maritime moodiness. When all goes well, as happened most extraordinarily in 1982, 1983, 1985, 1986, 1988, 1989 and 1990, then Bordeaux can combine quality with quantity to mouthwatering effect. All did not go well, by contrast, in 1991, 1992 and 1993. The 1990s have an immediate depth, warmth and generosity completely beyond the wines of the three subsequent years. Let no one ever tell you that vintages don't count in Bordeaux. They are the interest rates of the region; they change everything.

The wine furnace

There's been considerable criticism of Bordeaux in Britain from the wine press over the last few years, based chiefly on the fact that the region's cheaper bottles haven't been competing well with New World rivals. Perhaps they haven't; there is an extraordinary poverty gap in Bordeaux between the grandees in the plum appellations and the teeming masses which give the region its huge bulk, and in any case the 'claret ideal' of complexity and restraint can never really compete with superfruity New World models.

This criticism, though, ignores the astonishing manner in which fine-winemaking in Bordeaux has changed in the last decade: lower yields, older vines, more selectivity, riper picking, must concentration in place of chaptalisation, better oak and greater use of it at all stages of the fermentation process (including for malolactic fermentation: see page 19). It ignores, too, the spiralling prices achieved by Bordeaux's best wines on the international market. It ignores the massive corporate investments made in Bordeaux; it ignores the fact that Bordeaux has been, globally, wine's senior ambassador over the last decade, arousing an interest in wine in many countries where none existed before. It is, in short, a parochial view, based on the ludicrous assumption that a supermarket trolley in Tesco or Sainsbury's is the centre of the wine world.

The truth is that Bordeaux is offering a richer variety of wines at present than at any time in its history. The watershed was 1982. That was the year when nature dealt producers the ace of hearts: wines which, for Bordeaux, were unusually seductive, rich, voluptuous, lovely. They seized the wine-drinking imagination world-wide, and created a new horizon of possibilities for producers to aim for in Bordeaux. The excesses of the previous decades – tough tannins and whelping acids – began to slide from view; sloppily made wines were castigated with low prices; well-made wines broke price records. Merlot began to assume the importance in Bordeaux which it has always had in practice, but had never been given the credit for. Bordeaux realised it has a sensual side. The quest for exhilarating, seductive, hedonist's claret began, and it hasn't stopped since. The fact that Pomerol-based Michel Rolland is now the world's most influential wine consultant is not accidental.

These are some of the reasons why the *en primeur* market for '95 Bordeaux was such a frenzied one. Those who love good wine and whose means allow them to look beyond supermarkets and off licences to find it have realised that Bordeaux is undergoing a period of experiment, innovation and self-confidence found in few other parts of the world at present. It may be, indeed, that there are excesses at work; that the quest for flesh and extract is eclipsing some of the quieter virtues and disfiguring the sense of *terroir*. On balance, though, the gain looks to be the drinker's; Bordeaux is giving us more than ever before.

Orienteering

'Bordeaux', the catch-all, wine-stain-like appellation filling most of the Gironde département, fences in a flock of other appellations. The Médoc and Haut-Médoc occupy the flat, gravelly vineyards found on the western (left) bank of the vast and muddy Gironde estuary. Within the Médoc (Bordeaux AOCs enfold each other like Russian dolls) are the communes of St-Estèphe, Pauillac, St-Julien, Listrac, Moulis and Margaux, and it is here that almost all of the properties included in the 1855 classification (see below) are sited. Claret in the Médoc is dominated by the Cabernet Sauvignon grape, giving a wine which varies from rich yet taut after a fine vintage to one that is thin and bony after a poor vintage (or, as often happens with claret, when it has been over-aged). There are broad communal differences, too: Margaux is delicate and elegant; St Julien poised, mid-weight; Pauillac beefy; St Estèphe firm. Listrac and Moulis are second-rank communes built like lesser St Estèphe.

Encircling Bordeaux itself and stretching away along the western (left) bank of the Garonne are the vineyards of the Graves (including sub-zones Pessac-Léognan, Cérons, Barsac and Sauternes). Cabernet Sauvignon-dominated reds of softer, earthier style share this stage with broad-beamed, rather stately dry white wines and luscious, voluptuously rich sweet ones. The best Barsac and Sauternes, however, hang more precariously on the benefit of meteorology than any other wines anywhere in the world. There are more lean years than fat.

The Gironde estuary is formed by two seigneurial rivers, the Garonne and the Dordogne, which drain France's central highlands. The area between them, as they near estuarine fusion, is the Entre-Deux-Mers ('between two seas'), fringed by a number of other smaller appellations. Nothing from this region is particularly long-lasting, but young Sauvignon Blanc-based whites can be fresh and pretty here, while Premières Côtes de Bordeaux, Cadillac, Loupiac and Sainte-Croix-du-Mont can occasionally produce sweet whites which offer keen value.

On the north (right) bank of the Dordogne lies the cluster of appellations where Merlot (which in overall terms is the most widely planted grape variety in Bordeaux) dominates. Most expensively in Pomerol; most expansively in St Emilion and its 'satellite' appellations, as well as in Côtes de Castillon, perhaps Bordeaux's best-value red AOC at present. Merlot-based claret is friendlier, richer, softer, plummier and meatier than Cabernet-Sauvignon-based claret.

Fronsac and Canon-Fronsac are two blips where Cabernet Franc takes the lead, producing a chunkier, fuller-bodied wine than it ever manages in the Loire valley. Note, too, that Cabernet Franc is important in St Emilion (most famously for Château Cheval-Blanc, which contains more Cabernet Franc than Merlot). Bourg and Blaye, finally, which face the Médoc with what must be a measure of envy from the eastern (right) bank of the Gironde estuary, produce lightish claret from an almost equal mixture of the two main red-wine varieties.

Classed Growths

In 1855, Bordeaux's wine brokers – the middlemen whose intimate knowledge of the vineyards governs their earnings – classified the best vineyards of the Médoc (plus one lordly interloper from the Graves, Château Haut-Brion) into five strata or 'growths'. This classification (regularly reprinted in books on the subject and usually featured on labels) has acted as a marketing tool ever since. Is it still accurate? Yes; and no. Yes, because the brokers gauged the potential of each site with remarkable precision. No, because the site boundaries have, in a number of cases, changed, as has ownership and therefore the success or otherwise in realising each site's potential. In the section that follows, all classed growths given entries (the worst performers are excluded) are coded #, ## or ###. The ## symbol indicates a property meriting its position *at present;* # indicates one meriting demotion; ### indicates one meriting promotion. I stress 'at present' since there are many wines available which were made by lazier or less skilled former owners; particularly stark cases of quality upswings are cited in entries.

There are other classificatory systems in Bordeaux, all of which are best ignored. Especially misleading is that of St Emilion, where the term 'Grand Cru' is used far too casually, bearing in mind its burgundian overtones, and where 'Premiers Grands Crus Classés' are not necessarily the best wines. Reference books, magazine tastings and merchants' advice will be much more useful than classifications in pointing you in the direction of better-than-average wines.

L'Angélus, St-Emilion Wines much improved since '86. Lush, full, prodigal. One of the best '93s, a show-stopping '94 and a fine '95.

d'Angludet, Margaux Patchy, but comely when on form (as in 1989 and 1983).

d'Arche, Sauternes Flattering; full-flavoured.

d'Armailhac, Pauillac 5th growth## Well-tempered wine, though it has lacked Pauillac beefiness ('95 is deeper). Formerly called Mouton-Baronne-Philippe.

l'Arrosée, St Emilion Generous, richly upholstered wines at best, though inconsistent. Good *terroir;* cellars could do with renovation.

Ausone, St Emilion Tiny property producing wines of authority and depth: St Emilion flavours, but often Médocain structure. For long ageing; sometimes ungrateful when young. However '95 marks a new start: Michel Rolland, the key Bordeaux oenologist of the 1990s (see **Bon Pasteur**), has taken over from Pascal Delbeck, producing a lusher, more flattering wine.

Bahans-Haut-Brion, GRAVES   Second wine of Haut-Brion, sometimes close behind the grand vin, yet other vintages rather slender ('94, '95).

Balestard la Tonnelle, ST EMILION   Soft, ripe, good value.

Bastor-Lamontagne, SAUTERNES   Not the richest Sauternes, but more consistent than many, and often good value.

Batailley, PAUILLAC 5TH GROWTH##   Four-square, chunky, solid when good: '94 and '95 both disappointing, though.

Beauregard, POMEROL   Deliciously balanced wines from this fast improving property: '94 and '95 both very good.

Beau-Séjour-Bécot, ST EMILION   Ambitious, oaky wines since '85.

Beauséjour-Duffau-Lagarosse, ST EMILION   Small quantities, but coming on a storm of late: voluptuous yet well-shaped wines, with especially good 1990.

Beau-Site, ST ESTÈPHE   Solid; good value.

Belair, ST EMILION   Sited near to Ausone, and some of the same sinew beneath its surface warmth and richness. Soft-styled in '94 and '95.

de Belcier, CÔTES DE CASTILLON   Supple, tasty claret.

Bertinerie, CÔTES DE BLAYE   Creamy whites and full-fruited reds. Top cuvées called Haut-Bertinerie.

Beychevelle, ST JULIEN 4TH GROWTH##   Delicacy and restraint rather than muscle. Very good '82 and '86, but can be slender in lesser years.

Blanzac, CÔTES DU CASTILLON   First-rate Merlot-based wine: delicious '90.

Bonnet, ENTRE-DEUX-MERS   Enormous property, but high standards.

Le Bon Pasteur, POMEROL   Some of the best winemaking in Pomerol, beginning with silky, toffeed '82, from Michel Rolland. Definitive unction.

Boyd-Cantenac, MARGAUX 3RD GROWTH#   Pleasant though shallow wines.

Branaire, ST JULIEN 4TH GROWTH#   Patchy standards, but at best ('89) a full yet velvety style, both supple and expressive. Now up to scratch with high effort wines.

Brane-Cantenac, MARGAUX 2ND GROWTH#   Big property, but inadequate rigour results in variable wines. '86 was best of the 80s.

La Cabanne, POMEROL   Light in '80s; now deeper.

Cadet-Piola, ST EMILION   Sturdy.

Calon-Ségur, ST ESTÈPHE 3RD GROWTH#   When on song ('88) a generous, untrendy, surprisingly long-lived wine. Nonetheless below potential, which insiders consider some of the greatest in Médoc, as bottles from the '20s and '40s prove. Does the gutsy '95 (regarded by many as the sleeper of the vintage) signify a new start?

Canon, CANON-FRONSAC Given a good vintage, deep and feisty.

Canon, ST EMILION Full-bodied and concentrated in good vintages. Often tannic: give it time. '95 much better than '94.

Canon-de-Brem, CANON-FRONSAC Moueix wine: structured and punchy.

Canon-la-Gaffelière, ST EMILION Brilliantly fleshy wines since mid-'80s, peaking with a magisterial '90. In German ownership. '94 and '95 rather stern.

Canon-Moueix, CANON-FRONSAC New purchase; good value.

Cantemerle, MACAU 5TH GROWTH# Light-bodied, pretty claret with occasional fleshy epiphanies (as in '89).

Cantenac-Brown, MARGAUX 3RD GROWTH# Poised to improve under Jean-Michel Cazes, '86 and '90 merit ## with lush fruit supported by structured tannins. Still lacks sureness of touch, though: '94 was bony.

Carbonnieux, GRAVES Large, historic estate, but reds and dry whites are over-polite, lacking excitement.

Carsin, PREMIÈRES CÔTES DE BORDEAUX Talked-about property with Australian winemaker, but for me the treatment overwhelms the fruit.

Certan de May, POMEROL Expensive, but appealing, exotic fruit gave good results during '80s.

Chartreuse, SAUTERNES Not a classed growth, but high standards (succulent '89 from Waitrose and '90 from Sainsbury's and Oddbins both great buys).

Chasse-Spleen, MOULIS Steady generosity of flavour. '89 outstanding. Less sure-footed in '90s.

Chauvin, ST EMILION Improving property, turning in good wines in '94 and '95.

Cheval-Blanc, ST EMILION Superb, richly fruited, almost chocolatey wine from a higher percentage of Cabernet Franc than Merlot. The '90 was, in '94, the most seductive young claret I have ever tasted. Since '90, though, Cheval Blanc has had a lighter, silk-stocking style.

Domaine de Chevalier, GRAVES Generally fair red and outstandingly complex dry white wines from this small property.

Cissac, CISSAC Lean style, now looking masochistically old-fashioned.

Citran, HAUT-MÉDOC Rapidly improving wine (since Japanese purchase in '87): lush, oaky style.

Clerc-Milon, PAUILLAC 5TH GROWTH## Mouton-owned and well-sited, Clerc-Milon has usually produced soft, polite, mid-term wines. '95 was more serious.

Climens, BARSAC Exemplary balance and concentration, with superb '88, '90 and (unusually) '91.

Clinet, POMEROL From '85, a pace-setter: extravagance and exoticism leashed to firm extracts. '93, '94 and '95 better than most.

Clos du Clocher, POMEROL Easy-drinking, rich claret.

Clos l'Eglise, POMEROL Lighter, finer grained than is now the Pomerol norm.

Clos Floridène, GRAVES Oaked white from Denis Dubourdieu: firm and stylish.

Clos Fourtet, ST EMILION Inconsistent, but at best ('90, '94) chewy and chunky.

Clos des Jacobins, ST EMILION Consistently well-made, supple, friendly wine.

Clos du Marquis, ST JULIEN Second wine of Léoville-Las-Cases, with more stuffing than most.

Clos de l'Oratoire, ST EMILION Feathery, milky style.

Clos René, POMEROL Soft and rich.

La Conseillante, POMEROL Lush, supple and accessible. '89 and '90 both outstanding; '94 and '95 great fun.

Cos d'Estournel, ST ESTÈPHE 2ND GROWTH## Concentrated, square-jawed wine lent charm by the lusher fruit style and fresh oak of the 80s. ### in '82, '85, '86 and '90. '94 and '95 less square-jawed; more intense, refined and elegant, though well-supported by tannins. Unfiltered since '93.

Cos Labory, ST ESTÈPHE 5TH GROWTH# Often light, simple wines, but recent efforts suggest form may be returning: ## in '89 and '90.

Coufran, HAUT-MÉDOC Soft, full, Merlot-rich wine.

La Couspade, ST EMILION New start in sexy, soft, modern style.

Coutet, BARSAC Brighter, fresher fruit than some, and increased concentration at end of 80s ('89 unusually good). Cuvée Madame is the crème de la crème, produced only in top vintages (beginning in '43): rivals Yquem.

Le Crock, ST ESTÈPHE Sturdy, tannic wines, given a good vintage.

La Croix, POMEROL Not the deepest, but balanced and pleasurable.

La Croix du Casse, POMEROL Top value of late: dark and delicious. Clinet-owned.

La Croix du Gay, POMEROL Downy wines, acquiring greater depth recently.

La Croix St Georges, POMEROL Good-value buy from the Janoueix stable.

Dauzac, MARGAUX High efforts: finding its way.

La Dominique, ST EMILION Heady, sensual wine, though without profundities.

Doisy-Daëne, BARSAC Traditionally light, yet '88, '89 and '90 all superb.

Doisy-Védrines, BARSAC Sometimes coarse and simple, though '89 is good.

Domaine de l'Eglise, POMEROL Lush, sometimes over-lush ('90).

Ducru-Beaucaillou, ST JULIEN 2ND GROWTH## Ducru is less overtly showy than its peers, but its quiet classicism is one of the pillars of the Médoc. '94 and '95 seem to mark a change of style towards fashionable lushness.

Duhart-Milon-Rothschild, PAUILLAC 4TH GROWTH## Lafite-owned; like Lafite itself, elegant rather than muscular.

Durfort-Vivens, MARGAUX 2ND GROWTH# Ignominious past, but '89 and the finely balanced '95 suggest encouraging improvements.

l'Eglise-Clinet, POMEROL Concentrated, sumptuous wines throughout the 80s continuing a long tradition of excellence. A star in '95.

l'Evangile, POMEROL Pushing back the boundaries of Merlot: perfumed, hugely fruited, generous tannins.

Ferrière, MARGAUX 3RD GROWTH# Small, rarely seen, often slight, but '93 (in some Sainsbury stores) was balanced and expressive.

Fieuzal, GRAVES Comely, accessible and allusive red wines, with fresh, classy Sauvignon-led whites.

Figeac, ST EMILION Some vintage swings, but at best ('82, '86, '90, '94) a claret of deep-fruited, firmly phrased expressivity.

Filhot, SAUTERNES Pleasant but undemanding.

La Fleur de Gay, POMEROL Much sought-after wine made with craft and care.

La Fleur Pétrus, POMEROL Carefully made neighbour to Pétrus: rich, spicy.

Les Forts de Latour, PAUILLAC Second-wine of Latour. Sometimes disappointing in lesser years; well up to cru classé standard in the good ones ('82, '90).

Franc-Mayne, ST EMILION Improving under new ownership; good-looking '90.

La Gaffelière, ST EMILION Choice, well-articulated, comfortable wine. A new Rolland consultancy (from '95).

Le Gay, POMEROL Among the sturdiest and fiercest of Pomerols.

Gazin, POMEROL Thinnish prior to '88; now sleek and well-upholstered. Both '94 and '95 very impressive.

Gilette, SAUTERNES Singular Sauternes, only bottled and released when fully aged (in concrete tanks).

Giscours, MARGAUX 3RD GROWTH# Disappointing in 80s and 90s after fine 70s, but warmly flavoured '89 and '90 both merit ##. Changing ownership.

Gloria, ST JULIEN Consistently enjoyable claret; good value.

Grand Mayne, ST EMILION Superfruited, richly oaked style: fun. '94 and '95 both need long cellaring.

Grand-Puy-Ducasse, PAUILLAC 5TH GROWTH## Carefully made of late, with fresh curranty fruit and dapper tannins.

Grand-Puy-Lacoste, PAUILLAC 5TH GROWTH## Great fidelity to vintage characteristics within meaty style; worth ### in good years ('82, '86, '89 and '90).

Gressier-Grand-Poujeaux, MOULIS Some solid wines in the record book, but now loose-textured, slipping.

Gruaud-Larose, ST JULIEN 2ND GROWTH## Generally tannic, stern yet full-fruited wines (### between '82 and '86).

Guiraud, SAUTERNES Untrammeled, saturated style with lots of spicy new oak. '90 thick and good.

La Gurgue, MARGAUX Lively, fruity claret.

Haut-Bages-Averous, PAUILLAC Second wine of Lynch-Bages: soft and easy.

Haut-Bages-Libéral, PAUILLAC 5TH GROWTH## Good value; straightforward, with emphasis on fruit flavours. Poor '94 though.

Haut-Bailly, GRAVES Consistent quality and good value; pure, tapered, creamy flavours. '95 excellent.

Haut-Batailley, PAUILLAC 5TH GROWTH## Less meaty than some; blackcurranty elegance.

Haut-Beauséjour, ST ESTÈPHE Roederer-owned. Good wine since '94.

Haut-Bergeron, SAUTERNES Fine wines in the good years. See feature.

Haut-Bertinerie, see Bertinerie

Haut-Bonfils, BORDEAUX Ryman-made wine: '94 Semillon over-oaked and under-fruited.

Haut-Brion, GRAVES 1ST GROWTH## The only non-Médoc included in the 1855 classification, now surrounded by suburban Bordeaux. Along with Latour, the most consistent first-growth, and perhaps more aromatically refined than any. Haut-Brion ended the '80s with three sumptuous and seductive yet well-articulated, classically proportioned wines ('88, '89, '90).

Haut-Marbuzet, ST ESTÈPHE Generous, lavishly oaked wines of 5th growth standard.

d'Issan, MARGAUX 3RD GROWTH## Lovely château, beautiful labels, but patchy wines (# in '86 and '88). Perfumed, elegant when on form ('83, '85, '90, '94, '95).

Labégorce-Zédé, MARGAUX Inconsistent, but good vintages ('85, '89, '90) are plumply appealing.

Lafaurie-Peyraguey, SAUTERNES Exceptionally good, fat and oily from '83 onwards. A Cordier property.

Lafite-Rothschild, PAUILLAC 1ST GROWTH## A fallible first-growth, but when on song (as throughout the 80s) can outclass its peers for aromatic enchantment and poised, contained yet searing flavour. My favourite '95 primeur.

Lafleur, POMEROL As with Le Gay (same ownership), a massive, dense style, unafraid of tannin. Tiny production; stellar prices.

Lafon-Rochet, ST ESTÈPHE 4TH GROWTH## Sometimes over-armoured with tannins, but through the 80s the fruit has been there to match. Particularly good, accessible '94 and '95.

Lagrange, ST JULIEN 3RD GROWTH## Disappointing until '83 (routinely #); from '85 exciting (### in '86 and '90) thanks to Suntory investment. Settling into a tidy, cleanly defined, sweetly fruited style.

La Lagune, LUDON 3RD GROWTH# Limpid blackcurrant fruit melting into warm, spicy oak has made this (in '80s) as delicious a classed growth as any. Recently lighter, though: '94 and '95 are a disappointment.

Lamothe-Guignard, SAUTERNES Good value long-term wines, outstanding '89, '90.

Lanessan, CUSSAC Well-run property producing flavoury, herby claret of 5th growth standard.

Langoa-Barton, ST JULIEN 3RD GROWTH## Unfashionable, often overlooked, but full of quiet claretty virtue. Showier in '95.

Larcis-Ducasse, St Emilion Firm structured, authoritative.

Larmande, St Emilion Quality surge in 80s; now built to seduce.

Larose-Trintaudon, Haut-Médoc The Médoc's biggest property, producing wholesome, balanced wine.

Lascombes, Margaux 2nd growth# Modern standards only recently attained (## in '85 and from '88) with gracious, scented yet structured wines.

Latour, Pauillac 1st growth## Grand, statuesque wines slowly ripening towards a richly fruited yet always sober maturity. Very fine in '82, '86 and '90; some wavering in '83, '85 and '88; yet generally consistent, and often the best of the first growths in mean vintages. Clear leader in '94.

Latour-Martillac, Graves Clean, keen reds and whites.

Latour-à-Pomerol, Pomerol Plums-in-cream.

Léoville-Barton, St Julien 2nd growth## Concentrated wine in which the fruit is tannin-sifted into early quiescence, but all comes good in the end. The '90, '94 and '95 are all stunners, making Léoville-Barton a super-second.

Léoville-Las-Cases, St Julien 2nd growth### Wines from which nothing is omitted, but which need time to marshal these often turbulent forces. '82 legendary, but all the '80s good. '95 another stormer.

Léoville-Poyferré, St Julien 2nd growth## Poor wines in the '70s, but much improved in the 80s: black fruit wheeled in to support soft tannins. '95 a silky, mid-term wine.

Liversan, Haut-Médoc Smart, rich wine crossing into fifth-growth territory from time to time (excellent '88).

Loudenne, Médoc British outpost (Gilbey's) in far north of Médoc. Pleasant but unambitious red and white wines.

La Louvière, Graves Warm-fleshed red and occasionally exotic white.

Lynch-Bages, Pauillac 5th growth### An over-achiever of late, with black, bear-like wines in '89 and '90, and an impressive '91, too. '94 and '95 are slightly raw in youth.

Lynch-Moussas, Pauillac 5th growth# Mainly young vines; still a light wine, though deepening.

Magdelaine, St Emilion One of the severer St Emilions: sometimes over-tannic, yet when on form ('82, '89, '90) multi-dimensioned and age-worthy.

Malartic-Lagravière, Graves Slender, willowy style for both red and white (which now includes Semillon). Laurent Perrier-owned.

Malescot-St-Exupéry, Margaux 3rd growth# Many mean wines in its log book, but since '88 has begun finding the fruit to line its tannins; '90, '94 and '95 are ##.

de Malle, Sauternes The '76 was the first Sauternes I ever fell in love with, seduced by its glutting, lanolin embrace. It's still a good buy: the '88 and '90 are lovely plump young things, ready for dalliance.

Marbuzet, ST ESTÈPHE Formerly the balanced second wine of Cos d'Estournel; now a property in its own right again. Cleanly expressed, mid-weight wines.

Margaux, MARGAUX 1ST GROWTH## Many disappointing wines between '61 and '78, but during the '80s honouring its site with wines of enticing, floral perfume and intense, silk-wrapped fruit. Breathtaking in '82, '86 and '90. White Pavillon Blanc the best of the Médoc.

Marquis de Terme, MARGAUX 4TH GROWTH## Now sweet, succulent and accessible, though only # until '85.

Maucaillou, MOULIS Well-fruited and textured wine.

Méaume, BORDEAUX SUPÉRIEURE English-owned, with a dark red better than the appellation par.

Meyney, ST ESTÈPHE Well into 5th or 4th growth standard, this is firm chewy claret for those with cellar space.

La Mission–Haut–Brion, GRAVES Small, extraordinarily consistent château producing firm, sombre, fruit-quilted, gravy-like wines for the long haul.

Monbousquet, ST EMILION Ambitious wines in New Wave, super-lush style.

Monbrison, MARGAUX Good performer throughout 80s: profound wine of classed-growth standard. Less happy results in '90s.

Montrose, ST ESTÈPHE 2ND GROWTH## The inky, depth-charging '89 and '90 seem to mark a return to Montrose's traditionally battle-clad, cellar-seeking style. Light '88, '85 and '83 were #; '86 was a deliciously beefy blip. '94, unusually for St Estèphe, seems better than '95.

Moulin St Georges, ST EMILION Small property owned by Vauthier family (part-owners of Ausone) producing wines in lush, contemporary style.

Mouton–Cadet Big wine brand. Fair though never a bargain.

Mouton–Rothschild, PAUILLAC 1ST GROWTH## The most exotic, opulent and unbridled of the first growths when on song – magnificently so, during the early and mid-eighties. A more subdued wine at the end of the eighties, as if the property were in mourning for the Baron, who died that year, though '90 is beginning to turn on the charm. '94 and, especially, '95 both up with the best.

Nairac, SAUTERNES Rich wines, but the oak sometimes lords it over the fruit.

Nenin, POMEROL Soothing '94 and '95 worth buying.

Les Ormes de Pez, ST ESTÈPHE In Lynch-Bages ownership: plump, generous, round-contoured, good value. '94 and '95 both tannic, cellar-seeking.

Palmer, MARGAUX 3RD GROWTH## Deep, supple, comely Merlot-rich wines which in some vintages ('83, '89, '95) are ### and rival super-seconds.

Pape–Clément, GRAVES After terrible disappointments between '76 and '84, this château has refound inspiration with graceful, tapered yet deep-rooted wines. '88 and '90 particularly good, while '94 and '95 both fine. Delicious, almost Viognier-like white, too.

Patache d'Aux, MÉDOC Good safe fall-back claret.

Pavie, St Emilion   Firm sobriety characterises this authoritative wine when young; time unpeels the fruit. '95 much better than '94.

Pavie-Decesse, St Emilion   Staunch yet well-balanced; fine throughout mid and late 80s, though needs a spell in the cellar.

Pavie-Macquin, St Emilion   Competition has provoked excellence among the Pavies: Macquin, too, is rugged, yet backed by rich fruit. Rolland consults.

Petit Village, Pomerol   Smooth, low-acid, almost caricaturally lush Pomerol in good vintages; rather light in lesser ones (avoid '94).

Pétrus, Pomerol   The most expensive of all clarets. Why? Pure pleasure. You don't even have to wait, though the rewards are much greater for those who do, with truffley, Havana warmth lending dangerous allure to the thick black fruits of youth. Yet even Pétrus isn't infallible: the '76-'86 period was patchy.

de Pez, St Estèphe   English-style (understated, firm) claret of 5th growth standard. Roederer-owned; '95 a promising début.

Phélan-Ségur, St Estèphe   Difficulties in the early '80s, but lately a full-bodied, meaty, satisfying and underpriced wine (though disappointing '95).

Pibran, Pauillac   Rewarding, roasty, earthy and deep (though '94 a bit slender).

Pichon-Lalande, Pauillac 2nd growth###   Among the softest, gentlest and most graceful of the Médoc's stars, a wine to bathe your tongue in. Some quality variations, though '82, '86, '89, '94 and '95 all very fine.

Pichon-Longueville, Pauillac 2nd growth##   Often known as Pichon Baron, this wine was disappointing (#) until '82, on par until '86 (##), and rose to ### for '88, '89 and, especially, '90, under the tutelage of Jean-Michel Cazes of Lynch-Bages. '94 and '95, though, have brought toughish youngsters (##).

Le Pin, Pomerol   Minuscule quantities; cult status: liquid hedonism. The '93 (the only one I've tried) was spicy and deliciously balanced.

Pitray, Côtes de Castillon   Leading property in this fine-value AOC.

Pontet-Canet, Pauillac 5th growth##   Increasingly deep, tannic wine for this property with mediocre (#) pre-'80s past. Both '94 and '95 exceptionally good in New Wave, soft-centred style.

Potensac, Médoc   Stumpy, strutting little wines in same ownership as Léoville-Las-Cases.

Poujeaux, Moulis   Reliable, firmly constituted, with sweet oaken edges.

Prieuré-Lichine, Margaux 4th growth##   Deftly made, well-articulated, well-balanced, gently scented wine: a drinker's choice. Advice from Rolland has added to the pleasure: a good purchase in '94 and '95 for early drinking.

Rabaud-Promis, Sauternes   Great recent turn of speed from this estate, now making ('86, '88, '89, '90) rich, succulent and powerful wines.

Rauzan-Ségla, Margaux 2nd growth##   Major sock-raising exercise since '83; previously # or worse. In '88, '89, '90, '94 and '95 this was one of the sturdiest, most intensely flavoured wines in Margaux. Owned by Chanel family.

Rauzan-Gassies, MARGAUX 2ND GROWTH# Machine-picked, ramshackle wines.

Raymond-Lafon, SAUTERNES Absolute commitment to quality. Top '90.

Reynon, PREMIÈRES CÔTES Superb old-vine Sauvignon Vieilles Vignes, which I prefer to the oaky Clos Floridène.

Ricaud, LOUPIAC One of best non-Sauternes sweet wines.

Rieussec, SAUTERNES Quickly darkening, super-weighty wine: one of the stars.

La Rivière, FRONSAC Fairy-tale château producing some of Fronsac's sturdiest clarets. Recent change of ownership.

Roc de Cambes, CÔTES DE BOURG Appellation leader, run by François Mitjavile of Tertre-Rôteboeuf.

Roquetaillade-la-Grange, GRAVES Decent, well-rounded wines: I remember loving the red '85 in its youth, though the bloom faded quickly.

Segonzac, PREMIÈRES CÔTES DE BLAYE Good, try-harder property in quiet Blaye.

St Pierre, ST JULIEN 4TH GROWTH## Soft, contemporary claret.

de Sales, POMEROL Large property (there's even enough for the UK) turning out consistently ripe, plump, straightforward wines (though a flop in '94).

Sigalas-Rabaud, SAUTERNES Generally quite fresh and elegant in style, though '88 and '89 are richly upholstered. Cordier-owned.

Siran, MARGAUX Try-harder property, though the results are sometimes tough and ungrateful.

Smith-Haut-Lafitte, GRAVES Change of ownership and major investments here have resulted in a steady quality increase during the '90s: '90, '94 and '95 all very impressive.

Sociando-Mallet, HAUT-MÉDOC Knocks as regularly at the door of the classed growths as any: rich fruits meshed with generous oak. '82 and '90 both superb, long-term wines.

de Sours, BORDEAUX SUPÉRIEURE Good drinker's claret; excellent rosé.

Soutard, ST EMILION Conservatively made, steel-sinewed, but fruit to balance.

Suduiraut, SAUTERNES A sensual steamroller in good years ('76, '82, '86, '88, '89), though others can disappoint ('83 and '85).

Talbot, ST JULIEN 4TH GROWTH## Usually a solid, faithful, guard-dog claret. '86 outstanding; since then a slight lightening. White wine, too, called Caillou Blanc.

du Tertre, MARGAUX 5TH GROWTH## Pleasantly soft-fruited, yet holds well.

Le Tertre-Rôteboeuf, ST EMILION Showy, concentrated and thoroughly exciting wines from very low-yielding vines picked as ripe as possible: '95 exemplary.

Teyssier, ST EMILION English-made; promising quality.

Thieuley, BORDEAUX Crisp, fresh white. Cuvée François Courselle is oaky.

La Tour Blanche, SAUTERNES Student-made wines; suddenly on form in '88, 89 and '90 with concentrated, oak-honed wines after years of modest results.

La Tour de By, Médoc Good, warm, accessible claret-drinker's claret.

La Tour-Haut-Brion, Graves Generally firm, forceful wine, though '89 and '90 are softer in contour.

La Tour Haut-Caussan, Médoc Big-dimensioned wines.

La Tour du Haut-Moulin, Médoc Usually exciting, with vintage fidelity.

La Tour-Martillac, Graves Organic claret-producer (uncommon), yet an uncertain winemaking touch.

La Tour-Séguy, Bourg Good flavours for price.

Troplong-Mondot, St Emilion Fresh-flavoured, finely detailed wines. Superb '90 here, while '94 and '95 up the ante again: massively extracted, ambitious.

Trotanoy, Pomerol A good pedigree (in Moueix hands), but rather a light run from the sumptuous '82 to the deep, tight '90. '95, fine, too.

Trottevieille, St Emilion Steadily improving through '80s; now characterised by crunchy, spicy tannins and firm extracts.

Valandraud, St Emilion Huge ambition and effort is producing showy wines for 'the Le Pin of St Emilion'. Time will tell.

Vieux Château Certan, Pomerol Fragrant and fruity, cleanly defined: Pomerol for Médoc-lovers. The '90, however, has regional unction. Exceptionally good '94 and '95.

d'Yquem, Sauternes Undisputed king of Bordeaux's sweet wines, as complex as it is rich, with superb ageing potential. Quality mirrors vintage closely, so the greats of the '80s are '83, '86 and '88 ... but 1921 is still going strong. Tiny yields (a glass per vine) and universal celebrity mean spire-high prices.

Vintages (claret)
1995 ★★★; 1994 ★★; 1993 ★; 1992 ★; 1991 ★★; 1990 ★★★★;
1989 ★★★★; 1988 ★★★; 1987 ★; 1986 ★★★★; 1985 ★★★.

Previous vintages ranking 3 or 4
1983 ★★★; 1982 ★★★★; 1978 ★★★; 1976 ★★★; 1975 ★★★; 1970 ★★★★;
1966 ★★★★; 1961 ★★★★; 1959 ★★★.

Vintages (Sauternes)
1995 ★★★; 1994 ★★; 1993 ★; 1992 ★; 1991 ★★; 1990 ★★★; 1989 ★★★; 1988 ★★★★;
1987 ★; 1986 ★★★★; 1985 ★★★.

Previous vintages ranking 3 or 4
1983 ★★★★; 1982 ★★★; 1976 ★★★★; 1975 ★★★★; 1971 ★★★; 1967 ★★★★; 1962
★★★; 1959 ★★★★.

Specialist retailers
Roberson has a fine browsing range; also good are John Armit, Bibendum, Berry Bros, Corney and Barrow, Davisons, Fortnum and Mason, Goedhuis and Justerini & Brooks among others. Serious investors should consult Farr Vintners, whose access to stock seems unbeatable.

One sweet day

A tractor lurched into the cellar, its trailer bearing perhaps fifty or sixty little trays of rotten grapes. Outside, dusk was drawing on pinkly, at the end of a warm October day when honeyed sunshine had cut long, mobile shadows around the roadside poplars. A student fed the trays of grapes into the destemmer, and the air filled with dust, banks of it, billowing up from the corrupted fruit, screening the rosy felicities of the vineyard sunset with fine fungal soot.

This was Château La Tour Blanche, Sauternes' agricultural school, on the late afternoon of October 9th 1995. Sauternes is that part of Bordeaux which specialises in making unctuous white wines from grapes sweetly shrivelled by 'noble rot', *Botrytis cinerea*. The only anxiety of the director, Jean-Paul Jausserand, was that the grapes actually contained too much sugar, which might give him fermentation problems resulting in a finished wine too sweet and too low in alcohol. Hassles like this are welcome. Normally his difficulties are of quite another order.

Life for the Sauternes winemaker can be a tortured and humiliating business. In most years, things go badly, and the harvest is more or less a failure. When things do go well (the last really good year was 1990), growers still end up with less wine to sell than everybody else. Sauternes occupies two per cent of Bordeaux's vineyard land but only produces 0.8 per cent of its wine. Put another way, most of Bordeaux's vines yield half a bottle of wine a year; at Château d'Yquem, it's a glass per vine.

Properties in Sauternes are known as *danseuses* (dancers) – a worldly reference to their tendency to swallow wads of cash in return for small transports of occasional but intense delight. Traditionally, Sauternes families keep going by owning tracts of the Landes Forest which lies between the vines and the sea.

It was now dark. The limestone buildings on the town square in Sauternes were still warm to the touch. A tasting had been prepared. Growers were in attendance: thin men, modestly dressed, making wines without the renown of d'Yquem of Suduiraut, yet often excellent; I particularly liked the richly buttery 1986 and 1990 wines made by Robert Lamothe at Château Haut-Bergeron. It doesn't have to be grand to be good.

The tasting over, we stepped outside. A full moon now hung in the sky, draining the gold from the limestone and charging it with milk, and I was driven away down country lanes for one of the strangest dinners of my life. It was a *table d'hôte*, a meal prepared for the public in a private house – in this case, one of endearing ancestral squalour. Our *hôte* was in fact a *hôtesse*, Eliane Gay, a middle-aged lady with a childlike smile and a sing-song voice, dressed in a sweatshirt and tracksuit bottoms; the house had been her great-grandfather's. Gaspar, her dog, lay on the sofa with his legs wide open, exhausted after a day (Eliane told us) spent leading goats around, something he did purely for the pleasure of leading goats around. The stove roared, and we drank Sauternes with every course: not as bad as you'd think, and good both with asparagus and cheese.

Nature's call meant just that: Eliane led me into the garden and said that no one was looking. I could see strange, draped chairs huddled in a semi-circle for some obscure nocturnal conference, while beyond the garden the moon glittered on the Garonne; the little river Ciron joined it just here, and tinkled coldly. I tinkled warmly. "*C'est reposant!*" said Eliane, beaming, as I went back in. Gaspar turned and slept on.

Burgundy

Into the labyrinth

Wine books normally assume a tone of resigned world-weariness at this point. Burgundy, they sigh, is the most exciting red wine in the world – on occasion. Six bottles out of seven, by contrast, are dull, whether through meteorological malchance, viticultural greediness or winemaking ineptitude. Pursuing great burgundy requires a gambler's reckless fortitude.

This is still, broadly speaking, true, though there are some encouraging changes underway. I was very surprised to see the generally unexciting red '94s offered *en primeur* in early 1996, but '93 (red), '92 (white) and '90 (both) were all, in part if not in whole, felicitous vintages. The large merchant houses which have done so much to homogenise and impoverish burgundy's variety are foundering or reforming. Among the smaller grower-producers, well-trained, well-travelled and enthusiastic sons are taking over from unthinking, narrow-horizoned fathers. Burgundy is deeper, cleaner, more excitingly perfumed and more resonantly fruity than it used to be.

Decoding the label

Other difficulties for the consumer are perennial. The appellation system here is more complicated than anywhere else in France. In part, this is a beautiful struggle: site research has been pursued down the centuries here with obsessive precision, and the appellation system marks the summing-up, in pyramid shape, of these ceaseless enquiries. Grand Cru vineyards (labelled with their names alone) constitute the pinnacle of the pyramid; next come Premier Cru vineyards (labelled 'Premier Cru' plus, optionally, a vineyard name); next village wines (labelled with village names, most of which are confusingly hyphenated with the names of certain Grand Cru vineyards, and some of which may also be garnished with vineyard or 'lieu-dit' names); finally regional or sub-regional wines. The full list of Burgundy's appellations is not printed here, but will be found in larger reference books (see page 30).

Even supposing you managed to master the minutiae of Burgundy's appellations, there are still hundreds of producers' names to come to terms with. Printed below is a non-exhaustive selection of the best. Please write to tell me if you have growers or producers you are particularly enthusiastic about, or find disappointing.

Almost all white burgundy is made from Chardonnay (a minute amount of Pinot Blanc and Pinot Gris is used), and all red burgundy from Pinot Noir. Aligoté (a grape giving sharper white wines than does Chardonnay) makes a labelled varietal wine here, too; this is the wine to use for an authentic Kir. Bourgogne Passe-Tout-Grains is a red made from a mixture of one-third Pinot Noir and two-thirds Gamay.

'Burgundy' as a geographical entity is composed of four distinct regions. Furthest north is Chablis. Its famous wines should be, and sometimes are, the most mouthwatering and fine-honed of white burgundies. Much Chablis, by contrast, is mere varietal Chardonnay: milked from high-yielding vines, chaptalised to dropsy, lacking all regional style and true intensity.

Next comes the Côte d'Or, divided into the Côte de Nuits and Côte de Beaune. This is Burgundy's heartland: a necklace of dull little villages strung along an unspectacular, wood-capped slope. Beneath the sometimes pale, sometimes stony, sometimes brownish soils of that slope lies a geological terrine of unusual intricacy – reflected in wines of great variousness. The best red burgundies encapsulate a triumphant paradox: delicacy and perfume allied to force and power. White Côte d'Or burgundy is generally fatter and richer than Chablis, lushly so in the case of Meursault, nuttily so in the case of Montrachet.

South of the Côte d'Or lies the Côte Chalonnaise, a small group of villages where firm, chunky, often coarse-grained red wines gradually give way, moving south, to clean-limbed, deeply flavoured whites. The Mâconnais is overwhelmingly a white-wine-producing area (red Mâcon, from Gamay, is a dull affair). It's fashionable to criticise the Mâconnais, but most have a distinctively burgundian vinosity to them, a bone structure behind the warm blandishments of their fruit, which make them worthwhile and appealingly priced. The best – some Pouilly-Fuissé, some St-Véran – can rival and surpass lesser Côte d'Or white burgundy and much basic Chablis.

Ambroise, NUITS Hugely extractive, punchy wines.

Amiot Bonfils, CHASSAGNE Concentrated, deeply fruited white wines; not shy of oak. Lightish, penetrating reds.

Amiot-Servelle, CHAMBOLLE Graceful, ripe '93s.

Marquis d'Angerville, VOLNAY Elegance and depth.

Domaine de l'Arlot, PRÉMEAUX Cleanly, clearly expressed red wines of purity and depth, though they seem to be exploring the limits of varietal expression rather than trying to be red burgundy.

Jean–Claude Bachelet, ST AUBIN Traditional white wines from Puligny-Montrachet: concentrated, highly allusive, more oxidative than many.

Barthod–Noellat, CHAMBOLLE Firm, articulate, carefully made for aging.

Bitouzet–Prieur, VOLNAY Superb, tight-grained Meursault.

Blain–Gagnard, CHASSAGNE A delicate, restrained approach gives fine, tapered white wines and elegant reds.

Jean–Marc Boillot, POMMARD Grippy, spicy, peppery, juniper-scented reds and concentrated, extrovert whites.

Lucien Boillot, GEVREY Harmonious, spicy, mid-weight wines.

Boisset, BEAUNE Large merchant and stockholder who has hoovered up Viénot, Bouchard Aîné, Jaffelin and Chauvenet among others. A stock-exchange listing, implying that dividend hunger which is usually incompatible with great wines. Variable wine standards; I enjoyed the floral '92 Charles de France Chardonnay.

André Bonhomme, MÂCON Full-flavoured Mâcon-Viré with deliciously unyielding, stony core.

Bonneau du Martray, PERNAND The largest chunk of Corton-Charlemagne, yet rarely the best. Fine wine nonetheless, especially in good vintages.

Bouchard Père et Fils, BEAUNE Fine vineyard estate, yet a bust with the law, a bad fire and a tarnishing range combined to ground this old company. Now controlled by canny Champenois Joseph Henriot: things should improve.

J-M Brocard, CHABLIS Straightforward, well-made, intense wine from old vines.

Henri & Gilles Buisson, ST ROMAIN Delicious '85 'Sous Roche', sweet, soft and aromatic, was one of the best bottles of Burgundy I drank this year.

Carillon, PULIGNY Stony, almost austere whites, rewarding with time.

Caves de Buxy, CÔTE CHALONNAISE Reliable source of unfussy, good-value white burgundy.

La Chablisienne, CHABLIS This cooperative is an excellent source of good-value Chablis.

Chandon de Briailles, SAVIGNY Delicate, perfumed wines, typical of this village.

Chartron et Trébuchet, PULIGNY Good new-wave merchant with a remarkably consistent range of white burgundies in complex, vinous style. '93 Rully La Chaume tastes of orange, aniseed and flowers.

Jean Chauvenet, NUITS-ST-GEORGES It is notoriously hard to find good Nuits: Chauvenet's sweet-scented, ripely fruity examples are an exception.

Chopin-Groffier, PRÉMEAUX Complex, deep wines of consistently high quality.

Bruno Clair, MARSANNAY Elegant, accessible and urbane wines with good depth.

Coche-Dury, MEURSAULT Consistent, concentrated, unflabby wine, much sought-after.

Marc Colin, ST AUBIN Carefully crafted, unshowy, concentrated white wines.

Colin-Deleger, CHASSAGNE Good vintage and vineyard differentiation within a generally expressive, intense style.

Domaine du Comte Armand, POMMARD Severe, weighty wines in good years; plump, comely ones in lighter years.

Jean-Jacques Confuron, PRÉMEAUX Recent renaissance in quality: tiny yields now producing very fine wines, even in poor years.

Coste-Caumartin, POMMARD Unapologetically tannic, almost bitter wines when young; for long ageing.

Dauvissat, CHABLIS Carefully formed Chablis with discreet oak softening stony fruit.

Daniel Defaix, CHABLIS Long lees ageing but no oak gives complexity within a steely frame. Even when rich ('90), keeps elegance.

Jean-Paul Droin, CHABLIS Ample oak and expressive, floral fruit.

Joseph Drouhin, BEAUNE Well-mannered, passionless but reliable merchant range. Japanese-owned.

Maurice & Claude Dugat, GEVREY Tiny quantities, but deep, sumptuous style.

Domaine Dujac, MOREY Pure thoroughbreds: never deep in colour, but splendidly perfumed and richly fruited wines. Chambolle '92 has great presence; '93 Morey typically pure and long.

Maurice Ecard, SAVIGNY Graceful, true to Savigny style and good value.

René Engel, VOSNE Aromatic, classy, mid-weight wines from a fine spread of vineyards.

Michel Esmonin, GEVREY Father-and-daughter team producing a small but vigorous range of wines led by Gevrey-Clos-St-Jacques.

Faiveley, NUITS ST GEORGES One of the best of the region's merchants: consistently deeply flavoured wines, with good vineyard differentiation, though perhaps a lack of finesse and subtlety. Punchy, aggressive Mercurey wines offer the best value (though not in '93). Deep Meursault reliable.

William Fèvre, CHABLIS Flattering, oaky style can quickly grow wearisome, though examples from the best vineyards sink with age into classicism.

Ferret Pouilly-Fuissé Intensity and concentration.

Fontaine-Gagnard, CHASSAGNE Understated, weighty, old style whites, requiring cellaring for full expression.

Château de Fuissé, MÂCON Top-class Pouilly-Fuissé at Côte d'Or prices, yet the Vieilles Vignes cuvée could stand without shame among the best Meursault. St Véran and Mâcon both good.

Jean-Noël Gagnard, CHASSAGNE A combination of restraint and richness marks Gagnard's superb whites; his Bâtard needs time, but is a beacon. Skilled fruit handling means some excellent wines from lesser years, too.

Granger, MERCUREY Honest, peppery Vieilles Vignes is worth trying.

Jean Grivot, VOSNE Mixed quality, but the best (e.g. Les Beaumonts) is dense.

Robert Groffier, GEVREY Soft and tasty wines.

Jean Gros, VOSNE Best wines (like Richebourg) concentrated and perfumed; lesser wines lack substance.

Gros Frère et Soeur, VOSNE Fat, fruity-oaky wines initially; now softer, sometimes sharp.

Guffens-Heynen, MÂCON Ambitious, dense wines, hard work to drink young but promising much.

Jaffelin, BEAUNE Promising at end of '80s, but recent purchase by Boisset (a merchant house noted more for commercial acumen than oenological excellence) may check progress.

Louis Jadot, BEAUNE Huge spread of vineyards in the portfolio of this merchant, but rivals the best efforts of growers in most sites. Unfashionable Beaune reds can provide top value (especially Clos des Ursules). Whites are remarkably consistent, and Jadot's Montrachet is as concentratedly seductive as its legendary name suggests.

Jayer-Gilles, MAGNY-LÈS-VILLERS Exciting depth of fruit throughout the range, even Hautes Côtes.

François Jobard, MEURSAULT Finely detailed, restrained, meticulously precise wines for long ageing.

Joblot, GIVRY One of the best producers of the Côte Chalonnaise, and a vociferous philosopher of wine: generous fruit sheathed in unapologetic oak.

Michel Juillot, MERCUREY One of the few producers to avoid clumsiness with Mercurey: clean, deep fruit.

Labouré-Roi, Nuits-St-Georges As with so many merchants, a measure of saminess among the wines, yet the emphasis on fruit flavours and accessibility gives them an easy and occasionally exciting appeal.

Michel Lafarge, Volnay Silky yet richly fruited wines.

Domaine des Comtes Lafon, Meursault Fine vineyard sites, low yields and careful winemaking make these reference Meursaults. Volnay reds are soft but deep and rewarding.

Laroche, Chablis Big landowner producing a range of wines; lesser ones have no oak; best vineyards some discreet oak. Fair to good quality.

Louis Latour, Beaune Good, occasionally superb white burgundy (Mâcon to Montrachet), though can be overplump and flabby too (e.g Puligny Premier Cru '89); dull, unfocussed reds.

Laurent, Nuits Sumptuous, oaky, rich wines produced with lots of lees contact by an ex-pâtissier.

Lechcneaut, Nuits Up-and-coming producer: resonant wines.

Philippe Leclerc, Gevrey Colourful character making intense, highly extractive wines with (Premiers Crus) ageing in new oak.

Leflaive, Puligny Some inconsistency during the second half of the 80s, but from '90 onwards a return to high standards. Now semi-organic production. '93 Bienvenues-Bâtard-Montrachet structured and taut, needing cellaring.

Olivier Leflaive Frères, Puligny 'New wave' merchant with strict *terroir*-based approach with portfolio of fine white burgundies and fair though not yet outstanding reds.

Domaine Lejeune, Pommard Superbly punchy wines, with a fiery core beneath the rich, dark fruits.

Leroy, Vosne Hugely ambitious, hugely expensive wines designed to rival those of the Domaine de la Romanée-Conti (of which Leroy's owner, Lalou Bize-Leroy, is former co-proprietor); biodynamic cultivation from '91. Tiny yields give wines of massive concentration and extract, for long ageing.

Georges Lignier, Morey Expressive, juicy, pleasant wines, though lacking in substance — and excitement.

Hubert Lignier, Morey Small quantities but exceptionally good quality.

Lumpp, Givry Concentrated and uncompromising wines in the sometimes mealy Chalonnais context.

Machard de Gramont, Nuits Chunky wines from scattered vineyard holdings.

Manciat-Poncet, Pouilly-Fuissé Whites of great substance, esp. Vieilles Vignes.

Matrot, Meursault Young grower with healthy contempt for oak, permitting clear vineyard differentiation.

Maume, Gevrey Dense, almost tough top wines; soft but meaty Bourgogne.

Méo-Camuzet, Vosne Grand, urbane and expensive, though sometimes overly 'international' and oak-glossy in style.

Olivier Merlin, MÂCON Good wines, especially Vieilles Vignes cuvées.

Prince de Mérode, LADOIX Light, elegant, perfumed wines, acquiring more depth from '90. '93s unlovely, though.

Louis Michel, CHABLIS Stainless-steel-fermented Chablis of cutting purity and stony depth. Not a butter pat in sight ...

Michelot, MEURSAULT Plump wines, drinkable early.

Mongeard–Mugneret, VOSNE Formerly firm, chewy wines, but recently lighter in style, riding too heavily on oak.

Hubert de Montille, VOLNAY Hugely tannic, severe reds for long ageing. Do they soften?

Bernard Morey, CHASSAGNE Sound, expressive white wines.

Marc Morey, CHASSAGNE Fine winemaking; clean, floral style (white).

Pierre Morey, MEURSAULT Lush, full-bodied whites.

Albert Morot, BEAUNE Finely crafted, tight-textured red wines.

Denis Mortet, GEVREY Lesser red wines lush and soft; wines from top sites are fat, stuffed with almost-sweet, shattered black fruits. Uncertain touch in '93, though.

André Mussy, POMMARD Mussy's Beaune Epenottes and Montrevenots are far deeper than most; earthy, full-bodied Pommard, too.

Philippe Naddef, COUCHEY Contemporary red burgundy – lots of fruit, lots of oak. Stylish and good.

Michel Niellon, CHASSAGNE Buxom, yet supported by lively acids and firm fruit.

Ponsot, MOREY Inconsistent, but the best years ('80, '85, '90) are concentrated, with exciting, wild flavours (red). '92 Gevrey Cuvée de l'Abeille sour and thin. Very good '93s, though, expecially Clos de la Roche Vieilles Vignes and Clos St Denis.

Pothier–Rieusset, POMMARD Consistent, structured and often tannic wines, but with keen acid balance.

Pousse d'Or, VOLNAY Formerly deep and sonorous red, but hasn't shone in late '80s.

Jacques Prieur, MEURSAULT Fine vineyards, but disappointing wines until late '80s. Recent changes (from '88) have brought improvements; top whites now very fine. Laurent-Perrier-owned.

Henri Prudhon, ST AUBIN Beautifully fruited reds from this undervalued village.

Michel Prunier, AUXEY-DURESSES Ripe, rich wines from another of Burgundy's better-value villages (red and white).

Ramonet, CHASSAGNE Extrovert, unbridled white burgundy from superb vineyards, and clean, graceful reds.

Raveneau, CHABLIS Inspiring, exemplary Chablis of assured, stony classicism: regional benchmarks.

Domaine Daniel Rion et Fils, PRÉMEAUX Dark, sober reds, relaxing with the years. Unusually weighty Aligoté, too.

Antonin Rodet, MERCUREY Merchant house controlled by Laurent-Perrier; generally trustworthy. Domaine bottlings among the best from the Côte Chalonnaise.

Domaine Rollin, PERNAND Finely balanced white wines, more successful with top vineyards (like jasmine-scented Corton-Charlemagne) than with village wines.

Domaine de la Romanée-Conti, VOSNE Wines (mostly red) made, like Pétrus or d'Yquem, without compromise. In good years unctuously fruity and sleekly oaked to begin, ageing towards a carnal prime, yet some unaccountable variations (e.g. '92s). Much sought-after by investors and collectors, so beyond most pockets.

Ropiteau, MONTAGNY Carefully made, sinewy wines.

Joseph Roty, GEVREY Lots of tannins, but many of them from wood.

Emmanuel Rouget, FLAGEY Magnificent wines from Henri Jayer's successor: fine, sheer, sumptuous fruit, densely packed, authoritative.

Guy Roulot, MEURSAULT The village at its most comely and honeyed. Nutty, rich, four-square.

Georges Roumier, CHAMBOLLE Great fidelity to *terroir* in a richly diverse range.

Armand Rousseau, GEVREY Concentrated, muscular Chambertin and Chambertin-Clos de Bèze lead a diverse and occasionally disappointing range.

Etienne Sauzet, PULIGNY Slimmed-down domain, but wines remain among the most poised of all white burgundies, with richness and finesse both on board.

Baron Thénard, GIVRY Grandiose bottles, but dull, light wines.

Jean Thévenet, MÂCON Monk-like fanatic producing concentrated, intense wines.

Tollot Beaut, CHOREY Fine vineyard holdings, but the wines can lean too heavily on oak, drying their fruit.

Truchot-Martin, MOREY Fine wines in light, fragrant style.

Valette, POUILLY-FUISSÉ Textbook style and depth, with discreet use of oak.

Verget, MÂCON Merchant-vinification business of Guffens-Heynen: small range, but quality excellent, including top Côte d'Or sites.

Aubert de Villaine, BOUZERON Intense, zesty Aligoté and firm Chardonnay from the 'home' vineyards of the DRC administrator.

Comte de Vogüé, CHAMBOLLE An enviably situated estate, yet very patchy wines until '89. Now better structure and depth of fruit.

Vintages (red)
1995 ★★★; 1994 ★★; 1993 ★★★; 1992 ★★; 1991 ★★; 1990 ★★★★; 1989 ★★★; 1988 ★★; 1987 ★★; 1986 ★; 1985 ★★★.

Vintages (white)
1995 ★★★; 1994 ★★; 1993 ★; 1992 ★★★★; 1991 ★; 1990 ★★★; 1989 ★★★; 1988 ★★; 1987 ★; 1986 ★★★; 1985 ★★★

Specialist retailers:
London is well-served by burgundy specialists: John Armit, Adam Bancroft, Bibendum, Corney & Barrow (DRC), Domaine Direct, Goedhuis, Haynes Hanson & Clarke, Justerini & Brooks, Laytons, Morris & Verdin, La Réserve and Howard Ripley among others.

Rubbing knuckles

This was Burgundy, sure enough. I stood in front of a large house whose plaster was slowly peeling and falling. An old lady walked slowly across a courtyard. I was waiting for her son, one of eight children; he had six of his own. Another grower fulminated, his eyes bright with righteous rage, against those who became rich by talking rather than making things. "Making things is all that matters. Everything's adrift. We're living in a virtual world!" When I asked how he treated his wines after fermentation, he said "I leave the sodding things alone," and laughed uproariously. "It's so easy to make good wine. It's growing good grapes that's difficult."

I visited the cellars of the Château de Rully, a national monument open to the public, and a hound of Baskerville proportions lurched, slavered and barked at the end of a chain in furious and psychotic welcome. Another grower described a village controversy which had blown up concerning a wine tasting. He was receiving anonymous letters. "A spent cartridge came through the post yesterday, with a note saying 'The next one's for you'. Charming, eh?" He stubbed his cigar out and said he was going fishing. With his gun.

The contrast with Bordeaux, in other words, is total. In Bordeaux, more or less well-moneyed and not infrequently aristocratic owners live in châteaux perched like islands in the middle of large lakes of vines; neighbours might wave a distant bonjour to each other twice a year. Burgundy is a land of villages surrounded by vineyards, and the growers, not necessarily less wealthy but usually earthier in background and temperament, rub shoulders, elbows and occasionally knuckles, both at home and out in the vines.

I was visiting the Côte Chalonnaise. Burgundy is divided into four bits, north to south: Chablis, then the Côte d'Or (where the priciest bottles come from), followed by the Côte Chalonnaise and finally the Mâcon region. In the old days, wines from the Côte Chalonnaise tended to get mixed into blending vats further north to 'stretch' top names; nowadays this doesn't (or shouldn't) happen. Nonetheless the Côte Chalonnaise still helps out on the generic burgundy front: Sainsbury's big-selling White Burgundy is sourced from Mercurey-based Antonin Rodet, and is a blend of Côte Chalonnaise and Côte de Beaune wines. The region has five villages, each with an AOC in its own right: Mercurey and Givry, both mainly red burgundy with a little white; Rully, for both; and Montagny for white wine alone. Bouzeron is for white wine made from the Aligoté rather than the Chardonnay grape. Half an hour north on a bicycle will get you to vineyards producing some of the most expensive wines in the world: Montrachet, Meursault, Volnay, Pommard. What happens in the Côte Chalonnaise is that the continuous slope or côte on which the great wines grow becomes fractured and discontinous. Some of the region's producers feel their wines could be the equal of anything produced further north, but because they can't ask higher prices for them they are unable to make the quality decisions (fastidious viticulture, cellar investment) which would enable the vineyards to reach their full potential. I'm sceptical about this. I have never tasted anything even potentially sublime or lyrical from the Côte Chalonnaise. They are Yorkshireman's burgundies: gruff, square-edged, solid. Many Côte d'Or bottles at twice the price, however, bring you all the flesh and warmth of a whippet. Solidity, in this context, is a virtue.

Champagne
Millenial panic

The story's been rumbling on for about 18 months now: it goes something like this. New Year's Eve 1999 will, even if miscalculatedly, be a night to remember. Most human beings never get the chance to celebrate the turn of a century, let alone the turn of a millenium. The celebratory drink of choice is champagne. The world and its aunt, therefore, are going to want to pop a bottle on that night. Champagne is a small and unexpandable area. Horror: shortage!

The Champenois assure us all that it's not a problem, and that they are taking steps to meet demand. Their business is one in which logistics plays a large part anyway, and they're a terribly serious, hard-working lot, so perhaps it's true. Perhaps, though, there are anxieties: production thresholds have been increased, and the old question of whether or not to expand the champagne AOC area is back on the agenda. Just to be on the safe side, some canny merchants (like Selfridges) have launched millenial champagne offers to ensure devotees of supplies of the good stuff. This, indeed, is the key to the problem: a millenial night deserves not just champagne, but good champagne, which in value for money terms means vintage champagne, and it is this which may well be in short supply. You need to take care over storage (champagne is a delicate wine which hates light, warmth, vibrations or gross temperature fluctuations), but stock up with the best 1985 vintage champagne if you can find it; 15 years' age would be ideal for something mellowly millenial. Otherwise it's probably better to wait for the 1990s to come on to the market over the next year or so – a superb vintage, one of the century's best. They won't have finished their ageing trajectory by 31.12.99, but they should at least be on song by then. See the producer listing for choice marques.

A mouthful of freshness

No other wine illustrates as well as does champagne the French genius for accepting an offering from the earth, then teasing, troubling, twisting and turning it towards perfection. The earth offered, in this case, some rather thin, muddy and sour pink-red wines. They weren't abominable, though – there was a sort of mean, lean length to them that set medieval heads nodding in approval even while lips were pursed with their viperous acidity. Out of these unpromising materials, over long decades, through painstaking and corner-turning researches, came champagne: a mouthful of swarming, creamy freshness.

How is it made? Take chalk-grown Pinot Noir, Pinot Meunier and Chardonnay grapes, and make thin, sharp but fine-grained white wines with them. Bottle these wines with a little yeast and sugar; let them slowly referment, sealed in their bottles, sublimating their gases. Then leave the wine to slumber on the yeast deposits produced by this refermentation for long months. Eventually, of course, the deposits have to be removed. Turn the bottles upside down, freeze the necks, and then reinvert the bottles: gas pressure ejects the frozen plug of sediment. Swiftly add a little sweet wine; seal with the corks. Two small miracles have taken place: not only is the wine pregnant with a fine froth of foamy bubbles, but its initial sour thinness has been fattened and filled out (in the best cases with great grace) by the grainy flavour of dead yeast and the finishing addition of sweet wine.

As even this short resumé shows, champagne is, in comparison with most wines, highly processed. This in turn means that production is concentrated in the hands of a comparatively small number of large companies. Growers' champagnes do exist, and can offer good value; few of them, though, bother to export (see under 'Growers' champagnes' in the listing below).

And label information? As ever, the most important information is the producer's name. Most champagne is called 'non-vintage', and is blended from the wines of a single, recent year plus some older 'reserve' wines. Vintage champagne is usually deeper than non-vintage champagne, and will always be more rounded and expressive if you can age it for a further year or so in cool, dark conditions. 'Prestige cuvées' (Dom Pérignon, Cristal and the like) are impressive, though often drunk too young when their youth makes them seem unimpressive; given their high cost, straight vintage champagnes can offer better value. Blanc de Blancs champagne is made from Chardonnay alone, and Blanc de Noirs from black grapes alone (usually Pinot Noir). All the champagne region's vineyards are graded according to their supposed merits on a scale from 80% to 100%; Grand Cru champagne refers to one made from the fruit of vineyards graded at 100%, and Premier Cru from the fruit of vineyards graded between 90% and 100%. The legal ageing minima are three years for vintage champagne and 12 months for non-vintage champagne; most good producers will exceed these minima.

Ayala About five years ago this marque was a bargain; now only the price appeals. Green and unpredictable.

Barancourt Demanding but sometimes very fine, especially Rosé. Recently, however, sold to Vranken-Lafite, whose champagnes have always disappointed me.

Beaumet Quiet, low-profile, but good quality: clean, ripe Brut non-vintage, vinous Vintage, chewy Rosé. Aka Jeanmaire and (at M&S) Oudinot.

Beaumont des Crayères One of the best of Champagne's cooperatives, producing lean yet honeyed non-vintage Cuvée de Réserve. Shame about the labelling.

Billecart-Salmon Delicate, graceful Champagnes, yet the Vintage Cuvée Nicolas Françoise Billecart and Blanc de Blancs both age superbly. Beautifully packaged Rosé is understated, elegant, lingering.

H. Blin Well-balanced, vigorous Champagne from a Marne Valley cooperative (high percentage of Pinot Meunier).

Bollinger Grand, severe, sometimes difficult champagne; when well-aged (both before and preferably after release), peerless for disarming rigour of flavour. Grande Année '88 typically sombre and deep.

Canard-Duchêne Swaggering presentation, but timid quality for non-vintage. Vintage '88 Patrimoine has much better depth.

De Castellane Good high-priced champagnes, non-vintage Brut lacks sureness of touch.

Charbaut Once good; now coarse. Acquired by Vranken-Lafitte.

Deutz Non-vintage Brut recently upgraded and reblended to give vigorous, vinous, powerful Cuvée Classic. Cuvée William Deutz combines enticement and weightiness. Investment from Roederer should help further.

Devaux Assiduous cooperative in the Aube (sited half-way to Chablis) producing generously full flavoured, vinous champagnes offering good value for money.

Drappier Another Aube-based producer: non-vintage Carte d'Or much improved of late, and now round and tasty; Vintage '89 comely, enticing and sweet-edged.

Duval-Leroy Big merchant house supplying a number of UK supermarkets with own-brand champagnes of reliable quality and graceful style.

Nicolas Feuillatte This person exists, but the wines are those of Champagne's largest cooperative, the CVC. Soft, easy, rather mushy style.

Georges Gardet Deep, chunky, full-bellied, rounded Pinot-led champagnes.

Gosset Small, top-quality house, recently taken over by the ultra-wealthy Cointreau family. Vigorous, earthy, exuberant style throughout, especially in multi-vintage Grande Réserve; characterful vintage wines look set for greater consistency under Cointreau ownership (see feature).

Alfred Gratien Almost defiantly old-fashioned house using wood for fermentation, no malolactic and ageing under corks. If drunk too soon, non-vintage can seem shrill and brittle; with age (the '85 is superb at present), the whole range epitomises the piercing refinement Champagne-lovers seek.

Growers' Champagnes At best, characterful and complex, well worth trying, though often essays in the potential of a particular grape variety in a particular *terroir*. At worst, complete rubbish: acidic, cidery, coarse. Here is a selection (I consider those with an asterisk to offer better value than big names at an equivalent price): Albert Beerens (Aube), Henri Billiot (Ambonnay), André Clouet (Bouzy), Laurent Demazières (Chigny-les-Roses), Marcel Forest (Trigny), Michel Genet* (Chouilly), René Geoffroy (Cumières), Pierre Gimmonet* (Cuis), André Jacquart (Le Mesnil), Larmandier-Bernier* (Vertus), Jean Moutardier (Le Breuil), Alain Robert (Le Mesnil), See also **Jacques Selosse** and **Vilmart**.

Charles Heidsieck Marque brilliantly turned around by blender Daniel Thibault and the resources of Rémy-Cointreau. The non-vintage Brut Réserve is now among the most routinely complex of all, made in a creamy, grainy, vanillic style with honeyed fruit, and excellent value; vintage '88 shows more yeast than most. Blanc de Blancs (Cuvée des Millénaires) very fine, too. Weak labelling lets the side down.

Heidsieck Monopole Non-vintage Dry Monopole is ungracious and hard. The 1985 vintage of Diamant Bleu, too, is strangely simple and appley.

Henriot Recently enfranchised from the Moët group by Joseph Henriot, this house produces fine, tight-grained Blanc de Blancs, Rosé and vintage ('88 almost severe); non-vintage Souverain Brut built in elegant, tasteful, dapper style.

Jacquart Brand of CRVC cooperative producing two non-vintages: Brut Tradition, soft and full; and Brut Seléction, a citrus-zesty Chardonnay-driven blend.

Jacquesson Low-profile but good quality: the non-vintage is close-textured and vinous, while the 1990 vintage is a deep, grainy classic which will age well.

Jeanmaire See **Beaumet**

Krug No compromises for Krug's artisans: fermentation in wood; hugely complicated blends; the caress of age, amply, for all. Grande Cuvée often nears perfection for richness and complexity of flavour, eclipsing (when first released, anyway) some of the vintage wines. The Rosé is daringly pale yet deeply dry and winey, for me one of the most profound of all champagnes. Clos du Mesnil Blanc de Blancs I find a disappointment. All wretchedly expensive and beautifully packaged.

Lanson Owned by own-label specialists Marne & Champagne with a shareholding from Allied, Lanson is in transition. Non-vintage stays challenging, herby yet ripe, with decent depth. Is the 1989 vintage softer than usual? Time will tell.

Laurent-Perrier Consistency has been one of Laurent-Perrier's hallmarks, though whether this can survive its present financial difficulties remains to be seen (the Champagne arm of the group, which includes Rodet and Prieur in Burgundy and Château Malartic-Lagravière in Bordeaux, is reported not to have made a profit for three years). L-P's problem is its paucity of vineyard holdings: 90 per cent of its grapes are purchased. Perhaps IDV's shareholding will help. Brut LP, the non-vintage, is usually well-balanced, graceful, supple; the Ultra Brut is unsweetened, lean yet ripe; Grand Siècle, its multi-vintage prestige wine, is fine-grained and creamy. Its Rosé Brut, made by maceration rather than by the (more usual) blending in of red wine and given a generous 'dosage' of sweetening wine, is a crowd-pleaser.

Mercier Mercier manages to occupy the 'bargain' niche for luxury products with easy, accessible, sweet-scented, soft, Bouncy-Castle-style Champagnes.

Moët & Chandon The non-vintage Brut Impériale has improved hugely of late, its previously soft, rather soupy edges given extra definition, grain and crispness (though not enough to shock, of course – sales of 20 million bottles a year mean it must be accessible). The vintage is always a warm, bready Champagne (the '86 is already delicously nutty, almost buttery, while the '88 is beginning to mellow out); Dom Pérignon, by contrast, is driving, deep, sabre-like, challenging, particularly when young – but very fine-boned and beguiling at 15 to 20 years.

Mumm Cellarmaster Pierre-Yves Hareng describes the key quality of Cordon Rouge as 'power', but that isn't my experience of it. At best it's clean, fresh, roundly fruity; never crisp or cutting. Recent releases seem to have improved, with some aromatic brioche notes. Mumm de Cramant (a single-village Blanc de Blancs) is inconsistent in quality, and the hideously bottled Cuvée René Lalou is rather heavy and brutal. The great champagne from this house is unquestionably Grand Cordon: the '85 is honeyed, nutty and intense.

Oudinot see Beaumet.

Bruno Paillard Delicate, dry champagnes from this pale and interesting house.

Joseph Perrier Plump, dapper, yeasty, lemony, characterful champagnes;. Recently freshened up further towards excellence; 1989 vintage showing well for its age.

Perrier-Jouët Belle Epoque, the prestige cuvée in a pretty, flowery Art Nouveau bottle, is expressive yet delicate; I also enjoy the chunkier Blason de France. The non-vintage Grand Brut seems simple.

Philipponat 'Royale Réserve' non-vintage is a little raw at present, but the '88 Cuvée Spéciale is concentrated and good.

Piper-Heidsieck Mid-priced champagnes of crisp style undergoing renovation at present – but with some way to go. Still over-sherbetty. The '85 vintage, by contrast, is rich, full and classy.

Pol Roger   Pleasant champagnes, but some lack depth and rigour at present. Blanc de Blancs has great charm, and '88 vintage is expressive and articulate.

Pommery   Delicate, fine-grained yet surreptitiously penetrating Champagnes. Quality good at present. The '89 vintage graceful and balanced.

Roederer   Well-built, round-contoured champagnes of remarkable consistency. Cristal, the clear-glass-bottled prestige cuvée, can achieve great complexity, though (like so many Champagnes at this level) if drunk too soon seems strangely inarticulate. Roederer's well-rounded style sometimes means a lack of aroma and overall definition in the non-vintage.

Ruinart   Appley, vinous, well-constituted Chardonnay-style non-vintage (actually more Pinot than Chardonnay, but the Chardonnay works harder), creamy yet rousing vintage (the '90 is superb) and delicate, complex, allusive Dom Ruinart (a Blanc de Blancs). Non-vintage rosé (a three-variety blend) is satisfying and blackberryish; the only wine I query is the Chardonnay-dominated Dom Ruinart Rosé – that custardy creaminess just seems wrong in a coppery pink wine.

Salon   Blanc de Blancs from Le Mesnil, now owned by Laurent-Perrier. Great snob appeal – but justified by the nutty swimminess of well-aged examples.

Jacques Selosse   Leading grower, based in Avize, fermenting all his wines and ageing all his reserves in oak. Extraordinary aromatic richness (beeswax, flowers, frankincense) and a deep, pleasingly oxidative style. Could the New World take note?

Taittinger   Generally a creamy, biscuity Chardonnay-dominated style. Brut Réserve and Comtes de Champagne (the prestige wine) variable, but enticing when on form.

Pierre Vaudon   Reliable, soft champagne from Union Champagne co-op. (Also known as St Gall.)

De Venoge   Sound, well-mannered champagnes, best for purring Blanc de Blancs.

Veuve Clicquot   A house which has achieved great things over the last few years: reliably full-flavoured non-vintage Brut, and garrulous, earthy vintage wines (like the sumptuous '85). These need lots of time. Prestige cuvée La Grande Dame both muscular and delicate, perfect for long cellaring. The Widow takes the Demi-Sec style of sweeter Champagne seriously enough to release both a bread-and-plum flavoured non-vintage and a more deeply fruity and impressively thrusting 1988 vintage.

Vilmart   Top grower based in Rilly-la-Montagne: a fine range, beating most grandes marques for value-for-money.

Vintages (in Champagne, only declared in good years)
1990 ★★★★; 1989 ★★★★; 1988 ★★★; 1986 ★★★; 1985 ★★★★; 1983 ★★;
1982 ★★★★; 1981 ★★; 1979 ★★★; 1976 ★★★★.

Specialist retailers
Luxury-goods stores like Fortnum & Mason or Selfridges have the best ranges. Oddbins, Majestic and so on are best if you want to buy in quantity, since discounts are ubiquitous.

Jungle juice

It was about five years ago, I suppose. A dark night; all the workers had gone home. Antoine Gosset stood behind his desk, shuffled a few of his papers, then sighed heavily. "Champagne," he said, with an unguarded look, "is a jungle."

I never forgot that moment. Partly because the remark was transparently honest, in a region where honesty is often stifled under the mask of commercial triumphalism. It was also timely – since Champagne was just waking up to the post-eighties recessionary hangover. And it was the cry of the minnow surrounded by dentally luxuriant pike. Survival of the richest is the law of the Champagne jungle.

Gosset is one of the oldest companies in Champagne, as it happens; and it produces the kind of champagne which I like: uncompromising, exuberant, vigorous, flavour-drenched. Gosset isn't one of those champagnes which pass across the tongue in such a huff of urbanity that you can't remember afterwards whether it actually deigned to taste of anything; Gosset demands a response.

All this came to mind when I met the new boss of Gosset the other day. She's a bright, combative but fair-minded woman called Béatrice Cointreau. The Gosset family, as Antoine's sigh had suggested, had been looking for a way out for some time, since the financial strain of the Champagne jungle was beginning to tell. And the Cointreau family?

Béatrice wouldn't reveal much, but the least one can assume is that, having sold both Cointreau and its shareholding in Rémy-Martin (Béatrice's mother had a family interest in Rémy, and she remains the biggest landowner in the best part of Cognac), the family is wealthy enough to bare a few teeth of its own at cruising predators.

But privacy is put first. "We're not show-offs. We're interested in doing things. We're not important in ourselves; it's what we're doing that's important," says Béatrice fiercely. She has French degrees in law and marketing, and a degree from Cornell in management, yet it's her 'peasant origins' which she speaks most proudly of. "I'm the little girl of two winegrowers and I'm very proud of that."

She's ambitious for Gosset – "Gosset has to be the Pétrus or the Yquem of Champagne" – but is realistic enough to realise that this will take time. "You have to give time to time," she says, this nugget of peasant wisdom suggesting a respect for the natural processes of change, even when (as in a company) they are rooted in people rather than the external environment. She believes, above all, in her people, who "can change anything. Everyone is important; everyone must look for their own perfection." Admirable principles – providing you have the resources, and can extend the trust, to put them into action.

I recently tasted through the range of Gosset champagnes, and was reminded just how good they are – though at present this reflects credit on the Gosset family itself rather than the new Cointreau regime (whose first wines will begin to appear around the time when this book reaches shop shelves). The Brut Réserve has all the vigour and strike which constitutes the house style; punchy, yet rounded and lingering too. The Grande Réserve Brut is more expensive, but you'll find a champagne of remarkable, clock-maker's complexity inside its curvingly thigh-like bottle. Characterful vintages, too.

Base quality good, resources plentiful, ambition not wanting: look out, jungle.

Corsica
Island of herbs

Undistinguished table wine and inarticulate rosé accounts for over half of Corsica's wine production. Its better quality AOC red wines, however, are medium-bodied and subtle, infused with a hauntingly herby character over chocolatey fruit; the buoyant tourist trade keeps prices high enough to render them an unenticing prospect for British importers, sadly. These reds are based on Niellucio (Tuscany's Sangiovese) and the native Sciacarello, as well as the familiar southern French Grenache. Whites, from Vermentino (Rolle), can be delicately aniseedy if well made; they are otherwise neutral. Other, non-Corsican varietals such as Cabernet, Merlot, Syrah and Mourvèdre can put on an exciting turn of speed without losing a sense of place for the regional Vins de Pays (Ile de Beauté); there is less innate understanding of white wines on Corsica, and Chardonnay and Sauvignon are often dullish. Good producers include Arena, Clos de Bernardi, Gentile, Leccia and Peraldi. L'Albitru is a Chardonnay produced by Hugh Ryman in cooperation with the Union des Vignerons de l'Ile de Beauté.

Jura
The old curiosity shop

Each year I keep a little file in which I note the dozen or so wines which succeed in overvaulting my expectations, shaking my composure and proving, by some inexplicable symbolic and emotional process, that life is (for all its terrors and horrors) an experience of slow glory.

Early in '96 I pulled a bottle out of the rack which, truth to tell, I had been dreading: a varietal Savagnin, vintage 1985, from the Domaine de la Pinte. Savagnin isn't always an easy variety to understand or enjoy, and the property had rather a sad, lonely and unloved air when I visited. I pulled the cork and slopped the wine into a glass.

It was magnificent; hugely better than the 1989 Puligny-Montrachet Premier Cru from Louis Latour which I had opened on the previous day. It smelled of toast and nuts; it tasted full, strong, architectural, both broad-shouldered and keen-edged. I slumped in amazement before it.

Relics from the forgotten forest

The Jura is a quiet, wood-dappled step on France's alpine stairway. Like some forgotten forest in disputed ownership supporting a tangle of species which the modern world would otherwise have tidied away into oblivion, the Jura's relative isolation means that it continues to produce a range of fascinating vinous relics. Chief among these is *vin jaune,* a wine produced from the low-yielding Savagnin (a wild country cousin of the Traminer) which is aged for six years in casks containing an air space and sometimes a thin yeasty film, before being bottled in 62-cl bottles called *clavelins. Vin jaune* is often quite mistakenly compared to fino sherry: fino sherry is a low-acid fortified wine protected from oxidation by its thick yeast film, for immediate drinking; vin jaune is a high-acid, heavily oxidised unfortified wine designed for long bottle ageing (indeed it is sour and

93

dull when drunk young). After 10 or more years in bottle, *vin jaune* acquires a scent of wild mushrooms and rich, flavoury complexities to match its otherwise searing acidity; nonetheless it is most palatable served with rich, creamy food, and should never be drunk alone as an aperitif. The best *vin jaune* is that of Château-Chalon, though all the region's appellations (Côtes du Jura, L'Etoile, Arbois) produce it.

Other Jura specialities include ordinary white wines made from Savagnin or Chardonnay produced in local style by ageing them in former *vin jaune* casks, as well as small quantities of *vin de paille* (dessert wine made by drying grapes on straw mats before crushing and vinifying them) and macvin, local grape must fortified with local marc. (Marc is a brandy produced by distilling the residues – skins, pips and so on – of fermentation).

Jura red wines made from Pinot Noir may resemble light burgundies, but the more typical regional red wines are those based on Poulsard and Trousseau. Poulsard is the nearest thing in existence to a rosé grape, producing extremely light, teasingly scented red wines (sometimes described, winningly, as coral). Trousseau (improbably synonymous with Portugal's Bastardo) gives deeper, tougher, more iron-clad wines. Rosé wine is here referred to as *vin gris*. The region also sensibly turns the higher acid wines of poorer vintages into decent sparkling wine.

Good producers include Château d'Arlay, Château l'Etoile, Fruitière Vinicole d'Arbois, Grand Frères, Jean Macle, Domaine de la Pinte and Domaines Rolet. Henri Maire is by far the region's biggest producer, and an astute mail-order specialist in France. Maire's wines are variable in quality, but the company has undoubtedly done much to keep the fragile wine flora of the Jura alive.

Languedoc-Roussillon

The high road and the low road

Nothing testifies more persuasively to the intrinsic vigour of France's wine culture than the speed and success with which Languedoc-Roussillon has turned itself from a limping also-ran into pace-setter – and global pace-setter. Some of the most exciting wines I have tasted in the last three years from any corner of the earth have come from Languedoc: dense, dark and savage, tasting of fire and thorns, stones and cinders, iron and thyme, earth and smoke.

Are these the famous Vins de Pays? Not at all. Languedoc's Vins de Pays are very good, it's true, but the Chardonnays and Cabernets and what-have-you made by itinerant English and Australians belong to a politer, more internationally acceptable school of wine than the ones which appeal to me. This is the low road towards success, sure and meritorious, but lacking a little in daring.

The high road is the way of the regional appellations: blends of traditional grape varieties from old, low-yielding vines grown on stony hillside vineyards. And often made, I might add, by beautiful wastrels, displaced academics, eccentrics, dreamers, misanthropes and babblers. The remoter spots of the south, wind-fissured, seemingly barren, appeal to marginals. The appellation system, so often criticised, has served them well, lending the disparate a common banner to sell under, sustaining individual effort, and defending that which is rewardingly difficult against marauding simplicity.

In truth, of course, both the low road and the high road are still atypical; in volume terms much of Languedoc-Roussillon labours on with factory viticulture for table-wine production or, more probably, subsidised distillation. Economically doomed, such wines are no longer even able to excuse themselves on the basis of a lack of role models.

The vast majority of Languedoc-Roussillon's best wines are red, made from Grenache, Syrah, Mourvèdre, Cinsault and Carignan (the last variety occasionally or in part). The traditional whites are less interesting; Rhône valley varieties like Marsanne and Viognier should in the long run provide great things in appropriate sites. Sauvignon Blanc is often heavy, seldom exciting. Chardonnay from Languedoc can be varietally correct, but I have yet to taste an exciting bottle from this part of the world.

Corbières is where many of the best wines begin life, but Minervois, Faugères, Coteaux de Languedoc (with its individually distinguished *terroirs*), Côtes du Roussillon and Costières de Nîmes (a fine *terroir* for Syrah) all regularly produce exciting bottles, too. This region, incidentally, is where the best wines in the world made by carbonic maceration are produced, attaining a profundity of perfume and a seriousness behind ravishingly textured fruit which Beaujolais is quite unable to match.

Finally, of course, there are the sweet Vins Doux Naturels, the best of them from Muscat: heady, perfumed extravagance. Red Banyuls and Maury can be delicious, but to palates schooled on even the second-best port, anything but the top wines of these appellations seem irrelevant.

Domaine des Armouries, Corbières Concentrated wine from old vines.

Arnaud de Villeneuve, Côtes de Roussillon Good cooperative-produced cuvées: peppery red and haunting, waxy white.

Domaine de la Baume/Chais Baumière Hardy-owned property producing varietal Vins de Pays. Best for enjoyable, clean-fruited reds (like warm, big-limbed Merlot) with more natural grace than the Australian role models.

Château de Belle-Coste, Costières de Nîmes Fine, floral-spicy Viognier-based white.

Domaine de Belvezet, Côtes du Vivarais Punchy, Syrah-based red.

Château Paul Blanc, Costières de Nîmes Dark, perfumed Syrah: this is a wonderful buy.

Château de Calissanne, Coteaux du Languedoc Dark, intense wines. Clos Victoire has huge depth.

Château de Campuget, Costières de Nîmes Vivid wines, especially old-vine Cuvée Prestige.

Domaine Capion Neighbour of Mas de Daumas Gassac producing superb yet little-known reds, bottled without filtration. Merlot and Cabernet-Merlot blends are particularly good.

Château de Caraguilhes, CORBIÈRES Lighter than some, but great style.

Domaine de la Casenove, CÔTES DU ROUSSILLON Sound spicy wines, with fine old-vines Cuvée du Commandant Jaubert.

Clos de Paulilles see Val d'Orbieu.

Domaine des Combelles, MINERVOIS Allusive, exciting reds.

Cuvée Mythique see Val d'Orbieu

Daniel Domergue, MINERVOIS Cultural archivist as well as fine winemaker, Domergue's washday-fresh Carignanissime is as good as Carignan gets, while the Clos des Centeilles and Campagne des Centeilles are elegant, earthy blends.

Ermitage du Pic St Loup, COTEAUX DU LANGUEDOC Fresh fruit given satisfying regional complexity.

Château des Estanilles, FAUGÈRES Michel Louison produces a pure Mourvèdre and pure Syrah of huge, perfumed depth. Expensive, but justifiably so.

Château Flaugerges, COTEAUX DU LANGUEDOC Strong, gutsy, herby wine.

Figaro Unexceptional, reliable Vins de Pays in which Aimé Guibert of Mas de Daumas Gassac has a hand, produced at Villeveyrac cooperative.

Foncalieu Go-ahead cooperative supplying Asda with its Montagne Noire range and Waitrose with Winter Hill. Reds are best.

Fortant de France see Skalli.

Galet Vineyards Competent Vins de Pays include soft, mellow, fennel-like Grenache Blanc and chewy Roussanne; Viognier is dull. Made by Guy Anderson and Thierry Boudinaud for Rhône merchant Gabriel Meffre. Lost Valley label is for blends.

Château de Gourgazaud, MINERVOIS Reliably beefy wine.

Domaine du Grand Crès, CORBIÈRES Elegant, sweet style.

Château Haut-Fabrèges, FAUGÈRES Low yields and complex blends make this property one of the appellation leaders.

James Herrick High-effort Chardonnays, yet better by far is the new red Cuvée Simone, sweet-scented and grippy.

Domaine de l'Hortus, COTEAUX DU LANGUEDOC Deep, spicy wine from this much-improved appellation. Cuvée Classique and top wine Grand Cuvée have splendid savoury depth.

Château de Jau, CÔTES DE ROUSSILLON Mainly straightforward quaffing wine, but best cuvées have a darker streak to them.

Jeanjean Unpretentious merchant house bottling impressive, authentic regional wines.

Laperouse Joint Penfolds/Val d'Orbieu wines: structured, fresh, grippy '94 red blend, but '94 white is nondescript and sweetish.

Château de Lastours, CORBIÈRES Basic cuvées are uninteresting, but the top wines, particularly the Cuvée Simone Descamps and the 'Château de Lastours' (only produced in good years) are superb, complex wines. Produced by mentally handicapped workers in a small village setting.

Louis Latour   Well-made Ardèche Chardonnays. Grand Ardèche is tallow-coloured, buttery and rich.

Listel see Val d'Orbieu

Domaine de Mandeville   French, American-trained winemaker offering well-defined Vins de Pays varietals: floral Viognier, concentrated Cabernet Sauvignon, deep plummy Merlot and pungent Syrah.

Mas Amiel, MAURY   As good as it gets: cooked-fruit and chocolate flavours.

Mas des Bressades, COSTIÈRES DE NÎMES   Wonderful Syrah perfumes give this wine impact and sheen.

Mas Blanc, BANYULS AND COLLIOURE   High-priced, richly textured sweet Banyuls and stone-fruited dry red Collioure.

Mas Brugière, COTEAUX DU LANGUEDOC   Gutsy classy reds from a Syrah-Grenache-Mourvèdre blend.

Mas Cal Demoura, COTEAUX DU LANGUEDOC   Impressive old-vine wine from the father of Olivier Jullien (see Mas Jullien and feature).

Mas de Daumas Gassac   Hugely successful Cabernet-led red blend sold as Vins de Pays. Dark, extractive style grown on unusual mineral-rich red glacial soil. So far, I have found these wines inarticulate, lacking the soaring expressivity local grape varieties surrender here. Rosé very dull, but white is perfumed and good, though very expensive. See also **Terraces de Landoc.**

Mas Jullien, COTEAUX DU LANGUEDOC   Exciting, uncompromising reds from different vineyard sites, and a crisp, floral white too. See feature.

Mas Morties, COTEAUX DU LANGUEDOC-PIC ST LOUP   Brilliant Syrah from this fast-rising star.

Mas Sagala, CÔTES DU ROUSSILLON   Soft, spicy, regional style aplenty.

Meffre   Rhône producer of late offering decent varietal Vins de Pays from Oc's east. Rather dull contributions to Thresher's Southlands series, though.

Montagne Noire see Foncalieu.

Château Pech-Céleyran, COTEAUX DU LANGUEDOC   Tangy, herby red.

Domaine Jacques Pons, FAUGÈRES   Cuvée de la Fleur de Passion is an enticingly perfumed carbonic-maceration wine.

Prieuré de St-Jean de Bebian, COTEAUX DU LANGUEDOC   Massive, sometimes over-tannic wines produced in the past by a touchy eccentric, but charged with the stony, fiery qualities of the region. The property is now owned by French wine journalist Chantal Lecouty.

Producteurs de Blanquette de Limoux, BLANQUETTE DE LIMOUX   Pleasant aniseedy fizz.

Domaine de Rivoyre see Hugh Ryman

Château Routas, CôTEAUX VAROIS Cuvée Truffière; a rich, oaky Cab-Syrah blend.

Hugh Ryman Super-competent Cabernet and Chardonnay under the Domaine des Tuileries and Domaine de Rivoyre labels. Ryman also makes damn fine rosé; some whites, though (like '95 Domaine du Bousquet Chardonnay/Sauvignon Blanc) can be too sweet. Range set to expand.

Domaine Ste Eulalie, MINERVOIS Consistent producer of mid-weight, expressively spicy reds.

Sarda-Malet, CôTES DU ROUSSILLON The 'black label' red is sturdy.

La Serre Well-made straightforward Vins de Pays: Merlot is best.

Skalli (Fortant de France) This industrial-scale producer of Vins de Pays varietals has had considerable success, though I find its wines dull and unexciting, with little or no regional style.

Southern Cross see Val d'Orbieu.

Terraces de Landoc Underwhelming '94 Aramon produced by Aimé Guibert (see Mas de Daumas Gassac) illustrates the deficiencies of the variety.

Château La Tour de Beraud, COSTIÈRES DE NîMES Pungent Syrah-based red, like a minor Crozes-Hermitage.

Domaine des Tuileries see Hugh Ryman.

Val d'Orbieu An enormous conglomerate of cooperatives and individual producers which this year has swallowed up the perennially underachieving Listel (I hope it gives it a good chewing over). Generally dynamic in outlook; good wines include la Voulte-Gasparets (especially oaked Cuvée Reservée and the pure Carignan Roman Pauc) from Corbières and the stylish, extract-laden Cuvée Mythique. Clos de Paulilles is a label for generally overpriced Collioure and some good Banyuls and Rivesaltes. Southern Cross Chardonnay-Grenache is an intelligent blend with some of the fat of the south in it.

Domaines Virginie Franco-Belgian operation based near Béziers producing Vins de Pays varietals. '93 Gold Medal Cabernet Sauvignon had exciting depth, but '94 is less good. Viognier, Marsanne and now Roussanne all worthwhile; Vermentino duller. '94 Pinot Noir was un-Pinot-like but a gutsy wine.

Château la Voulte-Gasparets see Val d'Orbieu.

Winter Hill see Foncalieu.

Vintages:
1995 ★★★; 1994 ★★★★; 1993 ★★★; 1992 ★★; 1991 ★★★★; 1990 ★★★; 1989 ★★★; 1988 ★★★; 1987 ★★; 1986 ★★.

Specialist retailers:
Supermarkets tend to prefer easy Vins de Pays options to AOC wines (though both are stocked); chains (Oddbins, Wine Rack) and merchants (Lea & Sandeman, La Vigneronne, mail-order from Adnams) are the best places to find the finest wines of Languedoc-Roussillon.

Land of the dispossessed

When the mist came down, we could have been in Scotland. The car followed tiny lanes cut through beds of weeping rock; the only vegetation was knotty scrub from which, intermittently, a single hag-fingered tree had struggled to assert itself and been beaten down by the wind for its pains.

"It's harsh, it's uncompromising, it's savage," said Nick Bradford, formerly an Aberdeen University anthropologist, latterly a wine-maker in Corbières, as we ate a salad sprinkled with shards of dried liver. "This is the land of the dispossessed."

I understood more the next day. "You're looking at someone whose grandfather was humiliated by the world of wine and whose father was humiliated by the world of wine. We are ready to do anything. If you have ideas, if you like what we are doing, tell us. We're ready to listen. But if you don't, if you despise what we are doing, get out." Can't put it straighter than that, can you?

The second speaker was Olivier Jullien. Unlike Nick Bradford, Olivier Jullien comes from a wine-making family which has lived out the vicissitudes of Languedoc over the past 100 years. "There are no balanced winemakers here," he says, rocking with mirth. You think the mirth indicates balance? "Laughter is the mask of despair," is his next remark. They just don't say that kind of thing in Bordeaux.

Languedoc is the large patch of France's deep south which runs east from Marseille before turning south towards Catalonia. In the early 19th century, the growers claim, the hills of this area produced wines as good as anywhere else in the country. Then two newcomers arrived: phylloxera (an

insect which devastated the vineyards) and railway trains. When the new vineyards were planted, after the insect's destructive passage, they were in the flat land of the plains, and the grape variety was high-yielding, low-quality Aramon. Wagonloads of plonk rolled north.

It's only in recent years that the area has fought its way back from this legacy of mediocrity. And how: some of my favourite red wines of the past five years have come from down here. What I love about them is their lack of compromise: they seem the product of stones and fire as much as of grapes, full of violent and vivid flavours. They've sold well in Britain.

So why the gloom? "I'm getting very depressed about this 'varietal wine' thing," says Nick Bradford. "Suddenly varietal wines are all that anybody wants. It's another way in which this region will be exploited by those outside it."

Corbières, Minervois, Faugères; all these are appellations d'origine contrôlée or AOCs. The AOC rules here require wines to be made from a blend of grape varieties.

But there is an alternative. Make wine from just one grape variety, make it above all typical of that variety rather than its place of origin, and label it with the grape variety as a Vin de Pays. A number of outside investors (including the much-feared Australians) have come in and done just that, on a near-factory scale. These wines have been so successful that the growers within the AOC framework are beginning to perceive them as a threat.

Rightly or wrongly? I believe there is a sort of historical paranoia at work here. France's best AOC wines stand or fall on one quality: complexity. Varietal Vins de Pays, with a few small-scale exceptions, do not aim for complexity, but for simpler, fruitier virtues. There's room for both.

The Loire valley

The watering mouth

The Loire follows a leisurely course from its source in France's southern high lands through the country's heart – where the best French is spoken, the whitest towns have been raised from the river's pale pebbles, and the most sensually enticing buildings ever confected straddle hamlets of water and coutured gardens. It reaches the sea in an oily, demotic flourish.

Most of the Loire's wines are white, linked not only by the river's thread but also by quivering, tongue-creasing acidity. From Sancerre and Pouilly-Fumé in the Upper Loire to Muscadet at the river's mouth, the ideal remains the same: fresh, dry pungency, a stony firmness, the piscatorial vocation. Only in the central Loire does a richer, honeyed sweetness, the mellower spectrum of summer fruits, broaden this picture; even then by benefit of a generous season alone; even then without relinquishing a chasing, sweeping, balancing acidity.

The grape varieties of the valley are, typically, easier to master than its intricate pattern of appellations. Sauvignon Blanc and Chenin Blanc jointly preside. Sauvignon Blanc has a narrower range, but enjoys greater common acclaim: this is the severe, flinty avatar of New Zealand's herbacious lush. It is used for Sancerre and Pouilly-Fumé, but also for a number of lesser appellations, and sometimes as a named varietal. Chenin Blanc has a wide range and, at its best, is capable of delivering wines of dazzling intensity and rich-fruited complexity; but it's also moody and capricious, and can be ungratefully raw and coarse when the weather has been inclement or the winemaker sloppy. It makes the region's sparkling wines, semi-dry wines and dessert wines, as well as what is (for me) the valley's best dry wine, and indeed France's most underrated fine wine: Savennières. Vouvray, Saumur and Anjou are its home.

The third of the Loire's major varieties is the Melon de Bourgogne, used for Muscadet. As a variety, it's almost self-effacingly neutral; yet this self-effacement generates, when solicitously vinified, a wine of deliciously bright, lemony cleanness, often given a sigh of bready warmth by the flavoury echo from its yeast lees *(sur lie)*. Muscadet, astonishingly, accounts for 40 per cent of all French wine exports, echoing the success of Soave and Frascati from Italy. The lesson? That mass appeal in wine, as in literature and entertainment, lies in the bland, the unexceptional and, more than occasionally, the mediocre.

The Loire valley's minority red wines are chiefly made from Cabernet Franc, and freshness is again the key to these. A good, young Chinon or Bourgeuil always reminds me of the shock of summer rain in the furtive, mossy recesses of a wood. Best take them young, though: all the aged examples I've tried have been thin, sharp and fruitless. Softer, paler Gamay plays a supporting role more successfully than the valley's rather wan and insubstantial Pinot Noir.

Copious quantities of rosé are produced in the Loire. Since most of it is made, and bought, as a medium-dry commodity wine, it rarely excites. The infrequent exceptions are dry Pinot Noir rosés.

Domaine des Aubuisières, Vouvray Clarity, purity and charm from this mainly organic domain.

Donatien Bahuaud, Muscadet   Hard-working merchant sourcing good Muscadet; less good for other appellations.

Domaine des Baumard, Quarts de Chaume and Savennières   Fine, long-lived sweet wines from the former (and occasionally the latter) appellation and complex, heady dry Savennières from the shared Clos du Papillon.

Guy Bossard, Muscadet   Intelligent, scrupulous producer of organic Muscadet.

Bourgeois, Sancerre   Clean, flinty wines.

Bouvet-Ladubay, Saumur   Consistent sparkling wines from this Taittinger-owned producer.

Marc Brédif, Vouvray   Merchant-grower owned by Ladoucette producing sound, sometimes exciting wines.

Champalou, Vouvray   Young husband-and-wife team producing fresh yet complex wine.

Chéreau-Carré, Muscadet   Reliable, keen-edged wines.

Château de Cléray, Muscadet   Assiduous: carefully made, definitive Muscadet.

Paul Cotat, Sancerre   Consistent, true Sancerre.

Couly-Dutheil, Chinon   Fresh, mouthwatering reds.

Didier Dagueneau, Pouilly-Fumé   Wines for the aficionado: much fancy work with sites, yields and oak to push the appellation out towards its limits – of flavour and price.

Pierre-Jacques Druet, Bourgueil   Expressive, lively, curranty reds.

Château d'Epiré, Savennières   Not top notch, but does have the intensity of the AOC.

Foreau see Clos Nordin.

Marquis de Goulaine, Muscadet   Classically fresh, pungent *sur lie* Muscadet.

Château Gaudrelle, Vouvray   Wax-scented Vouvray of concentration and style.

Gratien & Meyer   Good, sometimes excellent sparkling wines from this company with one foot in Champagne, one in the Loire.

Château de la Grille, Chinon   Deep, peppery wines from the Gosset family (whose own Champagne roots are now, sadly, severed).

Huët, Vouvray   The appellation leader: superb wines from three sites, plus a yeasty, complex sparkling wine. This estate is now run, like the finest property in Savennières (that of Joly), along biodynamic lines (a form of organic viticulture based on the agriculture lectures of Rudolph Steiner).

Charles Joguet, Chinon   Red wines as structured and age-worthy as anything produced in the valley.

Nicolas Joly/Clos de la Coulée de Serrant, Savennières   Slow-developing dry wines of intense floral style and improbable substance, produced along uncompromising biodynamic lines. Superb if aged. Joly considers them best at room temperature.

Ladoucette, Pouilly-Fumé and (Comte Lafond) Sancerre High-impact winemaking, but absurdly high prices.

Henry Marionnet, Touraine Reliable producer in this often good-value appellation, now with a finger in a Chilean pie: Terra Noble.

Alphonse Mellot, Sancerre Fuller, fatter style than some, with use of oak.

Château Moncontour, Vouvray Clean, sensitive winemaking from this reliable producer for both still and sparkling wines.

Moulin–Touchais, Coteaux de Layon Often fine museum wines, proof of the remarkable longevity of good Chenin Blanc. Deft, limpid style gives superbly balanced wines without rawness or coarseness.

Clos Naudin, Vouvray Superb wines. Even lesser years age well.

Château de l'Oiselinière, Muscadet Good producer whose oaked cuvées can take on near-burgundian finesse.

Henri Pellé, Menetou-Salon Sauvignon-based white every bit as stonily mouthwatering as Sancerre – and now, unfortunately, just as expensive.

Prince Poniatowski, Vouvray Complex, finely balanced sweet wines.

Guy Saget Generally reliable wines from this merchant house; Sancerre good.

Soulez, Savennières Part-owners of La Roche-aux-Moines, the second great cru of Savennières. Elegant wines for mid-term keeping.

Château de Tracy, Pouilly-Fumé Soft, expressive style; truly smoky. Expensive.

Domaine Vacheron, Sancerre Intense, floral, sweet-grassy Sancerre. Red only occasionally good, and poor value.

André Vatan, Sancerre Mouthwatering, flinty wine.

Edmond Vatan, Sancerre Clos de la Néore, from organic vineyards, is fine.

Vintages:
1995 ★★★; 1994 ★★; 1993 ★★; 1992 ★; 1991 ★; 1990 ★★★★; 1989 ★★★★; 1988 ★★★; 1987 ★; 1986 ★★.

Specialist retailers:
The wine list of the restaurant RSJ, 13a Coin St SE1 is one of the best places in London to find good Loire wine; Adam Bancroft, Bibendum and the Waterloo Wine Company also have good selections. This, though, is a wine region which many retailers neglect. Mail-order merchants Adnams, Lay & Wheeler, The Wine Society and Yapp all stock characterful ranges of Loire wines.

Provence
Taking it easy

Provence does produce some excitingly dense, smoky reds, especially from the Bandol appellation; nevertheless most of the region's wines are a disappointment. Surely, you would think, one of the comeliest spots on the Mediterranean could do better than pale, flavourless rosé; than submissive, vaguely lemony white; than hopeful but irresolute red?

The two phenomena may be interconnected. Provence has never had to try very hard to sell its wine outside the region; the summer tide washes a path to every growers' door. Those wines which have slipped the net and made their way to Paris or London have generally sold on the region's lustrous image or the purchaser's memories of love on a carpet of pine needles rather than by the lure of raw flavour.

Land prices are high, moreover, prodding up wine prices beyond what intrinsic quality would merit. Most of the region's appellations underperform to a greater or lesser extent, so producers' names are more than usually crucial in finding worthwhile wines. Which exist: hills of pale limestone; dry, regular warmth; the cool, remedial Mistral; varieties like Mourvèdre and Grenache as well as the more recent Syrah and Cabernet Sauvignon: these propitious elements can come together in wines which combine the classic appeal of the deeply fruited, tannin-stiffened red with herb scents and an intrinsic savoury warmth. (For the promising appellation of Costières de Nîmes, see Languedoc–Roussillon.)

Domaine Bastide Blanche BANDOL Dense, expressive reds. Very good '93s.

Domaine Champagna, CÔTES DE VENTOUX Denser, more lavishly fruited wines than the appellation norm.

Château de Crémat, BELLET Tiny appellation, pleasant wines (the pale rosé is nutty). Crazy prices.

Mas de la Dame, COTEAUX D'AIX-EN-PROVENCE-LES-BAUX Improving wines, now deep and chewy, some of them made with advice from Colombo (see Rhône Valley).

Domaines Ott, CÔTES DE PROVENCE and BANDOL Large producer: consistent wines of medium depth. Top rosé from Château de Selle is intimidatingly expensive but dense, nutty and concentrated.

Domaine de Pibarnon, BANDOL Rich, olive-scented red wines.

Château Pigoudet, COTEAUX D'AIX-EN-PROVENCE Smooth, floral reds, expensively packaged.

Château Pradeaux, BANDOL Powerful, uncompromising wines.

Domaine Ray-Jane, BANDOL Council-house name, but sturdy, authentic wine.

Domaine Richeaume, CÔTES DE PROVENCE German grower-producer of two memorable organic reds, one Syrah-based and one Cabernet-based.

Mas de la Rouvière, BANDOL Sound, chewy wine, though overpriced.

Château de Selle see Domaines Ott

Château Simone, PALETTE The major property in this tiny appellation produces a full-flavoured white, dull rosé and deep but muddled red.

Domaine Tempier, BANDOL Among the appellation's best: deep, stewy, Mourvèdre-rich reds, and some good rosé, too.

Domaine de Trévallon, COTEAUX D'AIX-EN-PROVENCE-LES-BAUX The region's finest producer: pile-driving red wines whose dark, sumptuous fruit has a mineralised, herb-infused complexity. From low-yielding Cabernet Sauvignon and Syrah vines grown in a harsh, stony and savage landscape.

Château Val-Joanis, Côtes du Lubéron   Ambitious producer in a generally undistinguished appellation: best cuvées perfumed and well-fruited.

Château Vannières, Bandol   Savoury warmth shaped towards elegance.

Château Vignelaure, Coteaux d'Aix-en-Provence   Tangy, mid-weight reds more interesting than the whites or rosés. Now owned by Rystone (Hugh Ryman and Esmé Johnstone), so possible changes afoot.

Vintages:
1995 ★★★; 1994 ★★; 1993 ★★; 1992 ★★ ; 1991 ★; 1990 ★★★★; 1989 ★★★★; 1988 ★★★; 1987 ★; 1986 ★★★.

The Rhône Valley
Coming from behind

To speak of the Rhône valley crus even ten years ago in the same breath as one intoned the villages of Bordeaux or Burgundy was regarded as eccentric or irreverent. Now, were you to say (as well you might) that you prefer a Syrah-based red wine from the Northern Rhône to anything made from Cabernet Sauvignon or Pinot Noir, wine-trade eyebrows would remain in their customary positions, and once in a while there would even be a gentle nodding of heads. The grandeur of the Rhône is acceptable and accepted.

Great Syrah-based wine from Hermitage, Côte-Rôtie, Cornas, and occasionally Crozes-Hermitage and St Joseph, surrenders aromas which seem more carnally exciting than those of any other red wine on earth: a heady mix of burnt earth (sometimes burnt rubber, too), black fruits and thick cream, with a piercing and disarming floral sheen. In the mouth there's a draught of blackcurrant and blackberry fruit (cream-smooth again) supported by quick tannins; when the wine is young the warmth of the tongue seems to liberate flower perfumes, while older wines sink and decline graciously through a repertoire of often decadently animal allusions. New oak is used today, though this was not traditional in the region; opinions are mixed as to the success of this, but when successful it adds an extra layer of richness to the wine, and seems certain to become ubiquitous for all of the region's top bottlings. The finest white wines from the Northern Rhône, too, combine a seductive florality with width, grain and texture; in them the taste of new bread often lurks beneath that of ripe-fleshed apricots and peaches. They can be every sip as great as Grand Cru white burgundy. White Hermitage and Crozes-Hermitage are based on Marsanne and Roussanne; Condrieu is the home of now-fashionable, globetrotting Viognier, and the place where it performs most exotically.

The great appellation of the southern Rhône is Châteauneuf-du-Pape. Despite being celebrated for its permitted range of 13 different grape varieties, Châteauneuf is above all the place where Grenache reaches its apogee – which is why, of all dry red wines, this is naturally the sweetest, and sometimes the soupiest. The flavour allusions Grenache makes are to raisins and chocolate; its tannins can be fiery, but rarely tough. Great Châteauneuf is the softest of red wines; as Robert Parker has pointed out, this means that it has a longer drinking window than any other fine red wine. Its white equivalent, made with Grenache Blanc, Bourboulenc and Clairette, is (from the best producers, alas few in number) as good a wine as these grapes ever produce: nutty, fat, with a haunting whisper of blossom. The main hazard with Châteauneuf is inconsistency, even within the confines of a single property: there is a tradition in the region of bottling at different dates for different markets, customers and whims. Take care when buying older Châteauneuf.

Vivacious Syrah and plump, sweet, glycerous Grenache: these are the poles between which most of the Rhône's lesser red wines swing, from the bruising Gigondas down to the slightest Côtes du Rhône (an appellation with as wide a quality variation as any in France). Pure Syrah Vins de Pays from the Rhône are often an excellent buy.

Those experimenting with Rhône wines in 1996 and 1997 should note that 1992 and 1993 were both extremely difficult vintages for the Northern Rhône, and there are many disappointing wines on sale at present. Wait, if you can, for the much better 1994s and 1995s.

Château d'Aqueria, Lirac Soft, meaty reds.

Thierry Allemand, Cornas Softer wines than some, but great depth of fruit.

Domaine des Anges, Côtes du Ventoux Spicy, Grenache-based wines.

Gilles Barge, Côte Rôtie Inconsistent: deep-fruited though sometimes raw.

Pierre Barge, Côte Rôtie Expressive and aromatic.

Château de Beaucastel, Châteauneuf-du-Pape Exceptional wines, both in qualitative terms and because of higher-than-usual percentages of Syrah, Counoise and Mourvèdre in the wine (indeed the top wine, Hommage à Jacques Perrin, contains 60% Mourvèdre). Richly flavoured, sometimes tannic Châteauneuf for long ageing: '94 and '95 both set to be great wines, as are '90, '89, '85 and '81. Superb white version, with separate old-vines pure Roussanne cuvée deliciously nutty. Coudoulet is a deeply fruity, ageworthy Côtes du Rhône, and La Vieille Ferme a gutsy Côtes du Ventoux red (and duller Lubéron white).

Domaine de Beaurenard, Châteauneuf-du-Pape Soft but succulent wines. Boisrenard is the top cuvée (with new oak).

Albert Belle, Crozes-Hermitage Richly constituted Crozes; a fine, dense Hermitage.

Domaine de Belugue, Côtes du Rhône-Villages Deep, gutsy wine made by Jean-Luc Sweerts from Avontuur in South Africa.

Henri Bonneau, Châteauneuf-du-Pape Wines of great density and power: the manliest of all Grenache-based styles. Réserve des Celestins is the top cuvée.

Bosquet des Papes, Châteauneuf-du-Pape Well-balanced wines with supple fruit. Cuvée Chantemerle is lusher and deeper.

Les Cailloux, Châteauneuf-du-Pape Richly fruited, succulent Châteauneuf, epecially the Cuvée Centenaire (from centenarian vines).

Cave des Clairmonts, CROZES-HERMITAGE Cooperative turning out well-made wines even in difficult vintages (the '92 Crozes has remarkable softness).

Cave de Tain-l'Hermitage, CROZES-HERMITAGE Source of much supermarket Crozes-Hermitage, often good value.

Domaine de Cayron, GIGONDAS Top producer for this appellation: exotically sweet, flavour-saturated wines.

Chapoutier, HERMITAGE Since the late 80s, one of the pace-setters for red and white Hermitage, with excellent Côte-Rôtie, Crozes and St Joseph, fair Châteauneuf and decent Côtes du Rhône. Nutty, floral white Hermitage Chante Alouette and dark, sweetly oaked Hermitage La Sizeranne (plus super-cuvées white l'Orée and red Le Pavillon) now appellation benchmarks. Châteauneuf (la Bernardine and low-yield, old-vine Barbe-Rac) much improved of late. Moving towards biodynamic viticulture (see **Loire valley, Huët**) amid local controversy.

Domaine de la Charbonnière, CHÂTEAUNEUF-DU-PAPE Rapidly improving.

J.L. Chave, HERMITAGE Gérard Chave is the grand old man of Hermitage, and a wonderful example of how the 'ordinary', scrupulous winemaker, deeply imbued with local traditions and a feeling for land, can create finer wines than any gaggle of consultants with access to reservoirs of capital. Intense, deep, sinewy red Hermitage needing ten years in all but the lightest vintages, and blossom-charged white, also needing time before it chatters and turns nutty. Now assisted by his son Jean-Louis.

Auguste Clape, CORNAS As Chave (above) to Hermitage, so Clape to Cornas. Intrinsically chewier red wines, less soaring fruit, but generous and warming. '94 white Marsanne Côtes du Rhône was a treat – fat and succulent.

Clos de Papes, CHÂTEAUNEUF-DU-PAPE Like Beaucastel, a high proportion of Mourvèdre giving some of the most muscular, assertive and age-worthy red wines of the region (1990 particularly good). Top vintages need 10 years.

Jean-Luc Colombo, CORNAS Urbane but stylish and deeply fruited wines from Les Ruchets; Terres Brûlées is slightly softer. Look out, too, for expensive but consistent, perfumed examples of St Joseph. Good Côtes du Rhône (and Côtes du Roussillon).

Pierre Coursodon, ST JOSEPH Pure Syrah spice sings out of Coursodon's wines.

Yves Cuilleron, CONDRIEU New name, producing superbly defined wines (and fine St Joseph, too).

Château de Curson, CROZES-HERMITAGE Enthusiastic young grower (Etienne Pochon) producing generously fruity wines.

Delas, HERMITAGE Full-flavoured, direct but sometimes spiky, graceless wines; red Hermitage (Marquise de la Tourette), Crozes and St Joseph usually best value. Condrieu very good, by contrast.

Domaine Durban, MUSCAT DE BEAUMES-DE-VENISE Top producer of this fortified sweet wine: sumptuously rich, but keeps tangy poise.

Domaine des Entrefaux, CROZES-HERMITAGE Excitingly chewy, spicy wines.

Bernard Faurie, HERMITAGE Small holdings: traditional vinification and harvest patience make this a successful estate in some years ('93). Green and hard at times.

Michel Ferraton, CROZES-HERMITAGE I find these wines coarse and disagreeable, though some admire them.

Domaine Font de Michelle, CHÂTEAUNEUF-DU-PAPE Rapidly improving wines, peppery and herby, though not cheap.

Château Fortia, CHÂTEAUNEUF-DU-PAPE Historic estate, but wines have been dull and irresolute for nearly two decades. Arrival of Colombo (q.v.) for '93 and '94 vintages has given much better results.

Château de la Gardine, CHÂTEAUNEUF-DU-PAPE Oaky and urbane: untypical but good nonetheless.

Marius Gentaz-Dervieux, CÔTE-RÔTIE Authentic, pure and perfumed wines, unmuddied by new oak.

Alain Graillot, CROZES-HERMITAGE Regional newcomer, but has shown what Crozes is capable of with profoundly scented and excitingly deep wines, especially La Guiraude ('88, '89 and '90 all very fine). Now a small parcel of Hermitage, too.

Domaine du Grand Moulas, CÔTES DU RHÔNE-VILLAGES One of the best of this appellation's wines: scented, soft, warming.

Domaine du Grand Tinel, CHÂTEAUNEUF-DU-PAPE Inconsistent, but at best an exuberant, sweetly spicy wine.

Château Grillet A property with an appellation (for Viognier-based white) of its own: generally disappointing and overpriced.

Bernard Gripa, ST JOSEPH Good wines, with scent and weight.

J.L. Grippat, ST JOSEPH Some of the best of all St Joseph (look out for tarry Cuvée des Hospices), though like most producers defeated by '93. Lush Hermitage, softer than many, and scented whites.

Guigal, CÔTE RÔTIE Since being dubbed 'this planet's greatest winemaker' by Robert Parker, Guigal's wines have romped heavenwards in price, and the best (his three single-vineyard Côte Rôties – La Landonne, La Mouline and La Turque) are only available to the very wealthy. They are the appellation's richest wines, late harvested from tiny yields and given copious new oak. Best value from Guigal are his generous, almost fiery Gigondas and Châteauneuf wines. The Côtes du Rhône is widely available and a sound bottle, though others (e.g. Grand Moulas) have more personality.

Paul Jaboulet Aîné, HERMITAGE A merchant range of remarkable consistency during the 1980s, though sometimes some of the lesser wines have been low on excitement. Jaboulet's best wine is the Hermitage La Chapelle (extraordinary in '89 and '90), and the Crozes-Hemitage Thalabert is often great value, ageing superbly; in the '90s, however, there have been some disappointments.

Jamet, CÔTE-RÔTIE Exciting wines, if rather beefy and tannin-shrouded.

Domaine de la Janasse, CHÂTEAUNEUF-DU-PAPE Dense and sumptuous wines from this rising star, peaking with Cuvée Vieilles Vignes.

Robert Jasmin, CÔTE-RÔTIE Inconsistent, but the best bottles are lush.

Marcel Juge, CORNAS Lighter, politer Cornas than most.

Domaine Maby, LIRAC More tightly knit, complex wines than the norm.

Domaine de Marcoux, CHÂTEAUNEUF-DU-PAPE Densely fruited, soft-textured style from biodynamically-farmed vineyards. Vieilles Vignes cuvées are superb.

Domaine de la Mordorée, CHÂTEAUNEUF-DU-PAPE Classic silkiness and purity of flavour across the range.

Robert Michel, CORNAS Beefy, traditional, cellar-seeking style.

Domaine de la Nerthe, CHÂTEAUNEUF-DU-PAPE Grand property, with wines to match; Cuvée des Cadettes particularly toothsome, though new oak can obtrude.

Domaine du Pegau, CHÂTEAUNEUF-DU-PAPE Unselfconsciously gutsy, fiery, extract-laden wines.

Père Anselme, CHÂTEAUNEUF-DU-PAPE Merchant house producing consistent, pleasant, softly spicy wine.

André Perret, CONDRIEU Freesias and peaches combine in Perret's superb Condrieu. St Joseph les Grisières, too, a deeply fruited, exciting wine (though not in '93).

Domaine Pochon see Château de Curson

Château Rayas, CHÂTEAUNEUF-DU-PAPE One of the wonders of the wine world: a superb range emanating from the grubby, squalid cellar of an arch-eccentric, Jacques Reynaud. Rayas and Pignan (second wine) are both pure Grenache, and represent the variety's sweet, unctuous apogee (the '89 and '90 are already legendary). Rayas Blanc is perfumed and rich, and needs age. The Fonsalette Côtes du Rhône wines are superb, too, especially the earthy, slow-ageing Cuvée Syrah. Bottle variation is, however, a problem, and Reynaud's admirable late-harvesting practices have, ironically, meant diluted '93 and '94 wines (due to October rain).

Domaine de la Remejeanne, CÔTES DU RHÔNE Deep flavoured, as too few wines in this AOC are.

René Rostaing, CÔTE RÔTIE Concentrated, skilfully made wines, smooth, deep and spicy, with successes even in difficult vintages. Fine Condrieu La Bonnette.

Domaine Saint–Gayan, GIGONDAS Typically muscular, punchy red wines. Full-fruited Rasteau Côtes du Rhône-Villages, too.

Domaine de la Solitude, CHÂTEAUNEUF-DU-PAPE Fine estate, but some disappointing wines during the '80s. Better quality of late.

Henri Sorrel, HERMITAGE Punchy, rustic style, but plenty of fruit behind.

Marc Sorrel, HERMITAGE Impressive depth, but over-savage, splintery style, high in acids and tannins, is hard to love.

Steinmaier, CÔTES DU RHÔNE Soft, spicy and glycerous.

Château du Trignon, SABLET-CÔTES DU RHÔNE-VILLAGES Well-made, medium-bodied, lightly peppery wines.

de Vallouit, HERMITAGE Merchant range, much improved in '80s. Hermitage Greffières, Côte Rôtie Roziers and Vagonier, and St Joseph Les Anges all deep, top-notch wines. Cornas less good.

Georges Vernay, Condrieu Lush, honeysuckle-scented whites. Côte Rôtie disappointing, though.

Noël Verset, Cornas Generous, round-contoured wines.

Vidal-Fleury, Côte-Rôtie Merchant, now Guigal-owned. Improving range; Côte Rôtie (especially La Chatillonne) and Muscat de Beaumes-de-Venise best.

La Vieille Ferme see Château de Beaucastel

Le Vieux Donjon, Châteauneuf-du-Pape Well-sited domain producing concentrated, herby wines of late (e.g. '90, '93, '94). Good in off-vintages, too.

Domaine du Vieux Télégraphe, Châteauneuf-du-Pape Grenache-dominated blend, very good in '70s and early '80s but less impressive since, though meaty-sweet '90 and, especially, lush, intense '94 suggest a return to form. Cuvée Prestige, from '94, has a higher percentage of Mourvèdre. Vieux Mas de Papes is a second wine.

Domaine François Villard, Condrieu Low yields give wines of great perfume and intensity. Good white St Joseph, too.

Alain Voge, Cornas Scrupulous producer: intense Vieilles Vignes cuvée better than internationalised Cuvée Barriques.

Vintages (Northern Rhône):
1995 ★★★★; 1994 ★★★; 1993 ★; 1992 ★; 1991 ★★★; 1990 ★★★; 1989 ★★★★; 1988 ★★★; 1987 ★★; 1986 ★★; 1985 ★★★.

Vintages (Southern Rhône):
1995 ★★★★; 1994 ★★★; 1993 ★★★; 1992 ★; 1991 ★; 1990 ★★★★; 1989 ★★★★; 1988 ★★★; 1987 ★; 1986 ★★; 1985 ★★★.

Specialist retailers:
Adam Bancroft, Bibendum, Justerini & Brooks, OW Loeb, La Réserve and Roberson all have good ranges; Yapp is the chief mail-order specialist.

Savoie

A sip of fresh air

Imagine a huge, U-shaped, breezy valley, and two brooding, craggy mountains to either side of it. Scatter a little rubble and scree at the base of the crags, plant the scree with vines, and you have a typical Savoie vineyard. The wines such vineyards produce are light, shimmering and delicate, with a lightly salty, nettle-brisk flavour. We don't see many of them in Britain, since France's alpine ski resorts require most of the region's production to anaesthetize sprained backs, knees and ankles.

Savoie's appellation system is an oppressively complicated one. Most of its wines are white, produced from four grape varieties: Jacquère, Altesse (known locally as Roussette), Chasselas and Roussanne (known locally as Bergeron). A number of different cru names are used, some indicating one grape variety and some another. Most typical, perhaps, are the flinty, stony Jacquère-based wines of Abymes and Apremont, a good glass of which is aerially bracing, and the fuller, quince-fruited Roussette de Savoie wines from the small zone of Marestel (or the rarely seen Montherminod). Chasselas-based wines like Crépy, Vin de Savoie-Marin or Vin de Savoie-Ripaille may taste of white almonds and pale butter. Red wines are produced, too: light and quaffy from Gamay and Pinot Noir; richer, darker and more ferrous from Mondeuse (once thought to be the grape variety known as Refosco in Fruili, but now considered indigenous and unique). Sparkling wines are important to the region, so much so that some of the branded sparkling wines are now made with grapes sourced from other parts of France. The crisp, biscuity Seyssel leads the local appellations for fizz, based on yet another regional grape, the Molette, with a little extra Altesse. Most Savoie sparklers, though, are Jacquère-based − floral, delicate, pretty. As an alternative to champagne, they are less hard and harsh than the Loire's or Burgundy's sparkling wines, yet can have surprising depth of flavour.

Producers' names to look out for include Raymond Barlet, Pierre Boniface, Eugène Carrel, Cave Coopérative de Chautagne, Michel Grisard, Edmond Jacquin, Louis Magnin, Maison Mollex, André and Michel Quénard, Château de Ripaille, Domaine de la Tour de Villard and Varichon et Clerc.

South West France

Dark tales from the high country

Gathered together under this banner are an assortment of curiosities from deepest regional France. Nowhere is further from Paris and the Parisian mentality than this region − or these regions − of woodland and woodsmoke, goosefat and garlic; and of ruddy-faced, fireside excess.

The opening appellations of the South West belong to Bordeaux's back yard: Bergerac, Côtes de Duras and Côtes du Marmandais, where slight-framed though often tasty clarets are made. Monbazillac goes about the difficult business of trying to produce good yet inexpensive dessert wines; its irregular successes have a silky grace to them (1990 is thought to have been the best vintage there since the 1940s).

The rest of the region is one in which rivers begin their descent from their sources. These high-country wines have a long tradition but a troubled history; access to markets was controlled by those lucky enough to find themselves at the river's mouth, and all the major rivers here, save the Basque Adour, end at Bordeaux. Cahors, for example, sited around the twisting Lot, provided half the wine to leave Bordeaux in the fourteenth century. Today it is a small fraction of that. The major grape variety used here is the Malbec, a Bordeaux variety which plays a major role elsewhere only in the wines of Argentina. Cahors' historical reputation was for 'black' wine, made in part with cooked must or oven-baked grapes. Modern Cahors evades the kitchen yet remains dark, plummy and savoury; its tannins are often tempered now by carbonic maceration (see page 19). Look out for the local Vin de Pays des Coteaux de Quercy, which often offers well-structured reds at a keen price.

On the high Tarn lies Gaillac and (nearer to Toulouse) Côtes du Frontonnais. Gaillac produces wines in every style: crisp, Mauzac-based whites, soft rosé and reds (only a few have the depth to combat a British winter), and some pretty, off-dry sparkling wines. Côtes du Frontonnais is for fruity, peppery reds based on the Négrette.

The South West's most important zone of vineyards is that of Gascony, which lies at the remote centre of the Bordeaux-Toulouse-Biarritz triangle. It was precisely because of this remoteness, and the fact that there were few suitable rivers available for trading its wine out to customers in a drinkable condition, that Armagnac came into being; modern times and transport have shown how good Gascony's undistilled wine can be. It begins on a Bordeaux note with Buzet (more clarety red), and ends with the often fierce, tough, Tannat-based reds of Madiran. In the large, Armagnac-producing zone between the two, Vin de Pays des Côtes de Gascogne is the name used for what used to be delicious, nettle-fresh whites but what is now more often a dull sort of French Liebfraumilch. Côtes de Saint-Mont, by contrast, offers some good, iron-stiffened reds.

Béarn, Jurançon and Irouléguy are France's last wines. Of the three, it is Jurançon's whites which are most often seen in Britain: complex dry and well-balanced sweet whites of disparate but occasionally entrancing flavour, where mango and pineapple thicken and crystallise in spices and honey. They find an echo in the Madiran zone with the hauntingly named Pacherenc du Vic-Bilh.

Château d'Aydie, MADIRAN Best wine from Domaine Laplace: 70% Tannat and long wood ageing give a spicy, richly textured wine. Good sweet Pacherenc du Vic-Bilh, too.

Domaine Barréjat, MADIRAN Old vines give a deeply flavoured though well-rounded wine.

Château Bellevue-la-Fôret, CÔTES-DU-FRONTONNAIS Appellation leader, producing fresh, juicy, peppery reds.

Domaine Bouscassé, MADIRAN Fine, old-vine Madiran given silky sheen from new wood, plus fine sweet Pacherenc du Vic-Bilh. See also **Château Montus.**

Domaine Brana, IROULÉGUY Steep sloping vineyards and tiny yields produce fruity, mid-weight reds and floral whites.

Domaine du Bru-Baché, JURANÇON Wood-aged but well-balanced wines, both dry and sweet.

Domaine Capmartin, MADIRAN Rich, truffley Madiran, especially top Cuvée du Couvent.

Domaine Cauhapé, JURANÇON The key producer in this appellation, Cauhapé produces zesty dry whites and fruit-studded but cleanly balanced sweet ones (Noblesse and Quintessence are super-sweet wines from exceptional vintages).

Cave Coopérative de Monbazillac, MONBAZILLAC Enterprising cooperative making half the appellation's wine, including often fine Château de Monbazillac.

Château de Cayrou, CAHORS Structured, traditional wine.

Château de Chambert, CAHORS Painstaking, hand-crafted wine. Good, but would be better with less oak.

Chapelle Lenclos, MADIRAN Young grower producing wines with softer tannins than many, backed by ample fruit.

Clos de Gamot, CAHORS Pure Malbec wine from old vines: dense and deep.

Clos Guirouilh, JURANÇON Fine, flower-scented dry and elegant sweet wine.

Clos Triguedina, CAHORS Ambitious, punchy, oaky, ferrous wines, especially top cuvée Prince Probus.

Château Court-les-Mûts, BERGERAC Well-made dry Bergerac wines and sweet Saussignac.

Côtes d'Olt, CAHORS Cooperative (numbered among whose members is the Queen of Denmark) controlling half the appellation's production. Some wines dull; better wines (yet still on supple side) from single properties such as Châteaux du Cayrou-Monpézat, Léret-Monpézat and les Bousses.

Jean Cros, GAILLAC The best of this appellation's reds until 1990: deep and manful. Disappointing since '90.

Yves Grassa/Château de Tariquet, CÔTES DE GASCOGNE Reliable and often exciting, zesty whites sold under a greater variety of names (so that everyone can have an 'exclusivity') than you would think possible.

Château de Haute-Serre, CAHORS Supple wine, but consistent and flavoury.

Château La Jaubertie, BERGERAC Now owned by Hugh Ryman and Esmé Johnstone, this property produces cleanly fruity wines with more personality than the appellation usually manages.

Domaine de Joliet, CÔTES DU FRONTONNAIS Bright, lively reds, from almost pure Négrette.

Domaine Laplace see **Château d'Aydie.**

Mas d'Aurel, GAILLAC Choice red and well-made sparkling wine.

Domaine Meinjarre, MADIRAN Half-Tannat, half-Cabernet Franc red in fresh style: third of Alain Brumont's wines (see **Château Montus**).

Domaine de Mendisokoa, IROULÉGUY Spicy, meaty, earthy reds.

Château Montus, MADIRAN Top estate of energetic, much-lauded Alain Brumont (see also **Domaine Bouscassé** and **Domaine Meinjarre**). Pure Tannat with lots of new wood gives muscular, swaggering but entertaining red; expensive.

Domaine de Pichard, MADIRAN Authentic, spicy wines, especially the Vigneau Pichard cuvée, with 70% Tannat and new oak.

Domaine de la Pineraie, CAHORS Dark, firm reds with meaty core for ageing.

Plaimont Producteurs, CÔTES DE SAINT-MONT One of France's most innovative cooperatives. Crisp, refreshing Vin de Pays des Côtes de Gascogne, tangy white and grippy red Côtes de Saint-Mont, and some beefy Madiran, too.

Domaine le Puts, CÔTES DE GASCOGNE Hugh Ryman-made wine: fresh, grapy, reliable white.

Château Tirecul, MONBAZILLAC Huge efforts; superb wines.

Trés Cantous/Roucou-Cantemerle, GAILLAC Robert Plageoles is one of the guardians of Gaillac's often ancient varieties and traditions, including a flor-aged Vin de Voile from Mauzac and a dessert Ondenc called Vin d'Autan.

Clos Uroulat, JURANÇON Clean, elegant sweet wines.

Les Vignerons Réunis des Côtes de Buzet Some 85 per cent of this appellation's wine is made by the cooperative, most of it claret-like red (best wine labelled Baron d'Ardeuil).

> **Vintages:**
> 1995 ★★★; 1994 ★★; 1993 ★★; 1992 ★; 1991 ★★; 1990 ★★★★; 1989 ★★★; 1988 ★★★; 1987 ★; 1986 ★★★; 1985 ★★★

Georgia

The viticulturalist's Klondike

Georgia (in the former Soviet Union) is a wine country of extraordinary antiquity, claiming some 500 indigenous grape varieties of its own (bred from the many wild vine types which are still found there). Thirty eight indigenous and international varieties are approved for viticulture, though winemaking is still, by French or Australian standards, primitive – which is why Georgia's wines are little seen outside the country. The most celebrated of the country's wines are tannic reds from the Kakheti region, made by fermentation followed by long maceration (up to four months) in buried earthenware jars. A start was made on export sales in 1996 with Chinebuli, a ruby liqueur wine from the Khirsa winery, and two Kakheti wines, Hereti (made from Rkatsitcli) and Teliani (from Cabernet Sauvignon), both made by the Tsinandali winery.

Germany

The price of difference

Do you remember the boy or girl whom everybody bullied at school? Because he behaved strangely, chosing not to speak, walk or rebel in the same way as everyone else; because she looked paler, or thinner, or fatter than was thought the girlish norm? They had as much to offer as you or I did, and perhaps more. It went undiscovered. Malevolence occluded their talents.

German wine is, for the moment, that boy, that girl. It's different from all other wines, down to the last drop. Those differences make it harder for us to understand and to use. We ignore it, make jokes about it, bully it. We're missing out.

The death of a swallow

I had hoped to be able to report good news for this edition: the corner turned, the renaissance finally underway. I can't. The truth is that Liebfraumilch and 'Hock' continue their destructive work, reducing the public perception of German wine from an exciting land of frontiers, challenges and extremes to a paddling pool for those who like wine to taste like fruit juice. The pound's weakness against the mark, symbolic of Britain's tumble down the European pecking order, makes our approaches to the best German wines still more tottering. The big German cooperatives and industrial merchants continue to write German wine law, and thus to throttle the export fortunes of smaller, higher quality producers. There are only two faint flames in the darkness.

The first is that Riesling from New World sources (chiefly Australia and New Zealand) continues to grow in popularity. It's ironic, but the best chance for the Germany's grand masters of Riesling is to ride piggy-back into fashionability carried by perky antipodean pupils.

The second is the death of a swallow. Remember Hirondelle? Millions of bottles of this chameleon wine (it was sourced from whichever country came up with the best prices) were sold in the '70s and early '80s; now it's no more than lost light drifting out into space. Liebfraumilch remains hugely popular, but for how much longer? In less than a decade those in the paddling pool may prefer to opt for hooch, alcoholic cream soda, transparent cider, alcho-jelly, sniffo-wine or some other slickly packaged dollop of liquid technology as yet just a gleam in a research chemist's eye. And then we'll come back to real German wine again, and discover we've lost a couple of decades of great drinking.

The meaning of cool

Germany is, in wine-growing terms, a cool country. Its fortune is its rivers: the Mosel, Rhine, Main, Neckar, Nahe and Ahr. They cut their serpentine way through the country's southern uplands, and in so doing provide sun-angled slopes and banks to give the vines the warmth they need to manufacture sugar. Nowhere is the quest for sweetness in grapes taken more seriously than in Germany; nowhere is sweetness in grapes measured more minutely, or treasured more zealously.

Germany's coolness has other implications. Its cool summers mean that its grapes (and especially the Riesling) rarely lose their lively acidities and fresh fruit flavours; its cool winters traditionally meant that fermentation stopped early, before all the sugar had been turned into alcohol. The roots of Germany's differences lie in its climate.

These are wines in which alcohol is an irrelevance – a vulgar, thumping beat to be kept in the background. What matters is balance, the way all the flavours in a wine are bound energetically together; moreover those flavours and their scented echo should be dewdrop-clear, crystal-crisp. Sweetness is used as a factor of balance and proof of triumphant, against-the-odds ripeness. German wine is for holding close against the tip of the tongue, the better to sense its arabesques of tingling fruit. Its low alcohol makes it the most intellectually stimulating wine in the world: you can still discuss 'The Magic Flute' sensibly after three glasses each.

There are faults in German wine, of course, particularly the tendency to douse bottles and wines with sulphur to an offensive degree. (If you sniff a wine and start coughing for no apparent reason, that's caused by free sulphur.) High yields make even expensive wines flabby and weak; the domestic obsession with food match-ing (to which German wines are not always well suited) has falsified and standard-ised the character of some previously great bottles. And the differences I stressed earlier can seem like faults: the lack of alcohol, for example, takes a while to get used to. But persist: you'll soon realise that these wines are the best aperitifs in the world for those intending to drink other, stronger wines with dinner.

There are many words on German wine labels; it is safe enough to ignore most. Look, though, for one of the following: Kabinett, Spätlese, Auslese. These words refer to the sweetness of the juice from which the wine was made: Kabinett juice is less rich than Spätlese juice, which is less rich than Auslese juice. They do not, necessarily, mean that the wine will taste sweet. If the words Trocken (dry) or Halbtrocken (off-dry) appear on the label, expect no or little sweetness; otherwise expect some. By contrast, the words Beerenauslese or Trockenbeerenauslese mean very sweet wine indeed. Eiswein ('ice wine' made from frozen berries) is as sweet, but balanced by mountainous acidity; drinking it is like sword-swallowing. For other terminology and vineyard site information, see **Further Reading**.

Mosel-Saar-Ruwer

Filigree grandeur

The Mosel, a river of intestinal convolutedness, runs from France and Luxembourg northeast towards Rhenish oblivion at Koblenz. Over the slow beat of the centuries it has tickled and nibbled and worried its course down hundreds of feet, leaving giant walls of slate to mark the valley's edge. Graft Riesling vines into those airy walls, as the canny, goat-legged locals have long done, and you will (given a good summer) produce wines which represent an ultimate. No others on earth are capable of summoning fruit so vividly and limpidly to mind. None are so light in alcohol, so delicately phrased, so crystalline. The best, too, are charged not only with brilliant fruit flavours but with a haunting mineral quality. Astonishingly enough, they age superbly, acquiring buttery autumnal richnesses as they do so.

Of course not all of the Mosel's vineyards are grafted into precipitous slate. Many vineyards of more recent cultivation are spread out over the flatlands of the river's previous courses. These sites, formerly used for cereals, produce wines of indifferent quality, yet the consumer has no way of differentiating (other than by recourse to one of the reference books listed on page 30) between traditional vineyards and latter-day imposters. This is one of several iniquities enshrined by German wine law.

The Ruwer is a little stream which runs into the Mosel just north of Trier, while the Saar is a rather bigger watercourse which has carved out rocky vineyards of its own down the centuries, joining the Mosel at Konz, south of Trier. In each case, Moselline delicacy is heightened still further: the Ruwer's wines marry restrained peach and floral characters with a distinct earthiness; the Saar's are steely, severe, pungent, unfolding as slowly as buds after winter.

Clemens Busch Top organic grower working in dryer styles.

Christoffel Erben Stylish wines from one of the river's top sites, Urziger Würzgarten.

Grans Fassian Classical delicacy at an attractive price.

Friedrich Wilhelm Gymnasium Good value from Karl Marx's old school.

Fritz Haag Consistent, precision excellence from one of the Mosel's master-winemakers and a great vineyard – the Brauneberger Juffer-Sonnenuhr.

Reinhold Haart The real Piesporter (from Goldtröpfchen), buxom with fruit.

Heymann-Löwenstein Full, dryish wines from the less widely planted Unter Mosel.

Von Hövel Rounder Saar wines than some.

Karlsmühle An exciting turn of speed recently with concentrated, multi-faceted wines from this Ruwer grower.

Karthäuserhof One of the two leading Ruwer estates, producing steely, fine-honed wines, more Saar-like than Moselline.

Heribert Kerpen Producer of intense Wehlener Sonnenuhr.

von Kesselstatt Large estate with a fine vineyard portfolio producing wines shimmering with clearly defined fruits.

Dr Loosen Intelligent, outspoken Ernie Loosen produces a fine range, from the minimalist limpidity of his Riesling Trocken (despite recent bottling problems) to the luscious, burnt depths of his Erdener Prälat wines. Don't hurry to drink.

Maximin Grünhaus A benchmark for the earthy, green-fruited style of the Ruwer. Perfect-pitch balance gives fine, long-lived wines.

Meulenhof Intense, impressive Erdener Treppchen stands out.

Milz-Laurentiushof Softer than some, but ample fruit.

Mönchhof Purity of flavour.

Egon Müller Succulent yet always balanced sweet wines at stellar prices. Only red burgundy can combine delicacy and power in this manner.

J.J. Prüm Flowery, graceful classics, rewarding long cellaring.

Reinert Textbook Saar clarity.

Max Ferd Richter Inconsistent, but at best lush and spicy.

Schloss Saarstein Crisp, clean wines, more accessible in youth than many.

Willi Schaefer Classic slow-developing Mosel Riesling.

Selbach-Oster Reliable range, with extravagantly fruity Zeltinger Sonnenuhr.

Wegeler-Deinhard Some great wines (Wehlener Sonnenuhr and Bernkasteler Doctor), but others lack intensity and focus.

Weins-Prüm Site differences can be clearly tasted in these wines from a fine spread of holdings.

Zilliken Saar producer whose piano-wire wines can slice your tongue (deliciously) to shreds. Give them time to express their slaty depths.

Vintages:
1995 ★★; 1994 ★★★★; 1993 ★★★; 1992 ★★★; 1991 ★★; 1990 ★★★★; 1989 ★★★★; 1988 ★★★; 1987 ★; 1986 ★★; 1985 ★★★.

Specialist retailers:
Merchants have the best selection: Berry Bros, Fortnum & Mason, Justerini & Brooks, O.W. Loeb, and by mail order from Adnams, Lay & Wheeler. Among high-street chains, Oddbins' selection is small but strategically acute; other chains settle for the occasional good bottle. Supermarket German wine selections are cheap and poor.

Rheingau
Turbid river, limpid wine

For some 30 km between Mainz and Rüdesheim, the great watery highway of the Rhine abandons its northerly trajectory and turns west, stymied by the Taunus mountains. The westward-running river and its tributaries have created, on its northern side, sun-lavished south-facing slopes. There is no other stretch of German soil so propitiously sited as this; vines have clothed it for eight hundred years. This is the home of Riesling and the heart of German winegrowing.

The wines of the Rheingau are stronger and fuller than those of the Mosel, with perceptibly higher alcohol levels. In place of the felted softness and delicacy of the Middle Mosel, there is the hard clarity of sheet ice. The soils of the Rheingau are mixed, providing a spectrum of mineral flavours to ballast the fine, sheer, sumptuous fruit. Dry wines are more successful here than in the Mosel; 'Charta' is the name for an association of producers of dry wines meeting set criteria for roundness and harmony. Not all of their wines are inspiring, but the best do correspond to the balanced, classical Rheingau ideal.

Where the Rheingau has suffered in the last few years is not, as in the Mosel and elsewhere, with widespread vineyard planting on unsuitable land, but with a general complacency among the great aristocratic estates of the region. Assured sales on the strength of historic names have meant that unexciting wine, often produced from over-high yields, has betrayed the legacy of fine vineyards which these estates hold. It is the aspiring smaller estates, often with vineyards of less glittering potential, who have produced many of the best wines.

Look out for the term Erstes Gewächs on labels of Rheingau wine. This means 'First Growth', and is a voluntary description which may be used on wines of Auslese quality or higher in either dry or sweet form from certain classified vineyards. Classification of vineyards is a troublesome but worthwhile exercise, as the Bordeaux and Burgundy examples prove; what does seem bizarre, by contrast, is the denial that a vineyard's personality might be memorably expressed in Kabinett or Spätlese form. These epiphanies of delicacy are, for me, the truest and loveliest German wines of all.

Geheimrat Aschrott'sche Erben Improved of late: milk-soft, full-flavoured wines from Hochheim (from whence, originally, 'hock' – now merely a synonym for Rhine wine).

Becker Deep, mineral flavours which respond well to cellaring.

Breuer Clean, careful, intense, racy wines from the Rüdesheimer Berg Schlossberg and elsewhere.

Domdechant Werner Richer fruit and fuller textures than the Rheingau norm from this Hochheim-based producer.

Eser (Johannishof) Classical, fine-spun balance from the heart of the Rheingau. Very good Charta wines; all the range ages well.

Freiherr zu Knyphausen Another quiet classicist producing admirably consistent wines.

Kesseler Leading producer based in Assmannshausen, first stop round the bend after Rüdesheim, where vivid, crunchy Pinot Noir is a speciality.

Künstler Hochheim-based estate producing full, bready, peachy wines.

Langwerth von Simmern Delicate, choice wines, especially fine and mineral-charged from the high Rauenthaler Baiken site.

Leitz Small but well-sited holdings and innovative winemaking provide some concentrated wines.

Ress Sound Hattenheimer Nussbrunnen and Rüdesheimer Berg Schlossberg.

Schloss Johannisberg The region's most historic estate. Inconsistent for some years, with only the sweeter wines intense and memorable, but recent improvements suggest a general raising of standards.

Schloss Reinhartshausen Supple, expressive and increasingly consistent wines, especially from Erbacher Marcobrunn and elegant Hattenheimer Wisselbrunnen. Organic wines from the Rhine island of Mariannanaue are sold with a white and orange label.

Schloss Schönborn Another major landholder in Erbacher Marcobrunn, Schönborn's wines have, at best, an earthy, driving intensity. Scattered landholdings mean some inconsistency.

Schloss Vollrads Sometimes rather thin wines for the Rheingau, but memorable at higher categories. Recent financial problems. A change of management team may improve matters.

Staatsweingüter Kloster Eberbach Inconsistent, but bell-clear wines from the great Steinberger vineyard are essential reference drinking.

Wegeler-Deinhard Flavoury Charta wines and palate-slicing ice wines.

Weil Delicate and graceful, yet enormously penetrating wines, among the Rheingau's most seductive.

Vintages:
1995 ★★; 1994 ★★★; 1993 ★★★; 1992 ★★★; 1991 ★★; 1990 ★★★★; 1989 ★★★★; 1988 ★★★; 1987 ★; 1986 ★★; 1985 ★★★.

Specialist retailers:
See Mosel-Saar-Ruwer.

Nahe
Backwoods bargains

The Nahe, a green-quilted pocket tucked away between Rheinhessen and the Mosel, is a good name to remember for those thirsting for the classical ideal of German wine (tinkling clarity, mouthwatering fruits) but without the funds necessary to empty the best cellars of the Mosel and Rheingau. The Nahe and its burbling tributaries have carved out some fine and sometimes spectacular vineyards (northern Europe's highest cliffs, the Rotenfels, nourish vines on their scree); the best growers here are as scrupulous as anywhere in Germany; and the region's complex geology and soils give a wide range of styles and flavours, often showing the intense mineralisation which the Riesling, above all varieties, is capable of expressing.

Paul Anheuser A wide range of increasingly soft-focus wines.

Crusius Traiser Bastei – that scree vineyard – produces mineral-charged, fresh-burnt stars, but the whole range is carefully made and reflects site differences with an accuracy unthinkable as yet in the New World. Fine fruit definition in the Schlossböckelheimer Felsenberg wines.

Diel Journalist and showman Armin Diel's wines can ape oaky French models to a misguided extent, but the classically made Spätlesen and Auslesen from Dorsheimer Goldloch are pure, intense and exciting.

Hermann Dönnhoff Some of the most finely crafted wines in the region, with especially memorable Oberhäuser Brücke and Niederhäuser Hermannshöhle. Piercing and deep.

Krüger-Rumpf Adventurous dry wines.

Adolf Lotzbeyer Rich, almost Pfalz-like style.

Reichsgraf von Plettenberg The restrained, garden-fresh Nahe style, accessibly priced.

Prinz du Salm-Dalberg The world's oldest wine estate, now working organically. Fresh, well balanced wines.

Staatliche Weinbaudomäne Niederhausen–Schlossböckelheim This indigestibly-named state domain has produced some of Germany's best wines in the 1980s – spicy, full, yet with mouthwatering crispness and definition. There's been a slip in quality from 1988, yet the potential of its steep vineyards is still palpable in its richer wines.

Bürgermeister Willi Schweinhardt Fresh, fruity, straightforward wines.

Vintages
1995 ★★; 1994 ★★; 1993 ★★★★; 1992 ★★★★; 1991 ★★; 1990 ★★★★; 1989 ★★★★; 1988 ★★★; 1987 ★; 1986 ★★; 1985 ★★★.

Specialist retailers
See Mosel-Saar-Ruwer.

Rheinpfalz

Bacchus in lederhosen

Sunny Pfalz (in English the Palatinate) produces tankerloads of simple, often spicy wines from varieties other than Riesling (chiefly Müller-Thurgau). It is also home to finer, more intriguing wines in two styles. The first style constitutes Pfalz's classics: broad, busty, hip-swingingly fruity wines based on Riesling, chiefly grown in the central section of the region, the Mittelhaardt. German Riesling is rarely as spicy as it is here, nor is it, in its sweeter categories, as syrupy, heady and luscious. The second wine style has been created by the innovators:

growers who see beyond the walls of Fortress Riesling, and who are determined to produce whatever most memorably represents their generous little corner of German earth. The keynote of their work is uncompromising viticulture combined with watchful inactivity in the cellar (a combination which lies behind most great wines): growing superb fruit, then allowing it to express itself in the wine as it will. This group of growers, led by the remarkable Hans-Günter Schwarz of Müller-Catoir, show what German wine might achieve if it was driven by vision and imagination rather than by the economic short-termism of cooperative members chiefly interested in renewing their Mercedes each year.

Basserman-Jordan Classic: the pouting lower lip of the Pfalz given aristocratically clean, elegant lines.

Bergdolt Innovator: powerhouse dry wines.

Biffar Innovator: expressive, high-definition wines from good Mittelhaardt vineyards; also dry *sur lie* Weissburgunder (Pinot Blanc).

von Buhl Classic. Japanese endeavour is attempting to bring about a renaissance in this fine old estate's wines – which during the eighties lost their way due to family indifference. See page 201.

Bürklin-Wolf Classic. Less consistent than Basserman-Jordan, the Bürklin-Wolf wines are brisker than the regional norm when on form. Wine from the best sites only now appears under the Bürklin-Wolf label; the rest as Villa Eckel.

Koehler-Ruprecht Innovator. A try-anything-once grower, Bernd Philippi produces rigorously structured dry wines as well as sweeter ones with the density of medicine balls. The zanier wines (such as oak-aged reds and whites and a Sauternes-style oak-aged sweet white called Elysium) are sold under the Philippi name; the Koehler-Ruprecht label is used for dry classics from the Kallstädter Saumagen and elsewhere.

Lingenfelder Innovator. Broad-backed, fruit-dense wines from what, in lesser hands, would be quite ordinary vineyards. Reference-point Scheurebe; Riesling more delicate.

Messmer Innovator. Generously fruited wines in dryish style include good Gewürztraminer and splendidly peachy Scheurebe.

Müller-Catoir Innovator – though the estate might contest this description. The innovation consists in a complete lack of compromise: ripeness, here, is pursued fanatically, and the wines then allowed to develop as far through fermentation as their inclination takes them. The results seem impossibly perfumed, fruit-stuffed, dripping with sweetness. Scheurebe, Rieslaner and Muskateller can all outpunch the Riesling, though I have never come across a poor wine under this label.

Philippi see **Koehler-Ruprecht**.

St Ursula Innovative producer of inexpensive yet well-made dry wines.

Villa Eckel see **Bürklin-Wolf**.

> **Vintages.**
>
> 1995 ★★; 1994 ★★★; 1993 ★★★; 1992 ★★★★; 1991 ★★; 1990 ★★★★; 1989 ★★★★;
> 1988 ★★★; 1987 ★; 1986 ★★; 1985 ★★★.
>
> **Specialist retailers:**
> See Mosel-Saar-Ruwer.

Rheinhessen
Diamonds in the mud

It is in the flat, muddy fields of Rheinhessen that most of Germany's torrent of
poor wine has its source. This is viticulture at its most industrial: high-yielding
Müller-Thurgau and Silvaner trucked off to huge merchant warehouses in
the Mosel where chemists produce wine according to analysis figures while the
salesmen take their cues from a heavy-jowled accountant. Yet Rheinhessen
does have good vineyards, among the greatest in Germany: they're found in a
sloped tongue of red earth (the Roter Hang) which gazes down on the
Rhine between Nackenheim and Oppenheim (the Rheinfront). The top wines
here have a soft and silky intensity. In the far northeast of the region, too,
Bingen produces good wines, in a fresher, more structured style closer to that
of the Rheingau.

Brüder Dr Becker Characterful organic wines.

Gunderloch Concentrated, chewy yet fine-boned wines from a friendly
husband-and-wife team. Dessert wines from the Nackenheimer Rothenberg live
up to a legendary tradition.

Guntrum Comfortable merchant wines, and full-flavoured estate wines.

Heyl zu Herrnsheim Carefully crafted, perfumed, softly contoured
wines from organic vineyards. Partnership with merchants Valckenberg has
meant that Peter von Weymarn, who runs Heyl, is now looking after the
Wormser Liebfrauenstift-Kirchenstück – the birthplace of Liebfraumilch – and
converting it to organic production.

Keller Unpropitious sites, but low yields and careful winemaking provide characterful Riesling, good-value Silvaner and sumptuous dessert wines.

Okonomierat J. Geil Erben Fine dry Silvaner of unusual scentedness, plus
unsubtle but exciting dessert Huxelrebe.

St Antony Some of the best dry Riesling in the country from good sites on the
Rheinfront. Owned by MAN trucks.

Schales Family winery proving that even the Rheinhessen's lesser vineyards
have potential if carefully cropped: good dry Riesling, Weissburgunder and sweet
Huxelrebe.

Schneider Characterful and generous wines from Niersteiner Hipping and
other sites.

Villa Sachsen Purchased from Nestlé by Prinz zu Salm-Dalberg (see Nahe), this estate has some of Bingen's best vineyards (Binger Scharlachberg); improvements imminent.

Vintages:
1995 ★★; 1994 ★★★; 1993 ★★★; 1992 ★★★; 1991 ★★; 1990 ★★★★; 1989 ★★★★; 1988 ★★★; 1987 ★; 1986 ★★; 1985 ★★★.

Specialist retailers:
See Mosel-Saar-Ruwer.

Rest of Germany
The electric scrotum

Germany's remaining vineyard regions are, from north to south, Saale-Unstrut and Sachsen, the Ahr, the Mittelrhein, Franconia, Hessische Bergstrasse, Baden and Württemberg. Of these, it is Franconia which produces the most interesting wines: dry, intensely nervy, sappy wines which seem to express themselves by sending an electrical charge across the tongue rather than the waves of fruit more common elsewhere in the country. Their rounded, flask-like bottles are said to be modelled on the scrotum of a goat, and to Mateus-educated British eyes give off all the wrong signals: sentimentality and sweetness rather than (as would be more appropriate) danger and severity. Top Franken producers include Castell, Juliusspital and Wirsching.

Baden produces some of Germany's biggest wines, often dry in style, but quality is patchy: look out for the wines of Bercher, Dr Heger, the oak-loving Karl-Heinz Johner (whose career began at Lamberhurst in Kent) and Gräflich Wolf Metternich'sches Weingut, as well as some from the top cooperatives such as Buhl, Durbach and Bickensohl.

Much of Württemberg's wine is of appalling quality, thin and dilute, but good wines are produced by Graf Adelmann, Dautel, Drautz-Able, Furst zu Hohenlohe-Ohringen and Graf von Neipperg (Canon-la-Gaffelière in St Emilion is also in Neipperg ownership). The wines of Saale-Unstrut and Sachsen, too, are inconsistent, though efforts to improve standards there are in hand: look out for Lützkendorff in Saale-Unstrut and Schloss Proschwitz, Ulrich and Zimmerling in Sachsen.

The Mittelrhein (Bastian, Jost, Kauer, Ratzenberger and Weingart) and Hessische-Bergstrasse (Domäne Bensheim/Staatsweingut Bergstrasse) can produce good if slender Nahe-like wines. Red wines of light but surprisingly rounded fruit are the Ahr speciality; Meyer-Näkel is a name to remember.

Vintages:
1995 ★★; 1994 ★★★; 1993 ★★★; 1992 ★★★; 1991 ★★; 1990 ★★★★; 1989 ★★★.

Specialist retailers:
See Mosel-Saar-Ruwer.

Greece

Getting it together

Anyone who knows Greece will be familiar with the perfectly commingled feelings of delight and exasperation which its wines, like every other manifestation of its national life, provoke. Delight, of course, that the viticultural bloodline which connects our modern-day drinking with that of Homer's heroes remains unbroken, and that Greece can still produce the kind of mellow, sweet whites and sea-dark, savoury reds with which the great moments of Odysseus' traumatic return are punctuated. Exasperation, of course, that it doesn't do so more often.

The problems faced by modern-day winemakers in Greece – remoteness, heat, drought, and the inertia brought on by all three among winegrowers and cooperative members – are considerable. The difficulties do not finish once the wines are bottled. Anyone who has ever holidayed in Greece will be familiar with the gaggle of dusty wines on the shelves of tiny supermarkets run by gentle, innumerate widows, and even pallets containered straight out of the country can arrive in Britain in a tired state. Yet Greece is not only maintaining its viticultural traditions (and laudably resisting Chardonnization and Cabernetification), but the quality of some leading Greek wines has noticeably improved in the last few years. This is due both to the efforts of determined individuals as well as to Greece's larger wine companies which manage, by what seems to me near-miraculous means, to gather together and blend the pick of the country's far-flung specialities.

Retsina is certainly Greece's most celebrated wine, though it is not to everyone's taste (I relish it). It is made principally from the Saviatiano grape variety, the juice of which is mixed with around 0.15 per cent Aleppo pine resin (see feature). The best of it comes from Attica and Messoghia, to the north and south of Athens, as well as in Viotia and on the island of Evia. Attica is also the home of a number of Greece's new boutique wineries: their achievements are inconsistent as yet, though they have been useful in jolting the larger companies out of somnolence and inertia.

Northern Greece (Greek Macedonia and Thrace) is noted for Naoussa, a dark, chewy red based on Xynomavro; Goumenissa is similar but a little lighter, its Xynomavro blended with Negoska grapes. On the central prong of the trident-like Halkidiki peninsula lies the Côtes de Meliton, an appellation whose French name reflected its main producer's initial ambitions and aspirations (see Domaine Carras below).

In Central Greece (Thessaly and Epirius), little interesting wine is produced; the best is Xynomavro-based Rapsani, grown on the foothills of Mount Olympus.

The Peloponnese is the engine of Greek viticulture, with the bulk of the country's production of currants (the word itself derived from their varietal name, Korinthiaki), as well as several of its more interesting wines. Red Nemea, made from Agiogitiko grapes, is the name to look out for – it's potentially even deeper than Naoussa. Mantinia produces some good white wines, and Patras in the Northern Peloponnese two celebrated fortified wines – a sweet Muscat, and the tawny-port-like red Mavrodaphne (the nineteenth-century invention of a Bavarian, Gustav Clauss) – as well as the dry white simply called Patras.

Among the wine-producing Greek islands are Cephalonia (where white Robola and fortified Mavrodaphne and Muscat are traditional), Paros (Mandelaria-based reds) and Santorini (sharp, Assyrtiko-based whites and a little dried-grape Vissanto). Greece's best Muscats come from the island of Samos (and Samos Muscat is, curiously enough, an essential ingredient in the fine French apéritif Noilly Prat); others are produced on Lemnos. Rhodes and Crete are both big wine producers, though quality is very variable.

Total Greek production puts it behind Australia and ahead of Chile; the area under vines has shrunk by nearly 40 per cent in a decade, the biggest reduction within the EU, and will shrink further still in the years ahead as around a sixth of its crop is still unwanted by anyone (and distilled by the Union). The Greeks themselves, like most Mediterranean peoples, are drinking less wine and more beer than they used to as marketing and distribution developments eclipse deep local traditions.

Achaia–Clauss Best for Peloponnese specialities, including perfumed Mantinia and luscious Mavrodaphne. Ben Riggs of Wirra-Wirra (see **South Australia**) has made eight wines here from blends of native and international varieties.

Boutari A large company whose range includes good Cretan white wine (Kretikos), crisp white from Santorini, the blended Lac des Roches, a plummy Paros red, reliable Nemea, and the fine Grande Réserve, a single-estate Naoussa with dry-leaf-and-tobacco scents and a deliciously leathery flavour.

Calliga Some very strange packaging, but good red Ktima and white Robola from Cephalonia.

Cambas Sound retsina; other wines unreliable.

Domaine Carras, HALKIDIKI No-expense-spared, large-scale enterprise originally designed to produce ambitious, French-style wines but increasingly working with indigenous varieties. Among the reds, I prefer the pure Limnio to the rather dry, pruney Château Carras (from a Bordeaux blend of varieties plus Limnio). Blanc de Blancs and Melissanthi whites can be good.

Gentilini, CEPHALONIA Boutique-scale whites from mainly indigenous varieties. Much effort, but rather variable quality for their high prices.

Domaine Hatzimichali, VIOTIA Sited near Mount Parnassus, this is probably Greece's leading wine estate, and the one which has had best success with 'international' varietals like Chardonnay, Cabernet and Merlot. Expensive, well-made wines with real freshness.

Kourtakis Producer of some of Greece's best Retsina, as well as Kouros white from Patras, a fresher-than-usual white Cretan Country Wine, a good, punchy Nemea under the brand name Kouros, and some Samos Muscat.

Samos Cooperative The source of all Samos Muscat, including that sold by other wine companies. Generally good value. Nectar is unfortified, from raisined grapes; Samos Vin Doux Naturel and Samos Doux are both fortified.

Tsantalis Good Samos Muscat, but best are the Nemea and Naoussa.

Pine time

We met Christos Lagelou by the church. It was 14 September, the celebration of the Honoured Cross in Greece, a festival during which priests hurl crosses into the sea and divers plunge after them. Then we had a coffee, then some snacks. We ate diffidently, still cloaked in British etiquette. Soon Christos was stabbing huge lumps of cheese and fat olives on the end of a fork and thrusting them into our mouths, so keen was he to see us enjoy his hospitality.

He guarded the food with a pink plastic fly swat, lunging excitedly at the small forest flies wherever they settled, on ground, table or human limb. When the struggle became too heated, his wife Lambrini took the swat from him and agitated it quietly, in diplomatic warning to both flies and husband to keep combat within seemly limits.

We drank his own retsina, drawn from a barrel and served from a jug. It smelled of the pines we could see rooted in the mountainside above us, tissue-pale in the brilliance of midday, and tasted piercing and clean.

So it should have done. From a ramshackle shed behind Christos's house comes enough resin to flavour the astonishing 24 million bottles of retsina which the largest producer in Greece, Kourtakis, sends to market annually. If Christos can't find a spare lump or two of resin, nobody can.

The resin-harvesting operation is one of classic Greek simplicity. A small cut is made in Aleppo pine trees with a double-headed pick, then a tin collecting tray is knocked into the bark with the same pick. Soon the resin begins to dribble down into the tray. Every three weeks or so, between May and October, a new cut is made a few inches above the previous, now closed, wound. And so on up the tree, which soon begins to resemble a badly laddered stocking. The resin is colourless when it first seeps from the tree, but it dries and crystallizes into sticky white lumps, like cake icing.

On arrival at the Kourtakis winery at Ritsona, north of Thebes (a two-dog town, by the way: parricide and incest must be hard to avoid there), it is mixed with freshly pressed grape juice before it begins fermenting. The heat of the ferment dissolves it. Afterwards the resin residues settle with the lees.

Almost all retsina is made from the Savatiano grape, a variety whose chief virtue is that it can tolerate the fierce, rainless Attica summer. High-yielding and low in acidity, on its own it makes dull wine. Resin, of course, is just resin — Christos confirmed that quality is standard, regardless of the exact site or size of the tree.

Yet, like the plain parents of a beautiful child, together these two elements create something rather better than either in isolation. Part of the pleasure of retsina is that the resin, like mint, creates a pseudo-cooling effect on the tongue. Even warm, it refreshes; indeed, it should never be served colder than cool. (The injuction to serve retsina well chilled is what makes it taste like thinned turps.)

Its aftertaste is one of delicate, piny bitterness, not dissimilar to the taste left by hops (which are sometimes described as resinous) in beer. It elbows Savatiano wine into acquiring a lemony lilt. It goes well with much more than dolmades; anything Mediterranean tastes better, to me, with retsina. But then, to me, retsina is more than just wine: it is one of our last unbroken sensory links with the ancient world.

Hungary

Return to the fold

Hungary's had a good year. Sales of its wines in Britain are increasing, and not simply by dint of exploiting the all-important but increasingly mediocre £2.99 market. The country's openness to Western initiatives has given us a range to choose from, and Hungary's top wines nearly always offer as much value, and a lot more excitement, than the cheapest bottles.

Bureaucratically, Hungary is preparing sensibly enough for EU membership with revised wine laws which divide the country up into 20 regions within four main geographical areas. More important in practice is the founding of *hegyközségek tanács* or wine councils based on what are known as 'interprofessions': this brings together all of those involved in wine production (growers, wineries and merchants) to fight Hungary's corner in the world rather than each other. (British agricultural production desperately needs such groupings.)

The only discordant note of the year came when mildew problems caused a 25 per cent drop in the 1995 crop. Up went grape prices, with the result that ducking the £2.99 door lintel which leads to almost half the British wine market will be harder than ever before.

As I mentioned in this Guide last year, Hungary's competitors are not only its East European neighbours, but the countries of the New World, too. This poses the sort of bifurcated challenge also faced by France's Languedoc: does Hungary lunge for the international varietal market, or should it chose — a much stonier path — the slow resuscitation of its singular indigenous wines? Economic imperatives dictate that international varietals are, for the time being, carrying the day in most regions save Tokaj. Hungarian Chardonnay can be nice enough; but anyone who cares about wine should elect to try first a Hárslevelü, a Furmint or a Kéknyelü, where such choice exists. These wines can have a wonderful richness, a passive, chewy substance to them, hidden behind pale-complexioned fruit. The old wine-trade adage 'Bulgaria for reds, Hungary for whites' still holds largely true: Hungary's whites have natural balance, softness and freshness, while the reds tend to be firmer or sharper. Use this as a guide rather than gospel, though: Hungary is full of surprises.

Tokaj

The Grand Duke's return

Tokaj lies in the northeastern corner of Hungary, where the river Bodrog unwinds amid the quiescent ruins of former volcanoes. Like Sauternes and Rhine wine, Tokaji is made from grapes (largely Furmint, with some Hárslevelü, Muskotály and Orémusz) affected by noble rot (see page 78). Harvesters separate the botrytis-affected grapes (known as *aszú*) from those unaffected or only partly affected by rot; the latter are made into a dry base wine *(szamorodni)*. Aszú is then added to the *szamorodni*, and a slow and dithering refermentation begins, traditionally in incompletely filled casks — though this 'oxidization' of Tokaji production is being tempered towards a fresher, non-oxidized modernity.

Tokaj has been flattered by a remarkable flurry of international investment since 1989, much of it from Bordeaux (see feature). In the great 1993 vintage, foreign investors bought 80 per cent of all the *aszú* available in the region. A move towards the production of non-oxidized Tokaji has been one of the main changes wrought by the investors and their winemakers; only Tokaji Renaissance and some private growers persist in producing oxidized Tokaji. The heavily oxidized style of the period since 1945 seems doomed; there may be a role, however, for the light oxidation of Tokaji as factor of complexity in the future.

How sweet the final wine is depends on how much *aszú* has been added, measured in 'tubs' *(puttonyos):* three is barely medium-dry; six is very sweet, though balanced by lively acids. *Aszú* Eszencia is sweeter still, almost pure aszú fruit, lightly fermented; while what is now called Nektar (formerly Eszencia), widely considered to prolong life even as the doctors are drawing up their invoices, is composed of the syrup (so sweet it disdains fermention) which seeps from the unmilled *aszú* berries. Tokaji flavours usually include autumn-apple notes and a dressing of tangy honey; the sweeter examples are lusciously fruited yet keenly balanced. Older, oxidized examples have a sherry-like tang.

Tokaj's historic wine estates are still in mid-renovation, and it is in any case too soon for post-Communist Tokaji to be marketed. Tokaji wines at present on sale under domain labels are usually selected purchases from former Tokaji Wine Trust stocks; only the table wines post-date the arrival of the foreigners. Look out, though, for the first 1993s when they reach the market over the coming year or two. All Tokaji is sold in half-litre bottles.

Disznókö A 130-hectare first-growth estate near Mád owned by AXA Millésimes, a French insurance company, and overseen by Jean-Michel Cazes of Château Lynch-Bages (see page 73). Full, leafy Furmint and soft Orémusz (a Furmint-Bouvier cross) leads fresh new table-wine releases; selected Tokaji includes a superbly balanced 1988 6 puttonyos. Wines in preparation very promising (see feature).

Edes Term for *szamorodni* Tokaji sweetened by passing it over ground *aszú* paste and aged in barrel for two years. Unaged version is called *forditas*.

Forditas see **Edes.**

Hétszölö This 45-hectare vineyard on loess, rather than the usual clay, is now owned by another French insurance company, Grand Millésimes de France; the property includes the former Imperial State Cellars. Extensive replanting in process. Dessewffy is the name used for purchases from the Tokaji Wine Trust, including an intense 1988 4 puttonyos and a fresh 1983 5 puttonyos.

Château Megyer Yet another French insurance company, G.A.N., with 80 hectares of land formerly in the possession of the Rakoczi family. First releases of Furmint table wine are pure, rich in extract and intense. Jean-Michel Arcaute of Château Clinet (see page 69) manages, and Michel Rolland consults.

Oremus A property purchased by Vega Sicilia (see **Spain**). The '93 Mandulás Furmint is a strange sour-buttery wine.

Château Pajzos A property bought by a private consortium from Bordeaux led by Jean-Michel Arcaute and Michel Rolland (see **Château Megyer**). First table-wine releases and young Tokaji promising.

Royal Tokay Wine Company A joint venture between Western interests (spearheaded by Peter Vinding-Diers, with backing from Hugh Johnson among others) and 63 growers sited near the village of Mád. Wines are sold, where appropriate, under cru names (some of which were classified in 1700). The 1990 Birsalmás 5 puttonyos is superb.

Szaraz Term for dry versions of szamorodni wine.

Tokaji Renaissance (Tokaj Kereskedöház) Previously holding a monopoly position in Tokaj, the former Tokaji Wine Trust or Borkombinát is in the process of privatisation. Large stocks of older wines are variable in quality, but include many (Museum wines) that are great. Tokaji Renaissance continues to make its wines by oxidative processes.

Vintages:
1995 ★★★; 1994 ★; 1993 ★★★★; 1992 ★★; 1991 ★; 1990 ★★★; 1989 ★★; 1988 ★★★; 1987 ★; 1986 ★★; 1985 ★★.

Specialist retailers:
Berry Bros, Fortnum & Mason and Lea & Sandeman all have good Tokaji ranges.

Other Hungarian Wines
Keeping its promises

Most Hungarian wine comes from the country's Great Plain (Alföld), a broad and monotonous swathe of sandy land occupying the centre of the country. Better quality wines – and among them most Hungarian wine exports – are sourced from hillier sites to the north of the country (around Gyöngyös, Debrö, Eger and, further west, Mór), along the shores of Lake Balaton in Western Hungary (Badacsony), on the Austrian border (Sopron), and to the south (Mecsek and Villány).

Reds from native varieties such as the Kadarka (Bulgaria's Gamza) and the Kékfrankos (Austria's Blaufränkisch) tend to be light, as is Hungarian Pinot Noir; Merlot and Cabernet (the former has been in Hungary longer) produce deeper, plummier, grippier reds. They can also be thin and sharp. It is Hungary's whites which provide most intrigue: Furmint, Szürkebarát (Pinot Gris) and Kéknyelü, especially from Badacsony, can be spicy, full, fat and earthy. The Ezerjó variety produces perfumed wines at Mór; Hárslevelü is at its most complex and sweetly expressive away from Tokaj at Debrö. Olaszrizling (Welschriesling) can be fruitier in Hungary than elsewhere. In the main, what British supermarkets buyers are looking for from Hungary is Chardonnay; these may not have much Hungarian character, but their levels of soft, fresh fruit often make them a better bet than cheap hot-climate Chardonnay. Also proving popular on British wine-shop shelves are inexpensive, doughy-spicy whites – from Gewürztraminer, Muscat and the native Irsai Oliver.

Balatonboglár Excellent wines have been produced at this Balaton winery by Kym Milne M.W. under the Chapel Hill label including spicy Irsai Oliver and fine Chardonnay. Cabernet Sauvignon, by contrast, has lacked wealth of flavour. The German Henkell sparkling-wine company now has the major shareholding.

Château Bataapati see European Wine Producers Group.

Cool Ridge see Nagyréde

Danubiana Hungarian subsidiary of St Ursula (see **Rheinpfalz**) producing clean, well fruited wines in a number of locations. St Ursula purchased the Gyöngyös winery in early 1995 and has invested £1.5 million in it since then.

Deer Leap see Neszmély

Egervin Mediocre quality, though the region has great potential.

Egri Bikavér Or **'Bull's Blood'**. A light, raspberryish wine (made from Cabernet, Kadarka and – mainly – Kékfrankos) which rarely lives up to the fiery, thick-necked promise of its name.

European Wine Producers Group The EWT includes among its shareholders Piero Antinori and, in a joint venture with the Volgyseg Nepe cooperative, is producing crisp, fresh varietals from 100 hectares at Château Bataapati at Mocseny in Szekszárd (near Mecsek).

Tibor G'al As winemaker for Ornellaia (see **Central Italy**), G'al should know what to do with good fruit (from Eger). Oak muddied the fruit in his first release of Chardonnay, but the Kékfrankos and Cabernet were smoky, rasping, and challengingly good.

Gyöngyös Winery in the north where Hugh Ryman and on-site winemaker Adrian Wing has galvanised the locals. Initial Chardonnay and Sauvignon was over-sweet, but latest releases have a firmer foundation of fruit. Will new investment from St Ursula bring further improvements? See also **Danubiana.**

Hungarovin Massive trading house sited near Budapest, now owned by Henkell of Germany. Generally dismal standard as yet, though Balatonboglár (q.v.) link and £600,000 investment in Pazonand winery may begin to bring quality dividends.

Mecsekalji see Neszmély.

Nagyréde Fresh varietals (including the crisp, salty Zenit) from this cooperative in Matra mountains. Balanced, creamy oaked '94 Cool Ridge Chardonnay from Kym Milne M.W. was superb value, and local winemaker Benjamin Bardos's '95 Pinot Gris is fresh and chewy.

Neszmély Massive investment in this cooperative north of Mór on the Slovenian border has helped create some excellent white wines from Hungarian and Western varietals, formerly made with help from Nick Butler but now a purely Hungarian act. Safeway's River Duna Irsai Oliver and Special Cuvée Sauvignon Blanc are both very good, as is Waitrose's Deer Leap range of whites, while Asda's Mecsekalji wines offer sound value.

River Duna see Neszmély.

River Route Danube-basin wines from the Carl Reh group, with input from Britain's Angela Muir M.W., include a juicy Merlot from the Szekszárd winery.

Villany-Siklos This winery is a source of softly fruity Cabernet and Merlot (used by Safeway and Asda among others), some of it made by Nick Butler. Reserve wines can be richly chewy.

Vintages:
1995 ★★; 1994 ★★★; 1993 ★★★; 1992 ★★; 1991 ★★; 1990 ★★★★; 1989 ★★★;
1988 ★★★; 1987 ★; 1986 ★★; 1985 ★★★.

Farewell, potato man

Up until then, the weather had been dull and cloudy. On the last evening, Tokaj began to resemble my mental picture: a peach-pink dusk, sturdy yellow houses luminous in the early darkness, night vapours milky on the black river Bodrog. The dogs of Tokaj barked to each other across the vineyards, delinquents among them chasing cars and lorries down the street with suicidal exuberance. Goods trains groaned. There was only one pedestrian, my dinner companion and I apart, on the main street. He leant down to examine a brass plaque on a wooden door as we passed him.

I'd always wanted to come here, ever since I saw the picture in Johnson's *World Atlas of Wine* (substituted, alas, in the latest editions in deference to Hungarian sensitivities) which showed casks being trundled up a pitted track by horsecart amid thick mists, while a potato-shaped man wearing many layers of rough clothing and a brown woolly hat gazes at the camera with a look of undisguised distrust. In an obscure way, the photograph seemed to sum up the lure of Tokaj: the only one of history's great wines to fall within the ambit of both west (Vienna, Paris) and east (Moscow, St Petersburg); a relic of the past grown, by its remoteness and the fallibilities of communism, into a mournful disrepair.

I got there in the end, anyway. Just in time to find the world of the potato man and the pitted track disappear completely. The historic estates of the Tokaji region have almost all been sold or leased to foreign investors, most of them French. The former owner of these estates, the Borkombinát (now known as Tokaji Renaissance) has hung onto one estate only; there are also several cooperatives.

The vast majority of the region's vineyards are owned by weekend growers.

Stylistically, too, the wines familiar to the potato man are disappearing into history. Tokaji made the Borkombinát way had lots of oxidation and lots of pasteurisation. This made it safe and simple; the intrinsic quality of the raw materials ensured passably high quality.

The first thing the foreign investors did was work out that without generous oxidation and repeated pasteurisation, Tokaji would taste a lot better. Proof? At about midday on September 26th, standing in the tasting room of the extraordinary shell-like winery which the Hungarian architect Ekler Deszo has constructed for French-owned Disznókö, I had it. The 1993 Aszú Eszencia produced by Disznókö was one of the most powerfully and beautifully flavoured sweet wines I have ever tasted. It will enthral drinkers as yet unborn long after I have been reduced to a puff of crematorium smoke. It is great.

The 1993 vintage was a fine if chaotic one in Tokaj. That Aszú Eszencia, and an equally good 1993 Szamorodni Edes and 6 Puttonyos Aszú, will not be available for a while yet; what has been available for long enough to have become Unoaked White Wine of the Year in the previous edition of this guide was the 1993 Disznókö Furmint, a dry white wine of remarkable substance.

My wife, who is Polish, was startled to hear that the French had been able to acquire outright the choicest morsels of a stretch of soil so cherished by Hungarians that it is mentioned in their national anthem; doubtless there are Hungarians who feel the same way. Yet the French revere both land and agriculture. I suspect what has happened will prove to be the speediest way to return Hungary's prime vineyard region to former greatness.

India

A jug of sparkling wine

India's constitution has as a declared aim the total prohibition of alcohol, but the country's enthusiasm for whisky alone makes this an increasingly distant prospect. Wine-production, however, is rudimentary in the subcontinent. Most (70 per cent) of the country's grapes are grown in Western Maharashtra, and almost all of them are destined for table use; Ugni Blanc and Chardonnay, however, are grown on limestone slopes near Narayangaon for a surprisingly successful champagne-method sparkling wine. The dry version is sold as Omar Khayyam, and a sweeter one as Marquise de Pompadour. Two table wines — the Chardonnay-based Chhabri and the Cabernet Sauvignon–based Anarkali — imported to the UK for Indian restaurant use are also grown in Maharashtra.

Israel

Scaling the heights

Now here's a perplexing situation. The land of Israel staggers beneath its burden of history and myth, and much of that intoxicating, scripturally sanctified baggage is wine-sodden. What Christian would not like to drink the wine of Canaa or Galilee after a thoughtful afternoon among the splintery, fissured olives of Gethsemane? What Jew would prefer a French kosher wine to one from the land from which (according to the Book of Numbers) Moses' spies returned bearing an enormous cluster of grapes suspended from a pole? Only the Palestinians, among the peoples of the place, feel no thrill of historical emotion when confronted by a glass of its wine.

Yet most of Israel is not, as it happens, very well suited to the production of good wine. It's flat and hot. The country's best wine, unquestionably, comes from the part taken by force from Syria in 1967: Golan Heights. This upland region of senescent volcanoes is cooler than the rest of Israel, and its fruit fresher, cleaner, more vibrant than that of the lowlands. If the Golan Heights are returned to Syria, some of the Middle East's best wines will be lost.

Kosher wine strictures are too elaborate to describe in detail here. Of their religious necessity we need not concern ourselves; in practical terms, however, they make the production of good wine harder than it might otherwise be — by delaying the correct moment for harvesting on some occasions, emptying the winery of personnel on the Sabbath, and putting commercial checks on wine businesses. All *mevushal* kosher wines have been pasteurized, which no good wine should ever be. With patience and a supple-minded supervising rabbi, however, kosher wine can still be good wine, as the Golan Heights Winery has proved.

Askalon Soft, raisiny reds sold under the Ben Ami and Segal labels.

Baron Courageous Jonathan Tishbi, the only grower ever to quit Carmel and go it alone, produces excellent Dry Muscat and Sauvignon Blanc, and a light but penetrating Cabernet Sauvignon. Baron, Tishbi and Maestro are the labels used.

Carmel Carmel is a giant cooperative which produces 90 per cent of all Israeli wine. Much of it is, from the wine-lover's point of view, dire *kiddush* (sacramental) wine, like Palwin No.4 and the rest. These are made from mixtures of must and wine, often from *labrusca* varieties. Yet in recent years, increasing emphasis has been put on dry varietal wines, organised into three strata: basic varietals (mainly sold in Britain as own-label wines — look out for Petite Syrah and Dry Muscat), the Carmel Vineyards range, and finally the Rothschild range, from which the Cabernet Sauvignons can be broodingly good. Kadmon, a sweet solera-aged fortified wine from Carignan, is wonderful, though hard to find.

Golan Heights Winery Israel's coolish-climate pace-setters. Excellent, Californian-style winemaking through three ranges: Golan at the bottom, then Gamla, with Yarden used for the best wines. Yarden Cabernets can be captivatingly soft and chocolatey, while Merlots are a little brisker: both are deep, fine wines which, despite their youth, suggest that the Golan is a *terroir* of real winemaking interest. Sauvignon Blanc and Chardonnay are less successful to my mind, but pleasant and personable wines nonetheless.

Italy

The curse of the gods

Poor Italy. It must be beginning to wonder exactly what it has done to deserve such retribution from the skies. If there are two more bad harvests in 1996 and 1997, the country can claim classical, seven-year-plague status.

The last great year in Italy was 1990. The 1991, 1992, 1993 and 1994 vintages were all, for Italy's key quality-wine regions, relatively disappointing: cool or rain-spoiled. Nonetheless in spring 1995 things suddenly looked very bright for Italy: exchange-rate swings meant that its wines became far more appealing than for some time for 'price-sensitive' markets like Britain's, while French nuclear tests in the South Pacific meant that Italian wine quickly replaced French in markets of relative wealth and environmental sensitivity, like Germany and Scandinavia. Demand, in other words, soared.

With consummately malevolent timing, Italy then had its smallest harvest for decades: just 52 million hectolitres (compared, for example, to 86 million hectolitres in 1979). The shortfall on the previous year's figure was the equivalent of more than twice Australia's production. The country was shafted.

Poor flowering and a bizarre cold, wet August were responsible; hailstorms in Barolo reduced crop levels further there. Ironically, what little fruit actually came through all this then flourished in an Indian summer of great generosity: 1995 quality in Barolo and Chianti is the best since 1990. Southern Italy, normally immune to the climatic vagaries of the northern and central parts of the country, was also hit badly by the wet and unseasonal August – at a moment, one might add, when general quality (thanks to flying winemakers and local entrepreneurs capitalizing on a thirsty market) was gaining altitude rapidly.

Grape prices rose; wine prices are now rising. The market advances of the last year or two are on hold. In churches all over Italy, winegrowers are saying quiet but heartfelt prayers for the 1996 harvest.

The way it was

Italy was named Oenotria by the Ancient Greeks; in Plato's day, therefore, it was already defined by the ubiquity and profusion of trained vines throughout its territory. The Italians, unlike the French, do not challenge, worry and interrogate what they have been given; they get on with enjoying it. Thus it was that, during the centuries when France was engineering and tooling its vineyards and their wines towards a provisional perfection, Italy carried on harvesting grapes, fermenting must and drinking wine as one of a number of simple, innocent agricultural activities. Barolo is now recognized as one of the world's great wines; its vines shared their soil with rows of wheat until the late 50s. Even today, you will find remote parts of Italy where vines are trained up trees at the edge of small-holdings, as they have been for thousands of years.

Since the end of World War Two, therefore, Italy has had a deal of catching up to do. Broadly speaking, the state of play at present is that Italians produce much good red wine and little good white. Northern Italian reds tend to be boisterous and aggressive; they are nearly always high in acidity, and often high in tannin, too. Southern Italian reds are at best sweeter and fuller, though poor, thin reds vastly outnumber good ones. Italian whites are rarely, nowadays, badly made; they simply lack character, which Italians for some reason view as misplaced in a white wine yet essential in a red.

Wine law

As in Germany, it is big producers with political clout who have written Italy's wine law, much to the detriment of smaller, high-quality wine growers. In theory, Italy's best wines fall in the DOCG (Denominazione de Origine Controllata e Garantita) category, then comes DOC (Denominazione de Origine Controllata), then IGT (Indicazione Geografica Tipica) and finally Vino da Tavola. Further details, such as grape variety and vineyard name, may be included in the top three categories. In practice, however, many of Italy's best wines still appear as Vino da Tavola – a category in which they found themselves under the old wine regime because they failed to conform to often unimaginative DOC strictures. In some places, new DOCs are being created to accommodate the more famous former 'super-Vini da Tavola': Langa Rosso, covering the Barolo and Barbaresco areas, is an example. You should also bear in mind that DOCG does not, despite its name, guarantee quality – much atrocious Chianti, for example, is DOCG. As ever, the producer's name is the surest guide.

Italians, finally, are often overly obsessed with the image and packaging of their wines, and inadequately scrupulous about the quality of what goes inside. Expensive, tapered glass bottles with minimalist labels may contain mild little wines.

Northern Italy
Unearthing the truffles

November is the time to go: thick fog turns an already chaotic landscape of hillocks, cuts and gulleys into a zone of moist, milky mystery out of which poplars and people loom and into which they fade with eerie facility. Each restaurant displays its sweat-scented treasure of truffles; each cellar hides its shocking cache of dark purple, plum-perfumed wine. The fields, now, are wan and chill; the light of summer is concentrated in the private places where humans hide a season's beneficence.

This is Piedmont, the home of what, for me, are unquestionably Italy's greatest wines. Nebbiolo is the grape used for Barolo and Barbaresco, as well as for the mountain wines of Valle d'Aosta (Carema and Gattinara are most widely seen) and for Lombardy's Valtellina. No other red grape on earth combines perfume with tannic cragginess as Nebbiolo can. Failed Nebbiolo wine is that which omits to fill these two extremes with the flavours of dark black fruits; successful Nebbiolo wine does so abundantly.

Dolcetto is a sweeter, softer grape variety; Barbera is more vigorous, more acidic, a furiously energetic wine in the mouth, shivering and fissuring, charged with flavours of raspberries and currants. Moscato provides deliciously grapy-sweet light relief. There are dozens of other varieties, too; see page 30 for books which will help guide you around all of them, and around Italy's bewildering maze of DOC names.

Trentino-Alto Adige marks Italy's portion of the Tyrol: a mountainous, German-speaking zone of light reds based on the Schiava (Trollinger) variety and deeper reds based on international varieties like Cabernet, as well as dark, local Lagrein and the bitter-sweet, iron-stiffened Teroldego Rotaliano. More important in the Italian context, though, are the region's salty-fresh white wines, from Chardonnay, Riesling, Pinot Grigio and other varieties.

Friuli, further east, is the only part of Italy whose white wines are of international significance – thanks to their pungent varietal style and deep, sometimes succulent fruit characters. These attainments are clear to all; Friulian whites as a consequence are not cheap. The best are generally sold under the Collio DOC; Grave del Friuli is less pricey, but can also be good. Sauvignon Blanc does well here, as do Pinot Bianco and Pinot Grigio; Tocai Friuliano, interestingly, is said to be synonymous with Sauvignonasse. If so, it gives more intriguing, longer-lasting, blossom-perfumed flavours in the green Friulian hills than it ever does in Chile's hot, fertile vineyards.

The hills of Venice's back country, finally, yield some of the best light red wines in the world. Good Valpolicella is a swoon of cherry-kernel scent and crisp cherry fruit: deliciousness incarnate. Recioto is a sweet, flavour-thickened version made by drying bunches of grapes before vinification, and Amarone the dry, strong, bitter-edged, philosopher's account of that. Ripasso Valpolicella is made by fermenting ordinary Valpolicella on the skins left over after Recioto or Amarone production. Bardolino is a light, near-rosé equivalent of Valpolicella, best quaffed *in situ;* Veneto's white is Soave, about which little complimentary can be said save for its own, honeyed Recioto versions. Lugana is a better, fuller white from close by, just over the border into Lombardy.

Northern Italy is where, logically enough, the country's best sparkling wines come from. 'Talento' is a new name intended to provide those made by the *méthode champenoise* (or, as it's known in Italy, the *metodo classico*) with a common sales banner.

Allegrini, Valpolicella Fine, single-estate range. Palazzo alle Torre is an almost tough-flavoured ripasso.

Elio Altare, Barolo A range of consistent excellence: deep wines, yet never fierce. Barolo Arborina is intense, sweet-fruited; Vigna Arborina is a barrique-aged Nebbiolo and Vigna Larigi a barrique-aged Barbera.

Anselmi, Soave Barrel-fermented Capitel Croce gives Soave a lemony, buttery style; good Recioto dei Capitelli.

Alasia, Piedmont Martin Shaw and on-site winemaker Matthew Thompson producing a range of varietals in conjunction with Claudio Manera of Araldica (q.v.): Chardonnay in oaked and unoaked styles, Arneis, Cortese del Piemonte, Barbera, Dolcetto and, most attractively of all, dry Muscaté Sec.

Araldica, Piedmont Large, 1,000-member consortium of three cooperatives. Ceppi Storici (old vines) Barbera can be moreish, though the bad weather of recent vintages has thinned the pleasure a bit.

Matteo Ascheri, Barolo Warmly oaky, accessible, international style of Barolo. Bric Mileui is a lavishly oaked Barbera-Nebbiolo blend.

Bava, Asti Good Piedmontese specialities, including oddball varietals.

Bertani, Valpolicella One of the most reliable of the large producers. Old Amarones are very fine.

Borgo Conventi see Puiatti

Borgogno, Barolo Brooding, old-style Barolo, often given long ageing.

Bidoli, Friuli Sound wines (such as vinous Ca'Pradai Chardonnay for Asda) made by Chile-based Gaetane Carron.

Bolla, Soave Dull in the main, though Bolla produces a good (but not cheap) Amarone and Valpolicella Classico Jago.

Boscaini, Valpolicella Large company, but generally good standards.

Ca' del Bosco, Franciacorta Estate near Brescia producing Italy's top-priced sparkling wines, lively red Franciacorta and a concentrated Bordeaux blend called Maurizio Zanella (the name of its shy, retiring creator).

Casa Girelli, Trentino Large range. Pleasant, unexceptional I Mesi and Canaletto whites but good bitter, ferrous Teroldego Rotaliano, fresh crisp Fontella Sangiovese delle Marche and Monte S.Urbano Amarone. Veduta wines (from Puglia) include a neutral white but a fresh, plummy red.

Càvit, Trentino Excellent cooperative grouping marketing Trentino's generally affordable and flavoursome varietals. Earthy Merlot and fruity, rounded Teroldega Rotaliano worth looking out for.

Ceretto, BAROLO Elegant, accessible, urbane style.

Pio Cesare, BAROLO Sound rather than exciting wines at present, though older vintages can be very good.

Domenico Clerico, BAROLO Young virtuoso producing Baroli of fine balance, exuberant Dolcetto, and barrique-aged Nebbiolo Arté.

Collavini, COLLIO Reliable merchant house, now making and marketing the noteworthy estate wines of Conte Attems (such as dark Cabernet Franc).

Aldo Conterno, BAROLO Grand range from a master winemaker: the Gérard Chave of Barolo. Gran Bussia is the top Barolo (best years only); Barbera Conca Tre Pile and Dolcetto Bussia Soprana both definitive.

Giacomo Conterno, BAROLO Monfortino and Cascina Francia are both large-scale, tannic, traditionally fashioned wines which age superbly.

Conterno Fantino, BAROLO Spicy, mid-weight wines. Monpra is smooth and plummy.

Enofriulia see Puiatti

Fontanafredda, BAROLO Graceful, expressive, tenor style of Barolo; consistent.

Gaja, BARBARESCO Expensive, much sought-after wines from both traditional local varieties and international varieties. Single-vineyard Barabareschi are the greatest wines in his range, especially Sorì Tildìn: power with elegance. The estate has recently been increased in size with acquisitions in the Cerequio vineyard (Gromis). See also **Pieve di Santa Restitua** in **Central Italy.**

Bruno Giacosa, BAROLO Massive wines in traditional style – don't hurry.

Giordano Large producer turning out creative supermarket blends (like Il Caberno, a Nebbiolo-Cabernet).

GIV Massive conglomerate, including Lamberti and Santi in Valpolicella; Folonari near Brescia; Nino Negri in Valtellina; Melini and Conti-Serristori in Chianti; Fontana Candida in Lazio and Bigi in Orvieto. Some good wines (like the '94 Sangiovese from Fiordaliso stocked by Waitrose); many dull ones.

Gravner, COLLIO Cleanly made, deeply flavoured wines made near Slovenia.

Guerrieri–Rizzardi, BARDOLINO I have always been disappointed by these thinly flavoured wines.

Franz Haas, ALTO ADIGE Intense varietals from an intense man.

Jermann, COLLIO Expensive, lushly fruity wines outside the DOC framework. Vintage Tunina is a five-varietal blend; Vinnae brings Ribolla together with Riesling and Malvasia. 'Where the Dreams have No End' is a barrel-fermented Chardonnay. Creamily good but overpriced.

Lageder, ALTO ADIGE Scrupulous, innovative producer of fine single-vineyard varietals and concentrated, fresh-flavoured Löwengang Cabernet and discreetly wooded Chardonnay. Basic Lageder wines are less challenging.

Maculan, BREGANZE Thoroughly interesting range, peaking with one of Italy's greatest dessert wines, the unclassified Torcolato, a barrique-aged recioto

Vespaiola of deliciously spicy allusiveness. Acininobili is from botrytis-affected grapes, and Dindarello is a dessert Moscato.

Marchese de Gresy, BARBARESCO Light, elegant, fragrant style.

Giuseppe Mascarello, BAROLO Wayward, impish producer of fine reds, especially Pian Romualdo Dolcetto and good-value Nebbiolo.

Geoff Merrill Australian who has produced some decent whites with GIV for Sainsbury's. Reds disappointing, though.

Nino Negri, VALTELLINA Scented, high-vineyard Nebbiolos which ease back on tannin. See **GIV**.

Pieropan, SOAVE As good as Soave gets, though I still feel it is only with recioto (here Le Colombare) that Soave really gets interesting.

Pojer & Sandri, TRENTINO Producers of carefully crafted non-DOC wines as well as superb grappa (distilled pomace).

Produttori del Barbaresco, BARBARESCO Quality-conscious cooperative whose wines genuinely rank with the best of the region.

Prunotto, BAROLO Barbera Pian Romualdo is my favourite wine from this producer – for its unusual roundedness; the rest of the range is good.

Puiatti, COLLIO Well-made varietals of pure, non-oaked style. Enofriulia and Villa del Borgo are less expensive ranges.

Ratti, BAROLO Pure flavours from well-sited vineyards.

Quintarelli, VALPOLICELLA Quintarelli's painstaking, artisanal methods produce astonishingly characterful (and expensive, and sometimes faulty) wines.

Le Ragose, VALPOLICELLA Fine-featured wines from high-sited vineyards.

Josetta Safirio, BAROLO Ghastly labels (with gnomes on); good wines.

Santa Margherita, VALPOLICELLA Large, consistent range; also controls Kettmeir in Alto Adige. Deep, savoury Malbec (spelt Malbech) from Veneto Orientale worth looking out for.

Schiopetto, COLLIO Fine, almost steely varietals responding well to age.

Serègo Alighieri, VALPOLICELLA The elegant wine of Dante's descendant, Pieralvise Serègo Alighieri, made by Masi and aged in cherrywood casks.

Tedeschi, VALPOLICELLA Exemplary range, worth every penny of the modest prices asked. Capitel San Rocco Ripasso is as richly, chewily fruity as Valpolicella can get.

Terre del Barolo, BAROLO Cooperative producing worthwhile basic Barolo at a reasonable price.

Tiefenbrunner, ALTO ADIGE Aromatic yet firm, full, mineral-salty white varietals include fine dry Goldmuskateller and the mountain-top Feldmarschall Müller-Thurgau.

Vajra, BAROLO Brilliantly controlled, polished wines. Dolcetto Coste e Fossati is multidimensioned, and dry Freisa weird and fascinating.

Venegazzù Unclassified mid-weight Bordeaux blend, softer than much Cabernet from the Veneto. Black label version is from old vines.

Vietti, BAROLO Unshowy but classic wines.

Roberto Voerzio, BAROLO Plump, fruit-drenched wines from different sites: Cerequio particularly good. Lush Dolcetto and Nebbiolo-Barbera blend Vigna La Serra both good value.

Zonin, GAMBELLARA Large, pan-Italian merchant house with generally reliable standards. Also owns the exciting Barboursville estate in Virginia, USA.

Vintages:
1995 ★★; 1994 ★★; 1993 ★★; 1992 ★; 1991 ★; 1990 ★★★★; 1989 ★★★★; 1988 ★★★; 1987 ★★; 1986 ★★★; 1985 ★★★★.

Specialist retailers:
Enotria-Winecellars is the great specialist. There are also good Italian ranges at John Armit, Laytons, Lea & Sandeman, La Réserve and by mail-order from Adnams.

Central Italy
Running the gauntlet

Sometimes I'm not sure whether I like Chianti or not. There have been Chiantis, of course, which I have enjoyed intensely: young dandies with delicate coffeeish wafts of aroma and bright thrusting flavours of cranberries and cherries, crisply turned out in their suits of acids and bitters and little tannic neckties. Or the older, wiser wines, the ones which have slowly found a dry balance, a soft warmth, a delicate repertoire of late summer allusions. But it's a wine I always approach with trepidation in tastings, especially those laid on by supermarkets. Cheap Chianti is the worst red wine to be widely imported into Britain: graceless and bony, howling with untempered acidity, shivering in its rags of thin fruit. Do people really enjoy modern, inexpensive, industrial Chianti? Or is it, like the watery bacon people buy, the bland frozen meals, the stale fish, the fluffy bread, the courgettes which taste of drains, the dreary, mealy potatoes and the tinned soups which resemble washing-up water, a giant con?

Until at least half of all Chianti is declassified and sold off as cut-price table wine, any notion that DOCG truly guarantees quality is as worthwhile as supposing wealth guarantees happiness.

There is more to Central Italy, of course, than Chianti. On the Adriatic side of the Apennines lies Emilia-Romagna, home to an exciting fizzy bitter red wine called Lambrusco. The Lambrusco popular in Britain, by contrast, is a sweet white soda-pop with a little alcohol in; authentic Lambrusco is hard to find here. The Marches, south of Emilia-Romagna, is best known for a good though sharp white called Verdicchio, some fresh and lively Sangiovese and an often excellent, deep-flavoured red called Rosso Cònero. Whereas Chianti is made from Sangiovese, Rosso Cònero is made from Montepulciano, in some ways a grape variety of greater potential. It is Montepulciano, too, which produces the best wines of Abruzzo and Molise, south of the Marches.

East of the Apennines, meanwhile, lie Tuscany, Umbria and Lazio. Sangiovese dominates Tuscany (even for the confusingly named Vino Nobile de Montepulciano, Montepulciano here being a place name rather than grape variety). There are, however, many clones of Sangiovese; one of the best is that grown around Montalcino and used for Brunello di Montalcino and its little brother Rosso, giving wines of easier natural balance than much Chianti, though their tannins often demand long cellaring. Chianti itself is zoned; Chianti Classico and Rufino have perhaps the most exciting potential, variably realised. International grape varieties are now grown in Tuscany, and these produce all the region's worthwhile white wines and a number of the best reds (for there is nothing at all wrong with Tuscany's superb sites and soils). Vin Santo is an oxidised, sweet or dry wine made from local white grapes (Malvasia, Trebbiano or Grechetto) hung up to dry. The resulting semi-raisins are then fermented in barrels in attics, with unpredictable results. Good vin santo will always be very expensive, arguably more expensive than its quality can ever warrant; there is now a DOC for it (Vin Santo del Chianti Classico), including a rosé version (Occhio di Pernice) which includes at least 50 per cent Sangiovese. Umbria's best known wine is the bland dry white Orvieto; Lazio's the bland dry white Frascati.

Altesino, Brunello di Montalcino   Fine wines of rich constitution. Cab-Sangiovese, Alte d'Altesi good value, full of bitter chocolate and berries.

Argiano, Brunello di Montalcino Improving wines; good value.

Avignonesi, Vino Nobile Wines made and packaged with huge flair. In addition to poised Vino Nobile, there is a Merlot which combines ripeness and firmness, expressive Chardonnay, and a Cabernet-plus-local-varieties blend called Grifi. Avignonesi vin santo, too, is definitive.

Badia a Coltibuono, Chianti Classico Old vines and low yields combine to produce deeply flavoured Chianti which ages well. Sangioveto (pure barrique-aged Sangiovese) is unapproachable in youth, rewarding later. Sella de Buscone is an oaky Chardonnay.

Barbi, Brunello di Montalcino Great wines in '60s and until the mid-'70s, then a disappointing run until '88, which marked a return to form.

Barone Cornacchia, Abruzzo Muscular Montepulciano d'Abruzzo, including fine Vigna Le Coste.

Bigi, Orvieto Large merchant house, now part of GIV (see **Northern Italy**). Marrano, an oaked Grechetto, is Bigi's most interesting wine.

Biondi-Santi, Brunello di Montalcino The estate which created the DOC, famous for both high prices and semi-commercial stocks of antique bottles. Winemaking during the 1970s produced unlovely, over-tannic yet weakly fruited wines; there were improvements during the 80s, however, and recent releases have been of wines of intensity and refinement.

Boscarelli, Vino Nobile Well-made rich wines.

Brolio, Chianti Classico Famous estate in a good site, but disappointing wines until recently, when (under English direction) things began to look up.

Cantina Tollo, ABRUZZO   Fruity cooperative-produced Montepulciano; also under Colle Secco label. Recently inconsistent.

Capezzana, CARMIGNANO   Leading producer of this herby Sangiovese-Cabernet blend, whose history stretches back to the eighteenth century. Barco Reale is a lighter version; Ghiaie della Furba is a Cab-Merlot blend. Good vin santo, too.

Caparzo, BRUNELLO DI MONTALCINO   Winery specialising in shorter maceration periods for a softer, almost creamy style. Personal experiment shows that the wines still age well: an '81 Rosso di Montalcino I'd cellared for a decade was superb in '95. La Casa is top wine.

Caprai, MONTEFALCO   An obscure, possibly native Umbrian, red grape called Sagrantino produces characterful if rough-shod wines in the Montefalco area, including Recioto-like sweet versions. Caprai is the leading producer.

Castellare, CHIANTI CLASSICO   Well-made Chianti; I Sodi di San Niccolò brings Sangiovese interestingly together with Malvasia Nera.

Castell'in Villa, CHIANTI CLASSICO   Sturdy stuff.

Castello della Sala, ORVIETO   Antinori-owned property producing an intriguing, experimental range which suggests Orvieto may have better things to offer.

Castello di Ama, CHIANTI CLASSICO   Concentrated but sometimes sharp wines with lots of oak.

Castello dei Rampolla, CHIANTI CLASSICO   Consistent, earthy Chianti of softer style than many.

Castello di Volpaia, CHIANTI CLASSICO   Expressive, supple, mid-weight Chianti.

Castello Vicchiomaggio, CHIANTI CLASSICO   English-owned property producing sound, savoury wines.

Cavacchioli, LAMBRUSCO   Good real Lambrusco (including the lively Vigna del Cristo Lambrusco di Sorbara).

Cecchi, CHIANTI   Large merchant house; occasional average-to-fair supplies to supermarkets and others large customers.

Cesari, ROMAGNA   Decent fruity Sangiovese di Romagna.

Chiarli, LAMBRUSCO   Merchant house with some exciting real Lambrusco brands, such as the single-vineyard Tenuta Generale Cialdina.

Col d'Orcia, BRUNELLO DI MONTALCINO   Classic age-worthy style.

Colle Secco see Cantina Tollo.

Colli di Catone, FRASCATI   Jazzy labels; good wines, with some of the fugitive white-almond character than makes me prefer Frascati (albeit marginally) to Orvieto and Soave, the other two members of Italy's great dull white triumvirate.

Conti Costanti, BRUNELLO DI MONTALCINO   Small production; intense flavours.

Felsina-Berardenga, CHIANTI CLASSICO   Deep-flavoured Chianti with a sweetness of fruit that is most unusual – and most welcome. Fontalloro, too, is soft and approachable for a pure barrique-aged Sangiovese.

Fontana Candida, FRASCATI Huge producer, now part of GIV (see **Northern Italy**). Single vineyard Santa Teresa is the most interesting wine of a dull bunch.

Fontodi, CHIANTI CLASSICO Exciting, spicy wines; Flaccianello is one of the best of all the oaky, pure Sangiovese wines.

Geografico, CHIANTI CLASSICO Try-harder co-op producing vibrant.

Graziano, LAMBRUSCO Top producer of boutique Lambrusco (it exists!).

Dino Illuminati, ABRUZZO Deep, well-structured, good-value Montepulciano.

Isole e Olena, CHIANTI CLASSICO Innovative estate whose creamy Chardonnay shows how good the region could be for white wines, given worthwhile varieties. Chianti, Cabernet Sauvignon, Syrah and vin santo all pure, fresh and scented; varietal Sangiovese Cepparello only produced in best years.

Lisini, BRUNELLO DI MONTALCINO Back on form after a bad patch.

Lungarotti, TORGIANO Dominant producer in this Umbrian DOC for Chianti-style blends, which results in softer, gentler wines with scents of supple leather. Large range includes Cabernet, Pinot Grigio and Chardonnay, but quality has lost its former edge.

Di Majo Norante, MOLISE The region's only private producer, making warmly rustic Montepulciano and a range of other wines.

Marchese de Frescobaldi, CHIANTI RUFINA Large, ancient, noble house with eight different properties led by Castello di Nipozzano, which includes the fragrant wine of the Montesodi vineyard. Pomino is a sub-zone of high land chiefly in Frescobaldi ownership whose DOC contains enough varietal leeway to get Chardonnay and Pinot Bianco into the white and Cabernet, Merlot and Pinot Noir in with Sangiovese in the red. Castelgiocondo Brunello is intense, classic.

Marchesi L & P Antinori, CHIANTI CLASSICO Old-established (600 years) aristocratic estate responsible for leading Tuscany into varietal plurality with Tignanello (Sangiovese-Cabernet), Solaia (Cabernet) and by marketing Sassicaia (q.v.). Nonetheless Chianti remains the core business, where consistent standards are maintained. Antinori's best-value Chianti at present comes from the leased Badia a Passignano estate (also Classico).

Melini, CHIANTI Merchant owned by GIV (see **Northern Italy**) with large range; quality average.

Monsanto, CHIANTI CLASSICO Deep, tight-grained Chianti, sometimes forbidding without age. Herby varietal Cabernet Nemo and spicy Sangiovese-Cabernet Tinscvil both more approachable.

Monte Vertine, TUSCANY Unconventional and pioneering grower whose grippy, slow-ageing Le Pergole Torte, a pure Sangiovese, has completely replaced his Chianti Classico. Good Vin Santo, too.

Ornellaia, BOLGHERI Lodovico Antinori's estate, neighbouring Sassicaia. A band of clay makes for excellent Merlot, which joins Cabernet Sauvignon and Cabernet Franc in the deft Ornellaia, and is bottled as a varietal for sumptuous Masseto. Le Volte is a lighter, juicier blend, and Poggio alle Gazze an overrated Sauvignon greened by early picking rather than by nature's edge.

Pallavicini, Frascati More nutty fullness than most.

Il Paradiso, Brunello di Montalcino Deep, rich, soft '90 worth seeking out.

La Parrina, Parrina Good-value Chianti-blend reds from this coastal DOC.

Pieve di Santa Restitua, Brunello di Montalcino Gaja (see **Northern Italy**) now has controlling interest in this estate, making it one to watch.

Il Poggione, Brunello di Montalcino Fine, dark, consistent wines.

Poliziano, Vino Nobile Sturdy, sound wines.

Querciabella, Chianti Classico Upfront, full-bodied style.

Rocca della Macìe, Chianti Classico Widely distributed Chianti of standard quality; Ser Gioveto Vino da Tavola is leathery and persuasive, though, and Riserva di Fizzano worthwhile in good years.

Ruffino, Chianti Classico Large company with a number of individual estates. Riserva Ducale Oro (with gold label) is the best Ruffino Chianti – soft, spicy and expressive. Characterful wines from international varieties sold as Cabreo.

Sassicaia, Bolgheri International war-horse vino da tavola from Cabernet Sauvignon and Cabernet Franc. Planted in cleared scrubland, the *terroir* has sung ever since in this classy, urbane wine. '85 very fine.

Selvapiana, Chianti Rufina Old vines and low yields give intense flavour.

Teruzzi & Puthod, San Gimignano Husband and wife team producing slickly marketed wines which nonetheless have more character than most of their Vernaccia peers.

Umani Ronchi, Rosso Cònero Three deep, plummy reds, Casal di Serra, San Lorenzo and Cùmaro, all worth looking out for. Also crisp white Verdicchio and impressive single-vineyard Casal di Serra Verdicchio. Basic Montepulciano, by contrast, is now rather dull.

Valentini, Abruzzo Eccentric producer achieving fine results with Montepulciano and – more surprisingly – the usually dull white Trebbiano.

Villa Banfi, Brunello di Montalcino Extraordinary estate whose construction involved the moving of mountains. Huge range of wines but so far little of real excellence: perhaps the focus is too diffuse. Some good supermarket blends though (like M&S's Sangiovese-Cabernet).

Villa Ligi, Marches This producer's Vernaculum is, for me, close to the essence of Italy's appeal: rose-perfumed, rose-coloured, intensely characterful *sui generis* wine from an obscure grape variety (Vernaccia di Serrapetrona).

Villa Pigna, Rosso Piceno Key producer in this little-exported DOC; best wine is pure Montepulciano Vellutato.

Villa Vetrice, Chianti Rufina Good value from this improving estate.

Vinattieri Innovative wines from purchased grapes made by Badia a Coltibuono team.

Vintages:
1995 ★★; 1994 ★★; 1993 ★★; 1992 ★; 1991 ★★; 1990 ★★★★; 1989 ★★★; 1988 ★★★; 1987 ★★; 1986 ★★; 1985 ★★★.

Specialist retailers:
See Northern Italy.

Southern Italy

Shaking and moving

Like France's Languedoc, Southern Italy (Sicily and Sardinia included) was for decades locked into viticultural mediocrity. Buyers wanted cheap wine, regardless of quality; poor grape varieties, easy sites and high yields became the norm. The market for wine sold like petrol has gradually dwindled, leaving growers impoverished, stranded in their old ways, reliant on EC subsidies, sitting at café tables staring at dim-witted game shows on badly tuned televisions. Sicily, in particular, remains a monstrous drain on European Community resources, with most of its wine grown to harvest subsidies, many of which in turn finance criminal activity.

Southern Italy is poorer and less developed than Southern France, so its renaissance is less uniform than Languedoc's. At present, under five per cent of its wine falls within DOC regulations. A renaissance has begun, though, aided by the meteorological misfortunes of Northern and Central Italy; the best inexpensive Italian wines from the vintages of the early '90s have come from the south of the country, and in particular Puglia, the heel of Italy (where red grapes outnumber white by four to one). Basilicata (the boot's instep) is also beginning to send us some exciting wines; Campania (the ankle) and Calabria (the toe) lag behind a little, but may follow soon. Good native grape varieties (Negroamaro, Malvasia Nera, Primitivo, Aglianico, Greco, Nero d'Avola) and sites of potential exist. The region has several key oenologists of its own, and flying winemakers like Kym Milne M.W. have produced some excellent wines, especially from local varieties. Many Southern Italians remain insular, and lack international perspectives; those that look outward and forward, though, have everything to play for. Our supermarkets, insatiably thirsty for good inexpensive wine, need them.

D'Angelo, Aglianico del Vulture Wonderful name; scented, soft-fruited, earthy red wine. Canneto is the barrique-aged top wine.

Marco de Bartoli, Marsala Innovative, intriguing though not always wholly convincing Marsala, both fortified and unfortified, plus an often superb, orange-sodden Moscato, from the tiny island of Pantelleria, called Bukkuram.

Calatrasi, Sicily I Grilli di Villa Thalia is a decent juicy-fruit red from an intriguing four-variety mix (Sangiovese, Cabernet, Syrah and Nero d'Avola).

Candido, Salice Salentino Delicious smoky DOC red; Capello di Prete, a pure Negroamaro, is excellent, and Duca d'Aragona, a Negroamaro-Montepulciano blend, better and fuller still. Decent Chardonnay, too; Sauvignon less successful.

Cantina Sociale Copertino, COPERTINO   Rapidly maturing but deliciously flavoury Negroamaro-based wines made by Severino Garofano, who also makes wine with Taurino and Candido.

Cantina Sociale Dolianova, SARDINIA   Full-flavoured red Cannonau and Monica. White Nuragus di Cagliari pleasantly aniseedy.

Cantina Sociale Santadi, SARDINIA   Some good red Carignan-based wines from low-yielding vines (Rocca Rubia, Terre Brune).

Donnafugata, SICILY   Well-made, prettily packaged wines. Full-flavoured Tancredi combines Cabernet and Nero d'Avola.

Florio, MARSALA   The largest Marsala producer, whose wines include the Woodhouse and Ingham marques. The silken ACI 1840 and dry, almondy, buttery Riserva Egadi are the top Marsale; Morsi di Luce Moscato from Pantelleria is honeyed and rich.

Leone di Castris, PUGLIA   Biggest private winery in Puglia. Slowly catching up with regional trend-setters.

Librandi, CIRÒ   Intriguing light red based on Gaglioppo.

Cantina Sociale Locorotondo, LOCOROTONDO   Huge, well-equipped cooperative (four million bottles per year) producing a sound, good-value range.

Mastroberardino, TAURASI   Campania's standard bearer, Mastroberardino produces a wide range of variable quality but antique pedigree. Red Aglianico-based Taurasi, full bodied and sweetly earthy, offers best value.

Mottura, SQUINZANO   Decent juicy red from Azienda Cooperativa Leuca.

Azienda Nuova Murgia, PUGLIA   Boutique operation with good organic wines.

Pellegrino, MARSALA   Good range of dry Marsala, peaking with Vergine Soleras and Vecchio Riserva Vergine 1880, both as searching and austere as the finest dry sherries. Good Passito di Pantelleria sadly withdrawn from sale while regulators argue about grape-drying methods; Moscato di Pantelleria is lighter, silkier.

Regaleali, SICILY   Rosso del Conte, an uncompromising, savagely flavoured blend of Nero d'Avola and Perricone, has for long been one of my favourite Mediterranean wines; Regaleali Rosso is a lesser, lighter version.

Duca di Salaparuta, SICILY   Corvo has for decades been a reliable trattoria fallback: these are big-blend wines from grapes grown all over the island. Duca Enrico is now the flagship wine: a deep, barrique-aged Nero d'Avola red from high-sited vineyards.

Sella & Mosca, SARDINIA   The island's quality pioneers, with a wide range of consistent wines. Marchese di Villamarina is a grand, sumptuously oaked and startlingly expensive wine.

Taurino, SALICE SALENTINO   Excellent, good-value reds of fine balance, especially Notarpanaro and sweet, deep Patriglione.

Torrevento, PUGLIA   Small, progressive winery producing promising wines in a restored monastery. C.S.Locorotondo's winemaker Pascuale Carparelli consults. The '94 Torre del Falco was full, fleshy, smoky and meaty: promising.

Terre di Ginestra, SICILY Prettily labelled, fresh-flavoured red and white from near Palermo.

Le Trulle, PUGLIA Sound range produced by Kym Milne M.W. with Augusto Càntele. Primitivo has gutsy, mineral style.

Japan

Masters of mimesis

Despite unpromising climatic conditions, the Japanese have produced wine using growing stratagems of characteristic ingenuity for over a millenium. Most are sweet and weak-flavoured, reliant on massive levels of chaptalisation for alcoholic balance, and often made from unsubtle *labrusca* grape varieties. Good 'Japanese' wines are made, however, by blending Japanese-grown must with top-quality South American or European must; and very occasionally the weather permits fine botrytis-affected dessert wines to be made in Japan. Yamagata, Yamanashi and Nagano provinces, in central Japan, are the main zones.

Lebanon

Through flame and fire

The Lebanon is a tiny country (about as big as Wales) dominated by a huge mountain range which divides it in two. The Mediterranean side of the mountain tumbles populously down to the sea. To the east lies the Bekaa valley – a high green hollow carved by the Litani river. Most of Lebanon's vineyards are to be found on the western side of the Bekaa, and the wine-making grapes they produce are excellent: soft-fruited, sweet-flavoured, freshened by cool mountain nights. The second-century Temple of Bacchus in Baalbek, at the head of the Bekaa, suggests that this has long been appreciated, at least locally. Opium poppies are the Bekaa's other, more sinister crop.

Multi-cultural, multi-ethnic, religiously plural Lebanon has lived through what was one of the longest, most vicious and most public of recent civil wars, even if not, finally, the most sanguinary. It has three main wine producers, Château Musar, Kefraya and Ksara, and all three continued their work throughout the war. This was most spectacularly difficult for Château Musar, since its winery (in the Christian zone of Ghazir, north of Beirut) was far from the vineyards, across every one of the war's shifting front lines: Musar's lorry drivers regularly risked their lives to bring the harvest home by an extraordinary and nerve-jangling tangle of routes. The Bekaa-sited Kefraya, meanwhile, occupied what was at times a battlefield, and its bearded French winemaker spent some time in Israeli jails, under suspicion of espionage, with Shia fundamentalists. No Lebanese red wine of the late 70s and 80s should be drunk without a thought as to its circumstances of birth.

Serge Hochar, Musar's winemaker, is a thoroughly extraordinary man whose approach owes more to psychology and philosophy (galvanised by a proximity to death) than to oenology. His red wines have sometimes been criticised on technical grounds, but they are hugely loved, fragrant, sweet, warm and savoury (made from Cabernet and Cinsaut) with an improbable ability to age. His whites, meanwhile, made from Obaideh and Merweh (which might be Chardonnay and Sauvignon Blanc, according to Hochar, or at least avatars of these varieties transported to France by home-bound crusaders) make no sense at all without age. They remind me of fine Rhône valley whites.

Kefraya's wines have not been seen much in Britain, but the company intends to develop sales here in the future. Rouge de Kefraya is a Cinsault-Carignan blend, and Château de Kefraya is made from Cabernet Sauvignon plus smaller amounts of Mourvèdre, Syrah and Grenache. There are also two good rosé wines, a soft carbonic-maceration red and a duller white.

Kefraya's majority shareholder is Walid Jumblatt, the Druze leader; the Druze are a Muslim sect, so this is one of the world's few Muslim-owned wineries. In Lebanon, as Serge Hochar once told me, anything is possible.

Luxembourg

Not worth a detour

The Mosel is an unusual river for the wine spotter. It flows from its French source northwards, along the Luxembourg border and into Germany, and the further north it gets, the better its wines are.

The reason for this is that in Germany, and particularly between Bernkastel and Zell, it has cut its course deeply and sinuously, leaving steep valley sides whose slopes bask in sunlight. The smaller, shallower Upper Mosel, and France's and Luxembourg's Moselle, are not so well-endowed with slopes. They have vines, but their fruit gives a sourer, thinner wine. Most of it is made from Müller-Thurgau, called Rivaner here, with Elbling, Riesling, Auxerrois and Pinot Gris making up the balance; yields are high, and chaptalisation maximal. The most important producer is the cooperative group known as Vinsmoselle. Sparkling wines can be good.

Macedonia

Early days

Macedonia, the former Yugoslav republic which lies between Greece and Serbia, has a worthwhile red-wine tradition, its best wines (as in Montenegro, for the time being still part of the Serbian-dominated rump Yugoslav Federation) being based on the sturdy Vranac grape variety. An Australian-trained English winemaker, Steve Clarke, is the co-founder of the Macedonian Wine Company: this has a three-year contract with major cooperatives, and is shipping out some enjoyably rustic reds with Bulgarian help.

Mexico

Sweating it out

The first American wine was made in Mexico in 1521, the year after the conquistadores landed. Despite this early start, wine-growing is not widespread today (Brazil has more land under vines than does Mexico), and most of the grape vines planted are for table grapes, raisins and brandy production. The best wines – gutsy, inexpensive reds from Petite Syrah, Cabernet and Zinfandel – are produced where higher ground mitigates fierce daytime heat; quality areas include Guadalupe, Zacatecas and Querétaro. The leading exporter to the UK is L.A.Cetto; Domecq and Santo Tomas are other big names.

Moldova

Bessarabian renaissance

Vines? They got 'em. Some 10 per cent of the entire land surface of Moldova is vineyard, and viticulture here, as in Georgia and Armenia, predates Western European vine-growing by several centuries. Ancient Bessarabia was later chosen as the site of the Romanov family's 600-hectare wine estate; its most recent role was as a major supplier of wines to the Soviet Union.

The landscape is one of gently rolling hills licked into shape by small, soft rivers; the climate is temperate; and the range of grape varieties in the vineyards includes most of those familiar to British wine drinkers, as well as the Russian Rkatsiteli and Saperavi and the Romanian Feteasca (over half Moldova's population is Romanian). In technical terms, however, Moldova has been less well-equipped than its neighbours outside the USSR, and lamentably backward by western standards.

That is changing. Inspired by the country's potential, and to some extent by elderly bottles of acerbic but deep flavoured red wine sourced from Cricova and Pucar, western investors (though no longer Penfolds of Australia) have arrived, equipment in tow. For the time being, the best Moldovan wines are clean but simply flavoured varietals made by Hugh Ryman's team at Hincesti and sold by a number of British supermarkets under the Kirkwood label. I feel that the quality of Hincesti fruit is not, at this stage, exciting enough to compete head-to-head with Hungary, Bulgaria or Romania. It would be good to see wines from other parts of Moldova in the UK.

Montenegro

see Serbia

Morocco

Pour it again, Sam

Morocco seems to feel less anguished about wine-growing than Algeria does, and produces a wider range of wines than Tunisia. Nonetheless the waning of French influence in the area has seen a loss of direction and lack of investment in Morocco's wine industry, with consequent deterioration in the quality of wines produced. This is a shame. Casablanca's Gris du Boulaouane was never up to much (no wine made from Criolla ever is), but who could resist drinking a pale rosé made at the desert's edge? Red wines were often genuinely good, with those from the high-sited Meknès-Fès area (Guerrouane and Beni M'tir) deep but with an intrinsic balance; Tarik was a good brand. Berkane in the east, once famous for a fine dessert Muscat, is another area of promise. Perhaps things are again beginning to pick up: after Morocco's complete disappearance from the British market, both Majestic and Asda have begun to stock good Moroccan reds at rock-bottom prices during the last couple of years. Let's hope we now see something a little more expensive, and a lot better in quality, sent our way. Most of Morocco's production is, perhaps problematically, in the hands of state enterprises; Celliers de Meknès is the leading private producer.

New Zealand

Discoveries in time

I visited New Zealand in January 1996. Previously, I had known the country only through its bottles; this was a chance to deepen and round out my knowledge of its soils and climate — and the hopes and aspirations of its winemakers. I got to know ferns, too, and the gentle ways of flightless avians, and the sweet taste of fresh air and the cleanly sheepy smell of lanolin face-cream; and I could begin to imagine (begin, at least) a life in which the local take-away didn't mean an identikit McDonalds but a 'one-stop ram shop'; a life where you didn't go for a walk in threadbare, dog-fouled parks on Sunday but climbed into the back of a pick-up, thundered dustily off up mountain tracks and then river-rafted down two or three white-flecked miles with only a beady-eyed, thermal-riding Australasian harrier for company; a life where the journey to town is taken in tremulous dragonfly aeroplanes; a life where shyness is endemic.

It wasn't an ideal moment: 1995 was, for many of New Zealand's key wines, a poor, rain-spoiled harvest. Indeed the reality of bad weather, unusual in the New World context, was Discovery One. New Zealand's two islands are surrounded by a great deal of water, and water means meteorological unpredictability. The prevailing wind and rain may come from the west (which is why the vineyards line the sunrise side of the country), yet the east is quite capable of swirling up a storm at any time, too. A cyclone, later downgraded to a severe depression, tumbled in while I was in New Zealand, wrecking the stone-fruit harvest with three days of hammering rain and tree-bending wind in 'sunny' Hawkes Bay.

Bad weather, of course, is not necessarily bad news in winemaking terms; 90 per cent of the world's greatest wines come from areas where clouds and their cargo regularly spoil a year's work. It is meteorological brinkmanship which give great results. But it does have to be factored into the bottom line, which leads to ...

Discovery Two: expense. New Zealand's wines cannot be cheap. This is not a clockwork climate; these are not factory vineyards. Chardonnay costs £500 a ton more in New Zealand than it does in Australia. Moreover the country's strong dollar (33p in 1992; 43p as I write) has given the bottom line a further pummelling. Head-to-head confrontation with Australia, Chile and South Africa at £3.49, £3.99 or £4.49 is right off the Kiwi menu. A good Marlborough Sauvignon (Dashwood or Wairau River, say) is already up past £8; the best Chardonnays and the best reds cost a lot more than that. Even New Zealand's second-rate wines are expensive by UK standards. Britain has had the pick of New Zealand's wine thus far, but no longer. The sad reality is that many of these wines are going to scuttle off to other markets in the next few years. We're not rich enough; we can't afford them.

Discovery Three was discovery itself. The poet Ted Hughes once described his excitement when, in his first spring in a new house, thousands of daffodils rose up out of the earth: he had become, unknowingly, their steward. This is roughly analogous to the feeling many New Zealand winegrowers have in discovering the slow secrets of their soils and climates. I particularly remember the cloud-silvering brightness of the sky: surely light of this quality must be one reason why New Zealand's best wines taste so extraordinarily vivid, so starkly defined, so lightning fresh? I was no less astonished looking down at the evidence of geological youthfulness. The river gravels of parts of Hawkes Bay or Marlborough are not, as in the Médoc, a close-grained, soil-glued assembly, but a heap of stones. Just stones. Vineyard sites like these have become hot property in the last few years, but no one knows what their long-term future will be. Other soils, of course, are rich; others sandy; others tight clay. The point is that there is rarely the geological complexity you get with older land masses, the mixing and muddling which happens over millions (so easy to say, so hard to imagine) of years. The geology of Burgundy or Alsace is Byzantine by comparison. As with New Zealand's bright, clear light, there must be flavour implications: vibrancy, purity, impact, perhaps at the expense of nuance and subtlety? That's the way it looks at present, but we'll see.

North Island

Gearing up

Auckland, now a vast, Los Angeles-style sprawl housing one in three New Zealanders, is the historic home of the wine industry and still (in Henderson, Huapai and Kumeu) the place where many key wineries have their main base. This, though, is largely for logistical and marketing purposes: hit the Auckland wine trail and you're far more likely to be offered Marlborough or Hawkes Bay wine than a locally grown product. The sub-tropical conditions make vine growing difficult, and land is worth far more as bungalow blocks than as vineyards; nonetheless, as producers like Kumeu River or Collards demonstrate, locally grown wines can have fine depth and intricacy. Waiheke Island, a short ferry ride from the city centre, is a great red hope for New Zealand; its microclimate is dryer and warmer than that of the mainland and it is already producing some of New Zealand's best Cabernets and Cabernet blends. These will always be very expensive: the land area available is tiny.

Gisborne (Poverty Bay) is the North Island's Cinderella area, the nearest New Zealand gets to a Riverland; it has a soothing line in creamy Chardonnays, though, and in James Millton it has one of the country's most thoughtful and innovative wine-growers. Huge Hawkes Bay, by contrast, has a little bit of everything, and as a result lacks a clear regional profile. When you ask winemakers working for the big companies where they'd most like to be given a vineyard, though, the answer is usually Hawkes Bay. Its track record with Chardonnay is proven; its Sauvignons are more adaptable than Marlborough's; and the latest reds (like some of Montana's 1995 Cabernet vineyard selections) are dark and sturdily constructed. Just give it time.

Martinborough, towards the bottom of the North Island, is the source of the greatest red wines I tasted during my visit: the balanced and lyrical 1994 Pinot Noirs of Ata Rangi and Martinborough Vineyards. Chardonnay is also superb hereabouts; the lack of big-company interest in the region gives it, too, a pleasingly relaxed, 'alternative' atmosphere. The best Pinots from here and from Marlborough make the widespread plantings of Cabernet and even Merlot throughout the country look like a ghastly mistake.

Ata Rangi, MARTINBOROUGH   Rich, sumptuous Pinot Noir (plus outstanding Reserves) and creamy, sinewy Chardonnay; Celèbre is a spicy Cab-Syrah-Merlot.

Babich, HENDERSON   Large, consistent company. Oaked whites something of a speciality (Mara Estate Sauvignon and Irongate Chardonnay both very good), and reds from Mara Estate (super-stony Hawkes Bay vineyards) promising too – '94 Merlot has real sweetness of fruit.

Collards, HENDERSON   Some of the best Chenin Blanc outside France, and good unshowy Chardonnay. Locally grown Rothesay Vineyard wines are complex.

Cooks, HENDERSON   Corbans-owned. This 'inexpensive' brand illustrates the difficulties New Zealand has in competing with other New World producers at under £5: the whites are simple and trivial and the Cabernet slender and grassy. Winemaker's Reserve Chardonnay from Marlborough, however, offers good value.

Coopers Creek, HUAPAI/AUCKLAND   Vigorous and innovative producer, leading with intense Sauvignons and concentrated, graceful Rieslings.

Corbans, HENDERSON   Second-biggest in the country and ultimately owned by Heineken. Private Bin range is impressive (look out for chocolatey Merlot/Cabernet and rich, finely balanced Chardonnay, both from Marlborough), while Stoneleigh Riesling and Sauvignon Blanc from Marlborough are cleanly and challengingly expressive. Cottage Block Chardonnay from Gisborne is looking promisingly complex. Cheap Waimanu white is poor.

Delegat's, HENDERSON Despite the address, a Hawke's Bay specialist, with Marlborough wines sold as Oyster Bay. Winemaker Brent Marris is one of New Zealand's most talented, getting soft, grainy subtleties into wines like the long-flavoured '94 Hawkes Bay Proprietor's Reserve Chardonnay and the almost voluptuous '94 Hawkes Bay Proprietor's Reserve Merlot. The Oyster Bay Chardonnay is always good ('95 one of this vintage's few real successes).

Dry River, MARTINBOROUGH Top Pinot and Riesling producer, sadly not imported to the UK at present.

Esk Valley, HAWKE'S BAY Part of Villa Maria group. Red-wine specialists whose top wines are worth seeking out: they include a meaty '94 Merlot Reserve and 'The Terraces': a sweet-fruited four-variety blend grown on some of New Zealand's steepest vineyard land (surrounding winery). Decent Chardonnay; wooded Chenin less successful.

Goldwater, WAIHEKE ISLAND Fleshy, spicy Cabernet-Merlot is exceptionally good. Marlborough Chardonnay is rich and alcoholic, with more substance than most. Dog Point Sauvignon is less good: young vines, no oak.

Kaituna Hills An M&S label: fair though not exciting wines.

Kemblefield, HAWKES BAY Intense Chardonnay from this Californian-in-exile.

Kumeu River, KUMEU Complicated, Burgundian-style nutty-buttery Chardonnay, subtler and profounder than many of its peers, leads a provoking range.

Lincoln, HENDERSON Straightfoward, pleasant whites; red variable.

Martinborough, MARTINBOROUGH Soft but intense, pure and true Pinot Noir is among New Zealand's best. Delicate Riesling and Sauvignon Blanc and creamy Chardonnay, too.

Matua Valley, HUAPAI/AUCKLAND Wide range. Sauvignon Blanc generally very good ('95 Waimaku Reserve has a complex, Graves-like style); Smith-Dartmoor vineyard in Hawkes Bay turns out zingy Chardonnay, whereas Judd Estate (from Gisborne) has a softer, creamier touch. Top Ararimu wines don't yet justify their prices: the dark '94 Cab-Merlot (from Smith-Dartmoor) still lacks a little upholstery, while the fruit of the '93 Chardonnay (from Waimaku) seems overburdened by winery interventions. See also Shingle Peak (South Island).

Millton, GISBORNE Organic producer for some wines; questing approach for all. Not everything works, but the barrel-fermented Chardonnay is gracious, mouth-filling and nuanced, the Chenin Blanc has interesting flavours if a slightly muddled style, and there is a superb '94 dessert wine in preparation.

Montana, HAWKES BAY & GISBORNE New Zealand's giant, with bases and influence almost everywhere save Martinborough (see also **South Island**). Fair to good quality at most levels: Lindauer is a reliable sparkler, basic white varietals are still the best launch-pad for discovering NZ, while the basic Cabernet is much improved, meriting its tiptoe across the £5 threshold. The mid-priced Saints range, used for restaurant sales in NZ, includes a soft, full '95 Gisborne Chardonnay. Ormond Estate Chardonnay (also from Gisborne) is fat, nutty and full, while

151

Church Road (from Hawkes Bay) has a more intense, vivacious style. Top-of-the-range reds are still finding their way, but '95 samples from the Phoenix vineyard in Hawkes Bay suggest that great things are just around the corner.

Morton Estate, WAIKATO Full-flavoured, rich, succulent White Label Chardonnay is steady in quality. Grassy Hawkes Bay Sauvignon Blanc and flavoury Black Label Cabernet-Merlot are both worth trying.

Mills Reef, BAY OF PLENTY Overblown and unsubtle style.

Ngatarawa, HAWKES BAY Glazebrook is top label; Stables second label. Good Chardonnay and fine, cleanly balanced dessert wines.

Nobilo, HUAPAI/AUCKLAND White Cloud (an off-dry Müller-Sauvignon) is dull though improving. Zesty Poverty Bay Chardonnay (familiar to British Airways passengers) has been a merited success, and Marlborough Reserve Chardonnay is full of enjoyably mouth-puckering lime. Local reds disappointing.

Palliser, MARTINBOROUGH Toasty, mid-weight Pinot Noirs too dry and bitter in style for me. Sauvignon Blanc has fine Loire-like intensity, and there are some zingy, citrussy Rieslings.

C.J. Pask, HAWKE'S BAY Lively though lean whites and reds from Chris Pask, a former grower turned producer.

De Redcliffe, WAIKATO Subtle, structured whites. '94 Pinot dry, hard and green, though.

Rongopai, WAIKATO Carefully made wines include autumn-leafy Sauvignon and impressively deep '94 Merlot-Malbec.

Sacred Hill, HAWKES BAY Adventurous approach yields an unusually complex wild-yeast Sauvignon Blanc Sauvage and late-harvest Sauvignon, as well as weighty Reserve Chardonnays.

Saints see Montana.

Selaks, KUMEU Straightforward, consistent range includes bright, clean Marlborough Riesling.

Stonyridge, WAIHEKE ISLAND Bordeaux-blend red tasting like decent claret from a lighter vintage. New Marlborough winery should move quality up a notch.

Te Kairanga, MARTINBOROUGH Aggressive, low pH Pinots lack voluptuousness and velvet; Chardonnays are creamier, though still on lean side.

Te Mata, HAWKE'S BAY Top-of-the-line Coleraine Cab-Merlot and Elston Chardonnay are expensive but concentrated and vinous, with a wealth of flavour. Castle Hill and Cape Crest Sauvignons were slender in '95; second-level Awatea Cabernet-Merlot is curranty and bright (perfumed '95 impressively structured, too). Syrah off to a good start.

Vidal, HAWKE'S BAY Villa Maria-owned. Fair range includes a soft and spicy Gewürztraminer.

Villa Maria, AUCKLAND Consistent range, with Reserve white wines costly but full and deep-flavoured, even some of the reds.

Vintages:
1996 ★★★; 1995 ★★; 1994 ★★★★; 1993 ★; 1992 ★; 1991 ★★★★; 1990 ★★★; 1989 ★★★★; 1988 ★★; 1987 ★★★★; 1986 ★★★; 1985 ★★★.

Specialist retailers:
Bottoms Up, The London Wine Emporium, Selfridges, Waterloo Wine Company and Wine Rack are leading specialists. NZ Direct (0171 482 0093), run by wine agent Margaret Harvey M.W., runs a mail-order operation with a good range of top names.

South Island

Moving down

There is more to South Island than Marlborough, though it's sometimes easy to forget that fact. Easy, because the effect of Marlborough, and particularly of its Sauvignon Blanc, on wine drinkers throughout the world apes the effect magnets have on iron filings. Those extraordinary aromas of smashed leaf and chopped grass, of buttered asparagus and fooled gooseberries, combined with crisp, green-apple flavours which leap into the mouth with naked abandon have proved hard to resist.

Yet the first vines of the modern era were planted in Marlborough as recently as 1973. It's sunny, stony, dry, windy and cool. The result is high acidity combined improbably with high sugar levels. Sauvignon loves it there, and grows like hogweed; Chardonnay produces sun-burnished, citric wines with heady alcohol levels; Riesling should be incandescent, and indeed some dessert wines have been, but lack of marketability has held the variety back. Early examples of Pinot Noir from Marlborough are also exciting, many showing the intrinsic balance which Cabernet will never achieve here; while the region can produce superb sparkling-wine base, too. All of that said, the fact remains that this is a tricky time to buy Marlborough's wines: 1995 was rain-sodden there, and the only good wines have been made by those prepared to sell most of their crop in bulk.

Nelson, near to Marlborough, is an area of individual rather than regional excellence: its best wines have great edginess and incisiveness. Christchurch and Waipara, further south still, are dangerously cool, and Central Otago has a continental climate. Viticulture in these last three regions is still in its infancy and results so far suggest a wide degree of vintage variation; yet when the season is sunny, Pinot Noir and Chardonnay can be superb.

Le Brun, MARLBOROUGH   Intense, deep-driving sparkling wines of exciting though inconsistent quality from this much-restructured business.

Cloudy Bay, MARLBOROUGH   Rich, asparagus-packed, deep-pile Cloudy Bay Sauvignon still sells out wherever it shows up (even '95 was good, by dint of great selectivity). Fine, sleek Chardonnay and the chewy, bready Pelorus sparkling wine are every bit as good, and the rising star (though not yet available in the UK) is Cloudy Bay's promising Pinot Noir.

Dashwood see Vavasour.

Fromm, MARLBOROUGH Organic, high-effort wines including fine Pinot Noir.

Giesen, CANTERBURY Botrytis-affected Rieslings and an exceptionally good '94 Reserve Pinot Noir lead the range from the largest producer in Canterbury.

Highfield, MARLBOROUGH Promisingly deep Sauvignon and Chardonnay from this winery established with Far East investment.

Hunters, MARLBOROUGH Now expensive, but the unoaked Sauvignon Blanc is pungent and piercing, while the Chardonnay is succulent and structured. Riesling has tropical charm; Pinot Noir and sparkler are promising.

Jackson Estate, MARLBOROUGH Heady, unbridled Sauvignon and occasionally fine, pungent Riesling (sold as Marlborough Dry). Pinot Noir, Chardonnay and sparkling wine made in over-dry style, lacking succulence and charm.

Montana, MARLBOROUGH The New Zealand giant (almost half the national output), with other footholds in Auckland, Gisborne and Hawke's Bay (see **North Island**). Montana pioneered Marlborough, and has reaped the rewards with benchmark Marlborough Sauvignon and Chardonnay priced more keenly than most. Quality swings merely reflect the vintage. Top-flight wines from Marlborough include a classy oaked Sauvignon from the Brancott Estate and buttery, elegant Renwick Chardonnay. The fine-grained Deutz Marlborough Cuvée sparkler takes the opposite (aperitif-style) tack to Cloudy Bay's plump Pelorus.

Nautilus, MARLBOROUGH Yalumba-owned. Marlborough Chardonnay richer and oakier than many; clean limey Sauvignon and expensive, deep-fruited sparkler both worth trying. Lovely marine labels.

Neudorf, NELSON Carefully made range, best for delicate, pithy Riesling and intense, lean-line, grapefruity Chardonnays.

Old Coach Road see Redwood Valley.

Oyster Bay see Delegat's (North Island).

Mark Rattray, WAIPARA Full, perfumed Pinot.

Redwood Valley, NELSON Sold as Seifried in New Zealand, and soon also as Old Coach Road in UK. Capable of both assured and shaky wines: Rieslings are best.

Richmond Ridge see Wairau River.

Rothbury, MARLBOROUGH A good start for the Aussies, with grassy, grapefruity Sauvignon and peachy Riesling.

St Helena, CANTERBURY Touch-and-go Pinot, but good when it goes.

Shingle Peak, MARLBOROUGH Matua Valley's (see **North Island**) Marlborough operation generally on the pace.

Stoneleigh, MARLBOROUGH see **Corbans, North Island.**

Vavasour, MARLBOROUGH Intense, classy Reserve Chardonnay and Pinot. Second label Dashwood features a very crisp, clean, high-definition Sauvignon Blanc (one of the more successful '95s).

Waipara Springs, WAIPARA Soft Riesling and exciting but unsubtle Chardonnay lead the range for me.

Waipara West, WAIPARA Excitingly stony, flinty, Upper-Loire-style Sauvignon and Chardonnay.

Wairau River, MARLBOROUGH Intense Sauvignon Blanc and Chardonnay usually among the best. Second label Richmond Ridge may suffer in years (like '95) when fruit quality varied a great deal.

Vintages:
1996 ★★★; 1995 ★; 1994 ★★★★; 1993 ★; 1992 ★★; 1991 ★★★★; 1990 ★★★; 1989 ★★★★; 1988 ★★; 1987 ★★★★; 1986 ★★★; 1985 ★★★.

Specialist retailers:
see North Island.

Portugal

Lucky country

Wine is one of Portugal's prime assets. It has been dealt, by inequitable nature, a far livelier hand of grape varieties than has its neighbour, Spain. British wine prospectors visited the country early: its seaboard made transport easy, and mutual friendship has been in the interest of both countries for the best part of a millenium. (Moreover there are temperamental affinities between these nations of gentle, wave-washed, sea-dreaming souls.) The British wine-hunters found the deep red wines they wanted, 'insured' them for shipping purposes with a bucket or two of brandy, and inadvertently invented a new wine altogether – port. When wine was dispatched from Portugal's luscious Atlantic island, Madeira, it seemed by an extraordinary hazard of fortune to be brought to perfection by the very treatment which would normally reduce it to alcoholic slop: interminable boat-jouneys to hotter climes still and back. Portugal is wine's lucky country.

Yet it doesn't feature with any particular prominence in our wine-buying firmament at present. Port is untrendy; madeira still more so. The best port is the most richly and explosively flavoured fortified wine in the world; the best madeira eclipses, for absolute intensity, every other wine in the world of whatever type or sort. They should occupy pride of place in every serious cellar.

Portugal's table wines, too, remain boxed away in two unfortunate pigeonholes: cheap wine or odd wine. A legacy of poverty, and the fact that winemaking in some of the best vineyard areas was exclusively in cooperative hands, meant that quality has often been well below its potential level, and packaging and marketing are (with the exception of Sogrape) not Portugal's forte. Anyone, though, who has tasted widely among the best table wines of the Douro, of Bairrada, of Dão and of the Alentejo knows that complexity and longevity are incised in them like lines in the palm. For the wine enthusiast, Portugal is a rich reservoir of unusual, unobvious, inconvenient and occasionally incomprehensible excellence.

Port

The libertine and the retirement home

If there is a more exciting wine to taste and to drink than young vintage port, I don't know it. If there is a more beautiful vineyard region than the Douro valley (where port is grown and made), I have yet to visit it. The reason why port doesn't receive the adulation enjoyed by claret or burgundy is, of course, because it is inconveniently strong and inconveniently sweet. Create the circumstances whereby sweetness and strength become desirable (broadly speaking, when the day's work is done, when the nights are dark, when the wind is chill) and this is a wine which demands your attention.

Port is made by taking grapes (black for most port; white for white port) and beating hell out of their skins in different ways, among which treading by a multitude of bare human feet in granite tanks has yet to be surpassed. Halfway through fermentation, high-strength brandy is added; the extractive and fermentative parts of the process are then over. The remaining grape sugars are 'frozen' into the wine by the brandy. Port goes into big wooden vats.

Its destiny then diverges. The blackest, smashiest, stemmiest, fruitiest, most knee-tremblingly powerful is declared 'Vintage' port and bottled after two years without filtering or processing. Lesser ports of this sort are blended and bottled as 'Crusting' port. Wines of the next quality go into casks for four years before being bottled to become 'Late Bottled Vintage'; unfiltered, crust-throwing versions are called 'Traditional' Late Bottled Vintage. Then come filtered blends of darkish hue and fruity style called 'Vintage Character', and finally the decent but unexceptional Ruby. Most houses' best vintage ports bear the company name alone, while more individual vintage ports, or those from lesser years, bear the name of the quinta (farm) from which they were sourced in whole or in part. An interesting trend over the last decade is the fact that quinta ports have been steadily rising in quality, aided by the fact that a number of individual grower-producers (such as Quinta do Infantado or Quinta de la Rosa) only sell under the quinta name. It is no longer safe to regard quinta Vintage port as being less good than those Vintage ports which bear a company name alone: the game is now an open one.

Another branch of the port family spends its whole life in wooden casks: Tawny port. Basic tawny, however, is usually a sort of young rosé port; serious tawny is either sold 'with an indication of age' (10, 20, 30 and over 40 years old), or with a vintage (Colheita port).

When should port be drunk? In most cases, as soon as possible. The only exception is vintage port, which usually becomes drinkable in my opinion at about its eighth birthday, and is at its best between 10 and 20 years old. I prefer it closer to 10 than 20, though this is considered mad by port traditionalists, who are often unhappy about broaching bottles before their 30th birthday. It seems to me that by then all the wild fruit and bacchanalian excess of the wine has disappeared into the gritty black crust. Its qualities remain apparent, of course, just as the good looking usually remain good looking as they age; but would you not rather meet a beautiful libertine in his or her unbridled youth than exchange sage reflections with them in a retirement home?

The nineties have been a good decade so far for Vintage port: 1991 was declared by some shippers and 1992 by others; I have (at the time of writing) just visited Portugal to look at early declarations of the 1994s, the first uniformly declared year since 1985. The best Vintage ports of 1991 include Dow, Graham's, Gould Campbell, Guimaraens, Niepoort, Quinta do Infantado, Quinta da Terra Feita, Quinta de Vargellas and Warre; the best of 1992 includes Churchill's Agua Alta, Quinta do Bomfim, Fonseca, Niepoort, Quinta do Infantado, Quinta do Passadouro, Quinta de la Rosa, Quinta do Vesuvio, Taylor and Quinta da Cavadinha. Among '94s, Dow, Fonseca, Taylor and Croft all look darkly promising and taste splendidly multi-dimensioned.

Barros, ALMEIDA Lightish ports under a number of names (Vieira de Sousa, Hutcheson, Douro Wine Shippers and Growers, Feuerheerd, Feist and Kopke – this last the oldest of all port companies). Mainly commodity ports, but Kopke Vintage '85 is deeper than usual.

Burmester Small company producing fine, delicate tawnies and the occasional good Vintage port (as in '85). Excellent fiery, peppery, thick-textured '89 LBV worth seeking out. Gilbert's is a sous-marque.

Cálem A recent turn of speed for this Portuguese company: rich, emphatic, quite woody tawnies (including good-value Colheitas); Vintages (since '85) up to scratch, based on fruit from Quinta da Foz.

Churchill Young shipper (first vintage '82) founded by a member of the Graham family (which no longer owns the Graham marque). Early Vintages inconsistent owing to cask problems in source quintas, now resolved. All are made in enjoyably red-blooded style; look out for resounding '87, '90 and '92 Vintages from Quinta da Agua Alta. White port rich, nutty and full.

Cockburn I find most Cockburn ports rather bland and 'commercial' in style, but Vintages are serious, tight and deep. 'Anno' LVB '90 is cleverly packaged but gutless.

Quinta do Crasto Aussie David Baverstock, ex-Croft and ex-Symington, looks set to produce exciting port here.

Croft Hugely disappointing under present multi-national ownership (IDV). Last good vintage was 1970, and that's now over the hill. The blackcurranty '94 marks a new start.

Delaforce Some elegant, lightish wines from Quinta da Corte; His Eminence's Choice a complex 10-year-old tawny while the memorably named Curious and Ancient is a nutty 20-year-old. IDV-owned.

Dow Impressive Vintage ports of classical, sober style, slightly dryer than some; Quinta do Bomfim wines marked by blackcurrant characters (whereas LBV seems more cherryish). '84 Bomfim Vintage exceptionally good (and better than Graham's Malvedos '84): salty, treacly, creamy. Supple, appealing

10 Year Old tawny, widely available in half bottles. Owned by the British Symington family.

Ferreira Sweet, voluptuous style suits tawnies (e.g. 20-year-old Duque de Bragança) better than Vintage, though look out for '83 Quinta do Seixo. Sogrape-owned.

Fonseca In same ownership as Taylor's, and in some recent years outperforming its stablemate (though steer clear of feeble '80 vintage); stunning '85. Whole range worth trying; all ports in rich, generous, uncompromising style. Bin 27 a muscular (though expensive) Vintage-Character-level blend.

Gould Campbell Often bargain Vintage ports (e.g. fine '77, '80 and '83) from this minor Symington marque.

Graham Port grandee, now in Symington ownership. Usually among richest, sweetest, most orchestral Vintage ports, with rest of range built in same style (LBV '90 is raisiny, caramelly). Six Grapes blend improved of late. Malvedos also a blend rather than a quinta wine, but rich and many-contoured.

Guimaraens A Fonseca sous-marque, with an excellent Vintage tradition: the '76 was legendary; the '91 looks good.

Quinta do Infantado Shaky start in mid-'80s for this grower-producer, but recent releases (e.g. '91 LBV and Vintage '92) have been muscular and deep.

Martinez Sister company to Cockburn, capable of turning out good-value ports of punchy, exciting style (look out for '90 LBV). Also bottles ports of top-sited, historic Quinta da Eira Velha (sumptuous '87).

Morgan Minor marque in IDV ownership (see **Croft**).

Niepoort Tiny, idiosyncratic house with high standards (and recent surge in quality under Dirk van der Niepoort's direction). Among the sweetest of all Vintage ports, yet always backed by firm tannins and deep fruit. Niepoort super-intends and markets (though does not own) Quinta do Passadouro, which made superb '92 debut. Also full-throttle LBV, burnished tawnies and classically sultry white port and Moscatel.

Quinta do Noval Inconsistent producer which has recently passed into the ownership of AXA, the French insurance group (and is managed by Briton Christian Seely). Generally soft, elegant style, but the core quinta has the potential for much more (as historic vintages − '66, '47, '45, '34, '27 and the legendary '31 prove). 'Nacional' is from a plot of ungrafted vines. Some good Colheita ports (e.g. aromatic, silky '76) have been the first fruits of the stable clean-out. Noval LB is a full-flavoured ruby brand. See feature.

Offley Forrester Formerly Bacardi-owned; now (with Ferreira) part of Sogrape. Historic Boa Vista estate provides enjoyable Vintage ports, and '88 LBV is gutsier than most.

Osborne This sherry house produces a small range of sound ports.

Quarles Harris Another minor Symington marque (see **Dow**) with good-value Vintage ports in beefy style: '83 great value if you can find it.

Ramos–Pinto Fine tawnies and soft Vintage and Vintage-style ports ('82 Vintage is drinking well at present, while '87 LBV has glowing depths). Now in the ownership of Champagne house Roederer.

Quinta da Romaneira Grower-producer still finding its feet.

Romariz An inexpensive Taylor marque.

Quinta de la Rosa Privately owned and (since '88) run, with high ambitions and a delicate, choice style. Light wines prior to '88 were made by Robertson (Sandeman).

Royal Oporto The name used on export markets by the Real Companhia Velha. Shockingly variable wines, and never more than light save in earliest infancy: avoid Vintage ports (sold as Royal Oporto and Hooper).

Rebello Valente A fine old name belonging to Robertson (in turn owned by Sandeman). Some great historic wines ('45, '67, '70) but flimsy of late.

Sandeman Seagram-owned. Creamy, soft style: enjoyable, but lacking in grandeur, though the tannic bite of the '89 LBV suggests a more ambitious approach. Quinta do Vau '88 is creamy and satisfying. Imperial tawny is light-coloured but lingeringly flavoured.

Silva & Cosens The (Symington) company officially owning Dow.

Smith Woodhouse Chunky Vintage wines, and worthwhile traditional Late-Bottled Vintage. Supplier of decent LBV and Vintage Character blends to many supermarkets. Symington-owned.

Taylor, Fladgate & Yeatman For long the house to beat for Vintage port: consistent, tight-drawn, deep-founded and authoritative. Quinta de Vargellas, its core farm, also very fine in lesser years. Fine '92 (which I helped tread − I never realised how painful the pips could be) already hard to find. LBV is a more commercial wine, but its hallmark velvet makes a lovely Christmas treat.

Quinta do Vesúvio Showpiece High Douro quinta formerly in Ferreira owner-ship but since early '90s run as a separate operation by the Symingtons. Dark, super-ripe, fruit-stuffed early releases all sell-outs.

Warre The softest and most pliant of the four major Symington brands, but still large-scale, well-stuffed ports. Seductive floral style in youth. Very good traditional LBV and Crusted port, while Quinta da Cavadinha beguilingly combines grace and power.

Vintages (for vintage port only):
1994 ★★★; 1992 ★★★; 1991 ★★; 1987 ★★; 1985 ★★★; 1983 ★★★; 1982 ★; 1980 ★★; 1977 ★★★★; 1975 ★; 1970 ★★★★; 1967 ★★; 1966 ★★★★; 1963 ★★★★; 1960 ★★; 1955 ★★★; 1948 ★★★★; 1947 ★★★; 1945 ★★★★; 1935 ★★★; 1934 ★★★; 1931 ★★★★; 1927 ★★★★; 1912 ★★★★; 1908 ★★★; 1904 ★★★; 1900 ★★★.

Specialist retailers:
Traditional and fine-wine merchants are the best places to find particular Vintage ports.

Sic transit

It is a bitter moment. All journalists must face this death of innocence; the best you can hope to do is postpone it for as long as possible. You set off one sprightly morning to interview some grand and important personage, then you realise with mounting horror as you read the background notes that he or she is six years younger than you are. The personage proves confident, assured, well-briefed etc., etc. while you mouth asinine questions. You return home slumped in your train seat, the nascent lines suddenly incised deeply in your face, the meandering buffoonery of your professional life as plain as tar.

Anyway, it's happened and that's that. The 33-year-old prodigy in question is called Christian Seely: dad involved in wine, reads English at Cambridge, sets up gift hamper company, does MBA at Fontainebleau's INSEAD, becomes brand manager for l'Oréal, becomes venture capitalist, then hears about ...

Before we get into that, let me tell you a little about the port world. Portugal and England (later Britain) have been 'perpetual friends' since 1151. Trading agreements in the seventeenth century led to extensive wine-prospecting by English and Scottish merchants in northern Portugal, and a number of port companies (Croft and Taylor among them) were founded then. Port became established as a fine wine during the eighteenth and nineteenth centuries, initially as a strong dry table wine — which was why Boswell and Johnson were able to demolish 'a couple of bottles' on the evening of June 25th 1763 in discussing the perambulation of Spain, ghosts, and whether or not Colly Cibber was a blockhead. Only during the mid-nineteenth century did it become, uniformly, a sweet fortified wine.

No other wine land in the world is dominated by the British to the same extent as the port region. France, though, is the big market for port nowadays, and the two most recent major port acquisitions have been by French companies. The champagne producer Roederer purchased Ramos-Pinto in 1990, and the French insurance group AXA bought Quinta do Noval in May 1993.

Enter young Seely. He heard about the Noval purchase; through his Dad he knew Jean-Michel Cazes, the Bordeaux éminence who superintends AXA's vineyard portfolio. Seely wrote to Cazes, expressing interest; they met; they clicked. This is how the company which owns one of the greatest farms in the Douro, where the Citizen Kane of vintage ports ('31 Noval Nacional) was produced, has come to be run by a 33-year-old Englishman who had never previously visited the region.

It's a bit early to say how well Seely is doing with Noval, since there is a three-year time lag between making and marketing even the cheapest ports, and the quality of the best ports will only show up in a decade or so.

The new regime found at least one winner in the Noval lodges, anyway: Quinta do Noval's 1976 colheita port won the Eros Award for Fortified Wine of the Year in last year's edition of this guide. It is an extraordinarily fragrant old wine with a silky, succulent, fine-grained flavour. Also good is the lush, sumptuous 1989 Late-Bottled Vintage, a drinkable eiderdown of plump, blackberryish fruit. Seely and his team need to work at getting more of that fresh fruit into the ruby LB, while other tawnies in the range are rather sweet and simple; Noval's '91 vintage, too, lacks freshness and roundness; the '94 is more promising. But why shouldn't he manage all this? After all, he's got time on his side.

Madeira

Terminator

Madeira is a sub-tropical mountain top adrift in an ocean. It rises up through six kilometers of Atlantic seawater, then carries straight on up to nearly double the height of Snowdon. The island is fecund, with the right growing conditions, somewhere or other, for almost everything. Madeira is self-sufficient in both avocados and Christmas trees.

Vines don't occupy much of its agricultural land: total production is less than that of Vouvray. Most of it is, frankly, rubbish: poor quality cooked wine for kitchen use. A small minority of Madeira's wines are fine.

Fine? These are wines which can leave the unsuspecting wine drinker shaken to the core, disorientated, with all the fixed points of his or her secure little world rearranged by their reeking aromas and intense, tongue-splitting, sense-jangling flavours. There are no wines anywhere to match them for concentration of flavour: they are essences, distilled by heat and time. Oh, and they're almost immortal, too. And no one knows about them.

No one, that is, apart from a few eccentric connoisseurs. These are Vintage madeiras: fortified, then aged in casks in hot attics for 20 or more years, and then bottled. They cost upwards of £50 a bottle, but wait, wait, listen: this is not expensive at all! A thimbleful or two is an acceptable helping, so intensely flavoured are they; once opened, the bottle will last without deterioration for months. Since madeira is on intimate terms with oxygen from the moment its fermentation and fortification is finished, a little more scarcely disconcerts it.

They are hard to find (though see **Specialist Retailers**). They cry out to be sold in exquisite, phial-like half-bottles or even quarter-bottles, in order to communicate the message that these are elixirs and essences; I hope the Symingtons (see below) will eventually do this. If Madeira's fortunes are ever to revive, it will be through a wider appreciation of its greatest (perhaps the world's greatest) wine.

Most madeira you will come across will be called something like Selected, Choice or Finest. Don't believe it; it isn't; it's simpering, milksop wine, made by 'cooking' the base wine in a tank like a giant kettle, before fortifying it and sweetening it. Five-year-old blends are pleasant enough, but undemanding. Reserve or 10-year-old blends are usually good, intense wines, with keen acidity to match their sweetness and oxidative reek; Special Reserve, Extra Reserve or 15-year-old wines are impressive, incisive and concentrated. Solera wines can rival vintage wines for quality, though remember that the date on the bottle is that of the solera's foundation rather than that of the wine inside. This style of Madeira is no longer allowed on the island under EU regulations.

You may also see one of four grape-variety names on the bottle: Sercial (dry), Verdelho (medium), Bual (sweet) and Malmsey (very sweet). No grape-variety name means that the wine is made from the chameleon Tinta Negra Mole variety. Bual and Malmsey are the most sought-after among Vintage madeiras, but Verdelho and Sercial can be just as exciting.

There are a large number of company names, but madeira's declining fortunes have seen most of them concentrated in the hands of one company: the Madeira

Wine Company. This is now jointly owned by the Symington family (see Port) with the Blandy family, proprietors of Reid's Hotel. In principle, the mainland involvement is an excellent thing, since the remarkable, almost paramilitarily efficient Symingtons are dedicated to quality but commercially acute enough to ensure they have the means of funding it, whereas the traditional Madeira owners all seem to have dreamed themselves into oblivion. When the Symingtons bought into the Madeira Wine Company, it was a run-down, ramshackle edifice, and it will take great efforts over a decade or more to refurbish it. Among its great marques are Blandy, Cossart Gordon, Leacock, Power Drury, Rutherford and Miles and Shortridge Lawton; the Symingtons seem to have rationalised this range down to just four: Blandy, Cossart Gordon, Leacock and Miles. Other, independent shippers supplying good madeira include Barbeito, Henriques and Henriques (whose indebtedness has meant new investment from the port region recently) and D'Oliveira. Harvey's and Sandeman's madeiras are sourced from Henriques and Henriques.

Vintages:

These are only made from propitious raw materials, so the year itself is not of great consequence: the older, the more ravishing, the more expensive. Legendary years, however, include 1860, 1863, 1879, 1908, 1910, 1931, 1933, 1950, 1954, 1961, 1966, 1969 and 1971.

Specialist retailers:

The best madeira is hard to find in Britain. Wine merchants like Berry Bros, Justerini & Brooks and Lea & Sandeman stock a small range, and Bottoms Up has made a cautious, minor speciality of top madeira over the last year or two. Easily the best historic range, though, is available by mail order from Patrick Grubb Selections, Orchard Lea House, Steeple Aston, Bicester OX6 3RT (01869 340229). The best (and cheapest, and most atmospheric) place to get more recent Vintages, by contrast, is at the Madeira Wine Company's shop in Funchal (the unmissable São Francisco Wine Lodges).

Portuguese wines

Curiouser and curiouser

Vines grow throughout Portugal, as often as not on a garden footing; every non-urban Portuguese is a smallholder. Where two or three thousand are gathered together, there you have an appellation – called, in Portuguese, either Denominação de Origem Controlada (DOC) or Indicação de Proveniência Regulamentada (IPR). There are eighteen of the former (the senior designation) and 29 of the latter, most of their names only ever heard in Britain as top-scoring questions in wine quizzes. This is not to denigrate them; one day we may come to appreciate the richness and variety they offer.

The country's least successful wines are made from the vineyards most familiar to tourists: the dull reds of the Algarve, whose four DOCs expect and deserve demotion to IPRs. The best wines of Portugal's south are those of the Alentejo (Vidigueira, Reguengos, Redondo and Borba): richly flavoured, softly fruited reds. The Ribatejo, Lisbon's hinterland, has six IPRs; most of its wine is rough and cheap, but the potential for quality is attested by the fact that many of Portugal's best *garrafeira* wines (often excellent aged blends sold under a merchant's name rather than under a regional name) are sourced here. Around Lisbon itself are the historic DOCs of Carcavalos (near-extinct fortified wines), Colares (near-exinct tough reds grown from ungrafted vines in sand) and Bucelas (buttery-sour white). To the south of Lisbon, meanwhile, fine fortified dessert Moscatels are produced on the Setúbal peninsula (their perfumed intensity the consequence of six months' skin maceration) while nearby Palmela produces lively red wine and fragrant dry Muscat.

Northern Portugal has three great red-wine DOCs: Bairrada, Dão and Douro. All three produce much more red wine than white, and the reds of both Bairrada and Dão can be tough and unyielding. They can also be intense, complex and rewarding – and excellent value for money. One day, both DOCs will produce great wine by design rather than by accident, something the Douro is already beginning to do. (The best port, after all, is merely great red wine sent off on a diversion.) Port's legacy is still so powerful that making red wine in the better parts of the valley is regarded as eccentric; the results, though, can be superb.

Of the white wines of these three regions, it is perhaps those of Bairrada – fragrant, leafy and fresh from the better producers – that hold most promise. Yet white Dão and white Douro, too, can have a deliciously subtle unctuous pungency when well made, like the best white Rhône wines.

The coastal stretch of Northern Portugal is *vinho verde* country. This 'green wine' is just what the name suggests: fresh almost to the point of rawness, low in alcohol, high in acidity, sometimes frothy – and often, for the export market, sweetened. Red *vinho verde* , rarely exported, is a hot contender for the title of most bizarre wine in the world: almost black in colour, hard, sour, with a sort of demonically jesting appeal. You drink it with sardines: the final joke. And it works! There are, lastly, more good reds of conventional style produced in the remote, inland mountain country of Trás-os-Montes.

Portuguese grape varieties merit a book on their own, with a chapter on names – one is called Dog Strangler, another Fly Droppings, another French Squire, another Small Parrot. The great varieties include Touriga Nacional and Touriga Francesa (used for port, Douro reds and Dão reds), Baga (used for Bairrada reds) and Castelão Francês (the red grape of the south, where it is also known as Periquita, João de Santarém or Trincadeira Preta). Tinta Roriz is Spain's Tempranillo; Tinta Barroca is a very thick-skinned, drought-resistant port variety also grown in South Africa. Among the whites, Loureiro and Alvarinho are both better than some of their *vinho verde* incarnations suggest, while Fernão Pires (also known as Maria Gomes) can be marvellously subtle and expressive. These are varieties we will see more of in the future.

Adega Coop de Borba, Borba Good Alentejo coop producing soft yet intriguing red; excellent value.

Alta Mesa, Estremadura Coarse, cheap wines.

Quinta da Aveleda, VINHO VERDE Big producer: Casal Garcia and Aveleda are semi-sweet; dry, authentic wines are Quinta de Aveleda and Grinalda.

Quinta da Bacalhoa, SETÚBAL Cabernet-based red wines from an American-owned property, marketed by JP Vinhos. Long-term British success. I have found this wine rather hard and ungrateful, though '90 was softer and richer.

Peter Bright/Bright Brothers Australian winemaker based in Portugal for many years, where he was the man behind the success of João Pires Dry Muscat. Understands Portuguese varieties well. Douro Red good and supple. See also Fiuza.

Quinta do Carmo, BORBA Fine property, now Rothschild owned, preponderantly made (another good wine-quiz question) from the red-juiced Alicante Bouschet variety, foot-trodden in tanks of pink marble. Oak lends complexity.

Quinta do Crasto, DOURO Richly fruited red from Tinta Roriz and Touriga Francesa.

Cartuxa, EVORA IPR Fat whites and lush, minty reds from this promising Alentejo property of monastic origin, now a charitable trust.

Carvalho, Ribeiro & Ferreira Merchant-firm based in Ribatejo turning out fine garrafeiras (see above) without regional origin, as well as soundly made, good-value regionally identified generics. Also owns Quinta do Serrado in Dão and Quinta Folgorosa in Torres Vedras IPR. Now part of Allied-Lyons (through a subsidiary).

Casa de Saima, BAIRRADA Sumptuous red and age-worthy whites.

Caves Aliança, BAIRRADA Reliable, up-to-date, well-made reds and whites, and sometimes better than that (e.g. '94 Bairrada Branco). Also Douro wines and soft, sweet Alabastro Alentejo red.

Caves São João, BAIRRADA Excellent wines with great ageing potential, sold under Frei João label (look out for Reservas). Good Porta dos Cavaleiros Dão.

Caves Velhas, BUCELAS Rather heavy Bucellas (sic) but some good *garrafeiras*. Owned by beer-producer Sagres.

Quinta da Cismeira, DOURO Spicy, soft reds.

Quinta do Côtto, DOURO Grande Escolha (best years only) is an exciting red wine of booming plummy flavour given long (sometimes over-long) oaking.

Ferreira, DOURO Sogrape-owned port producer which has shown the way forward for red table wines in the Douro with the scented, savoury and expensive Barca Velha (second wine Ferreirinha Reserva Especial), made from grapes grown in the Douro's wild backlands.

Finagra see Herdade do Esporão

Fiuza, RIBATEJO Winery working with Peter Bright (q.v.). Creamy barrel-fermented Chardonnay is both satisfying and fresh; Cabernet Sauvignon and Merlot both spoiled by high acidity.

J.M. da Fonseca Internacional, Setúbal Lancers Rosé and sparkling wine.

José Maria da Fonseca Sucessores, Setúbal One of the country's leading wine producers, with a fascinating range which includes definitive Setúbal; the lively, raspberryish Periquita (and its *garrafeira* version CO); the deeper, Cabernet-influenced reds of Quinta de Camarate (*garrafeira* labelled TE); deep, tarry Alentejo red JS Rosado Fernandes (part-fermented in clay pots) and gamey Tinto Velho, and Terras Altas and Casa da Insua from Dão.

Quinta de Foz de Arouce, Beiras Deep, challenging red.

Herdade do Esporão, Reguengos Ambitious Alentejo producer turning out delicious carbonic-maceration Alandra and bigger, plummier estate wines. David Baverstock (ex-Symington group; see also **Quinta do Crasto**) now making wines.

João Pires Dry Muscat, Setúbal Fragrant, off-dry white. See also **JP Vinhos.**

JP Vinhos, Setúbal Dynamic company initially called João Pires; the João Pires name has now been sold, with the rights to the dry Muscat brand, to IDV. Fascinating range of often individual wines originally created by Peter Bright (q.v.), including carbonic maceration red Quinta de Santa Amaro; tougher, sharpish Meia Pipa; oaky white Catarina; Chardonnay Cova de Ursa; an intriguing Late Harvest Fernão Pires; and two Alentejo wines, the oak- and chestnut-aged Tinta da Anfora and the old-vines Herdade de Santa Marta.

Quinta da Lagoalva, Ribatejo Satisfying plummy red at a good price, and oily-lemon white is good, too.

Leziria, Almeirim IPR Cheap wine from the Ribatejo.

Niepoort, Douro Exciting red and white wines in preparation.

Palácio de Brejoeira, Vinho Verde Expensive, much-sought-after wine: a peachy, varietal Alvarinho.

Quinta de Pancas, Alenquer IPR Exciting, richly fruited Porta da Luz and promising Cabernet: gutsy '92 very good.

Luis Pato, Bairrada The DOC's leading grower-producer, with a taste for experiment. Wines sometimes difficult; never dull. A new start in '95 with low yield, individual vineyard wines of softer style.

Pedras do Monte Well-made, prettily labelled, plum-fruited cheapie.

Quinta das Bágeiras, Bairrada Old-vine vineyard producing promising dark reds.

Quinta das Maias, Dão Partner vineyard to Quinta dos Roques (q.v.); impressive.

Quinta da Romeira, Bucelas Exciting new venture from Portuguese subsidiary of Tate & Lyle. To watch.

Quinta dos Roques, Dão Dark, intense reds and lively whites.

Quinta de la Rosa, Douro Soft, full-flavoured reds backed by ripe tannins – mostly, though '93 was over tannic with tenuous appley fruit.

Quinta de Sães, Dão Gutsy, rough-edged, authentic red; spicy white drinks well.

Ramos–Pinto, Douro Duas Quintas table wines some of the subtlest of the North.

Paulo da Silva, COLARES Leading producer both of Colares and branded wines from outside the DOC sold as Beira Mar (good '83 Reserva). Deep, slow-ageing prunes-and-bacon flavour, concentrated and interesting: was this what claret was like 150 years ago?

Sogrape The company whose fortune was founded on Mateus Rosé continues to keep up to date with well-made and slickly packaged regional wines, including some of the best Dão (Duque de Viseu); fine red and white Bairrada; some of the best estate *vinho verde* from Honra de Azevedo (as well as more commercial sweet Gazela and dry Chello); and textured, oak-aged Alentejo red Vinha do Monte. White Planalto and Vila Regia are clean, crisp Douro whites, though look out for the white Douro Reserva – a fatter, more interesting wine. The '94 vintage has the floral grace and apricot fruit of a good white Rhône, combined with fresh acidity: superb. Vila Regia red is fresh and fruity, while the Reserva version is deeper, with some oak influence. See also **Ferreira.**

Solar das Bouças, VINHO VERDE Good, Loureiro-led green wine from Van Zeller family, former owners of Quinta do Noval (see **port**).

Vale do Bomfim, DOURO Table wine from Dow's Douro home; the '90 red was decent, cedary, chewy.

Quinta do Vale da Raposa, DOURO Fresh, supple red.

Valle Pradinhos, VALPAÇOS IPR Classy, chewy red from the far north made by Ramos-Pinto's wine maker. Second wine Porta Velha.

Vintages
1995 ★★★; 1994 ★★★★; 1993 ★; 1992 ★★★; 1991 ★★★; 1990 ★★★; 1989 ★★★; 1988 ★★★; 1987 ★★★; 1986 ★★; 1985 ★★★★.

Specialist retailers
Sainsbury's have had a long relationship with JP Vinhos and Peter Bright, but other supermarkets seem primarily interested in Portugal as a source of cheap wine only.

Romania

Come and get it

Like its neighbour and chum Moldova, Romania is one of the vine-richest countries in Europe; it has some 200,000 hectares of vineyard, more than either Bulgaria and Hungary, and a lot of this land is well-sited (lying on the same latitude as the best parts of France, though with a more continental climate) and topographically interesting. Two key wine consultants and Masters of Wine – Angela Muir and Kym Milne – have both told me in the last year that, of all the countries of Eastern Europe, Romania strikes them as having the most potential. Muir spoke of the lie of the land; Milne recalled the taste of some of the grapes. Turning this potential into bottles of wannabe burgundy or couldbe claret, though, is a slow business, delayed further by our unwillingness to regard Romania as anything but a producer of cheap gluggers.

The Romanians are good at producing two sorts of wine: juicy, stewy, varietal ly vague but naturally well-balanced drinkers' reds; and sometimes fine-grained sweet whites. Romanians love old wine, too; soft-contoured bottles from the mid-eighties are still easily obtainable. Making crisp, dry, fresh-flavoured whites, by contrast, requires equipment which many Romanian wineries cannot yet afford, and techniques which many Romanian winemakers have yet to master.

The most impressive wines exported from Romania at present come from the Dealul Mare region which, as it happens, is the closest to Bucharest. Pinot Noir can be very good, varying in style from super-light and throat-stroking to soft, full, spicy and concentrated; Cabernet is also good: meaty and earthy. Merlot tends to be rather jammy. The best of Romania's native red varieties, Feteasca Neagra, usually fetches up as quite an earthy wine, too, with spicy, liquorice tones. (Romania has a rich viticultural heritage, and there are many native grape varieties which have yet to reach Britain.) Varietal definition, as I hinted above, isn't a great Romanian forte, and few wines have the classic notes which wine textbooks describe.

The best of the sweet whites are made from the Tamaîoasa variety, which botrytises well to produce flavours of intrinsic complexity and satisfying acid balance. The Grasa, too, makes fine, succulent, soft-bellied dessert wines. Dealul Mare's best wineries are Prahova, Rovit and Pietroasa.

The whole country is speckled with wine regions, and doubtless other wines of curiosity and excellence will emerge with time. Tirnave in the centre of the country and Murfatlar on the Black Sea are, with Dealul Mare, the most sizeable areas; Cotnari, in northern Romania near the Moldovan border, is regarded as the Romanian Sauternes district – its wine once rivalled Tokaji in fame and allure. Whenever a Romanian wine proves good, it will always offer excellent value; the best are bargains.

Serbia (Yugoslav Federation)

Dark hour

Serbia used to produce around a third of the wine of the former Yugoslavia. The best of it was red – from the native Prokupac blended with Pinot or Gamay in the Zupa region, or from Cabernet and Merlot in Vranje near the Bulgarian border. The finest wines of the former Yugoslavia, though, are those produced in Montenegro, a country still federated with Serbia: earthy, spicy Vranac. It still has great export potential, despite its political handicap.

Slovenia

Prize draw

In its swift and comparatively painless transition to independence, Slovenia has looked the luckiest of the former Yugoslav republics; in wine terms it certainly is. Little quality wine has emerged yet from the country, which is mostly geared at present to the production of the doughy but dull Laski Riesling. The fact, however, that one of its two major vineyard areas marks a continuation of Italy's Friuli (Primorski), and the other a continuation of Austria's Styria (the Drava valley), bodes extremely well for the future. Sauvignon Blanc and Merlot are expected to be prominent among Slovenia's leading varietals, together with the native Sipon (Furmint). Quality is already rising – but we may not see many of its wines since Austrian and Italian customers are already driving home with bootfuls of the best.

Slovakia

Surprise, surprise

When the first Czechoslovakian wines reached Britain, few tasters were not taken aback. Instead of the thin, sour, weedy and fault-ridden whites we were expecting, out poured some surprisingly plump, comely, self-assured white wines, seemingly grown in a misplaced outpost of Alsace. Slovakia has most of those vineyards today, and they're still good: dry, full-bodied, often spicy (especially Traminer and Irsai Oliver), and excellent value in comparison to similar wines from neighbouring Austria. Slovakian reds, too, can be fun in a tart, raspberryish sort of way (the region lies on the same latitude as Chablis, and we don't expect much red wine from there, do we?). Slovakia even has a couple of Tokaji villages up on the Hungarian border, though wines from these have yet to reach Britain.

South Africa

The morning after

Last year marked South African wine's honeymoon on the British market. This year sexy young SA has begun to discover wicked old GB's defects (parsimony on price and a fickleness of purchasing habits), while mature, indulgent GB has begun to grasp wilful, provocative SA's failings (inconsistency, frivolity, and a dislike of softness and subtlety of flavour). Nonetheless the marriage remains broadly happy. They keep floating containers at us, and we keep emptying them and pushing them back.

The key area for South Africa in Britain is still the supermarket white wine at under £4 (and sometimes under £3). There are now a huge number of labels of this sort, usually featuring a profile of a few mountains, a thorn tree and a proboscidian mammal, and called something ending in 'a'. They're technically adept but (as raw material costs rise in South Africa while prices stick here) getting less and less interesting: light, fresh, crisp and fruity is about as far as even the most verbally febrile commentator can go. Take care, South Africa: British supermarkets will suck you dry for this kind of product, and you'll then be left with a kind of New-World-Liebfraumilch image and no obvious path of consumer progression. The best wines of this sort, to my mind, have been those produced by Kym Milne MW for Thresher under the Winelands label, since they use raw materials intelligently and provide a graduated sequence of wines to enjoy from the off-dry Medium White (£2.99) up to the Bushvine Chenin (£4.49), Cabernet blend (£4.49) and Shiraz-Cabernet (£4.99), via interesting wines like the Cinsaut-Tinta Barocca (£3.99). Milne's Barrel-Fermented Chenin for Tesco (£3.99) was also a grown-up wine with real strength and depth of flavour.

Then what? Then there is a sort of hole in the middle between the cooperative-sourced cheapies and the grander estate wines. Those estates and producers who have stooped to fill it (Fairview, Villiera, Danie de Wet and others) have done well, though this success has often meant that their prices accelerate and UK sales consequently drop off (as with the superb Stellenzicht). Yet this is precisely the zone where Australia has profited, and in which South Africa should be focussing its efforts.

As far as the best wines are concerned, 1995 brought South Africa the trauma of defeat in the SAA Shield 'test match' against Australia. It was probably a salutary humbling, bringing home to winemakers what was pointed out in this introduction last year: far too many of South Africa's 'top' red wines are modelled on a kind of rugby-playing ideal – the impressive but ugly brute. They are not picked ripe enough; they are then over-extracted and over-wooded; the wood, too, is sometimes less clean than it should be. The result is dark, smouldering and undrinkable. Everyone loves intensity and depth of flavour, but it must be soft and approachable, even in youth. In the wine world, ugly ducklings grow into ugly swans. Aspirational white wines are in general more successful than reds (and I, for one, often prefer South Africa's fresh, cool-night acidity to Australia's chemistry-set version), yet even these lack consistency: Klein Constantia's Sauvignon Blanc, for example, or Dieu Donné's Chardonnay have been both magnificent and mediocre from vintage to vintage. Cap Classique sparkling wines (the name merely indicates that the Champagne method is used, with nine months' lees ageing) are few in number as yet, but off to a good start.

South Africa has twelve main wine-growing areas. Some have a clear sense of regional identity: Constantia and Walker Bay/Elgin are cooler climate regions where South Africa's freshest, most herbacious whites and lively, thrusting reds are produced, while Robertson's warm climate and lime-rich soils produce Chardonnay of luscious, creamy appeal. Other areas like Stellenbosch or Paarl appear too diverse to have any discernible regional style as yet.

Most of South Africa's repertoire of grape varieties are those used internationally. Chenin Blanc (locally called Steen) is by far the most widely planted variety; it produces a good basic quaffy white with a guava-like style to it rather than the raw cooking apple of cheap French Chenin; look out for 'bush vine' versions (i.e. older plantings), which can be more serious in flavour. Colombard is the other white staple; well handled, it can be fun. Sauvignon Blanc is on the up and up; the results are unpredictable, but when it is good (Graves-style from Plaisir du Merle; Sancerre-style from some of the Constantia producers) it seems to 'belong' more happily in South Africa than it does in California, Australia or even Chile. Chardonnay is still a comparatively new arrival, but provides some very promising bottles: nutty-buttery but with natural balance. Riesling is often used for dessert wines.

Among reds, both Cabernet and Merlot (though not yet widely planted) are used for the more aspirational wines; some are superb (see producers, below) but others are green, violent and unlovely. It is varieties like Cinsaut (as it is usually spelt there), Shiraz and, especially, Pinotage (a Pinot Noir-Cinsaut cross) which give the most interesting wines: tangy, savoury-sweet, soft textured. Pinot Noir itself is exciting in the right hands, while there are a couple of good Cabernet Francs, Gamays and Zinfandels from fanatics, too.

Finally, don't miss out on South Africa's fortified wines: both port styles (made from Tinta Barocca and other authentic port grape varieties) and sherry styles (including sweetening Muscadels and Jerepigos), often given extravagant pre-bottling age. They can be delicious and inexpensive.

Avontuur, STELLENBOSCH Rich, lemony 'Le Chardon' Chardonnay leads an eclectic range. '95 Pinotage has a nice leathery scent but lacks charm and roundness.

Backsberg, PAARL A winery that can turn out bullseye wines – Chardonnay, Merlot, Shiraz – but wide, experimental range leads to a lack of consistency.

Bellingham, FRANSCHHOEK Improved range. '95 Sauvignon Blanc has good crispness and freshness. This is the source for Waitrose's fair but not outstanding Diamond Hills range.

Bergkelder, STELLENBOSCH Big cooperative-cum-merchant group, bottling (not always flatteringly) for a number of estates such as Meerlust. Its own sparkler Pongracz is well made and delicately fruity; Stellenryck Cabernets, though, tend to be tough, old-style wines, their pleasure on hold. Other ranges include Fleur du Cap and Two Oceans.

Beyerskloof see Kanonkop.

Boschendal, PAARL It's the busty, broad-beamed, butter-soaked Chardonnay and tangy, zesty sparkling wines we see most of in Britain. Non-vintage red Le Pavillon rather hard in style, but offers fair value.

Bouchard–Finlayson, WALKER BAY Crisp Sauvignon, and risky, French-style, sometimes over-lean Chardonnay. Pinot Noir also very firm but (from Oak Valley in Elgin) perfumed and good.

Buitenverwachtung, CONSTANTIA Zesty Sauvignon Blanc and clean, limey Chardonnay are best.

Cabrière, FRANSCHHOEK Sparkling-wine specialist, selling under the Pierre Jourdan label. Brut Sauvage attempts Champagne-like severity and achieves cutting, dry vinosity; Brut is deep if slightly graceless; Blanc de Blancs has a creamy, sumptuous nose though seems unripe on the palate. Pinot Noir to watch.

Cape Vineyards Grouping of seven cooperatives supplying Rawsons wines for Kwiksave (and including Du Toitskloof for Waitrose).

Cathedral Cellars see KWV.

La Cotte, FRANSCHHOEK Pleasant cooperative-produced wines.

Delheim   Generally unexciting wines as yet, though '94 Cabernet Sauvignon and '94 Pinotage are better.

Diamond Hills see Bellingham.

Dieu Donné, FRANSCHHOEK   Impressive Chardonnays of taut, burgundian complexity in '92 and '93; '94 was a disappointment.

Diemersdal, DURBANVILLE   Good, expressive Shiraz from this estate acquired by Swiss-owned Sonop.

Eikehof, FRANSCHHOEK   Small, carefully made 'home farm' range from Dieu Donné's winemaker.

Neil Ellis   A winemaker sourcing fruit from different areas. Generally fine-grained, piercing style which works best for Sauvignon Blanc. Minty Cabernet Sauvignons sometimes too acidic.

Fairview, PAARL   One of the few producers to take Chenin Blanc seriously; good Semillon, sound Shiraz and easy-drinking Gamay stand out, too, in an inventive, accessible range. Even the Cabernet Sauvignon is made in a soft, supple style, and the Zinfandel/Cinsaut blend was unique and appealing. Serious Rosé one of the best on the market from anywhere.

Genus see Simonsvlei.

Glen Carlou, PAARL   Classy, complicated Chardonnay.

Goiya Kgeisje see Vredendal Cooperative

Hamilton Russell, WALKER BAY   Restrained, cosseted Pinot Noir and Chardonnay in European style, best with a little age. Sometimes ('93 Pinot) overworked and overcomplicated, eclipsing the fruit.

Hartenberg, STELLENBOSCH   Fine, buttered-apple Riesling best of the range so far.

Impala, OLIFANTS RIVER   Varietal range produced at Citrusdal cooperative (Goue Vallei) by Peter Flewellyn on behalf of Hugh Ryman.

Jordan, STELLENBOSCH   Classy Sauvignon Blanc and aspirational Chardonnay.

Pierre Jourdan see Cabrière.

Kanonkop, STELLENBOSCH   Winemaker Beyers Truter is more skilled at giving Pinotage a gutsy, sweet-edged classicism than any competitor. Kadette, a Cabernet-Pinotage blend, is a good buy, too, as is generous, earthy Bouwland. Bordeaux-blend Paul Sauer is chunky, for ageing, built on a core of rounded fruit. A new venture for Truter is Beyerskloof, specialising in accessible, fruit-driven Pinotage for export.

Klein Constantia, CONSTANTIA   Beautiful estate which has reinvented one of history's legendary dessert wines, Constantia, sold (in a beautiful dark bottle) as Vin de Constance — succulent, voluptuous and buttery. Sauvignon Blanc can be good on occasion; Riesling is one of South Africa's best; Cabernet lacks richness.

Kleindal   A négociant label (Vinimark is the company name) including lush, fine-value Pinotage.

Kumala   Disappointing inter-regional blends assembled by Bernard Fontannaz of Sonop. Chenin-Chardonnay rather weak; Cabernet-Shiraz thin and slight.

KWV, PAARL The giant cooperative which has traditionally underwritten South African grape overproduction and legislated for the wine industry. A huge range of wines, though few outstanding (fortified wines most prominent among them). Cathedral Cellars prestige range a particular disappointment.

Long Mountain Big brand, intended to be the Jacob's Creek of South Africa, sourced from a number of scattered cooperatives. Early results underwhelming though safe enough, which is what wine brands are all about.

Louisvale, STELLENBOSCH Delicate, floral Chardonnays, almost crisp.

Meerlust, STELLENBOSCH   Exasperatingly inconsistent: fine, sweet-fruited raw materials often end up thin, sour and hard in bottle. Merlot is best bet.

Mount Disa KWV-produced wines for Oddbins.

Mulderbosch, STELLENBOSCH Pace-setting Sauvignon in both unwooded and barrel-fermented versions, backed by oaky Chardonnay.

Nederburg, PAARL Large but unconvincing range.

Neethlingshof, STELLENBOSCH   Grand estate with massive investment from Singapore-based owner Hans-Joachim Schreiber, yet early releases were often slight, and were soon outclassed by sister winery Stellenzicht. Best for late-harvest dessert wines.

Plaisir de Merle, PAARL   Classy Sauvignon Blanc — lean, crisp fruit with discreet oak/lees input — and impressive, curranty Cabernet Sauvignon made an exciting debut in UK for these wines made from older vines with consultation help from Paul Pontallier of Château Margaux. Slick packaging also revolutionary among the generally frumpy South African bottles.

Pongracz see Bergkelder.

Rawsons see Cape Vineyards.

Rust-en-Vrede, STELLENBOSCH   Old-style, high-acid, massively concentrated, aggressive and unlikeable Estate Wine is much lauded in South Africa.

Rustenberg, STELLENBOSCH Generally thin reds, lacking suppleness and wealth of fruit. Change of winemaker may renovate style.

Savanha Merchant-style operation run by Aussie Graham Knox.

Saxenburg, STELLENBOSCH Coming on a storm of late; particularly good Shiraz.

Simonsig, STELLENBOSCH Generally consistent range. The '92 Kaapse Vonkel Brut is a pretty, well-made sparkler. Adelberg dull.

Simonsvlei, PAARL Forward-looking cooperative; hit-and-miss wines include Genus for Oddbins.

Sonop, PAARL   Swiss-run operation producing wines for the international market. Ranges include Cape Levant, Cape Soleil and Kumala.

Sinnya Dullish.

Steenberg, CONSTANTIA Widely travelled young winemaker has begun work at this grand, renovated estate with a commanding Sauvignon Blanc.

Stellenryk see Bergkelder.

Stellenvale Gilbeys label: creamy, bubblegum-like Chardonnay is fun.

Stellenzicht, STELLENBOSCH Some good late-harvest dessert wines and a brilliant series of salty, blackberryish Shiraz wines (South Africa's best) are the hits.

Thelema, STELLENBOSCH Deep-flavoured Sauvignon Blanc and nut-buttery Chardonnay more to my taste than dry-fruited, sharp Cabernet Sauvignon and sour Merlot.

Du Toitskloof, WORCESTER Decent cooperative wines in the main; the '95 Cabernet/Shiraz was sweet and tacky.

Twee Jonge Gezellen, TULBAGH Full-flavoured and increasingly complex sparkler Krone Borealis is best of range.

Uiterwyk, STELLENBOSCH A spell in St Emilion for red-winemaker Daniel de Waal has paid dividends with unbridled, extractive but fruit-supported Pinotage (the value alternative to Kanonkop) and ambitious Cabernet Sauvignon. Whites dull.

Uitkyk, STELLENBOSCH Clean, deep Sauvignon Blanc offers fair value.

Van Loveren, ROBERTSON Typically creamy Chardonnays (Spes Bona has less oak than estate version).

Vergelegen, SOMERSET WEST Huge investment in a historic property: wines to watch (including Yellowwood Ridge for Victoria Wines). Good Merlot.

Villiera, PAARL One of the most consistent of South African estates: crisp, appley Carte Rouge and complex, impressive Carte d'Or sparkling wines, crunchy Sauvignon Blanc, classy Blanc Fumé, well-made smoothish Merlot and gutsy Cabernet Sauvignon. The Bordeaux blend Cru Munro is concentrated and well-balanced. High-effort lightly oaked Chenin is sumptuous and impressive, too. Only Riesling is a slight disappointment.

Vinfruco, STELLENBOSCH Complicated ownership arrangement, but well-selected wines sold under various names (including the ominous Oak Village).

Vredendal Cooperative, OLIFANTS RIVER Goiya Kgeisje is a fresh, well-balanced, not quite dry, cheap, colourfully labelled white made half-way to Namibia and sold under an unpronounceable San name.

Warwick, STELLENBOSCH Great Cabernet Franc (piercing varietal style backed by chewy, almost fiery depth) is the best wine here, while straight Cabernet Sauvignon can also be sweeter and riper than most; the Bordeaux-blend Trilogy is sometimes (as in '91) acidic and unlovely, though impressive in terms of pure extract. Bush-Vine Pinotage coming on stream with a feisty, punchy '95.

De Wetshof, ROBERTSON Chardonnay virtuoso: creamy, smooth, supple, summer-fruited, densely woven wines under a variety of labels.

Wildekrans, WALKER BAY Deep, concentrated, almost sherbetty Chardonnay and Sauvignon. Pinotage esteemed by some; I find the '93 lacks a firm core of flavour, though it quaffs well enough.

Winelands Hugely impressive range from the Kym Milne team for Thresher, including spicy Medium Dry, deep Chenin, deeper Bush-Vine version, sweet and toothsome Cinsaut/Tinta Barocca (sic), gutsy Cabernet Sauvignon/Cabernet Franc and well-stuffed if slightly rubbery Pinotage. 'Premium' Shiraz-Cabernet offers great value if you like its slightly minty, inky, cool-weather style.

Woodlands Range for UK sourced variously and assembled (by Giorgio Dalla Cia of Meerlust) for complexity rather than simple impact. '90 Merlot/Cabernet was disappointingly thin and dry, though.

Yellowwood Ridge see Vergelegen.

Vintages
1996 ★★★; 1995 ★★★; 1994 ★★; 1993 ★★★; 1992 ★★★; 1991 ★★★★; 1990 ★★;
1989 ★★★; 1988 ★★; 1987 ★★★★; 1986 ★★★★; 1985 ★

Specialist retailers
The leading London specialist stockist is The South African Wine Centre.

Spain

Rise and shine

No country in the world has more vineyard land within its borders than Spain. It is, though, far from being number one in other respects: low, drought-striken productivity means that Italy and France both vinify more wine; and in quality terms, too, Spain has tended to lag behind its European and New World competitors. Whites have been heavy, dull, flat, oak-sodden; reds weak-coloured and dopy from an over-long siesta in an ancient cask. Criticism was met with the flat assertion that wine could be no better than this. The reality is that Stockholm's buses run on ethanol distilled from unwanted Spanish red.

Changes are underway, though. Ideas from abroad are now welcomed, as is practical help from itinerant winemakers trained in non-Spanish ways. Spain's low costs (the importer's euphemism for poverty) has been turned to its advantage with increasing slices of the price-conscious British market. The 1995 harvest (good in quality but with much reduced totals in all areas save Rioja, following savage spring frosts) may put this trend on hold temporarily, but the value will be back; indeed Rioja, with the splendid '94s and '95s to play with, looks like being a key value area in the next half-decade. It's not only value that's on offer, but absolute quality, too: when I tasted the Cabernet Sauvignon and Syrah wines of Dominio de Valdepusa late last year, I felt I'd found two truly great contemporary Spanish wines. Of course there have always been great Riojas, great Ribera del Duero wines and great sherries, but this was different: they were grown in a non-DO location, they were made with international perspectives, they brimmed with a sense of confidence and purpose. Spain, these wines said, is on its way.

Sherry

Wind from the sea

Spain is the second highest country in Europe – after Switzerland. The country's interior lies far up above sea level. Where rivers like the Guadalquivir or the smaller Guadalete reach the sea, there you have 'a corridor for wind', moistly inhaled from the water by Spain's white, arid heart.

The wind from the sea makes sherry. At least, so far as anyone knows. Sherry, like Sauternes, owes its existence to mould spores, thought to be chauffeured in from the ocean by the passage of vapour-laden air. This time the mould does not feast on the berries themselves, but on the new-made Palomino wine in its casks (here known as butts). It covers the wine in a pale, yeasty carpet called flor – 'flower'; and it is flor which gives fino and manzanilla sherry its distinctive crisp tang. Amontillado, true amontillado, is fino aged beyond the death of flor, though most commercial amontillado is merely a blend of sweetened sherries. Oloroso sherry is one on which flor was not permitted to grow, and which ages oxidatively, as madeira does. Palo cortado is a sort of hermaphrodite, half-fino, half-oloroso; and Pedro Ximenez (or PX) is the super-sweet sherry used for sweetening purposes, but occasionally bottled on its own. It tastes like a syrup of raisins and is popular poured like dark tar onto pale ice cream.

Sherry is fortified, though only just: most fino and manzanilla nowadays is 15.5% abv, tweaked up from its natural 14% abv; oloroso is usually 18% abv. Ageing provides almost all its flavour (biological mould-ageing for fino, chemical air-ageing for oloroso); and the means of ageing sherry consistently is called the solera system: a chain of butts which breaks a single portion of wine up into many fractions, mingling them with thousands of fractions of other wine of different ages as it does so.

Spain has no greater wine than this. The best fino has a fresh, pure breadiness which makes it the perfect partner for almost all foods, but particularly fish; manzanilla is cleaner and softer still. Both should be chilled, and drunk quickly, as you would drink a white wine. Oloroso is better without food, to provoke thought or reverie.

The past year has been an important one for sherry, bringing three pieces of good news and one of bad. Sombrely, 1995 was the fourth consecutive drought year in the region, and production sank by half as the parched vines struggled for survival. Happily, January 1 1996 marked the outlawing of the use of the term 'sherry' for British and Cypriot imposters (the concentrate-based concoctions must now be called Fortified British Wine and Cypriot Fortified Wine); there is now one duty band for sherry (15 per cent abv to 21 per cent abv), enabling producers to pitch the alcohol levels of their wines according to taste rather than excise criteria; and sales of sherry to Britain rose by 50,000 cases in 1995. Perhaps the message is getting through: sherry is the cheapest of the world's fine wines.

Barbadillo Manzanilla-producing company, part-owned by Harveys. Light, fresh, delicate style of sherry throughout the range, even including oloroso. Castillo de San Diego, its Palomino-based table wine, is useful for demonstrating the near-miraculous nature of sherry. How can something as fine and flavour-laden as sherry be transubstantiated out of base wine as dull and insipid as Castillo de San Diego? (This is no slight on Barbadillo, since Castillo de San Diego is well made; Palomino is just fatally dull in its pre-sherry state.)

Caballero This company is based in the third of sherry's towns, Puerto de Santa Maria, said to have a style of its own which combines the softness of manzanilla with the lemony tang of Jerez fino. Put it to the test with the Puerto Fino of John William Burdon, a Caballero-owned brand.

Croft A Jerez vandal, in my opinion, since its hugely successful Croft Original Pale Cream sherry is an inauthentic confection of trivial flavour which does nothing to draw the confused consumer towards the delights of true dry sherry; Particular and Delicado are also insipid, mawkish products. Croft produces a good Palo Cortado, but it's almost impossible to find.

Diez–Merito Fino Imperial and Victoria Regina oloroso are expensive but intense, as is the Don Zoilo range.

Domecq La Ina fino is one of the most reliable brands, lighter in style than Tio Pepe. Dry Oloroso Rio Viejo is good, too. Domecq's top sherries (51-1A amontillado and the sweetened Sibarita palo cortado) are deeply flavoured but expensive by comparison with their peers.

Garvey San Patricio fino has improved in Garvey's present German ownership, though it's easier to find in Stuttgart than Surbiton.

Gonzalez Byass Sherry's greatest name maintains exemplary standards. Tio Pepe is the fino against which others are measured; Alfonso is a light, choice dry oloroso. Amontillado del Ducque is a superb dry, authentic amontillado, while medium Apostoles and sweet Matusalem prove that, when the best raw materials are used, sweetened oloroso can have all the grandeur of fine vintage port or madeira. As it happens, Gonzalez Byass has been experimenting with the release of old, vintage sherry: these are essences, akin to vintage madeira, but dryer and harsher still.

Harveys The best Harveys sherries are those in the 1796 range, though they have always been hard to find. The sickly sweet Bristol Cream has had its day, despite the gimmicky new blue bottle; now Club Amontillado has become 'Club Classic' and Luncheon Dry is re-born as 'Dune'. Give us a break ...

Hidalgo Great manzanilla La Gitana and pleasant soft amontillado Napoleon.

Lustau Highly inventive company responsible for marketing 'almacenista' sherries (butts bought from private stockholders): light, flavoury, delicate, worth trying. The Landed Age sherries are less successful, and the huge total range (including own-label supplies) variable in quality: you get what you pay for.

Osborne Lively red-label Quinta fino

Palomino & Vergara Tio Mateo fino is excellent if you can find it.

Ponche Delicious orange-flavour liqueur produced in the Jerez area by Caballero and others.

Sandeman Basic sherries have been dull; new Soléo fino and 'Don' series may mark improvements. The top-line Imperial Corregidor oloroso and Royal Ambosante palo cortado are authoritatively intense.

Valdespino With Gonzalez Byass, the greatest of sherry producers, though on a much smaller scale. Everything in the range is worth trying (and usually worth double the asking price), but of particular note are the hugely bready Inocente fino; two complex amontillados, Tio Diego and Dom Tomás; the dry Don Gonzalo and richer Solera 1842 olorosos; Cardenal, an intense palo cortado; and finally Amontillado Coliseo – which, as its name suggests, is a sherry of herculean concentration, the legacy of 60 or so years of casky slumber.

Williams & Humbert A tackily labelled, mainly sweet range which includes two very good sherries: the large-framed, lemony Pando fino, and the deliciously austere Dos Cortados oloroso (sometimes described as a palo cortado).

Rioja
Softly, softly

Rioja is Spain's Bordeaux. Indeed Bordeaux helped make Rioja: the area's prominence dates from the times of the nineteenth-century phylloxera epidemic in France, when replacement sources of claret-like wine were needed. Nearby Rioja helped supply the demand – until it, too, succumbed to the tiny insect's depradations. The Bordeaux manner of producing deep flavoured, cask-aged red wines took on the distinctive sweet-edged warmth we associate with the word 'Rioja' because much of the wood used in the region was sourced from America (whose white oak is more vanilla-laden than France's tight-grained native oaks); and because the grapes grown in Rioja were the soft, strawberryish Tempranillo.

They still are, in the main, though Garnacha Tinta (Grenache) plays an important role in the least lauded of Rioja's sub-regions, the Rioja Baja; ironically Cabernet Sauvignon, too, is now on the increase, albeit at this stage on an 'experimental' basis. Quality has traditionally been flagged for the consumer by the use of terms describing ageing on the label: Sin Crianza means young wines with no barrel ageing; Crianza wines are aged for one year in barrel and one further year in vat, cask or bottle; Reserva means wines (supposedly from a good harvest) with one year in barrel and two years in vat, cask or bottle; and Gran Reserva should mean wines from the best years only, aged in barrel for two years and for another three in vat, cask or bottle. Modern winemakers feel, however, that ageing requirements of this sort are not necessarily the best route to quality, and some now ignore in particular the Crianza/Sin Crianza division, giving good quality wine, say, just six months in oak.

White rioja (one fifth of the region's production) is principally made from Viura, though the less widely grown Malvasia Riojana often gives more interesting flavours than Viura. Ageing requirements take a similar pattern to those for red wines, though the time spent ageing is less lengthy; nonetheless traditional white Rioja is heavily, often overly woody. A modern style of clean, crisp neutrality gained ground throughout the 80s, but in truth what was needed was a middle way between the two, which contemporary experiments with barrel fermentation (a technique leaving the wine less oak-saturated than does straight barrel ageing) may bring about.

Rioja retains its niche in the affections of the British wine-buying public because it produces the most approachable of all red wines: even the youngest, grandest Riojas are never frightening, and most you could sip in your sleep. The wines remain good value, too: many are still under £5. Moreover Rioja has been Spain's luckiest region over the last two years: the drought which affected most of Spain in '94 spared Rioja, which only suffered a 10 per cent drop in quantity; while the spring frosts of '95 spared Rioja, too, giving the region its largest harvest ever at a time when most parts of Spain saw their harvest cut by half. Quality for both vintages is good to very good.

AGE I find the Siglo range disappointingly light-flavoured.

Barón de Ley Single-estate production from a good site, but quality is patchy.

Berberana Increasingly go-ahead company experimenting with (inexpensive) younger wines like the fruit-rich 'Oak-Aged Tempranillo' (queer name, since the point is that it has less oak than usual). '92 Viura Crianza coarse and unlovely.

Bilbainas Dullish wines, chiefly seen in Britain under the Viña Pomal label.

Campillo I like the fine, expressive, strawberry-fragrant varietal Tempranillos from this Faustino-owned company enormously, though Gran Reserva '85 is perhaps a little too soft for true greatness.

Campo Viejo Generally reliable range from this large company, with good Reservas and Gran Reservas (especially Marqués de Villamagna). Albor is a light, easy mouthful of wine.

Contino Lush, full Rioja from a single-vineyard site sold as reserva only. Vinified and marketed by CVNE.

Cosme Palacio y Hermanos An early rebel against Rioja's ageing pigeonholes. Unambitious, but these sweet, soft wines offer generally fair value.

CVNE A name to look out for: wines packed with the accessible deliciousness of Rioja at its best; most sold under the Viña Real brand. Monopole white is now barrel-fermented, lending extra complexity.

Domecq The biggest vineyard owner in the region, producing reliable Domecq Domain and Marqués de Arienzo.

Faustino Martínez Tacky bottles, but expressive, carefully made wines.

Lagunilla Reliable; often good value.

López de Heredia My experience of these wines has been terrible: every bottle of the Viña Tondonia I have tried has been fault-ridden, coarse and hugely over-aged. Perhaps I have been unlucky, since others praise them highly. Viña Cubillo and Viña Bosconia are younger wines.

Marqués de Cáceres Modern-style wines, pleasant rather than profound. Moving, interestingly, to all-French oak.

Marqués de Griñon Soft, creamy wines offering good value.

Marqués de Murrieta Classic wines, both red and white: soft, warm, lavishly oaked. Castillo Ygay and Blanco Ygay are hymns to age.

Marqués de Riscal Bad patch mid-'70s to mid-'80s, but now generally consistent, sometimes exciting. Long Cabernet Sauvignon tradition here (back to nineteenth century) now finding expression in Baron de Chirel (Tempranillo-Cabernet blend, plus a bit of Graciano).

Martinez Bujanda One of my favourite Rioja producers: always clean wines with pure Tempranillo fruit gently shaped by oak (especially top Conde de Valdemar wines). Good barrel-fermented white, too.

Montecillo Good quality range. Use of French (rather than American) oak for Reserva Viña Monty and Gran Reservas lends complexity.

Muga Old-style wines, sometimes good but overly inconsistent; I find many washed out. Prado Enea is top red.

Navajas Inexpensive, pleasant, uncomplicated wines.

Orobio Comely young Tempranillo: see page 202.

Paternina Banda Azul is pleasant enough; older wines sold under Viña Vial label, which makes anglophones chuckle.

Remélluri Organic, single-estate Rioja. Deep wines.

La Rioja Alta This excellent producer specialises in Reserva (Arana is firmer, Ardanza fleshier) and Gran Reserva (904, with 890 in very best years) categories. Viña Ardanza white is full and lemony.

Riojanas Sound Rioja, both red and white. Rich Monte Real is always a treat.

Sierra Cantabria Supple, fine value reds and fresh whites.

Viña Pomal see **Bilbainas.**

Viña Valoria Prettily packaged range of soft, oaky pale and slender reds.

Viñas de Gain (Bodegas Artadi) Impressively deeply fruity Crianza '92 shows how Tempranillo can have some of Pinot Noir's lyricism. Rich '94 white very impressive, too.

Vintages

1995 ★★★★; 1994 ★★★★; 1993 ★★★; 1992 ★★; 1991 ★; 1990 ★★★; 1989 ★★★★; 1988 ★★★; 1987 ★★; 1986 ★★; 1985 ★★.

Fine earlier vintages: 1982, 1981, 1978, 1970, 1968, 1964.

Specialist retailers

Rioja is widely available; Moreno is the leading London specialist. Adnams and Laymont & Shaw (both mail-order) have particularly good ranges.

Other Spanish wines
Charting the deeps

Vineyards are ubiquitous throughout the Spanish countryside, from green and rainy Galicia down to sunburned Málaga. Even Mallorca has a few (Binisalem), though quality is dull. The Spanish equivalent of France's Appellation Contrôlée category is the Denominación de Origen; as in France, this is not a guarantee of quality, but it does provide a regional badge with stylistic implications which helps small producers and cooperatives up and down the country to market their wines. In general, Spain is good at producing light, easy-going reds and straightforward, cleanly made white wines; depth of flavour is the great challenge, and it is one Spain meets with increasing frequency.

Galicia, situated to the north of Portugal's vinho verde region, is in practical terms a continuation of 'green wine' country. Its wines can be perfumed and peachy (from DOs like Rías Baixas or Ribeiro), as fresh as vinho verde though rather fuller, and certainly among Spain's best; they don't, though, come cheap. Albariño, Loureira, Treixadura and Torrontés are the key grape varieties.

Three of Spain's most promising DOs are found in the basin of the river Duero, later to flow through port territory as the Douro. Ribera del Duero may be destined to rival Rioja one day: the same grape variety (Tempranillo, here called Tinto Fino) produces an altogether darker, intrinsically livelier wine than Rioja in this highland of cool nights. Toro produces fuller, sweeter reds than those of Ribera del Duero, but ones which carry the same promising levels of cladding; it can resemble a Spanish Châteauneuf-du-Pape. Rueda, between the two, is for crisp, acidic whites based on Verdejo, though Sauvignon Blanc performs even better here. There are also several first-class estates lying outside DO demarcations in this part of Northern Spain.

Rioja's neighbour and rival Navarra is a forward thinking, commercially minded region, well able to compete and often defeat Rioja at budget and mid-price levels. Its mainstay Garnacha is gradually being replaced with Tempranillo and Cabernet Sauvignon. High-sited Somontano lies to Navarra's east, and is just beginning to export its often lively wines: Chardonnay here looks promising. To the south of Navarra, meanwhile, are the up-and-coming red-wine regions of Campo de Borja and Calatayud.

Catalonia, further east still, has for long been a quality enclave within Spain: Cava, the country's soft and foamy sparkling wine, is one reason for this, but the Penedès DO itself and high-sited, inland Conca de Barbera both have fine potential for red and white wines. The Cava scene has been an entertaining one over the last year, as its two giants Freixenet and Codorníu made accusations of sleaze against each other: the former accused the latter of watering its vines and using Pinot Noir (both, it has to be said, probably quality-enhancing measures) after the latter had accused the former of releasing wine onto the market earlier than the nine months which the DO regulations stipulate. They've now kissed and made up, agreeing that the ageing regulations should remain in place while greater flexibility is required for varieties and vineyard management. The massive, medicinal reds of Priorato, finally, are among Spain's most exotic wines, and recent investments there suggest that it could become Spain's key area for boutique wineries and internationally aspiring fine-winemaking.

The southern half of Spain has less to offer at present, sherry excepted. La Mancha is an ochre wasteland of vines: poor, heat-parched things which struggle to yield at all. Yet even La Mancha (and its quality enclave Valdepeñas) can produce good reds from Cencibel (aka Tempranillo), as itinerant winemakers at work in the region have proved; the problem is that almost all of this huge region is planted with the no-hope white grape Airén. Jumilla and Utiel-Requena can produce a boisterous glass of red wine (Sainsbury's Jumilla has been good for many years), while Valencia and Málaga specialise in sweet wines. Málaga's are, at best, essences of raisin. Sadly, this may be a wine en route for extinction: the region's best producer, Scholtz Hermanos, was closed down last year by its gin-distilling corporate owner, and its invaluable wine stocks sold off and dispersed. Montilla-Moriles and Condado de Huelva produce sherry-style wines; dry Montilla can be excellent and offers extraordinary value for money. Tierra de Barros, finally, hard against the Portuguese border in Extremadura and not yet a DO, may prove to have a way with warm, rich reds.

Agramont see **Bodegas Principe de Viana**

Alvear, Montilla-Moriles Good-quality, usually inexpensive, typically delicate.

Arroyo, Ribera del Duero Well-equipped, up-and-coming winery producing rich, structured reds.

Baso, Navarra Lush reds from old Garnacha vines from Telmo Rodriguez of Remélluri (see **Rioja**).

Bornos, Rueda Clean, racy Sauvignon Blanc.

Peter Bright Stomping clove-flavoured alcoholic Jumilla (from Merlot and Monastrell) for Sainsbury's from this itinerant winemaker.

Callejo, Ribera del Duero Tinto Joven very good: lots of soft cherry fruit.

Casa de la Viña, Valdepeñas The region's most forward-looking winery producing deep, fruity wines, especially Solana (made with Don Lewis from Mitchelton in Victoria).

Bodegas Castano, Yecla Fresh, lime-scented white.

Castellblanch see **Freixenet.**

Castillo del Ebro, Navarra AGE-owned bodega producing supple wines.

Cellers de Scala Dei, Priorato Wonderfully weird cough-mixture-and-chocolate reds. Cartoixa Priorat is the top wine.

Chivite, Navarra Light, cherryish reds (Gran Fuedo) offer good value.

Clos Erasmus, Priorato Part of new renaissance of this region: long macerations and new oak make for a highly ambitious blend of Cabernet Sauvignon, Garnacha and Syrah.

Clos Mogador, Priorato Massive depth combines with exotic flavours from this pure Garnacha made from old, low-yielding vines by René Barbier.

Clos d'Orlac, PRIORATO Dense, slow-evolving blends of Cabernet Sauvignon and Garnacha, plus small quantities of Syrah, Merlot and Mazuelo given new wood.

Martin Codax, RÍAS BAIXAS Perfumed, fresh-flavoured Albariño.

Codorníu, CAVA One of the two Cava giants (Raimat, Rondel and Masía Bach are subsidiaries). Anna de Codorníu Chardonnay is aromatically more interesting than most, with well-balanced, lemony flavours.

Bodegas Concavins, CONCA DE BARBERA Smallish winery where Hugh Ryman and colleagues have been producing decent quaffing whites and some excitingly deep, fresh, claret-style reds.

Conde de Caralt see Freixenet.

Dominio de Valdepusa see Marqués de Griñon.

El Liso, LA MANCHA Soft, sweet, gentle, generous barrel-aged Tempranillo.

Enate, SOMONTANO Classy, balanced Chardonnay and Tempranillo-Cab Sauv from this up-and-coming region.

Bodegas Fariña, TORO The DO leader. Consistency has been a problem, but the '87 and '88 Gran Colegiata Reserva and '91 Colegiata both have the sweetly meaty, savoury, succulent quality of the DO at its best.

Freixenet, CAVA Second regional giant (subsidiaries include Castellblanch, Segura Viudas and Conde de Caralt). Big seller Cordon Negro now vintage-dated, is slightly deeper than previously white Monastrell Xarel-lo is very biscuity.

Gandia, VALENCIA Reliable source of orange-flavoured Moscatel.

Gracia, MONTILLA-MORILES Leading Montilla producer; deeper style than some.

Guelbenzu, NAVARRA Deeply fruited, rich reds which could sometimes benefit with extra racking (try decanting a few times to blow off the reductive aromas). Jardin is pure Garnacha for drinking young.

Gurpegui, NAVARRA Reliable wines under Monte Ory label.

Cavas Hill, CAVA Thrusting Cava and some good red Penedés wines of earthy, deep style (Gran Civet, Gran Toc).

Juve y Camps, CAVA Characterful, deep-flavoured fizz.

Lagar de Fornelos, RÍAS BAIXAS Soft, lingering '92 Albariño suggests good things to come.

Jean León, PENEDÈS Well-made though expensive international varietals.

Los Llanos, VALDEPEÑAS Very gentle reds (good value) and clean, dullish whites.

Hermanos Lurton, RUEDA French interlopers producing good Verdejo and superb Sauvignon Blanc.

Marqués de Griñon Innovative, California-trained producer based outside any DO area on the banks of the Tagus near Toledo. Superb Dominio de Valdepusa estate reds (Cabernet Sauvignon and Shiraz), lush and velvety, made with help from Michel Rolland; there is also a crisp white Verdejo from Rueda, a barrel-fermented Garnacha Blanca from Somontano and the expressive Durius red from Ribera del Duero and Graves like, non DOC white Durius. See also **Rioja.**

Marqués de Monistrol, Cava Consistent fizz.

Masia Bach, PENEDÈS Well-made Cabernet and Cabernet-based reds.

Masia Barril, PRIORATO Sweet-edged reds of high strength and massive limb.

Mauro Winery outside DO area (but sited near to Vega Sicilia, whose winemaker also consults). Small production but high quality: rich, shapely, concentrated fruit and French oak.

Monte Ory see **Gurpegui.**

Mont-Marçal, Cava Chardonnay sparkler is best; some fruity reds, too.

Ochoa, NAVARRA Technically adept but slightly passionless range.

Pago de Carraovejas, RIBERA DEL DUERO Newcomer bursting on the scene with punchy, gutsy '92.

Palacio de la Vega see **Vinícola Navarra.**

Parxet, ALELLA Pleasant, scented Marqués de Alella Chardonnay, and good complex vintage Cava.

Peñalba Lopez, RIBERA DEL DUERO Big-bodied, earthy, smoky wines meriting wider distribution.

Pesquera, RIBERA DEL DUERO Full-throttle, heavily extracted, lushly oaked reds. Expensive; sometimes charmless.

Bodegas Principe de Viana, NAVARRA I can't find the freshness I'd like on the Agramont white, but the red is warm and mouthfilling. The '92 Tempranillo-Cab Sauv is surprisingly burly. Old-vines Garnacha in preparation.

Protos see **Bodega Ribera Duero**

Raimat, COSTERS DEL SEGRE Fine, deep flavoured varietal Cabernet and Tempranillo lead the range. Avoid '88s and '89s (barrel problems). Inexpensive Gran Calesa and Carretela both first-rate smooth-fruited red wines. Sparkling Chardonnay is lemony.

Bodega Ribera Duero, RIBERA DEL DUERO Inconsistent and expensive, but when good (e.g. '87 Reserva) full-flavoured and age-worthy.

Santara see **Bodegas Concavins.**

Bodega de Sarría, NAVARRA Sweet, aromatic style.

Scholtz Hermanos, MÁLAGA This company, and with it perhaps the future of this historic wine, came to an end last year. There are still bottles about of this dark, treacly, toffee-and-raisin wine: buy it if you can. It will keep well for a decade or more.

Segura Viudas, Cava Crisp, clean Brut Reserva is good value.

Senorío de Sarría see **Bodega de Sarría**

Solana see **Casa de la Viña.**

Bodegas Felix Solís, VALDEPEÑAS Best for soft, easy reds: Viña Albali is top label. Gran Reserva '84 was a lovely soft, butterfly-wing wine. '95 Tempranillo dreadful, though: sour and short.

Sevisa, CAVA Cooperative supplying good own-label Cava to a number of British supermarkets.

Torre del Gall, CAVA Initial releases of this Moët-made sparkler were a disappointment, but the '92 vintage is carefully blended and sound.

Torres, PENEDÈS The best wines of the great pioneer, Miguel Torres, remain international benchmarks: expressive, finely balanced Mas la Plana Cabernet Sauvignon, complex Milmanda Chardonnay (from Conca de Barbera), the spicy Viña Esmeralda (Muscat and Gewürztraminer) and the creamy Fransola (Sauvignon Blanc and Parellada). However both Gran Sangredetoro and Gran Coronas, formerly favourites of mine, have been tasting lighter of late; and Mas Borras (Pinot Noir) and Las Torres (Merlot) fail to sing, too, though both are well made. Viña Sol is a hugely dull varietal Parellada; Gran Viña Sol adds a little Chardonnay fullness to it. New White Coronas (a Garnacha Blanca-Parellada blend) lacks depth and interest.

Valduero, RIBERA DEL DUERO Characterful, typically chewy reds.

Vega Sicilia, RIBERA DEL DUERO Spain's most sought-after wine, made from Tempranillo blended with Cabernet, Merlot and Malbec, the blend then being given lengthy wood and bottle ageing. Unico is the top wine: dark, oaky, sometimes tough; Valbuena, the second wine, is released as a 5-year-old and 3-year-old. Valbuena is particularly good in years (like '88) when no Unico is made.

Viña Albali see **Bodegas Felix Solís.**

Bodegas Viños de Leon, LEON Complex, rich Don Suero ages well.

Viñas del Vero, SOMONTANO Pinot Noir and Chardonnay not yet wholly successful (still too much oak) but encouraging freshness and balance.

Vinícola Navarra, NAVARRA Clean, well-made wines sold under the Palacio de la Vega label includes balanced, elegant Cabernet Sauvignon-Tempranillo. Now owned by Pernod-Ricard.

Bodegas Vitiviño, JUMILLA French-owned: full-flavoured Altos de Pío red.

Bodegas Vitorianas Winery outside any DO area producing cheap, oaky reds and rather sawdusty whites sold under the Don Darias and Don Hugo names. Owned by Faustino (see **Rioja**).

Vintages:
1995 ★★★; 1994 ★★★★; 1993 ★★★; 1992 ★★★; 1991 ★★; 1990 ★★★; 1989 ★★★; 1988 ★★; 1987 ★★★★; 1986 ★; 1985 ★★★.

Specialist retailers:
Moreno is London's chief specialist, and buyers for the big chains take an increasing interest in Spain. Laymont & Shaw has a good mail-order range.

Hugh and Hookie

Hookie met me at Barcelona airport: jeans, bleached shirt, muscular forearms, every inch the rugged Aussie. "Do you know Barcelona?" he asked. I didn't. "Pity." Nor did Hookie.

We belted out into the night down a series of grim motorways, reaching Espluga de Francoli by one in the morning. After a bit of banging, the night man let us into the hotel and gave us a beer. Hookie stayed up watching the tennis. I went to bed.

The next morning, Hugh Ryman turned up shortly after 8:30, having got up at 4 to drive from Bordeaux. He was looking more like Lord Peter Wimsey than ever: bright blue eyes permanently creased at the edges into a faint smile, moppish fair hair, clean good looks. We spent the day together, then he drove me back to Barcelona, before making off home to Bordeaux. His French wife Anne had had their third child, Edwin, a week earlier. Hugh was meant to be at home as much as possible, which doesn't come easily to a flying winemaker.

I'd met Hugh once before in London, and we'd argued a bit about the usual things: whether all this flying winemaker business will lead to a monotony of wine styles, whether the world needs another dozen Chardonnays, whether imposing Australian winemaking techniques on Moldovans is any better than trying to structure India along Whitehall lines. Hugh gave the usual, practical replies: compare before and after for quality, then give us time to create variety and work with native varieties. Oh, and ask the locals what they think. Which was why I was in Spain.

If ever a man was glad to see Hugh and Hookie turn up, it was Fernando Caballero. His friend and employer, the industrialist Luis Carbonell, had bought Bodegas Concavin, in the High Penedés. Selling the wine had been so difficult that Fernando had been drafted in from his previous job running an industrial laundry for Carbonell on Menorca, but even Fernando couldn't put the wine division into profit. A French broker who bought some of the wine in bulk mentioned Hugh Ryman to him.

Hugh didn't want to make wine in Spain — he wasn't impressed with the fruit quality, and he felt the country had a big marketing problem. When he came to meet Fernando, though, he discovered that there was Chardonnay, Cabernet, Merlot and Shiraz here; he was also impressed with the commitment and openness of Fernando and the young winemaker Josep Vadri. "The contract was worth peanuts, but it all depends whether you have the same ambitions and want to do the same thing." Hugh and Hookie got going.

They were startled by the results, especially since 1993 was not a bright year. The red wines, in particular, were so good that they decided they merited barrel fermentation and ageing.

Looking at the plant, it was clear how glamourless the work of a flying winemaker is. You make wine in a warehouse in the middle of nowhere with people who don't understand you. The local community thinks the company is now making wine to sell to Australia.

It was in Josep, though, the young winemaker there, that I could read the value of the enterprise. "Last year, it was the revolution," he explained to me in broken French. "I learned so many things. They [Hugh and Hookie] worked with me as a comrade." I could list the techniques which amazed him, but what I really remember is the gleam in his eyes, and the pride and excitement as we stole like cats after milk around the casks of deep red wine.

Switzerland

Top that

The Swiss like wine: their annual per capita consumption is greater than that of Spain or Greece, and more than four times the British total. Wherever vines are in with a chance of fructifying in mountain valleys or on lakeside terraces, the Swiss plant vineyards, and often instal baby funicular railways to service them. It is all, as you might imagine, very spick, very span.

Moreover the wines are good. Chasselas is the key (white) grape variety; it gives a more interesting wine here – soft, scented and buttery – than in any other country. Gamay and Pinot Noir display closer cousinage in Switzerland than elsewhere (indeed they are often blended): both are soft, clean and curranty. Merlot, in Italian-speaking Ticino, makes a fresh, bright cherry-plum wine; and even Müller-Thurgau (which the Swiss insist on calling Riesling x Sylvaner) has a grassy, clean-air appeal. The problems with Swiss wine are its chaos of nomenclature (Chasselas alone is also known as Gutedel, Fendant, Dorin and by various geographical names) and its expense (when exported to Britain, Swiss wines fetch up at roughly double what they are worth in relation to competitors). We might be able to put up with the former; we are never going to come to terms with the latter.

Tunisia

The ruins of Carthage

Tunisia has a long tradition of Muscat-production; some believe this dates back to Carthaginian times. Logically enough, Muscat is also the great speciality of Pantelleria, the Italian island which lies nearer to the Tunisian coastline than it does to Sicily's (see Southern Italy). Modern Tunisian Muscat is vinified in both sweet and dry forms (Muscat de Kélibia is dry, for example), but in general the country's red wines (such as those from Mornag and Magon) make a more diverting glass, if you can find them. UCCGT, a cooperative grouping, is the major producer: its brands include Château Mornag, Coteaux de Carthage and Sidi Saad.

Turkey

Eat up

There are vines all over Turkey: the country grows almost 10 times as many grapes as Australia does. But only three per cent of them ever get turned into wine; the rest are eaten as table grapes, dried or made into grape-juice concentrate. The majority of Turkey's wines are made in one of the state's 21 wineries, founded by Kemal Ataturk; Anatolian Buzbag is often thought choice, though

my one turn with it was an unhappy experience. Private wineries include Dolu
ca, Kavaklidere and the organic Diren. As in North Africa, conditions for wine
production are propitious; indeed these countries could rival much of the New
World if they wanted. But 'want' is the key; Islam's opposition to wine production is a great brake on progress.

Ukraine

Sweet secession

Ukraine's best wine is produced in the part of the Republic which considers
itself least Ukrainian: the Crimea. Here there is a long tradition, dating back
to the pioneering work of Count Mikhail Woronzov in the 1820s, of dessert wine
production, particularly from the former Imperial Massandra winery sited near
Livadia. This continues today. Nonetheless the only Massandra wines to reach
export markets so far have been the antique rarities from the cellar's museum.
The quality of many of these, made in creditable imitation of foreign styles like
port, madeira, sherry and tokay, is striking. Comtemporary Crimean wine is, thus,
a treat to come.

There are Ukrainian vineyards proper in the Nova Kakhovka area near the
Black Sea coast (between those of the Crimea and Moldova) where John
Worontschak (see England, Valley Vineyards and Harvest Wine Group) has been
working – he's an Australian of Ukrainian ancestry.

United States of America

Buried treasure

Two or three years ago, America couldn't seem to get to grips with the British
wine market. The wheel of fortune then spun a little; exchange-rate sunshine
shone; and for the past 12 months or so America has offered us good value at
around the £5 or £6 mark. Indeed Britain was the number-one importer of Californian wines in the first half of 1995, up 65 per cent on the same period in
1994. They've learnt what we like, in other words. Wines which are soft, fruity,
expressive – and cheap.

Problematically, though, grape prices for the 1995 harvest have risen by 20 per
cent or so in California for worthwhile varieties (and especially the Rhône varieties so suited to much of California's best vineyard land). One of two things will
now happen: almost all Californian wines will now cross the £5 barrier but
retain their quality level, or they'll stay at their present price and quality will
slip. Either way, sales will drop. Nice while it lasted, wasn't it?

There's another story to be told, too. If we were prepared to spend a bit more
money on wine (money, I might add, which we're perfectly happy to squander in
far larger quantities on other needless and dehumanising luxuries) then we
would quickly discover that California now produces some of the best wine in

the world between £10 and £25. The fashion swings and winery mania which formerly afflicted wine production in California have settled down; the state's winegrowing and winemaking have become, wisely, more primitive. Californians listen to their sites and soils more than in the past, letting the vineyard chose its own grape varieties; they interefere less in the winery, letting wines express themselves both in vat and (via the refusal to fine or filter) in bottle. The result is a wonderfully languid landscape of flavours, like the Mediterranean winelands without their bitter, stony asperities, the whole floating beneath a honeyed gauze of yellow, West-Coast light. The best of these wines can never be cheap, but reward experiment resonantly: find them via those merchants who persist with this difficult specialism (notably Morris & Verdin and Oddbins Fine Wine Shops).

Statistically, California is the wine state (over 90% of total US production) to the virtual exclusion, in export terms, of all others. Does this lend a homogeneity to US wine production? Not at all: California, if dumped in Europe, would stretch from London to Morocco; furthermore the fog-generating effect of its long Pacific coast on its confusion of valleys has no European parallel and means, in effect, that most viticultural conditions are available if the searcher looks long and hard enough.

The rest of America remains a land of opportunity for the would-be winemaker: people are doing it all over. Results are variable, but so what? Wine should be about fun – and fun is particularly necessary in America, a country which, for all its privilege and wealth, suffers from more everyday neurosis than most.

Napa

Highway 29: wine's Hollywood Boulevard

Napa is, in descending order of size, a county, a valley, an AVA (American Viti-cultural Area – a geographical designation), and a town. The valley's relative proximity to San Francisco and its long wine-growing history (intensive commercial viticulture began here in the 1880s) have made it the most famous name in Californian – and American – winegrowing.

Although only about 20 miles long, the climatic differences between its cool southern end (around the town of Napa) and its northern, Calistoga end are considerable; the valley contains a kaleidoscope of soil types. Sub-regional specialities (Cabernet Sauvignon from Oakville and Stag's Leap District; Chardonnay from Yountville) are already well-established. The Carneros valley to the southwest of Napa town, coolest of all and hence a prime source of fine Chardonnay and Pinot Noir, is shared between Napa and Sonoma counties.

A Napa style? Inky Cabernet set for long ageing has been, historically, Napa's great gift, but (as always in America) endeavour and aspiration create their own surprises.

Napa does not, however, come cheap; nor, finally, is it particularly innovative in the Californian context. The freaks and zanies work elsewhere; Napa's for businessmen and moguls.

Anderson's Conn Valley Tiny quantities of fine Cabernet Sauvignon and Valhalla Pinot Noir.

Atlas Peak Sangiovese disappointing and overpriced so far.

Araujo Overachieving Cabernet Sauvignon and Syrah from Eisele Vineyard, hard by hot Calistoga.

Beaulieu Historic grandeur; still good (especially Private Reserve Cabernet) but rarely great.

Beringer Consistently high standards across a wide range. Even the Fumé Blanc is good, thanks to fine balance (a Beringer hallmark) and clean fruit. Chewy, peppery Zin and basic Cabernet both good value; Meritage wines appropriately complex. Howell Mountain Merlot expensive but exciting (as usual for Napa, more Médoc than Pomerol in style) and ageworthy. Viognier, especially from Hudson Ranch, is out in the vanguard, and the Chardonnays are as honeyed and Mae-West-like as anyone could wish. Shame the packaging isn't better. Sold by owners Nestlé during the last year to Texas Pacific Group, an investment partnership: let's hope little changes.

Caymus Vineyard Expressive, resinous, warm-limbed Cabernet Sauvignon, among the Valley's most accessible — yet Special Selection wines very long-lived, too.

Clos du Val French-run (by Bernard Portet, elder brother of Dominique Portet of Taltarni in Australia), producing a supple, warm, well-ordered Cabernet. Chardonnay sweet-edged and spineless.

Dalla Valle New producer: fine reds from tiny yields. Maya (with a high proportion of Cabernet Franc) makes a plausible bid to be the Cheval Blanc of California.

Diamond Creek Rugged, son-of-a-gun single vineyard Cabernets which evolve slowly but profoundly — and sell for terrifying prices in infancy. Vintages from '85 on lighter, however, after a run of '70s monsters — no bad thing? Volcanic Hill (8 acres) biggest, Red Rock Terrace (7 acres) richest, and Gravelly Meadow (5 acres) softest.

Dominus Christian Moueix (Pétrus) at work on low-yield, late-harvested Napa fruit. The prices are high, but there is great depth, impressive consistency; few wines are ready for drinking yet. '91 and '94 already legendary, however. There is no 1993.

Duckhorn Vineyards Blockbuster, tannin-sheathed Merlots, more Médoc than Pomerol, are the speciality.

Dunn Dense, slow-ageing Cabernet.

Elyse Whacky, off-beat blends and stonking Zins.

Flora Springs Wines from '90s much better than previously: Bordeaux-blend Trilogy now deep and resonant.

Franciscan Good value red wines, especially Zinfandel. Bordeaux-blend Magnificat is softer and more accessible than many.

Frog's Leap   A good, provoking range: genuinely fresh-flavoured Sauvignon Blanc and fresher-than-usual Zin, too, backed by fiery Carneros Chardonnay and typically inky Napa Cabernet and Merlot.

Grgich Hills   Dry-farmed, hill-grown Zin usually very good, though fleshy Cabernet and Chardonnay grab the limelight.

Harlan   Tiny production of hugely ambitious red Cabernet-based blend, made with help from Pomerol guru Michel Rolland. First vintages are dense but accessible.

Havens   Try-harder Merlots lead the range.

Heitz   Martha's Vineyard Cabernet Sauvignon was a eucalyptussy California legend in the '70s; the '80s have been less consistent, though at best ('85, '86) still fine, for long ageing. Bella Oaks Cabernet and ordinary Cabernet can both be good.

Hess Collection   Clearly defined, aspirational wines; high standards through-out range. Sumptuous, glyceriney '93 Chardonnay particularly good.

Jade Mountain   Accessible, fruit-laden, mineral-silted Rhône varietals; expensive, though.

La Jota   Tiny production: concentrated Cabernet and Petite Syrah from low-yielding vines.

Robert Mondavi Winery   Consistent quality has been a Mondavi hallmark, but some recent releases have seemed disappointingly dull and directionless. However the tannic, nutmeggy '93 Unfiltered Zinfandel is deep, authentic and powerful, and recent Cabernet Sauvignon Reserves are of world class. Pinot Noir Reserves are fat and satisfying. Second-label Woodbridge wines have always been dull, and remain so.

Merryvale   Complex, francophile Chardonnays and dark, elegant Bordeaux-blend Profile.

Château Montelena   Old-established winery with fine track-record for big-gun Cabernet.

Mumm Cuvée Napa   Sound, good-value sparkling wines, with fruit flavours reined back to allow vinosity and yeasty complexities to come through.

Newton   Scrupulously made, richly flavoured Cabernet, Merlot and sweet, full, unfiltered Chardonnay from hill sites.

Niebaum–Coppola   Francis Ford Coppola and his wife Eleanor have now reconstituted the original Inglenook estate, founded in 1879. Pedigree vineyards produce the thunderous Cabernet-based blend Rubicon. See feature.

Opus One   Cabernet-based blends produced as a joint venture between Robert Mondavi and Baron Philippe de Rothschild of Mouton Rothschild. Classy and urbane, but overpriced. Dominus looks more exciting.

Pahlmeyer   Turning heads with new, exciting Merlot.

Pine Ridge   Fast-rising quality for Cabernet, Chardonnay and Merlot.

Joseph Phelps Big range of wines, but impressive standards from traditional single-vineyard Cabernets to fine Rhône varietals under Vin du Mistral selection label (such as spice-drizzled Viognier and chocolatey Syrah).

Kent Rasmussen Buttery Chard and ripely fruity Dolcetto and Pinot Noir.

Rockland Superb Petite Syrah and good Cabernet Sauvignon.

Saddleback Cellars Consistent quality for Cabernet, Chardonnay and Merlot.

Saintsbury Carneros producer of Pinot Noir and Chardonnay which combine Burgundian scent and polish with Californian base warmth and balance.

Schramsberg Ambitious, pricey champagne-method sparkling wines.

Screaming Eagle Hot newcomer with already legendary Cabernet Sauvignon sold, as with many of California's best new wines, by mail-order only.

Shafer Traditionally lingering, delicate wines (for Napa), but greater depth since 1991. Merlot a speciality; Firebreak is a Sangiovese-Cabernet.

Silver Oak A great tradition of unapologetically gutsy Cabernet Sauvignon.

Stag's Leap Wine Cellars Inconsistent, but at best (with Cask 23 and Stag's Leap Vineyard Cabernet Sauvignon) some of Napa's most aromatic, expressive reds. Improving, elegant Chardonnay.

Sterling Vineyards Big, Seagram-owned winery with a patchy track record. Recent bottles, like the supple '93 Winery Lake Pinot Noir or the dark, coal-dusty '92 Diamond Mountain Ranch Vineyard Cab Sauv show promising improvements and offer fine value.

Storybook Mountain Good Zinfandels, especially Howell Mountain and Reserve.

Sutter Home The massively successful sweetish White Zinfandel still seems a disgusting wine to me.

Swanson Good Sangiovese and Syrah as well as the usual Cabernet and Chardonnay.

Togni Succulent, rich style of Cabernet from Napa's *vigneron*.

Truchard Memorable Syrah.

Turley Cellars Stomping Petite Syrah and sweet-fruited Zinfandels superb. Vineyard owned by Helen Turley's brother (see **Marcassin**).

ZD Massive, cellar-seeking Cabernet and big-cleavage Chard.

Vintages:
1995 ★★; 1994 ★★★; 1993 ★★★; 1992= ★★★; 1991 ★★★★; 1990 ★★★★; 1989 ★; 1988 ★; 1987 ★★★; 1986 ★★★; 1985 ★★★★.

Specialist retailers:
Morris & Verdin, The Winery, The Wine Treasury and Oddbins Fine Wine Shops have good Californian (and North American) ranges. Among chains, Oddbins, Majestic and the Thresher group are closest to the ball.

Vines, vats, action ...

Half-way up a dry grass slope, near Gustave Niebaum's olive grove, was a slowly decomposing boat. I had the feeling I'd seen it before somewhere. "The crew were mostly just kids — rock and rollers with one foot in their graves," prompted assistant winemaker Scott McLeod. Philips? Lance? Mr Clean? Scott nodded. "And Chef — wrapped too tight for Vietnam; probably wrapped too tight for New Orleans."

In a barn attic we came across Kilgore's surfboards. "Charlie don't surf!" yelled Scott, imitating a hoarse Robert Duval in mid-flow. "Whadda you know about surfing, Major? You're from goddamned New Jersey!" Then there was a bamboo cage — Willard's prison — through which hopper ranted and Brando purred. Cue for another line. Did Scott know the whole of Apocalypse Now by heart? "Almost. Seen it 15 times." He smiled, and went hoarse again. "I love the smell of napalm in the morning ..."

We strolled down towards the vineyard, past the Thunderbird from *Rumblefish* and the bugging van from *The Conversation*. This was the first great vineyard I've ever visited with 100 phone lines, a 48-track digital sound studio and a winemaker who knows screenplays by heart.

But then there aren't many great vineyards owned by great movie directors. The European equivalent of Francis Ford Coppola's ownership of the historic Niebaum property would be Louis Malle in charge of Château Haut-Brion or Bertolucci at Biondi-Santi's Brunello property. In Europe, worlds like these rarely meet. In America, anything is still possible.

Coppola acquired the vineyard in late 1975. "I bought the property as a place in the country for my family," he says simply, but ingenuously. Italian blood is invariably thickened by wine, and investing in a property of this size in this location would have brought with it knowledge of its historic importance.

Gustave Niebaum, born Nybom, was a Finnish sea captain who, having made a speedy fortune in Alaska, decided to treat himself to a Napa wine estate in the grand European manner. The property he bought was called Inglenook. Niebaum made his first wine in 1882, in a cave built into Mount St John, still used today by Coppola's winemakers for barrel-ageing the estate's wines. Owning a vineyard dating back to 1882 is, in Californian wine terms, like having a few lines in the Book of Genesis refer to you by name. But there's more — Niebaum's great-nephew, John Daniel, was the man who created the great Inglenook Cabernet Sauvignons of the 1940s, made from fruit grown largely on the present Niebaum-Coppola estate.

The estate majors on just one wine: Rubicon, a classic Bordeaux blend of Cabernet Sauvignon, Cabernet Franc and Merlot. Coppola himself points out a number of analogies between wine-producing and film-making. "You have a period of gathering the fruit, which is the source-material for the footage required in film-making. Sometimes the fruit is great, but sometimes it gets damaged by rain, just as when you're shooting, you don't always get what you want. They both demand that you adhere to certain timetables. The difference is that wine moves to a slower cadence. You're looking at 30 to 40 years, not six to eighteen months."

Well, maybe. My own feeling is that, good as Rubicon is, even the best vintages will have faded before people stop watching The Godfather, and that's the time frame which counts. Film-making is an art; wine-making is no more than the loveliest of crafts.

Rest of California
There's wine in them thar hills

Napa is convenient, contained, coherent. But it's just a part – one small, neat square on the rangy chessboard of California's wine scene. Quantitatively, most of California's efforts are made elsewhere, in the Central Valley; and many believe that qualitatively, too, Napa's claim to preeminence is challenged with ever-growing regularity both by nearby Sonoma and the diverse growing areas of the Central Coast, between San Francisco and Los Angeles.

Sonoma Country is large and unwieldy, beginning at Carneros (see Napa) and fanning out through the Sonoma valley itself northwards into Russian River Valley, Green Valley, Dry Creek Valley, Alexander Valley and Knights Valley. Further north still lie the vineyards of Mendocino and Lake Counties. It is hard to generalise about such a large zone as this, but Dry Creek Zinfandel is an all-American classic, and some of the country's sexiest, sleekest Chardonnay comes from the Russian River Valley.

San Francisco Bay's urban spread is gradually jostling out the dull, flat Livermore valley to its east and (with more difficulty) the Santa Clara/Santa Cruz mountains to its west, where rugged hills produce some of America's most uncompromising Cabernets and Zins. Monterey, San Benito, San Luis Obispo and Paso Robles, further south, have yet to prove themselves, though much is happening there; Santa Barbara, north of Los Angeles, has produced some fine strawberryish Pinot Noirs from foggy sites as well as unusually drinkable versions of Cabernet and Rhône varieties.

The Central Valley is, a few good fortified wines aside, essentially a bulk production zone; the Sierra Foothills area, however, where the valley begins to romp up east of Sacramento into the forested heights of the Sierra Nevada, can produce rough, tough, frontiersmen's Zinfandel. Wines are made south of Los Angeles, especially in Temecula, but they are so far of local interest only, and sometimes not even that.

Arciero, Paso Robles Can-do winery working with Hugh Ryman to produce some impressive wines including sleek Chardonnay under Kings Canyon label.

Arrowood, Sonoma Wide and brainy range including sumptuous Malbec, fine Viognier and Pinot Blanc and luscious Late-Harvest Riesling.

Au Bon Climat, Santa Barbara Succulent Chardonnay and poised, focussed Pinot Noir, both of European complexity, have made the estate's name; Barbera looks set to be as good. Even Aligoté is rich and chewy.

Benziger, Sonoma Good value and accessibility across a broad range.

Bonny Doon, Santa Cruz Wittily labelled, frenetically innovative wines, the best of which (Clos de Gilroy, Cigare Volant, Old Telegram, Le Sophiste) are made from Rhône varietals. Not everything works: Pacific Rim Riesling, Chenin Blanc and Pinot Meunier all shaky.

Calera, San Benito Fragrant Viognier; concentrated, intense Chardonnay and graceful, penetrating but risky Pinot Noir, both peppery and silky.

California Direct Fleet-footed blending operation run by Jason Korman creating entry-point wines for the British market, including Grant Canyon (Asda), Havenscourt (Oddbins), Thornhill (Fuller's), South Bay (Sainsbury's) and Apple Hill (Majestic). Quality patchier this year than last.

Chalone, Monterey Deep-flavoured Chardonnay and Pinot Blanc.

Château St Jean, Sonoma Honeyed Chardonnays, some from single vineyard sites, made the winery's name, yet recent releases have been disappointing.

Cline, Contra Costa Côtes d'Oakley is a real Languedoc-in-California wine: herby intensity and a bitter finish. Splendid Zins peak with the Big Break.

Clos du Bois, Sonoma Cleanly fruited Chardonnay (especially Alexander Valley Calcaire and Dry Creek Flintwood), balanced by soft Merlot and Sauvignon Blanc. Cabernet is taken seriously: varietal Briarcrest and blended Marlstone.

Domaine Carneros, Carneros Taittinger-owned producer of reliable sparklers.

Dehlinger, Russian River Good-value producer meriting UK distribution.

Dry Creek Vineyard, Sonoma Known for Sauvignon Blanc, which is better defined here than the mushy California norm; Zin too simple for price.

Durney, Central Valley Impressively deep Cabernets lead the range.

Duxoup, Sonoma Gamay, Charbono (possibly Dolcetto – see **Northern Italy**) and Syrah all exuberant drinking.

Edmunds St John A fine Rhône-style range from various sources. Pallini Rosso combines Zinfandel and Grenache to sweetly spicy effect.

Ferrari-Carano, Sonoma Large range, but generally high quality. Claret-blend Reserve Red very deep, for long ageing.

Fetzer, Mendocino Large operation now owned by Brown-Forman (which makes Jack Daniels), but sourcing much (increasingly organic) fruit from the Fetzer family. Fair quality, though many wines rather dull and safe, even the formerly exciting Zinfandel, Petite Syrah and Merlot. Pure organic Bonterra began well, yet '92 Cabernet is much duller than the '91 Petite Syrah-Zin which preceded it, and '93 Chardonnay is overtreated and overoaked. Gewürztraminer flabby.

Firestone, Santa Barbara Prosperity Red is a juicy, well-balanced red offering excellent value; the white is sweeter, mushy. Firestone label wines are variable; supple Cabernet Sauvignon is best.

Fisher Vineyards, Sonoma Ripeness is all. Some of the richest of all California's Cabernet Sauvignon, and lush, early drinking Chardonnay.

Foppiano, Sonoma Good for Petite Syrah and Zin; other wines dull.

Gallo, Central Valley Basic varietals are still not the most exciting California wines around; quality is improving, though, with new up-market ranges: Turning Leaf and Sonoma wines, then Single Vineyard series, then the Estate wines.

Glen Ellen, Sonoma Commercial wines, but tasty ones (like sweet, soft '94 Proprietor's Reserve Merlot).

Havenscourt see **California Direct**. Good Zinfandel and Rôti.

Iron Horse, SONOMA Worthwhile sparkling wines in a restrained style.

Ironstone, SIERRA FOOTHILLS Good Cabernet Franc.

Kalin, MARIN Intriguing range made from purchased fruit in out-of-the-way sites, including fine sparkling wines. Chardonnays need time.

Kendall-Jackson, LAKE Improving range: reds now exciting and Chardonnay super-rich.

Kenwood, SONOMA Tight-grained, flavourful Cabernet and Merlot, and peppery Zin. Sauvignon Blanc trivial, though.

Kings Canyon see Arciero.

Kistler, SONOMA Expensive but virtuoso Chardonnay from individual sites: lavish, sumptuous, age-worthy. Pinot Noir almost as good.

Kunde, SONOMA Exciting Viognier and Chardonnay.

Madrona, SONOMA Classic Zinfandel.

Marcassin, SONOMA California's most intense and burgundian Chardonnay from uncompromising Helen Turley, the Michel Rolland of California. Tiny quantities, mostly sold direct.

Marietta Cellars, SONOMA Chunky Rhône-style reds.

Martinelli, RUSSIAN RIVER Impressive, heady Zinfandel and luscious Chardonnays from this former grower, now making wine with advice from Helen Turley .

Matanzas Creek, SONOMA Some of California's best Merlot; Sauvignon and Chardonnay less exciting.

Peter Michael, SONOMA Dense, concentrated, Cab-based Les Pavots ambitious but unyielding in youth. Fine range of Chardonnays in burgundian style, hitting all the right buttons for superstar status.

Noceto, AMADOR Grippy, serious Sangiovese with pretty labels.

Ojai, VENTURA Typical ash-scented, pepper Syrah, and Chardonnay Reserve fresh and juicy.

Peachy Canyon, PASO ROBLES Supple Merlots and Cabernets easier than many to drink. Zinfandel wonderfully ripe.

Pedroncelli, SONOMA Good value through the range.

Pepperwood Grove, NORTH COAST Cheapish, high-flavoured blends.

Prosperity see Firestone.

Quartet see Roederer Estate.

Quivira, SONOMA Real depth of flavour to the Asda-stocked Cabernet Cuvée.

Qupé, SANTA BARBARA Exciting range from Rhône valley varietals incuding beefy, meaty Syrah (moving up to powerhouse Bien Nacido Syrah) and floral, smooth Marsanne.

Ravenswood, SONOMA Brilliant low-yield, bell-clear Zinfandels, with Merlot and Chardonnay almost as good. Pickberry blend has huge depth.

Renaissance, YUBA Picturesque, philosophical vineyard out on a limb producing dark, chewy, resiny Cabernet and some burnt but not unattractive Rieslings.

Ridge, SANTA CLARA Monte Bello Cabernet is usually one of the state's benchmarks, ageing from a heroic youth towards an exotic old age; but it is with Zinfandel, Petite Syrah and Carignan that Ridge's grandeur and power are most spectacularly gauged. These are thrilling, sweet-scented, midnight-deep wines of world class.

Rochioli, RUSSIAN RIVER Warm, supple Pinot Noir.

Roederer Estate, MENDOCINO Superb sparkling wine from Anderson valley fruit sold as Quartet.

Sanford, SANTA BARBARA Consistently excellent Chardonnay and Pinot Noir. Easy to enjoy, yet deep, pure flavours capable of profundity.

Scharffenberger, MENDOCINO Delicate, supple, subtle sparkler.

Shooting Star see Jed Steele.

Simi, SONOMA Consistent; best for complex, mid-weight Cabernet, but all the range is good. Rolland consults.

Sonoma–Cutrer, SONOMA No-expense-spared Chardonnay specialist. Les Pierres, the best, does have stony interest beneath the lavish oak and creamy fruit.

Jed Steele, CLEAR LAKE Fine Chardonnay from various locations (Mendocino to Santa Barbara); Merlot and Zinfandel good, too. Shooting Star is second label.

Sean Thackray, MARIN Offbeat producer (in tiny quantities) of superb Rhône varietals given star-struck names.

Marimar Torres, SONOMA Sumptuous, unctuous Chardonnay; Pinot has been perfumed and graceful, though '93 vintage was a thin failure.

Vita Nova, SANTA BARBARA Au Bon Climat joins forces with Qupé to produce exciting blends from purchased fruit.

Vintages
1995 ★★★; 1994 ★★★; 1993 ★★★; 1992 ★★★; 1991 ★★★★; 1990 ★★★★; 1989 ★★;
1988 ★★; 1987 ★★★; 1986 ★★★; 1985 ★★★★

Specialist retailers
See Napa Valley.

Oregon
Grapes and other berries

The vineyards of Oregon are, in terms of landscape and climate, the most 'European' in America. Here you find gentle heat, dappled skies, relaxed and spontaneous rainfall; here cows ruminate, vineyards share hillsides with orchards, and the smell of fermenting wine mingles in the smoky late summer air with that of simmering jam.

Oregon first burst on the scene (in 1970 or so) with Pinot Noir which, in its pale perfumed freshness, bore a startling resemblance to burgundy. Pinot Noir is still Oregon's main theme, with Chardonnay, Riesling and Gewürztraminer providing white variations. Pinot Gris (non-oaked, its complexities the consequence of vineyard and lees ageing alone) is the latest enthusiasm: 35 of Oregon's 110 or so wineries produce it, and it now occupies around 10 per cent of the vineyard land planted. Initial optimism has been much qualified over the last two decades: Oregon (and specifically the Willamette valley) can have vicious spring frosts, grey summers and damp harvests, just like Burgundy. Without Europe's wine culture to fall back on, such conditions have all too often given sour, spiky Pinots of fearsome unloveliness backed by clankingly overoaked Chardonnay. When all goes well, by contrast (recent vintages have favoured Oregon), these can be America's most graceful, aerial reds and fresh-fruited whites.

Oregon producers

Among Oregon's best producers are Adelsheim (especially Elizabeth's Reserve Pinot Noir and Pinot Gris), Amity (Winemaker's Reserve Pinot Noir), Bethel Heights, Cameron, Cooper Mountain (especially Pinot Gris), Domaine Drouhin (great recent improvements), Edgefield, Elk Cove, Evesham Wood, Eyrie (Chardonnay and Pinot Gris, occasional Pinot Noir), St Innocent (Pinot Gris), King Estate (Pinot Gris), Montinore Vineyards (Pinot Gris), Oak Knoll (Pinot Noir), Panther Creek (Pinot Noir), Ponzi, Redhawk, Rex Hill, Domaine Serene, Sokol Blosser, Willamette Valley (Pinot Noir). Beaux Frères is the vineyard owned by Robert Parker's brother-in-law, producing reputedly excellent wines with help from the main man.

Vintages

1995 ★★; 1994 ★★★★; 1993 ★★; 1992 ★★★; 1991 ★★★; 1990 ★★★★; 1989 ★★; 1988 ★★★; 1987 ★; 1986 ★★; 1985 ★★★

Washington

Let there be vines

In populous Europe, vineyards exist because land must support human life, and vines crop best in hot, stony places. Much of America, by contrast, is empty desert. Viticulture, under such circumstances, is a novel form of cultivation requiring less water than most. If the wines taste good, so much the better. If not, pull 'em out.

The vineyards of Washington State's Yakima valley fall into this category: huge green discs in a monotonous wilderness of ice-scoured basalt, irrigated into being. The sun burns down by day, and the moon sucks away their warmth by night. It never rains in summer, and almost never during the rest of the year. In the winter, weeks pass at -20°C. This is what life is like for a vine, buried between the Rattlesnake Hills and the Horse Heaven Hills, staring at the stars. Some 40 per cent of Washington's wines come from the Yakima valley; the rest is grown in the Columbia valley to its northeast, and more temperate, moister Walla Walla to its east. These extreme conditions produce wines of intense but, in slightly bizarre flavour, of vivid yet fleshless style: Merlot, Cabernet Sauvignon and Chardonnay.

Washington producers

The scale, remoteness and extremity of conditions here means that most Washington wineries are large operations. Château Sainte-Michelle, Domaine Sainte-Michelle, Snoqualmie and Columbia Crest are all owned by the American Tobacco Company (through its subsidiary Stimson Lane); the best wines are the Château Sainte-Michelle single vineyard selections. Other big producers include Columbia Winery and Hogue Cellars. Leonetti, de Lille Cellars, Woodward Canyon, Quilceda Creek, Seven Hills, L'Ecole and Yakima River are good smaller producers.

Vintages

1995 ★★; 1994 ★★★; 1993 ★★★; 1992 ★★★; 1991 ★★; 1990 ★★; 1989 ★★★★; 1988 ★★★; 1987 ★★; 1986 ★; 1985 ★★

Rest of the USA

Hang loose

Arkansas, New Mexico, Texas, Virginia, Massachusetts ... Few American states do not produce wine, though sales are more often ensured by novelty value rather than by reasoned quality. Among the best names are Ste Chapelle in Idaho; Crosswoods in Connecticut; Basignani, Byrd and Boordy in Maryland; Gruet in New Mexico; Bridgehampton, Hargrave, Pindar and Lenz on Long Island in New York State, with Wagner, Millbrook, Palmer, Wiemer and Finger Lakes Wine Cellars on the mainland; Llano Estacado and Pheasant Ridge in Texas; Callaghan Vineyards in Arizona (Fullers stocked some of their porty Zin last year); and Horton, Piedmont, Williamsburg and Barboursville in Virginia.

Uruguay

Tannat, anyone?

This triangular country, wedged between two giants (Argentina and Brazil), is an enthusiastic producer and consumer of wine. Traditionally, the majority of its vinifera-based wines were based on the Tannat grape variety, responsible for France's leather-jacketed Madiran (brought across the seas by Basque settlers). Uruguay used to have more Tannat planted than France did, though vine virus has now reduced the country's dependence on this variety. Hybrid vines are also important, especially in the humid zones on the Brazilian border. Such wines as have been exported so far have been well-made and clean, with forceful reds.

Zimbabwe

Out of the flames

My Zimbabwe correspondent, Monty Friendship, tells me that there have been 'great leaps forward' since Flame Lily days. The two major producers are Afdis (Stapleford wines) and Cairns (Mukuyo).

Buying Wine

Eros Wines of the Year

The notion of a 'wine of the year', of course, is absurd: tastes differ; perceptions of value are fugitive; good wines are good in different and variable ways. Wine is not something which can be assessed objectively. It's absurd, then – but fun. These Wines of the Year are selected from the bottles I have enjoyed most in the last six months. In each case, the cited retailers assure me that the wines will be available at least until Christmas 1996.

EROS SPARKLING WINE

OF THE YEAR

Cava
Brunet
Penédes, Spain
Stocked by: Kwiksave (£4.99)
Score: 19/25

I meant to choose a Champagne for the millenium for this slot, but in the end this sparkling wine offered such outstanding value for money that my original plan went up in ... bubbles, I suppose. (If you're interested, though, think about storing Moët & Chandon's widely available 1990 vintage, as well as Taittinger's fine 1990, Ruinart's superb 1988 and 1990 vintages, and Gosset's powerful 1985 Grand Millésime.) The Cava Brunet is an outstanding example of its style, blowing away competition from Australia and elsewhere at this price level, and humiliating many more expensive Cavas. It's aromatically fresh and flowery – hawthorne and hay. In the mouth, too, it tastes fresh and graceful, fine-foamed, with the refreshment of gentle acidity and delicate yet firm structuring vinosity. Above all, there are none of the raw apple-core flavours which spoil so many Cavas in this gentle, subtle fizz.

EROS UNOAKED WHITE

WINE OF THE YEAR

Joint winners:

1994 Réserve Gewürztraminer
Cave de Turckheim
Alsace, France
Stocked by:
Thresher group (£5.99)
Score: 20/25

1995 Sancerre La Vraignonette
Paul Régis
Upper Loire, France
Stocked by: Waitrose (£6.99)
Score: 19/25

This category has been jointly taken this year by two French classics, both vividly typical of their appellations and, expressly in the first case and implicitly in the second, grape varieties. The Cave de Turckheim is one of the finest cooperatives in France (I enjoyed a smokily expressive bottle of its '86 Pinot Gris, aged in my cellar by accident, this year); Thresher has pushed for a reblend of its cuvée of the Gewürztraminer, and this exotically rose-scented, spice-laden wine is the result. Gewürz can be rather a gallumphing mouthful, but this version even has a little freshening acidity to give it edge: great value at this price.

The Sancerre is, in every way, the more challenging wine: freshly grassy scents, though rather more stripped back in style than New Zealand's Marlborough aficionados will be used to, with a rapier blade of nettley, stony, lemony flavour slicing its way across the tongue and excoriating the throat. I've docked a point from the wine for questionable ripeness, but I deeply admire its untrammeled and untimid expression of saliva-detonating acidity and, more generally, its austere, early-spring beauty. It dreams, at night, of oysters.

balance between the different flavour components of the wine; the point of blending, too, is to give a wine complexity of flavour. Balance and complexity mean that the oak doesn't dominate the flavour in a simplistic manner: this is a taut, chewy, vinous, sumptuously nutty wine with impressive depth of fruit (peach and dry lemon). It would make a good alternative to burgundy whenever a weighty white is needed; it will improve and soften over two or three years; it tastes like white Rioja ought to but rarely does. Strangely enough, its weight and dimensions make it unlike white Bordeaux, which has more delicacy than this. Compare it with the price of white burgundy, though, and you'll see it's a bargain.

EROS OAKED WHITE WINE OF THE YEAR

1994 Meritage White

Beringer
Knights Valley, California
Stocked by:
Majestic Wine Warehouses (£7.49)
Score: 20/25

'Meritage' is the synthetic term adopted in California for Bordeaux-style blends, which for white wines signifies a mix of Sauvignon Blanc and Semillon. As is the case with most great white Bordeaux wines, this has been fermented in French oak casks, and aged in casks, too, on the yeast lees. Oaked, then? You bet. Both in aroma and flavour you'll find a rich charge of top-quality oak. Yet one of the Beringer hallmarks is fine

EROS MEDIUM-DRY WHITE WINE OF THE YEAR

1994 Forster Pechstein Riesling Kabinett

Weingut Reichsrat von Buhl
Rheinpfalz, Germany
Stocked by:
Wine Rack and Bottoms Up (£7.99)
Score: 22/25

Good medium-dry white wine is extremely hard to make; many taste manipulated, confected or artificial. The Kabinett and Spätlese categories of fine German Riesling, by contrast, combine medium-dry levels of sweetness with impressively natural grace, charm and freshness. This wine, from a grand old Pfalz estate in renaissance, smells, at the time of writing, of soft fruits and baby talc; the aromas will improve and pull into focus over the next year or two. It is the wonderful shock of its flavour which impresses at present: an explosion of peach, grapefruit, melon and apple, with a generous sprinkling of those mineral after-flavours which the Riesling is uniquely capable of drawing out of the earth. Vivid, arresting, complex yet finally light and refreshing: I can imagine no better apéritif.

EROS SWEET WHITE WINE OF THE YEAR
1990 Château de la Chartreuse
Sauternes, France
Stocked by: Oddbins (£9.99 per half bottle; £18.99 per bottle) and Sainsbury (largest 38 stores: £9.95 per half bottle)
Score: 21/25

Having selected a half-bottle of Sauternes for this slot last year (the fine Bastor-Lamontagne '90), I meant to chose something different – until I tasted this. Frankly, while the wonderful 1990 Sauternes vintage is still available at a reasonable price, drinkers should take full advantage of it.

Château de la Chartreuse is one of the best of the region's non-classified properties: this deep buttercup-coloured wine has all of the gloriously unctuous scents of classic Sauternes (straw, runny honey and that strangely seductive sort of fattiness generally called 'lanolin'). In the mouth it's sweet, full of tangy honey yet lent complexity both by the bitter-edged botrytis flavours and by a quiet but persistent peachy acidity.

EROS SOFT RED WINE OF THE YEAR
1995 Tempranillo
Orobio
Rioja, Spain
Stocked by:
Oddbins (£4.49)
Score: 20/25

I can scarcely remember better Rioja than that which is in our shops at the moment: 1994 was a sensationally good year there, and 1995 wasn't far behind. When Tempranillo is well-handled, it is one of the softest and loveliest of all red grape varieties: try this wine to see what I mean. Dark colours; a sweet perfume of plum, strawberry and nutmeg; a soft and generous mouthful of strawberry fruit melting as swiftly on the tongue as chocolate or cream. After you've swallowed, those perfumes are back, wafting across your tongue and sweetening your breath.

EROS MIDWEIGHT RED WINE OF THE YEAR
1994 Malbec White Label
Bodega Norton
Argentina
Stocked by:
Oddbins (£4.99)
Score: 22/25

The second victor in the red-wine triple crown pulled off this year by Oddbins exemplifies Argentina's huge promise. This Malbec is a dark, slow-fuse kind of red: there's a minty-mineral nose and earthy, savoury, close-textured flavours. It's a hard wine, in other words, to plaster with analogies (the fruit, if you want, is somewhere between plum and prune, and there's a quiet chocolate drizzle in the background); its intensity and complexity, though, are absolutely remarkable at this price. This meal-time red (perfect for stews) should cost twice what it does. The white-label version, stocked by Oddbins alone, is unoaked; there is also a pink-label version available at some other retail outlets and in restaurants which sees some oak, and is slightly more expensive. My preference is for the purity of the unoaked version.

EROS FULL RED WINE

OF THE YEAR

Joint winners:

1993 Syrah, Dominio de Valdepusa

Marqués de Griñon
Toledo, Spain
Stocked by: Tesco (largest 77 stores: £8.49)
Score: 23/25

1994 Shiraz, The Dead Arm

D'Arenberg
McLaren Vale
South Australia
Stocked by: Oddbins (£9.99)
Score: 21/25

It was in October 1995 when I first tasted the wines of Dominio de Valde-pusa — the superb 1992 Cabernet Sauvignon, stocked at that time by Fullers. I was utterly seduced by its voluptuous fullness, its softness, its depth and its expressivity. The 1993 Cabernet doesn't seem quite as good, but in the meantime along has come this superb and barely-less-buxom Syrah. It's dark ruby in colour, with scents which seem to combine some of the smoky-bacon and burnt-rubber aromas of French Syrah with the earthiness and creaminess of Aus-tralian Shiraz. It has searing intensity in the mouth; the flavours of currants and sloes and drifting woodsmoke linger for the best part of a minute. Yet there is also a sweetness and a softness there, easing the wine over the tongue caressingly, despite the wine's intensity. This could hold its own among £15 bottles without diffi-culty. The fact that it is made from vines planted in April 1991, thus only two years old, is astonishing: the only explanation I have heard for this is that such young vines naturally give very low yields. (The 1994 vintage, untried at the time of writing but rumoured to be as good or better, should be available when this book is published from Fullers and others.

The vines which provide the fruit for D'Arenberg's Dead Arm Shiraz, by contrast, are around 100 years old (the full story of the name is told on the wine's fascinatingly informative back label). This is, quite simply, a classic bottle of Australia's greatest wine style: black-purple in colour; a nose on which the fine American oak leads at present, but which will eventually surrender more typical aromas of fire and minerals; and an appropriately thundering and primeval flavour: earth, salt, tar, black herbs, black pepper, black fruits ... black clouds in a lightning-lit sky. This is a great if challenging, almost medicinal wine.

EROS FORTIFIED WINE

OF THE YEAR

Sainsbury's Palo Cortado

Francisco Gonzalez Fernandez

Jerez, Spain

Stocked by: Sainsbury (largest 73 stores: £3.29 per half bottle)

Score: 23/25

Of all of the Eros Wines of the Year, this superb half-bottle offers best value in absolute terms: it's a fine wine at a giveaway price. It's described as a Palo Cortado: that strange hermaphroditic sherry in which some of the delicacy and nuttiness of the true amontillado is combined with the intensity and depth of an oloroso. It has the colour of antique oak, and smells of raisins, toasted almonds and dry peaches. In the mouth, you'll find more nuts, dried currants, peach skins and, obscurely but persistently, a quality to the flavour which reminds me (and I only find this in lighter sherries) of perfumed basmati rice. It's slightly sweet − enough to round out the edges without ever beginning to sate the palate. Perfect sipping, either before or after a meal.

Wine Merchants

John Armit Wines

5 Royalty Studios, 105 Lancaster Road, London W11 1QF
Tel: **0171 727 6846**   Fax: **0171 727 7133**

The case for classicism

For the novice, John Armit's sales pitch has rather a forbidding air: unmixed cases only, while the delivery charges suggest you might like to sign up for those in multiples of three or more. This is a business clearly aimed at the corporate client, or the drinker with a taste for the classics and the wherewithal to indulge it. If that category includes you, then Armit's selection of burgundies and clarets is among the best, and includes regular en primeur offers to help you lay hands on great wines at pre-stratospheric prices. The relationship wih Robert Parker blossomed further during 1996 with two lectures given by the great tipster on his way back from tasting '95 Bordeaux. Specific tips on the '95s were in short supply then, though as it turned out Parker's rationale for keeping stum on the '95s (that his pronouncements might distort the market) was hardly justified by events, since most châteaux waited for his scores before fixing their prices. Armit's offer of '95s was a serious one, though a number of key Pomerol successes were notable by their absence (Clinet, Eglise-Clinet, Evangile and Trotanoy), and extensive use was made of the 'price on application' rubric. I am told that fine-wine broking now accounts for almost half Armit's turnover, with private individuals enjoying the same prices as the trade. Away from the classics, Armit scores most heavily with California, Italy and Argentina. There is one classic, note, which Armit spurns entirely, claiming he neither likes it nor believes in its future: vintage port. I share neither his distaste nor his pessimism, though I suppose I admire him for having the courage of his conviction.

Worth a punt

White: 1995 Chardonnay Mulderbosch £108 per case; 1994 Rully Premier Cru Mont Palais, Olivier Leflaive £123 per case; 1994 Pavillon Blanc, Château Margaux £275; 1993 Meursault Les Luchets, Roulot £292 per case.

Red: 1990 Château de Lussac £93 per case; 1991 Malbec Weinert £111 per case; 1994 Zinfandel Ravenswood Vintner's Blend £115 per case; 1992 Cabernet Sauvignon Hess Collection £180; 1991 Savigny-lès-Beaune Les Guettes, Simon Bize £232 per case.

Sparkling: Beaumont des Crayères Champagne £190 per case.

NOT A SHOP

Hours
Mon-Fri
9.00am-6.00pm

Minimum sale
1 case (unmixed)

Credit cards
Access/Mastercard,
Visa

Discounts
Bin ends and
special offers

Delivery
1 case £10, 2 cases
£15, 3 or more
cases free

Glass hire
No

Tasting facilities
Annual tasting, and
in-house tastings
for corporate
clients

Storage facilities
£6 plus VAT per
case per year

Joint winner
EROS AWARD FOR SUPERMARKET

WINE SELECTION OF THE YEAR

Hours
Mon-Fri
9.00am-8.00pm;
Sat 9.00am-7.00pm;
Sun 10.00am-
4.00pm (may vary)

Minimum sale
No

Credit cards
Access/Mastercard,
Visa

Discounts
£2 per case (£4 if
case over £48)

Delivery
Direct mail service
now in operation:
ring for details

Glass hire
Free with order
(deposit required)

Tasting facilities
In-store tastings

Storage
facilities
No

Asda

Head Office: Asda House, Southbank, Great Wilson Street,
Leeds LS11 5AD   Tel: 01532 435435   Fax: 01532 418666

Basilisk of the aisles

Asda may not necessarily be first choice for those looking for rabbit loins or truffle juice, but its wine range remains a supermarket pace-setter for excitement and eclecticism and a compelling reason to shop here rather than down the road. The wine department is run with spark and passion by Nick Dymoke-Marr with help from Alistair Morrell and Illy Jaffar. Dymoke-Marr believes strongly in communication, and most of the department's innovations are designed to help his bottles talk eloquently to customers: organisation by taste and style rather than country; the roadshow of customer tastings; lots of leaflets; the wine-merchant-like 'bins and barrels' promotions; and a culture of encouraging talented departmental managers which has already produced one star – the legendary Dave Reid of Sunderland, now breaking new sales records at Harrogate. Dymoke-Marr isn't averse to a spot of direct selling himself: if you're collared by a bouncy chap with a basilisk gaze who turns your hesistant wanderings around the shelves into a sale of several hundred pounds (as he did one day in Taunton), you can guess who it is. You'll know when he comes out with his catchphrase: ' ... and by the way, my name's Nick.' The wines themselves are characterised by lots of style and character: diversity here really is diversity, rather than the badge engineering some other supermarkets go in for. Lots of the wines I love (see below); a few of the wines I hate, such as the sickly 1995 Sebastiani White Zinfandel (£3.99; 7/25) and loose-knit 1995 Sebastiani Red Zinfandel (£3.99; 11/25); the sour, thin Hungarian Kekfrankos (£2.79; 10/25); the ungrateful 1994 Château l'Eglise-Vieille (£4.99; 11/25); the feeble 1995 Kumala Chenin-Chardonnay (£3.49; 10/25); the boring, sour 1995 Remonte Navarra Blanco (£2.99; 10/25) and the emaciated 1995 Montepulciano Abruzzo from Tollo (£2.79; 9/25). Almost none leaves me indifferent. I admire the temerity with which Asda takes classy wines to the people – and sells them. No one who likes Chardonnay, for example, should fail to try the St Véran Domaine des Deux Roches; no one who likes good red wine should miss Quivira's Cabernet Cuvée; the delicate Scharffenberger sparkler makes a great way to turn a ten-pound note into a celebration; and the Penfolds Bin 389, the Stellenzicht wines and the Stanton & Killeen Liqueur Muscats are all, in their own ways, palate-thrillers. Good buying, good selling: Asda merits this year's joint Eros Award for Supermarket Wine Selection of the Year.

Worth a punt

White: 1995 Hungarian Muscat £2.79 (15/25); 1995 Spring Vale Blanc £2.99 (17/25); 1995 Northern Star German White £2.99 (15/25); 1995 Chardonnay-Grenache, Southern Cross £3.49 (15/25); 1994 Chardonnay, Ca' Pradai £3.79 (14/25); 1995 Carden Vale £3.99 (14/25); 1995 Riesling, Wild Boar Vineyards £3.99 (17/25); 1995 Chardonnay, Cono Sur £3.99 (16/25); 1995 Gewürztraminer, Fairview £3.99 (16/25); 1995 Chardonnay Barrel-Fermented, Fiuza £4.49 (14/25); 1995 Viognier, Cuckoo Hill £4.99 (14/25); 1994 Marsanne, Cranswick Oak-Aged £4.99 (15/25); 1995 Chardonnay Reserve, Rowan Brook £4.99 (15/25); 1995 St Véran 'Domaine des Deux Roches' £6.49 (19/25); 1995 Chardonnay, Rosemount Estate £6.49 (16/25); 1994 Chardonnay, Château Reynella £6.99 (18/25); 1995 Sancerre 'La Vigne des Rocs' Bourgeois £7.49 (14/25).

Rosé: 1995 Fairview Dry Rosé £3.49 (15/25).

Red: Asda Cape Red £2.99 (15/25); Asda Argentine Red £2.99 (15/25); 1995 Remonte Navarra £2.99 (16/25); 1995 Cabernet-Garnacha, Terra Alta £3.29 (14/25); 1995 Cabernet Malbec, Rowan Brook £3.49 (15/25); 1995 Mas Segala Côtes du Roussillon-Villages £3.99 (15/25); 1994 Domaine de Belugue Côtes du Rhône-Villages £3.99 (16/25); 1994 Domaine de Grangeneuve Coteaux du Tricastin £4.49 (15/25); 1995 Pinotage, Bouwland Bush Vine £4.49 (15/25); 1994 Cuvée Simone James Herrick £4.99 (21/25); 1995 Zinfandel, Stellenzicht £4.99 (16/25); 1995 Cabernet-Shiraz, Penfolds Bin 35 Rawsons Retreat £4.99 (16/25); 1995 Kanonkop Bouwland Red £4.99 (16/25); 1990 Señorio de Nava Crianza Ribera del Duero £5.69 (19/25); 1995 Pinot Noir Reserve, Cono Sur £5.99 (14/25); 1994 Domaine de la Baume Rouge £5.99 (15/25); 1992 Cabernet Cuvée Quivira £6.99 (18/25); 1993 Cabernet-Shiraz Bin 389 Penfolds £9.99 (21/25).

Sparkling: Seaview Australian Brut £5.99 (13/25); Scharffenberger Mendocino Brut £9.49 (16/25); Asda Champagne Brut £11.99 (15/25); Asda Champagne Rosé Brut £11.99 (15/25).

Fortified: Liqueur Muscat, Stanton & Killeen (half-bottle) £5.49 (20/25).

Hours
Mon-Sat
10.00am-6.00pm

Minimum sale
No

Credit cards
Access/Mastercard,
Visa, AmEx, Switch

Discounts
5% per case and
bin-end sales

Delivery
Free to E2 area and
mail-order service to
England and Wales

Glass hire
Free with order

Tasting facilities
Regular tastings
throughout year or
by request

**Storage
facilities**
No

Nearest tube
Bethnal Green

Balls Brothers Wine Centre

313 Cambridge Heath Road, London E2 9LQ
Tel: 0171 739 1642   Fax: 0171 729 0258

A safe case of wines

Those who have picked up one of the neat and tidy little lists which garnish the counters of Balls Brothers' wine bars (see page 273) can make their way to Bethnal Green to rummage around the list if they choose (a mail-order service is also offered). The merchant list offers a considerable expansion of the wine-bar version: French classics at its heart, but with increasing exploration of the strange and exotic (such as, this year, a push into Chile and South Africa). The company is also very pleased with what it's found in the South of France. Balls Brothers is the sole London member of the Merchant Vintners group, so you will find wines here available elsewhere only through some of the leading regional independents (like Adnams or Lay & Wheeler). 'Service is all' is the ringing phrase with which Geoffrey Balls concludes his introduction to the '96 wine list, stressing the qualifications of the sales team, so put them to the test.

Worth a punt

White: 1994 Marsanne, Domaine Virginie £4.95; 1994 Sémillon, Mitchell £6.65; 1994 Chablis Domaine des Manants £8.30; 1994 Pinot Gris Patergarten, Blanck £8.75.

Red: 1992 Cabernet Sauvignon, Portal del Alto £4.55; 1995 Côtes du Rhône Domaine du Grand Moulas £4.95; 1993 Merlot, Overgaauw £5.95; 1993 Cabernet Sauvignon/Malbec Leasingham Domaine £7.80.

Sparkling: Prosecco di Valdobbiadene, Ruggieri £6.95; Champagne Joseph Perrier Cuvée Royale £15.95.

Fortified: Manzanilla La Gitana (half bottle) £3.15; 1983 Dow Vintage Port £17.95; Amontillado Viejo, Hidalgo £23.50.

NOT A SHOP

Hours
Mon-Fri
8.00am-6.00pm

Minimum sale
1 case

Credit cards
Access/Mastercard,
Visa, Eurocard, Delta

Discounts
By negotiation

Adam Bancroft Associates

The Mansion House, 57 South Lambeth Road, London SW18 1RJ
Tel: 0171 793 1902   Fax 0171 793 1897

The wine sleuth

Master of Wine Adam Bancroft's list makes no pretensions to completeness: he merely tracks down what he considers to be worthwhile wines which, as often as not, nobody else has got hold of in order to pass them on via restaurants, other wine retailers to whom he sells, and through direct sales. Result? Lots of colour and interest; little dross. The difficulties of buying from France has meant a serious look at Italy this year with a much increased range; while on the New World front Australia's steadily rising stock is to bring South Africa into the frame. The list is thoughtful and succinct, providing good background information on the selected producers.

Worth a punt

White: 1995 Sauvignon de Touraine Manadet £5.95; 1995 Château Haut-Grelot Blanc £5.95; 1995 Sauvignon Collio Orientali Paolo Rossaro £8.25; 1995 St Véran Michel Chavet £8.50; 1994 Pouilly-Fuissé les Crays Michel Forest £16.95.

Red: 1994 Côtes du Roussillon Colombo £6.60; 1995 Mas Bruguière Fûts de Chêne £8.65; 1995 Dolcetto di Dogliani Siri d'Yermu Pecchenino £8.95; 1994 Gevrey-Chambertin Vieilles Vignes, Gallois £16.95.

Sparkling: Crémant de Loire Neau £9.45.

Delivery
Free in London
1 case or more; free nationwide 3 cases or more

Glass hire
Free with order

Tasting facilities
Biannual tastings

Storage facilities
No

Bentalls of Kingston

Wood Street, Kingston-upon-Thames, Surrey, KT1 1TX.
Tel: **0181 546 1001**   Fax: **0181 549 6163**

Weird and wonderful

This is a wine department with wide horizons. Buyer Andrew Willy is a great sleuth for strange excellence of the kind which makes wine drinking the fun we all know and love. In particular, he likes Portuguese wines, a sure sign for me of a taster who (as all should, but few do) cherishes complexity in wine even when it's unfashionable. Willy gets involved with food buying, too, which leads to creative synergies in terms of themed promotions and food-and-wine matching advice. The selection is not huge, but it is one of the best balanced to appear in this book.

Worth a punt

White: 1995 Chardonnay, Domaine Collin, Vin de Pays d'Oc £3.99; 1995 Albariño Lagar de Cervera, Rias Baixas (half-bottle) £4.49; 1994 Bairrada, Casa de Saima £6.99; 1992 Chardonnay, Isole e Olena £11.99; 1990 Chassagne-Montrachet, Paul Pillot £19.95.

Red: 1994 Chianti, Poggiano £4.49; 1992 Alenquer, Quinta d'Abrigada £6.99; 1990 Madiran, Château Peyros £7.99; 1990 Bairrada Garrafeira, Casa de Saima £12.99; 1985 Rioja Alta, Gran Reserva 904, La Rioja Alta £16.50; 1985 Château Poujeaux, Moulis £19.50.

Hours
Mon-Sat
9.30am-6.00pm
(Thurs 9.00am-9.00pm);
Sat 11.00am-5.00pm

Minimum sale
No

Credit cards
Access/Mastercard, Visa, AmEx, Switch, Bentalls Card

Discounts
5% per case

Delivery
Free locally

Glass hire
Free with order

Tasting facilities
Tutored tastings, Saturday in-store tastings, annual wine fair evening

Storage facilities
Free storage with purchase

Nearest BR station
Kingston

209

Sparkling: Jacques Selosse Grand Cru Champagne £22.50.

Fortified: 1980 Vintage Port, Dow's (half-bottle) £11.50; Bual Madeira, Henriques & Henriques £15.99; 1962 Colheita Port, Niepoort £75.

Hours
(St James's) Mon-Fri 9.00am-5.30pm
Warehouse:
Tues-Weds 10.00am-5.00pm; Thurs-Fri 10.00am-8.00pm; Sat 10.00am-4.00pm.

Minimum sale
None

Credit cards
Access/Mastercard, Visa, AmEx, Diners, JCB

Discounts
3% off 3-5 cases;
5% off 5-9 cases;
7.5% off 10+ cases

Delivery
Free nationwide
1 case or more

Glass hire
Cost on request

Tasting facilities
4 tastings per year in Central London

Storage facilities
Cost on request

Internet site
http://www.berry-bros.co-uk/

Nearest tube
Green Park

Berry Bros and Rudd

3 St James's Street, London SW1A 1EG   Tel: **0171 396 9600**
Teleorders: **0171 396 9669**   Fax: **0171 396 9641**
Terminal 3 Departures, Heathrow Airport   Tel: **0181 564 8361**
Berry's Wine Warehouse, Hamilton Close, Houndmills,
Basingstoke RG21 6YB   Tel: **01256 23566**   Fax: **01256 479558**

Some things never change

Like Berry Bros's extraordinary premises in St James's St, which will doubtless remain as clear an approximation of the eighteenth-century shopping experience as you'll find anywhere until we poison ourselves (not, of course, with wine) into sterility. And yet, and yet ... what is one to make of Berry Bros taking, far more swiftly than than many of its rivals, to the Internet? Perhaps I'm wrong; perhaps 3 St James's St will be a web-surfer's cyber-café by this time next year. For the time being, take advantage of Berry Bros for the delights of its list (designed for the waistcoat pocket), the high-quality ramble through winelands old and new that its range offers, and its generally reasonable prices. The plethora of half-bottles is welcomed by the temperamentally moderate (your author among them); hot areas include claret, burgundy, and some genuinely punt-worthy German wines.

Worth a punt

White: Berry's Californian Chardonnay £6.20 (15/25); 1993 Chablis, Tricon £9.45 (17/25); 1994 Riesling Kabinett Eltviller Sonnenberg, Langwerth von Simmern £9.85 (15/25); 1994 Riesling Kabinett, Erdener Treppchen, Loosen £11.32 (17/25); 1989 Riesling Cuvée Fredéric Emile, Trimbach £18.50 (20/25); 1994 Condrieu, Chapoutier £23.50 (20/25); 1992 Chassagne-Montrachet les Campgains, Niellon £35.15 (19/25).

Red: 1990 Château La Vieille France, Bordeaux Supérieur £5.80 (15/25); Berrys' Californian Cabernet Sauvignon £6.20 (15/25); 1992 Pinotage, Saxenburg, South Africa £7.10 (17/25); 1990 Vacquéyras, Domaine le Couroulu, Ricard £7.75 (17/25); 1990 Château de Maison Neuve, Montagne St Emilion £8.45 (16/25); 1990 Château Tour Pibran, Pauillac £9.25 (19/25); 1990 Mesoneros de Castilla, Arroyo £9.50 (15/25); 1990 Château Fleur Cardinale £10.50 (16/25); 1989 Château Fombrauge, St Emilion £12.45 (17/25); 1993 Pinot Noir, Wignalls, Western Australia £13.50 (15/25); 1989 Hermitage, Chapoutier £13.95 (19/25); 1990

Gevrey-Chambertin les Corbeaux, Boillot £27.50 (16/25).

Sparkling: Berry's Australian Quality Sparkling Wine Chardonnay/Pinot Noir £9.95 (15/25).

Fortified: La Seguidilla Manzanilla £7.85; Oloroso Añada 1918, Pilar Aranda y Latorre £12.50; Churchill Crusted Port, bottled 1987 £13.45; 1954 Bual Madeira, Henriques & Henriques £142.

Bibendum

113 Regents Park Road, London NW1 8UR   Tel: **0171 722 5577**   Fax: **0171 722 7354**

The Primrose Hill mob

Bibendum, for those readers not already familiar with the japes and aphorisms of bow-tied Willie Lebus (sorry about the gout, Willie, no, really, it's agony and we know it's nothing to do with your work), the complex viti-vinicultural theorems of Simon Farr, the saturnine pronouncements of Ben Collins, the exclamations of Dylan Parris and Laura Pragnall and the various and varying contributions of other habitués of Regents Park Road, is a sort of community as much as a business, an open-doored university of wine where tastings turn into seminars and seminars into parties and parties back into sales drives. It's a company which has done the London wine scene a lot of good, and British wine buying, too, has been greatly stimulated by Bibendum's increasingly active involvement with producers around the globe. The 1996 list (which shows the tasting room fascia during what appears to be a nuclear detonation) is entitled 'Return to the Roots'; this does not mean that all the New World wines have been thrown out, but is rather the company's attempt to draw drinkers' attention to the new anti-technology spirit abroad in vineyards and cellars everywhere. Well, fair enough, and it makes good reading (this is now an exceptionally well-organised and intelligent list), though what really counts is the quality of recent vintages and the producers featured, and here Bibendum's great strength is that it has few weaknesses − the sweep is wide enough to ensure that Italian vintage difficulties are, for example, compensated by a surge from Chile and Argentina. Indeed its main failing would be an exaggerated eclecticism; there is perhaps too brisk and merry a roundabout of producers, so that no sooner has one struck up a relationship with something good than it disappears, to be replaced by some new discovery or enthusiasm. Tasting facilities here are excellent − there are both free informal tastings on Friday evenings and Saturday lunchtimes, and grander tutored tastings of fine wines (for which a charge is made) trailed in the list. I was lucky enough to be on board for the 1988/1989/1990 Bordeaux Superstars' tastings: would any other merchant in depressed,

Hours
Mon-Thurs
10.00am-6.30pm;
Fri 10.00am-
8.00pm; Sat
9.30am-5.00pm

Minimum sale
1 case

Credit cards
Access/Mastercard,
Visa, AmEx, Switch

Discounts
No

Delivery
Free to mainland
England and Wales

Glass hire
Free with order
(mainland England)

**Tasting
facilities**
Regular tastings
held throughout
the year

**Storage
facilities**
£7.61 per case per
year

Email address
BIBENDUM @
Compuserve.com.uk

Nearest tube
Chalk Farm

pessimistic, impecunious Britain have organised that? There is a Bibendum Direct service for those who can't be bothered to do their own wine-shopping. Fine wines are now listed separately – a necessity, given the frenzied pace of price rises over the last year or two and the perennial difficulties of locating stock of the creamed cream. Bibendum's aim is to be an all-round, up-to-the-minute, cutting-edge wine merchant and, by and large, it succeeds.

Worth a punt

White: La Croix Blanc £3.50; 1995 Thrakkoma Chenin Blanc £4; 1995 Colombard/Chardonnay Red Cliffs £4.50; 1995 Orvieto Classico, Tenuta Antica Selva di Meana £6; 1993 Mâcon-Bussières Domaine de la Sarazinière £7; 1994 Crozes-Hermitage Blanc, Domaine du Colombier £8; 1994 Chablis, Legland £8.75; 1994 Chardonnay Lawson's Dry Hills £8.75; 1994 Sancerre 'Le Manoir', Neveu £9.75; 1995 Sauvignon Blanc, Carmenet £9.95 1994 Pouilly-Fuissé 'La Croix' , Denogent £11.75.

Rosé: 1995 Domaine du Poujol £5.50.

Red: 1994 Merlot La Serre £4; 1994 Malbec, Alamos Ridge £5; 1992 Château Brandeau, Côtes de Castillon £5.75; 1992 Barbera d'Asti Superiore, Litina, Cascina Castle't £6.75; 1994 Rosso di Montalcino, Talenti £8.50; 1994 Pinotage, Grangehurst £8.95; 1993 Gigondas Domaine de Font-Sane £9.75; 1992 Charbono, Duxoup £11.

Sparkling: Lonsdale Ridge £5.75; Chardonnay Brut, Charnay £7.85; Albert Beerens Brut Reserve Champagne £15; 1988 'R' de Ruinart Champagne £23.50.

Fortified: Oloroso Seco Napoleon, Hidalgo £8; 1987 Niepoort Vintage (half-bottles) £11; Niepoort 10 Years Old Tawny £15.

Bottoms Up

See Thresher

C. G. Bull & Taylor

2F Hewlett House, Havelock Terrace, London SW8 4AS
Tel: **0171 498 8022**   Fax: **0171 498 7851**

Small is tasty

This company, or more accurately its bloodline, has had a long and varied history since its foundation by Captain Bull in 1945; today its declared aim, 'to find those wines which really excite and stand out in tastings', is pursued through a steadily expanding list of largely well-chosen wines with as much emphasis as possible on 'small producers and growers'. Claret and burgundy form its core; there is, though, leavening from the French regions, from Spain

NOT A SHOP

Hours
Mon-Fri
9.00am-5.30pm

Minimum sale
1 mixed case

Credit cards
None

Discounts
By arrangement

Delivery
Free within Central London and on all orders over £100

Glass hire
Free with order

(especially Pesquera and Peñalba Lopez), and from the southern hemisphere (Neil Ellis from South Africa, Wirra-Wirra from Australia and Caliterra from Chile all merit sensory inspection).

Worth a punt

White: 1995 Domaine de Grachies, Jean-Claude Fontan, Vin de Pays des Côtes de Gascogne £3.85; 1994 Hautes Côtes de Beaune, Henri Gagnard £7.64; 1994 Montagny Premier Cru Les Guignottes, Domaine Michel £8.81; 1995 Sancerre les Roches, Vacheron £9.12; 1995 Casta Diva Cosecha Miel, Gutterez de la Vega, Alicante (50cl) £9.35.

Red: 1990 Rioja Crianza Lorinon, Bodegas Breton £5.85; 1994 Lirac, Domaines Tour des Chênes £6.70; 1993 Chianti Classico Roccaldo Acuti £9.25; 1992 Chassagne-Montrachet Premier Cru Morgeot, Lequin-Roussot £11.75; 1992 Pesquera Reserva, Ribera del Duero £15.94; 1982 Château Malescot-St-Exupéry, Margaux £25.46.

Sparkling: Marguet Bonnerave Grand Cru Champagne £11.75.

Tasting facilities
Corporate tastings by arrangement

Storage facilities
By arrangement

Bute Wines

2 Cottesmore Gardens, London W8 5PR   Tel: **0171 937 1629**
Fax: **0171 361 0061**

The Kensington phoenix

The Marchioness of Bute's singular wine company, having divested itself of some of its stock through Goedhuis & Co., is now being run exclusively through the W8 mail-order operation. A feisty 1995 Bordeaux offer has been issued, and a new list is, at the time of writing, in preparation. Jennifer Bute hopes that she will soon be back on track with sales of fine claret and burgundy for her discerning and patient clientele.

Worth a punt

The absence of a list makes this section difficult to complete, so it is best to discuss your needs directly with Lady Bute.

NOT A SHOP

Hours
9.00am–5.00pm

Minimum sale
1 unmixed case

Credit cards
None

Discounts
5% on 12 cases

Delivery
Free for 5 cases or more

Tasting facilities
Not at present

Storage facilities
£5 per case per year

Hours
Mon-Sat 10.00am-
11.00pm; Sun
12.00pm-3.00pm,
7.00pm-10.00pm
Minimum sale
No
Credit cards
None
Discounts
10% on most wines
by the case
Delivery
Free locally
Glass hire
Free with order
Tasting facilities
In-shop tastings
Storage facilities
No
Nearest tube
Stamford Brook

Chiswick Cellar

84 Chiswick High Road, London W4 1SY Tel: **0181 994 7989**

Lots of bottle

Mario Giorgetti's 'we never close' operation is one of London's best – the man likes wine, and takes an interest in the taste of what he buys as much as the deals he can get on it. If you can't find what you want, just ask.

Worth a punt

Chiswick Cellar has no list and the range is constantly being updated, so ask Mario Giorgetti's advice about his latest discoveries.

Clapham Cellars

See **La Réserve**

Hours
(W11): Mon-Sat
10.30am-8.00pm; Sun
11.00am-2.00pm
Minimum sale
None
Credit cards
Access/Mastercard,
Visa, AmEx
Discounts
Negotiable
Delivery
Free in London for 1
case or more; free
nationwide for 3 cases
or more
Glass hire
Free with order
**Tasting
facilities**
2 major tastings a
year; 6 special events
**Storage
facilities**
£5.20 a case + VAT
E-Mail address
Londonname@corbar.
co.uk
Nearest tube
Notting Hill Gate

Corney & Barrow

194 Kensington Park Road, London W11 2ES.
Tel: **0171 221 5122**   Fax: **0171 221 9371**
Head office and mail-order: 12 Helmet Row, London EC1V 3QJ
Tel: **0171 251 4051**   Fax: **0171 608 1373**

The Grand Old Duke of Old Street

For those who have the time and inclination to read wine lists, Corney & Barrow's stiff and sturdy ring-bound offering is one of the most informative and discursive available; indeed it's quite hard to locate the vulgarity of listed wines and prices in it as you squeak the pages to and fro. Holding the agency for both Pétrus and DRC obviously makes this a phone number of great interest to the platinum-card-holding classes; yet there are plenty of fine wines here with less weighty price tags dangling from them, Bordeaux's quieter districts being particularly well represented. Most parts of the world, even obscure Switzerland and cold Canada, get a steady look from the C&B buyers, though the German selection is much reduced from what it must once have been, while Spain and the States are over with surprising speed. Like most merchants at this level, I suspect that Corney & Barrow is deriving a larger and larger part of its income from fine-wine broking ("We now," I'm told, "have a team of seven"), and its impressive Bordeaux '95 offer must in part reflect the success of this team within a team, as well as the company's Bordeaux contacts and position in the pecking order. The sobering spectacle of Farr Vintners' success has not gone unnoticed on Helmet Row. The seasonal Fine Wine list is well worth requesting, particularly if you are looking for smaller quantities than a case of something or other; even single halves are duly listed. The special sale offers, too, are worth requesting: there are bargains to be had. Note, too, that the W11 shop carries a wider range of wines than is listed in the stiff little tome.

Worth a punt

White: 1995 La Combe de Grinou £5.76; 1995 Sauvignon Blanc Constantia Uitsig £7.94; 1994 Rully St Jacques, Aubert de Villaine £12.69; 1994 Chassagne-Montrachet, Olivier Leflaive £16.92.

Rosé: 1995 Château de Sours Rosé £7.44.

Red: 1994 Syrah, Domaine de la Jonction £4.41; 1990 Château Michel de Montaigne £6.76; 1991 Château St Brice £16.92; 1993 Château La Fleur Pétrus £27.85.

Fortified: Corney & Barrow's Fino £5.76.

Davison (J. T. Davies & Sons)

Head Office: 7 Aberdeen Road, Croydon, Surrey CR0 1EQ
Tel: **0181 681 3222**   Fax: **0181 760 0390**

Two and two makes ...

As this guide went to press last year, Davisons bought Mayor Sworder, the corporate specialist which was itself still in the process of digesting Russell & McIver; thus the independent wine trade shrinks. Happily, Mayor Sworder is still functioning as autonomously as it probably wishes within the familial embrace of Davisons, while Michael Davies professes himself very happy with his new acquisition: "Putting our 400 wines with 400 wines from Mayor Sworder and taking the 600 best has been a wonderfully rewarding experience." Davisons' customers should by now be noticing a difference, with the areas of most marked improvement being in regional France and Spain, with one or two hot New World acquisitions, too, like Norton and Navarro Correas from Argentina and the Mulderbosch Faithful Hound from South Africa. Davisons is a great spot to shop for well-aged (and well-stored) claret and port: you can still pick up worthwhile 1982s here, and the company is still selling good clarets from '78 and '79 (indeed the prices of more recent vintages make those '78s look snippy).

Hours
Mon-Sat
10.00am-2.00pm,
5.00pm-10.00pm;
Sun hours vary

Minimum sale
No

Credit cards
Access/Mastercard,
Visa, AmEx, Diners

Discounts
8.5% per case

Delivery
Free

Glass hire
Free with order

Tasting facilities
Weekly in-store tastings

Storage facilities
No

Worth a punt

White: 1995 Domaine de Lacquy, Vin de Pays des Terroirs Landais £4.25; 1994 Chardonnay Reserva Caliterra £6.49; 1995 Mâcon-Loché, Cave des Grands Crus £6.49; 1994 Chardonnay Bourgogne, Chavy £7.99; 1988 Château de Malle (sweet) £10.95; 1993

Mâcon-Clessé, Domaine Emilian Gillet £12.95.

Red: 1994 Conde de Castilla £3.95; 1994 Peter Lehmann Grenache £4.49; 1995 Mulderbosch Faithful Hound £6.49; 1994 Vacquéyras Château des Roques £6.75; 1990 Château Cardaillan £8.99; 1991 Cabernet Sauvignon Navarro Correas Colleccion Privada £9.75; 1990 Clos du Marquis £22.95.

Sparkling: Killawarra Brut £5.49; Pere Ventura Cava Brut Imperial £6.49; Charles Ellner Champagne £13.99.

Fortified: Inocente Fino, Valdespino £7.45; 1980 Warre Vintage Port £15.95.

Domaine Direct

NOT A SHOP

29 Wilmington Square, London WC1X 0EG   Tel: **0171 837 1142**   Fax: **0171 837 8605**

Hours
Mon-Fri
8.30am-5.00pm

Minimum sale
1 mixed case

Credit cards
Access/Mastercard,
Visa

Discounts
No

Delivery
Free in London; free
nationwide 3 cases
or more

Glass hire
No

**Tasting
facilities**
Biannual tastings for
private customers;
smaller monthly
tastings

**Storage
facilities**
£6.50+ VAT per case
per year

The great pursuit

Namely, Burgundy. If the wines of this exasperating and glorious little fillet of land are your passion, under no circumstances omit to contact Domaine Direct and solicit some sort of a mixed case from Hilary Gibbs or her assistant Priscilla Chase: this is one of London's best collections. As the company name suggests, these wines are overwhelmingly sourced from the small, individual growers who are responsible for much of the region's best: Tribut, Droin and Dauvissat in Chablis; Juillot in the Chalonnais; Vincent and Bonhomme in the Mâconnais; Roulot, Colin and Sauzet on the Côte de Beaune; Mortet, Roumier and Michelot on the Côte de Nuits. There is an 'Extra' list, too, for choice non-burgundian morsels like Leeuwin from Australia (one of the continent's best ten producers by any reckoning) and the Californian triumvirate of Spottswoode Cabernet, Etude Pinot Noir and Nalle's Zin. Backing for the most exciting new wine bar to open in London in the last year, The Crescent (see page 280), has come from Hilary Gibbs, though the sources for The Crescent's wines are laudably wide.

Worth a punt

White: 1994 Bourgogne Aligoté, Goisot £6.46; 1994 Beaujolais Blanc, Pivot £6.46; 1993 Mâcon-Viré Cuvée Speciale, Bonhomme £8.17; 1993 Chablis Vieilles Vignes, Durup £9.40; 1992 Chardonnay Leeuwin Art Series £16.39; 1994 Meursault les Luchets, Roulot £22.91.

Red: 1995 Côte de Brouilly, Pivot £7.93; 1991 Cabernet Sauvignon Leeuwin Estate Prelude £9.34; 1992 Mercurey, Juillot £11.46; 1993 Zinfandel, Nalle £12.63; 1993 Marsannay Premier Cru Les Longeroies, Mortet £14.69; 1992 Savigny-lès-Beaune Premier Cru La Dominode, Pavelot £15.22.

Drinks Cabin

See **Thresher**

El Vino

Mail order: Head Office: 1-2 Hare Place, Fleet St, London EC4
Tel: **0171 353 5384**   Fax: **0171 936 2367**   Also available on
retail basis at the sales counters of the tasting houses (see **page 283**).

Are you tasting tonight?

El Vino continues down its singular path as a wine merchant, offering (as only the two Reynier Wine Libraries – see page 294 – and La Réserve do at present) potential customers the chance to try anything in the range through its four 'tasting houses'. A further singularity is the style of the wines. If your delight is soft, smooth, supple, well-rounded, well-aged clarets and burgundies, the kind of wines which slip down without a murmur, stroking your throat to a purr as they do so, this is the place to find them. The company even calls one of its house reds Velvin. "We have thrown our management accountant out of the window," Graham Mitchell tells me, the proof of this defenestration being the fact that, in mid-1996, only one out of the company's 18 red burgundies dates from a harvest later than that of 1990, while (house clarets aside) there are only three 1991 red Bordeaux wines, everything else being from 1990 or earlier. El Vino has not entirely turned its back on modernity, though: New World (this quaint phrase rings truer here than elsewhere) selections incude good New Zealand whites and Australian reds. Corporate tastings are a further speciality. There is, in sum, no reason at all for buying a bottle from El Vino without previously ascertaining that you like the way it tastes.

Worth a punt

White: 1995 Sauvignon Blanc La Fortuna £4.75; 1994 Château La Nauze £6.25; 1995 Petit Chablis £8.25; 1993 Rully £9.20; 1994 Chablis Premier Cru Fourchaume £12.60; 1993 Mercurey Blanc Mauvarennes, Faiveley £12.95.

Red: 1990 Château Vieux Perinot £5.10; 1992 Côte de Beaune-Villages £8.75; 1991 Cabernet Sauvignon Beaulieu Vineyard £8.95; 1990 Mercurey Domaine Lorenzon £12.80; 1986 Crozes-Hermitage Domaine de Thalabert £14.95; 1985 Château Fonbadet £18.60.

Sparkling: Louis Boyier Champagne £14.85.

Fortified: No.1 Manzanilla £4.80; 1982 Offley Boa Vista Vintage Port £17.50.

Hours
Mon-Fri
9.00am-5.30pm

Minimum sale
No

Credit cards
Access/Mastercard,
Visa, AmEx

Discounts
£1.50 off a case up to £50; £3.00 off a case between £50 and £100; £4 off a case over £100

Delivery
Free for 2 cases or more; 1-4 bottles £5.75; 5-23 bottles £6.50; flat rate of £2.50 for 1-23 bottles in EC1, EC2, EC3, EC4 and WC2.

Glass hire
Free with order

Tasting facilities
Customer tastings and corporate tutored tastings on request

Storage facilities
£4.50 per case per year

Hours
Mon-Sat
10.00am-7.00pm

Minimum sale
No

Credit cards
Access/Mastercard,
Visa, Switch

Discounts
Collection discount
(30p per bottle);
£1 per case 5 cases
or more

Delivery
Free locally 1 case or
more; free outside
M25 2 cases or more

Glass hire
Free with order

**Tasting
facilities**
Tutored tasting
programme; June list
launch tasting and
November fair;
occasional dinners

**Storage
facilities**
By arrangement

**Nearest
BR station**
Wandsworth Town

Enotria Winecellars

153-155 Wandsworth High Street, London SW18 4JB
Tel: **0181 871 2668**   Fax: **0181 874 8380**

All things to all drinkers

So far as I can ascertain, the marriage between Enotria and Winecellars has been broadly satisfactory for retail customers; at any rate the Wandsworth retail shop continues to flourish (turnover is said to have doubled) with more independence than it previously enjoyed, and mail-order customers now have a truly enormous range of wines to choose from. I understand that the list, in fact, is now considered too unwieldy altogether, and will be split up into a series of mailings sent to customers throughout the year. The emphasis remains on Italy, of course, and all that one can hope for is a series of wonderful vintages between now and the new millenium to make up for the disasters since 1990. The Italian selection is complemented by a large range from elsewhere in Europe and the New World, and that old Winecellars hallmark of quality and individuality remains apparent in most of the selection.

Worth a punt

White: 1995 Chenin Blanc Stormy Cape, South Africa £4.99; 1995 Poacher's Blend, St Hallets £5.49; 1995 Arneis, Langhe, Alasia £6.99; 1994 Chablis, Grossot £9.99.

Red: 1994 Cabernet Sauvignon Reserve, MontGras, Chile £5.99; 1995 Costières de Nîmes Terre d'Argence, Château Mougues du Grés £6.99; 1995 Gamay, Wildflower, Lohr £7.99; 1993 Sangiovese, Noceto £10.79; 1990 Amarone Classico della Valpolicella, Allegrini £16.49.

Sparkling: Sonoma Pacific Blanc de Noir £10.99.

NOT A SHOP

Hours
Mon-Fri
10.00am-6.00pm

Minimum sale
£500

Credit cards
Access/Mastercard,
Visa

Discounts
On application

Delivery
£8.50 London only

Glass hire
No

Farr Vintners

19 Sussex St, London SW1V 4RR   Tel: **0171 828 1960**
Fax: **0171 828 3500**

View from the top

Farr Vintners is a wine merchant like no other. It deals exclusively in fine wines; most of its customers are overseas; it doesn't accept orders for less than £500; its biggest problem is finding stock, rather than selling it. There's barely a bottle in the place; it is, more than anything, a highly specialised tele-trading house. Yet the Vintners (now three in number, and none of them called Farr) take wine very seriously, taste widely and have unrivalled contacts; as with most great commercial successes, Farr Vintners has tackled a rapidly expanding and highly lucrative market with vision and professionalism. If you want to convert cash into blue-blooded wine for drinking or investment purposes, begin with this number. The emphasis is on claret, naturally enough – Bordeaux still produces a larger quantity of consistently great wine than any other region in the world. Structurally, too, Bordeaux's quality hierarchies are relatively easy to understand, an important factor in getting through to the world's wealthy (who are too busy making money to pore over wine books). There are smaller quantities of other great wines (like burgundies, particularly from Jean-Noel Gagnard and Leroy; Rhône wines from Beaucastel and others; even New Zealand wines from Kumeu River and Ata Rangi). The key event of the last year here was the '95 Bordeaux *en primeur* campaign which, for the first time in the UK, Farr Vintners dominated, producing a larger and more excitingly marketed offer than any rival; this was partly because '95 was a good vintage, but it cannot have escaped the quick-witted Stephen Browett that future stock needs can only be ensured by booking a place well up the queue at every stage of the Bordeaux sales process. Expect, therefore, more *en primeur* offers from Farr (leading, they would doubtless hope, to larger first-tranche allocations of the most sought-after wines). Sales advice (from Lindsay Hamilton, Jonathan Stephens and Gaylene Thompson) is straightforward and honest: they are more likely to put you off buying a bad wine or an overpriced wine than hype up a good one. If you have fine wine (particularly claret) to sell, buyer Browett would like to hear from you. Prices for both buyer and seller are right on the pulse of the market, so purchasers will find bargains by looking ahead of the market (at the time of writing, top '89s are attractive in relation to the unbottled '95s). What of value for money in all of this? For those on average British incomes, little of the Farr stocklist can be said to offer value for money. Yet if you want the best, this is what it now costs.

Worth a punt

Ring to discuss your requirements.

Fields

55 Sloane Avenue, London SW3 3DH   Tel: **0171 589 5753**

Mute appeal

Fields has a long and honourable record of bringing good wine to its local community; indeed it brings, through its agency, good wine to a larger community still. The shop is well-organised and pleasantly staffed; the wide range includes lots of half bottles, and notable areas of strength are burgundy and the South of France. More, alas, I cannot say, since Fields is proudly uncommunicative, and my attempts to find out more have been unreasonably rebuffed. Secret agents and informers are welcome to contact me.

Tasting facilities
Tastings and dinners for regular customers

Storage facilities
£5 per case per year

Hours
Mon-Sat 9.30am-8.00pm

Minimum sale
No

Credit cards
All major cards

Discounts
by arrangement

Delivery
Locally by arrangement

Glass hire
Free with order

Tasting facilities
Fri pm; all day Sat

Storage facilities
No

Nearest tube
South Ken/Sloane Sq

Worth a punt

Unfortunately, the company seems to be unwilling to cooperate with me in providing recommendations for readers of the Guide, so interested parties will have to ask (and pass judgement) for themselves.

Hours
Mon-Sat
9.30am-6.00pm

Minimum sale
No

Credit cards
All major cards

Discounts
1 bottle free per case
(unmixed)

Delivery
Free in London to
account holders and
orders over £50 plus
nationwide delivery

Glass hire
No

**Tasting
facilities**
In-store tastings;
customer dinners
and themed
evenings

**Storage
facilities**
£4.50 per case per
year

Nearest tube
Green Park/Piccadilly
Circus

Fortnum & Mason

181 Piccadilly, London W1A 1ER   Tel: **0171 734 8040**
Fax: **0171 437 3278**

Choice delights for mad moments

I always think that Annette Duce, F&M's buyer, has what must be the best job in the wine trade (though even she probably has grim sales targets to reach and a delicate game of office politics to play). My envy is based on a look throught the Fortnum list. Most wine buyers have to hit price points with decent bottles; Annette's double duty, by contrast, seems to be to buy the best at any price, and to have something good from everywhere worthwhile. So there's ten vintages of Yquem and lots of 1982 claret; the shop is a showcase for almost every Champagne you could want; vintage port, sherry, Chablis ... ample, all ample. Yet Australia is splendidly stocked, too, and you can find essential curiosities like vin jaune and English sparkling wine and Willi Opitz, too, including the now-celebrated 'Blip-Blop' c.d. Picking the wines to constitute F&M's own-label range must be a delight, since price is not the first consideration, as a glance through the suppliers (all now sensibly credited) shows: the Pauillac from Pichon-Lalande, the Margaux from Rauzan-Ségla, the red burgundy from Faiveley in Mercurey, the Sancerre from Vacheron, the Mosel from Dirk Richter. This, in sum, is a superb, wide-ranging and well-composed list, sold, I know, by knowledge-able and enthusiastic staff. Of course you'll need a bob or two ...

Worth a punt

White: 1995 Menetou-Salon 'Charnay' Jean-Max Roger £8.25; 1992 Brauneberger Juffer Sonnenuhr, Fritz Haag £14.95; 1990 Chassagne Montrachet Premier Cru Morgeot Ramonet £30.

Red: 1993 Mondot, Château Troplong-Mondot £11.95; 1989 Viña Ardanza Reserva, La Rioja Alta £11.95; 1993 Gevrey-Chambertin Groffier £20; 1994 Château La Tertre Rôteboeuf £27.50; 1990 Château Beaucastel, Châteauneuf-du-Pape £30.

Sparkling: Fortnum & Mason Champagne £17.45.

Fortified: Fortnum & Mason Pale Dry Manzanilla £6.75; 1990 Fortnum & Mason Late-Bottled Vintage Port £9.95; 1976 Colheita Port Quinta do Noval (half-bottle) £10.95; Royal Corregidor Rich Rare Oloroso Sherry Sandeman £13.25.

The Four Vintners

City Wine & Cigar Shop, 3 Fleet St, London EC4Y 1AU
Tel: **0171 353 7733**   Fax: **0171 353 7730**
(plus 5 further branches)

Corks away

The Four Vintners' letterhead shows the antique gentlemen in question sitting, shoes brightly buckled, while corks scythe through the air about them, in celebration perhaps of the new business and list expansion Nick Cater (in fact the sole vintner) says has come the company's way since the publication of the last Guide. The basement in the Fleet St premises has been opened up, expanding the range beyond the confines of the list for champagne, armagnac, madeira, port and cigars. Well-informed service remains the company aim.

Worth a punt

White: 1992 Montagny Premier Cru Vieilles Vignes, Philibert £8.99; 1994 Sancerre Domaine du Carrou £9.25; 1994 Pouilly-Fumé Comtesse d'Estutt d'Assay £11.25; 1994 Chablis Premier Cru Vaucopins Long Depaquit £12.75.

Red: 1991 Château le Temple £8.35; 1993 Morgon, Confrérie des Chevaliers du Tastevin £8.55; 1989 Château La Tour St Bonnet £10.45; 1993 Pommard Clos du Pavillon £15.25.

Sparkling: Champagne Jules Ferraud Cuvée de Réserve £12.99.

Fortified: Noval Extra Dry White Port £7.15.

Hours
Mon-Fri
9.00am-6.30pm

Minimum sale
No

Credit cards
Visa, AmEx, Diners

Discounts
10% per case

Delivery
Free within M25 for
4 cases or more, plus
nationwide service

Glass hire
Free with order

Tasting facilities
Biannual tastings by
invitation; others by
arrangement

Storage facilities
Free storage

Nearest tube
Temple

Fullers

Head Office: Griffin Brewery, Chiswick Lane South, London W4 2QB   Tel: **0181 996 2000**   Fax: **0181 996 2087**

Spot on

Fullers continues to be an extremely impressive wine merchant. All of the wines I have tasted from their range this year have been characterful, and most of those I've liked – which is all anyone can expect of a wine supplier. Some, moreover, have been outstanding, particularly from Spain and the South of France; buyer Roger Higgs sniffs out exciting new wines as quickly as any of his rivals (and former colleagues) at Oddbins, and uses Fullers' size astutely to pick up parcels of wine others may be too many-branched to touch. With the Los Fundos Chilean wines, he even managed to tackle the supermarkets on cut-price £2.99 wonders. Chardonnay remains a speciality; Syrah is becoming so. Longer opening hours, and new stores in Central London locations, put the Fullers package within the reach of more of London's wine-thirsty. (And beer thirsty, of

Hours
Mon-Sat 10.00am-
10.00pm; Sun
11.00am-10.00pm

Minimum sale
No

Credit cards
Access/Mastercard,
Visa

Discounts
1 bottle free per case
plus selected 10%
case discounts

Delivery
Local service

Glass hire
Free with order

Tasting facilities
Saturday in-store
tastings

Storage facilities
No

course; my brief here doesn't include beautiful ale, but Fuller's bottled range, stocked in full by the shops, is exemplary.)

Worth a punt

White: 1995 Sauvignon Blanc Berticot, Côtes de Duras £3.89; 1995 Pinot Grigio del Friuli, Pecile £4.75; 1995 Château Haut-Grélot £4.99; 1995 Chardonnay Santa Ines, Chile £4.99; 1994 Chardonnay Valdivieso Reserve £4.99; 1994 Chardonnay, Alamos Ridge, Argentina £4.99; 1992 Riesling Kabinett Serriger Herrenberg, Bert Simon £5.99; 1995 Sauvignon Blanc Neil Ellis, South Africa £6.99; 1994 St Véran Domaine des Deux Roches £7.49; 1994 Chardonnay Catena, Argentina £7.99; 1994 Chardonnay Augustus £8.99; 1995 Sancerre, Pinard £9.49; 1994 Chardonnay Devil's Lair, Western Australia £9.99.

Red: 1995 Castillo de Montblanc Tinto £3.29; 1994 Merlot Domaine de Raissac, Vin de Pays d'Oc £3.79; 1995 Merlot Concha y Toro, Chile £3.99; 1994 Monastrel Muri Veteres £4.25; 1994 Domaine de Belvezet £4.49; 1995 Pinot Noir Concha y Toro, Chile £4.99; 1995 Merlot Terre Noble, Chile £4.99; 1993 Domaine de La Grande Bellane, Valréas (organic) £5.99; 1993 Shiraz, Leasingham £6.99; 1993 Château Reynella Basket-Pressed Shiraz £7.99; 1992 Crozes-Hermitage Cuvée Louis Belle, Albert Belle £8.49; 1993 Syrah, Dominio de Valdepusa £8.99; 1992 Château Haut-Faugères £9.99; 1993 Zinfandel Mondavi Unfiltered £11.99.

Sparkling: Seaview Brut £5.99; 1993 Green Point £10.49; Château de Boursault Brut Champagne £14.99; Château de Boursault Rosé Champagne £15.99.

Fortified: 1988 Late Bottled Vintage Quinta do Crasto £7.99; Matusalem Oloroso Muy Viejo £16.99; 1985 Fonseca Vintage Port £19.99.

Gelston Castle Fine Wines

45 Warwick Square, London SW1V 2AJ. Tel: **0171 821 6841**
Fax: **0171 821 6350**
Main office: Castle Douglas, DG7 1QE. Tel: **01556 503012**
Fax: **01556 504183**

Voice in the wilderness

This is a wine merchant whose base is in Scotland's lowlands, whose stocks are held in Octavian's Wiltshire cellars, and whose London office marshals orders from the capital. It is run by Alexander Scott, a fine taster and thinker in this island's best sceptical traditions — so the list is constantly stimulating, as is the range, with its resolute plundering of the unfashionable and the misguidedly neglected. James King, formerly of J&B, oversees the London office, and Michael Schuster M.W., one of the coun-

NOT A SHOP

Hours
Mon-Fri
9.00am-6.00pm

Minimum sale
No

Credit cards
No

Discounts
By arrangement

Delivery
Free with orders of £150+, or £7 per consignment anywhere in UK

Glass hire
No

try's top tasters and wine educators, seems to be on board on a kind of consultative basis. Scott's understanding of, and commitment to, Burgundy, the Loire and German wine is remarkable; he has a stealthy, bargain-hunter's approach to claret (and Bordeaux is big enough for this to work well); and he has the ambition to stock enough cleverly chosen wines from other regions to make this a complete as well as a controversial list. No one who likes to think as they drink should be without a copy.

Tasting facilities
Regular client tastings: ask for invitations

Storage
£5.50 per case

Worth a punt

White: 1994 Pacherenc Sec, Berthoumieu £5.75; 1994 Rully Blanc Premier Cru Margotés, Jean-Claude Brelière £11.75; 1990 Riesling Grand Cru Rosacker Vieilles Vignes, Frédéric Mallo £12.50; 1992 Chablis Premier Cru Fourchaume, Duplessis £12.75; 1988 Hochheimer Herrnberg Riesling Spätlese Trocken, Künstler £13.

Red: 1995 Terras de Belmonte Tinto, Cova da Beira, Portugal £4.25; 1992 St Chinian Cuvée Spéciale, Mas Champart £6.25; 1992 Bandol Cuvée Spéciale, Domaine Tempier £12; 1993 Ladoix Rouge, Maurice Maratray £12.25; 1990 Vosne-Romanée, Confuron-Côtedidot £19.50; 1989 Gevrey-Chambertin Premier Cru Poissenot, Geantet-Pansiot £21.

Sparkling: Vouvray Brut, Foreau £8.50; Jean Lallement Champagne £14.70.

Fortified: 1995 Muscat de Rivesaltes, Domaine du Mas Crémat £6.95; Niepoort Vintage Character Port £8.75.

Gerry's

74 Old Compton St, London W1V 5PA   Tel: **0171 734 4215**

Pile it high

Hours
Mon-Fri 9.00am-7.00pm; Sat 9.00am-5.30pm

Minimum sale
No

G erry's (and Del Monico's before it) is a Soho landmark: the bottle-filled windows, the counter on which staff and customers lean to discuss purchases, the constant scurrying to and fro of men with cases of wines on trolleys to lubricate the quarter's desire for a good time (free same-day local delivery). Prices are keen; quality varies, but finding the good bottles is half the fun. The service may be stylistically different from that vaunted by Berry Bros but it's no less assiduous for all that.

Credit cards
None

Discounts
Negotiable on quantity orders

Delivery
Free same-day local service

Glass hire
Deposit with order

Worth a punt

Hard to say – since there's no list and the stock changes all the time. Michael and his merry men are happy to give advice.

Tasting facilities
Saturday tastings

Storage facilities
No

Nearest tube
Leicester Square

Hours
Mon-Fri
9.30am-6.00pm

Minimum sale
1 case (unmixed)

Credit cards
Access/Mastercard,
Visa, AmEx

Discounts
No

Delivery
Free in England 5
cases or more; also
nationwide service

Glass hire
Free with order over
£250

**Tasting
facilities**
1 large tasting per
year; biannual
dinners

**Storage
facilities**
£5.95 per case
per year

Goedhuis & Co

6 Rudolf Place, Miles St, London SW8 1RP   Tel: **0171 793 7900**   Fax: **0171 793 7170**

Tuck box

Jonathan Goedhuis's naturally sunny temperament has become pessimistic of late. Nothing to do with selling less wine, or selling it less well; if anything, rather, the opposite. Demand for the kind of fine wine in which Goedhuis specialises has risen steadily of late; a quarter of it, he now says, leaves the country. His pessimism is based on the fact that he fears it will never be replaced. And when the opportunity does come along to replace some of it, as with 1995 Bordeaux, Britain is spurned. "This time last year I was a Francophile," he recalls. "Due to the horrors of the 1995 *en primeur* campaign, I am rapidly turning into a Francophobe." Nonetheless the Goedhuis offer of Bordeaux '95s was a sporting one; there have also, in the last year, been some good 'open case' offers and bin-end clearance offers to add to the general list (strong on claret and burgundy; seasoned with wines from elsewhere – including, last year, three tranches of Lady Bute's legendary stocks). The Gardet champagne and Beaucastel Châteauneuf are both excellent.

Worth a punt

White: 1993 Bourgogne, Dussort £92.83 per case; 1992 Meursault Premier Cru Les Perrières, Fichet £276.13 per case; 1993 Puligny-Montrachet Premier Cru les Referts, Carillon £311.38 per case; 1994 Roussanne Vieilles Vignes Châteauneuf-du-Pape Beaucastel £329 per case.

Red: 1990 Château Greysac £137.48 per case; 1990 Château Haut Plantey £159.80 per case; 1992 Château Grand-Puy-Lacoste £164.50 per case; 1993 Châteauneuf-du-Pape Beaucastel £169.20 per case; 1990 Gevrey-Chambertin 'Corbeaux', Serafin £235 per case; 1993 Chambertin Clos de Bèze, Rousseau £763.75 per case; 1988 Clos de la Roche, Ponsot £822.50 per case.

Sparkling: Guy de Flavy Champagne £156.28 per case; Georges Gardet £182.13 per case.

Hours
Mon, Tues, Sat
10.00am-6.00pm;
Wed-Fri 10.00am-
7.00pm

Minimum sale
No

Credit cards
Access/Mastercard,
Visa, AmEx,
Diners, JCB

Harrods

87-135 Old Brompton Road, London SW1X 7XL
Tel: **0171 730 1234**   Fax: **0171 581 0470**

Bottling out

Harrods' wine department, as I know from numerous visits there, is grandly stocked. Prices are certainly not cheap, but few areas are neglected; classics from both worlds, new and old, rub shoulders in the refined and scented air. Alas, more than that I am unable to say since (like its neighbour and rival Harvey Nichols) Harrods seems to have slapped a news blackout on all information emanating from the wine department. Despite repeated requests for information, our questionnaire remained unanswered, no wine list has been forthcoming, and no statement of strategy has been received. The contrast with the communicative enthusiasm found in the wine departments of Selfridges and Fortnum & Mason is striking. We trust that personal callers will receive a better standard of service.

Harvey Nichols

109-125 Knightsbridge, London SW1 7RJ   Tel: **0171 235 5000**   Fax: 0171 235 5020

Rumours of grandeur

The wine department of Harvey Nichols is tiny in terms of floor space but extensive in terms of range, as those who eat regularly in the Fifth Floor restaurant will know (its full list arrays all of the shop's bottles, admirably enough, before the diner).

Sadly no details can be provided this year, since repeated phone calls and requests for information from Harvey Nichols' wine department have failed to yield any sort of response whatsoever.

Haynes, Hanson & Clark

25 Eccleston St, London SW1W 9NP   Tel: **0171 259 0102**   Fax: **0171 259 0103**

Neat and tidy

Haynes, Hanson and Clark is a London and Gloucestershire wine merchant which quietly gets on with searching out talented growers to contribute to its fine burgundy list (including Beaujolais not from Georges Duboeuf but from growers in the best crus); these are supported with good clarets, Loire wines and Rhône wines, and little vinous snippets from more or less everywhere else. The list is clearly laid-out and those on the mailing list receive regular offers of *en primeur* wines, new arrivals, bin ends, etc. H. H. &C wines have a habit of leading the field in tastings, and the emphasis is firmly on wines which drink well rather than the glitz-encrusted buzz-wines others increasingly specialise in. Neat operation.

Discounts
1 bottle free per case

Delivery
Various rates

Glass hire
No

Tasting facilities
With Gourmet Club

Storage facilities
No

Nearest tube
Knightsbridge

Hours
Mon-Fri 10.00am-8.00pm; Sat 10.00am-6.00pm

Minimum sale
No

Credit cards
All major cards

Discounts
5% on mixed cases; 1 bottle free per case on unmixed cases

Delivery
Free over £50, Central London

Glass hire
No

Tasting facilities
Occasional

Storage facilities
No

Nearest tube
Knightsbridge

Hours
Mon-Fri 9.00am-7.00pm; Sat 10.00am-6.00pm

Minimum sale
No

Credit cards
Access/Mastercard, Visa, Switch

Discounts
10% per case (unmixed)

Delivery
Free to central London; free nationwide 5 cases or more

Glass hire
Free with order

Tasting facilities
By invitation
Storage facilities
No
Nearest tube
Victoria

Worth a punt

White: 1995 Sauvignon Blanc Vin de Pays d'Oc, Domaine La Belonette £4.95; 1995 The Warden Dry White, Bedfordshire £5.48; 1995 Chardonnay Vin du Pays du Jardin de la France, Domaine Richou £6.35; 1995 Quincy, Rouzé £7.35; 1994 Chablis Premier Cru Côte de Lechet, Dampt £11.60.

Red: 1995 Vin de Pays de Vaucluse Domaine de l'Ameillaud £4.55; 1994 Vacquéyras, Château des Rocques £7.35; 1993 Bourgeuil Cuvée des Pins, Domaine Delaunay £7.90; 1995 Juliénas Le Bois du Chat, Descombes £8.65; 1991 Morey St Denis Domaine du Lambrays £18.20; 1990 Château Bourgneuf, Pomerol £22.80.

Sparkling: Pierre Vaudon Champagne £14.95.

Fortified: Manzanilla La Gitana, Hidalgo £4.95; 1982 Late-Bottled Vintage Port, Warre's £14.85.

Heath Street Wine Company

See La Réserve

Holland Park Wine Company

Hours
Mon-Sat
10.00am-8.30pm
Minimum sale
No
Credit cards:
Access/Mastercard,
Visa, AmEx, Delta,
Switch
Discounts
5% per case
Delivery
Free same-day
service to Central
London; free 48-
hour service
nationwide on orders
over £120
Glass hire
Free with order
Tasting facilities
Monthly tutored
tastings; biannual
wine school; in-store
tastings
Storage facilities
£5 + VAT per year
Nearest tube
Holland Park

12 Portland Road, London W11 4LA   Tel: **0171 221 9614**
Fax: **0171 221 9613**

Bright sparks

This buzzy little shop in the heart of catholic Holland Park remains a model of what the neighbourhood wine merchant ought to be. The range, like the universe, has 'expanded greatly last year in all directions,' I'm told by David Penny (who, together with ex-Roseworthy College graduate Gary Evans, helps owner James Handford M.W. run the shop); the South African and Argentinian selections have been a particular success. Other innovations include regular special-case offers, a standing-order case system, and a programme of tastings plus an introductory tasting course held at the St Francis of Assissi Community Centre. The 1995 en primeur jamboree didn't pass Holland Park by: d'Armailhac, Durfort-Vivens, Calon-Ségur and Prieuré-Lichine were among the worthwhile offerings. The biannually updated wine list could fit in jacket pocket or handbag, and all the wines are usefully annotated in (printed) longhand. Apart from good wine, the Company gets involved in good works and arts ventures locally.

Worth a punt

White: 1995 Chenin Blanc Drostdy-Hof, South Africa £4.60; 1995 Blanc de Brumont, Madiran £4.99; 1996 Sauvignon Blanc Neil Ellis, South Africa £7.99; 1994 Sancerre, Pinard £9.99; 1995

Chardonnay Pipers Brook, Tasmania £12.95; 1994 Chablis, Defaix £13.95; 1994 Chardonnay Au Bon Climat £14.95.

Red: 1994 Merlot, Domaine de Fraisse £4.69; 1989 Marius Reserva, Almansa £4.99; 1991 Merlot Weinert, Argentina £8.99; 1991 Madiran Montus, Alain Brumont £12.99; 1993 Châteauneuf-du-Pape les Cailloux, Brunel £13.69.

Sparkling: 1990 Brochet-Hervieux Champagne Rosé £19.99.

Fortified: Oloroso Viejo de Jerez, Lustau (half-bottle) £6.95; 1976 Colheita Port Quinta do Noval (half-bottle) £10.95; 1976 Fonseca-Guimaraens Vintage Port £21.50.

Huttons

See **Thresher**

Jeroboams

See **Stones of Belgravia**

EROS AWARD FOR

WINE MERCHANT OF THE YEAR

Justerini & Brooks

61 St James's Street, London SW1A 1LZ   Tel: **0171 493 8721**
Fax: **0171 499 4653**   Broking Dept. Tel: **0181 471 0002**   Broking Dept Fax: **0181 471 1006**

Rolling pastures of wine

For sheer choice, and for sheer choiceness of wines, Justerini & Brooks is near unbeatable. It is a connoisseur's list — there are one or two wines under £5, but to get the most out of what's on offer you should allow yourself fairly free rein in the £10-£25 price bracket. If you are an enthusiast for either burgundy or German wine, then you are likely to be familiar with J&B: its stock of both is definitive. Moreover many of the great wines are here; there is none of the spirit of failure which increasingly characterises British wine buying when great wines are at stake. Clarets are as well stocked here as anywhere; J&B's '95 *en primeur* offer was one of the country's three best, even if some of the wines were instantly unavailable. The French regions, Italy and Spain are all well-covered; only New World wine enthusiasts need have cause to fill cases elsewhere, and even they can keep in touch with some of the best of the southern hemisphere (like Ata Rangi's superb Pinot Noir) through the capacious J&B cellars. Broking is increasingly

Hours
Mon-Fri 9.00am-5.30pm

Minimum sale
No

Credit cards
Access/Mastercard, Visa, AmEx

Discounts
£1 per case on 2-4 cases; £2 per case on 5-7 cases; £3 per case on 8+ cases

Delivery
Free nationwide 2 cases or more; otherwise £9

Glass hire
Free with order

Tasting facilities
Specialist tastings of young burgundy or Rhone

Storage facilities
£6.50 per case per year

E-mail address
100340.1620@
compuserve.com
Nearest tube
Green Park

important here, as to all of its rivals; and the company is encouraging those who wish to drop in to 61 St James's St with mini bin-end sales and whisky and wines for tasting. The same-day bike-a-bottle service will send a leather-clad man off with the bottle of your choice for your wife, lover or mistress; the selected cellar plan, meanwhile, will build your own stocks via monthly banker's order or credit-card payments. I provide a few recommendations below, but if you're buying wines at this price and quality level, then it's best to seek advice from J&B's staff as you do so.

Worth a punt

White: 1994 Mâcon Uchizy, Talmard £6.95; 1993 Pouilly-Fuissé Vieilles Vignes, Manciat-Poncet £11.85; 1993 Riesling Kabinett Maximin Grünhauser Abtsberg £12.50; 1992 Chardonnay, Chalk Hill, California £12.95; 1990 Château Bastor-Lamontagne (sweet) £17.50; 1993 Chablis Grand Cru Les Clos, Dauvissat-Camus £19.90; 1993 Château Laville-Haut-Brion £30.

Red: 1990 Ribera del Duero Valduero Crianza £7.30; 1993 Bourgogne, Chevillon £8.95; 1993 Cabernet Sauvignon Coonawarra, Leconfield, South Australia £9; 1989 Château Fourcas-Loubaney, Listrac £10.50; 1993 Pinot Noir Ata Rangi, New Zealand £16.90; 1993 Pommard Premier Cru Les Boucherottes, Coste-Caumartin £19.90; 1990 Château Pichon-Longueville-Baron £39.50.

Sparkling: 1988 le Mesnil Blanc de Blancs Champagne £19.90.

Fortified: 1993 Gould Campbell Vintage Port £16.90.

Kwik Save

Hours
Mon, Tue 9.00am-
5.00pm; Wed
9.00am-6.00pm;
Thurs, Fri 9.00am-
8.00pm; Sat 9.00am-
5.30pm; Sun
10.00am-4.00pm
(selected stores only)

Minimum sale
No

Credit cards
Delta, Switch

Discounts
No

Delivery
No

Glass hire
No

Tasting facilities
No

Storage facilities
No

Head Office: Warren Drive, Prestatyn, Clwyd LL19 7HU
Tel: **01745 887111**   Fax: **01745 882504**

The bottom line

One of the delights of the alphabetical ordering of this section of the *Evening Standard Wine Guide* is that it makes neighbours of Justerini & Brooks and Kwik Save. It's like seeing a Reliant Robin parked next to a Rolls. Each does a different job of work; each does it well. Kwik Save's consultant Angela Muir M.W., in conjunction with the in-house buyers, has managed to put together a small but high quality range of wines at startling prices: I arrived at the '96 summer tasting something of a sceptic, and left a convert. Not everything is good, of course: wines to avoid include the repellent, unnaturally flavoured California Cellars White (£2.99, 9/25) and Red (£2.99, 8/25); the thin, hard Valpolicella Venier (£2.99, 10/25); the sulphurous Marino white from Spain (£2.79, 9/25); and, sadly, the strange, sweet-and-sour 1994 Cabernet Sauvignon from Macedonia (£2.69, 10/25). I was taken aback, however, by how many good wines, especially red, there were at these kind of prices (the best are listed below), and heartened to hear that Kwik Save customers are prepared to punt on wines at over £3 (the company says that sales of some wines actually increased with the price, so it is obviously possible to have too much of a good thing). We are assured that the 'lightweight margins policy', a delicious euphemism where none was necessary, operates throughout the list.

Worth a punt

White: Riesling & Dimiat Country Wine, Khan Krum, Bulgaria £2.59 (16/25); Vin de Pays de l'Hérault, Domaine Virginie £2.69 (17/25); 1995 Chardonnay-Sauvignon Blanc, Preslav £2.79 (17/25); 1995 Hungarian Pinot Gris £2.99 (15/25); 1995 Bordeaux Sauvignon Cuvée VE, Calvet £2.99 (16/25); 1995 Classic Réserve Chardonnay, Angove's £4.29 (16/25).

Red: Les Garrigues, Vin de Pays des Cevennes £2.69 (15/25); Mendoza Red, Argentina £2.69 (15/25); 1995 Merlot & Cabernet Sauvignon, Liubimetz, Bulgaria £2.79 (18/25); 1993 Cabernet Sauvignon, Burgas, Bulgaria £2.89 (21/25); Promesa Tinto Joven, Cosecheros y Criadores £2.89 (19/25); 1995 Pinot Noir Young Vatted, Romania £2.89 (14/25); 1995 Merlot Young Vatted, Romania £2.99 (19/25); 1992 Gamza Réserve, Suhindol, Bulgaria £2.99 (15/25); 1995 José Neiva, Portugal £2.99 (15/25); Merlot Skylark Hill, Vin de Pays d'Oc £2.99 (18/25); Montepulciano d'Abruzzo, Venier £2.99 (15/25); 1992 Cabernet Sauvignon Reserve, Elhovo, Bulgaria £3.09 (15/25); Cabernet Sauvignon/Shiraz Skylark Hill, Vins de Pays d'Oc £3.19 (14/25); 1994 Domaine des Bruyères, Côtes de Malpère £3.49 (15/25); 1994 Tempranillo Berberana £3.89 (18/25).

Sparkling: Cava Brunet £4.99 (18/25); Bonnet Brut Héritage Champagne £12.99 (17/25).

Laytons Wine Vaults

20 Midland Road, London NW1 2AD   Tel: **0171 388 4567**
Fax: **0171 383 7419**
Laytons/André Simon shops: 50-52 Elizabeth St, London SW1W 9PB
Tel: **0171 730 8108**   Fax: **0171 730 9284**
21 Motcomb St, London SW1X 8LB   Tel: **0171 235 3723**   Fax: **0171 235 2062**

The cellar-searchers

The Laytons operation has two halves: one is the capacious vaults, over which trains for the north rumble, and from which wines are sold on a mixed-case basis; the other half is constituted

Hours
Vaults: Mon-Fri
9.30am-7.00pm;
Sat 9.30am-7.00pm

Shops: Mon-Fri
9.30am-6.30pm;
Sat 10.00am-1.00pm

Minimum sale
Vaults: 1 case
(mixed)

Shops: no

Credit cards
Access/Mastercard,
Visa, AmEx, Diners,
Switch

Discounts
Wholesale prices available

Delivery
Free nationwide on orders over £150; £10 flat fee for less than £150

Glass hire
Free with order

Tasting facilities
Regular tastings

Storage facilities
£7 + VAT per case per annum

Nearest tube
Vaults:
King's Cross,
St Pancras
Elizabeth St:
Victoria
Motcomb St:
Knightsbridge

by two up-market wine shops from which interesting bottles find their way to well-polished dinner tables. The list has its reference points, but much changes from season to season according to what Graham Chidgey and colleagues have sniffed out: burgundy is a particular strength, and Italian wine is becoming so (thanks to Palazzo Chidgey, the holiday home). The approach to claret is committed but selective, and other wines are bought when taste warrants. Communicative lists are made memorable by the paintbrush of Mrs Chidgey. The London delivery service is designed to be as responsive as any, and as is the case for all members of The Bunch (a grouping of independent merchants), customers' reserves are clearly labelled and stored separately from the Laytons' stocks.

Worth a punt

White: 1995 Château de la Pelissière Vieilles Vignes, Bordeaux £5.29; 1995 Burgundian Chardonnay Oak Aged Vieilles Vignes, Chartron & Trébuchet £6.95; 1993 Chavignol Blanc Sancerre, Cotat £13.32; 1994 Meursault, Domaine Geneviève Perrin £15.18; 1993 Puligny-Montrachet, Chartron & Trébuchet £19.39.

Red: Les Marrons, Vin de Pays de Vaucluse £5.58; Laytons Oak-Aged Claret £6.56; 1994 Vino Cuore, Cabanon £9.50; 1993 Connétable Talbot £12.24; 1993 Châteauneuf-du-Pape, Bosquet des Papes £13.51; 1993 Gualdo del Re, Cabella-Rossi £13.71; 1993 Chambolle-Musigny, Dujac £23.40.

Sparkling: Laytons Champagne £14.10; Deutz Cuvée Classique Champagne £19.39.

Fortified: Manzanilla de Sanlucar, Barbadillo £6.75; 1977 Quarles Harris Vintage Port £18.40.

Hours
Mon-Fri 9.00am-8.30pm; Sat 10.00am-8.30pm

Minimum sale
No

Credit cards
Access/Mastercard, Visa, AmEx, Switch

Discounts
5%-12% per case (mixed)

Delivery
Free in Central London; free nationwide on orders over £150

Glass hire
Free with order

Lea & Sandeman

301 Fulham Road, London SW10 9QH   Tel: **0171 376 4767**
Fax: **0171 351 0275**
211 Kensington Church St, London W8 7LX   Tel: **0171 221 1982**
Fax: **0171 221 1985**
51 Barnes High St, London SW13 9LN   Tel: **0171 878 8643**
Fax: **0171 878 6522**

Undeterred

There is fear and loathing among the wine merchants. The supermarkets and chains will soon have a near-monopoly on bread-and-butter wines; the brokers are stealing more and more of the fine-wine pie. What does the merchant-in-the-middle do? Cry into his spotted, breast-pocket hankie, rail against the supermarkets and brokers, repeat the 'service service' mantra until sleep comes, and pare down his list? Not if you're called Lea or Sandeman, you don't. These two (Charles and Patrick, respectively) have rolled their sleeves up and got on with what all merchants used, at least, to claim to do: touring wine regions, finding good wines, making pleasant shops and writing enticing lists, then talking to customers, discovering what they want, and selling it to them. The energy and enthusiasm you'll find here is more and more unusual among the merchant classes. Most bottles stocked by Lea and S are complex and unusual; burgundies, clarets, Southern French and Italian wines are all superb. This last year has seen the Loire given a welcome upgrade, and the 'older bits of the New World' are said to be under scrutiny. The package is remarkably complete: sweet wines, whisky, armagnac, cigars ... they got 'em. These would be lovely shops in which to be let loose with two crisp new £50 notes.

Worth a punt

White: 1995 Sauvignon de Touraine, Domaine des Cabotières £5.95; 1994 Gewürztraminer Cuvée Réservée, Schaetzel £5.95; 1995 Viognier, Domaine La Condamine l'Evêque £6.95; 1995 Saumur Château de Villeneuve, Domaine Chevallier £6.95; 1994 Savennières Clos de la Coulaine, Château de Pierre Bise £9.95; 1994 Rully Premier Cru la Pucelle, Jacqueson £12.34; 1994 Coteaux du Layon Beaulieu L'Anclaie Séléction des Grains Nobles, Château de Pierre Bise (sweet) £14.95; 1992 Meursault Les Chavalières, Jobard £21.50.

Rosé: 1995 Merlot Château Tour de Gendres £5.50.

Red: 1994 Domaine Piquemal, Cuvée Pierre Audonnet, Vin de Pays des Coteaux Catalans £5.50; 1993 Cabernet Sauvignon Cuvée Bascou, Domaine la Condamine l'Evêque £5.95; 1994 Château La Mothe du Barry, Bordeaux £5.95; 1993 Cairanne, Alary £7.95; 1994 Dolcetto Diano d'Alba Bricco Maiolica £7.95; 1993 Château Montaiguillon, Montagne St Emilion £9.95; 1993 Pommard Premier Cru Clos des Epeneaux, Comte Armand £29.95.

Sparkling: Domaine de l'Aigle Brut Chardonnay-Pinot Noir £7.95; 1995 Elci Aleatico Le Pupille (half-litre, red) £8.95; Legras Grand Cru Blanc de Blancs Champagne £16.95.

Fortified: all Valdespino sherries (various prices); 1988 Churchill's Traditional Late-Bottled Vintage £9.95.

O. W. Loeb

64 Southwark Bridge Road, London SE1 0AS   Tel: **0171 928 7750**   Fax: **0171 928 1855**

Aladdin's cellar

Loeb tells me its intention is to concentrate its efforts on 'traditional wine merchanting (private customers and restaurant

---

Tasting facilities
Regular tastings

Storage facilities
No

Nearest tube
Fulham Road: South Kensington + bus Kensington Church St: Notting Hill Gate Barnes High St: Barnes Bridge BR

NOT A SHOP

Hours
Mon-Fri 9.00am-5.30pm (telephone enquiries only)

Minimum sale
No

Credit cards
None

Discounts
No

Delivery
Free delivery 1 case or more in Central London

Tasting facilities
No

Storage facilities
£5.50 + VAT per unsplit case per annum

business)' more in the future, and less on its agency role. Good news for private purchasers, then, since there is an extraordinary concentration of fine stock at the end of this telephone line: Eser, von Schubert, J. J. Prüm, Egon Müller, Karthäuserhof, Willi Haag and others from Germany; Hugel and Faller from Alsace; Jaboulet and Rayas from the Rhône; Ramonet, Sauzet, Marquis d'Angerville, Tollot-Beaut, Gouges, Dujac and Rousseau from Burgundy. A deal of claret, too; even the occasional snip, via the 'remnant offer'. (Smith Woodhouse '85 at £13.51. Cheaper than Oddbins.) Send for Loeb's luscious little list.

Worth a punt

White: 1991 Riesling Kabinett Brauneberger Juffer, Willi Haag £7.35; 1995 Pouilly-Fumé Le Calvaire, Renaud-Bossuat £7.55; 1993 Auxey-Duresses, J. Pascal £9.20; 1994 Chassagne-Montrachet, Niellon £17.45; 1990 Vouvray Clos Naudin Moelleux Réserve, Foreau (sweet) £33.40.

Red: 1994 Merlot Le Faucon Bleu, Vins de Pays d'Oc £4.15; 1994 Corbières, Château Pasquier £4.35; 1990 Château Reysson, Haut-Médoc £8.95; 1994 Hermitage La Chapelle, Jaboulet £23.50; 1990 Corton, Tollot-Beaut £28.90.

Hours
Mon-Fri 10.00am-7.00pm; Sat 10.00am-5.00pm

Minimum sale
No

Credit cards
Access/Mastercard, Visa, AmEx, Diners, Switch

Discounts
5% per case (mixed or unmixed)

Delivery
Free within M25 1 case or more; free outside M25 3 cases or more (1-2 cases £5 per case)

Glass hire
Free with order

Tasting facilities
Regular tutored tastings

Storage facilities
No

Nearest tube
Vauxhall

London Wine Emporium

86 Goding Street, Vauxhall Cross, London SE11 5ES
Tel: **0171 587 1302**   Fax: **0171 587 0982**

Emporium building

This warehouse-style operation, pugnaciously sited next to Majestic in scenic Vauxhall, is well worth a visit, particularly if you're interested in lesser known wines from the New World. David Rigg, one of the managers, has had winemaking experience in Margaret River, and Australian stocks are good; New Zealand and South Africa have also been trawled extensively, and this year has brought a catch from Chile. Since the last issue of this guide, Norman Price has taken over from Colin Barnes. Lots of information; lots of enthusiasm; even lots of parking.

Worth a punt

White: 1995 Sauvignon Blanc Santa Helena, Chile ££3.99; 1994 Chardonnay, Pierro, Western Australia £5.19; 1995 Vernaccia di San Gimignano, Ambra delle Torri £5.19; Dry Muscat à Petits Grains, Cape Charlotte £5.25; Riesling Watervale, Fay Mckenzie £5.40; 1992 Chardonnay Corella Ridge, Seppelts £5.69.

Red: 1995 Cabernet Sauvignon, Santa Helena, Chile £3.99; 1990 Château les Maréchaux, Bordeaux £4.74; 1994 Pinot Noir White Heron, Washington State £6.64; 1993 Shiraz Peppertree,

Mitchells £8.54; 1985 Savigny-lès-Beaune Premier Cru Les Guettes, Doudet Naudin £14.15.

Sparkling: 1993 Pinot Chardonnay Brut, Yaldara £7.59; Joseph Perrier Champagne £12.99; Ployez Jacquemart Champagne £16.14.

Fortified: try the superb selection of Australian Liqueur Muscats (£5.49-£28.79).

Majestic Wine Warehouses

Head Office: Odhams Trading Estate, St Albans Road, Watford, Hertfordshire WD2 5RE   Tel **01923 816999**
Fax: **01923 819105**

Get stocked

Majestic's expansion continues: now 57 stores and rising. There's something about wandering around one of these heapy warehouses, leaning nonchalantly on the trolley and dropping in bottles as one might sixpences down a well, which is close to the core of wine's appeal. It's an exploration of delicious uncertainty, a promise of weeks of drinking discovery. Majestic is a useful place to stock up with beers and mineral water, too; indeed all it's really missing on the Calais experience is the kind of duty rates our European partners enjoy. Not all the bottles are good, of course, but half the fun is panning out the disaster purchases (steer well clear of Louis Page's horribly thin 1994 Pinot Noir, the awful Waimanu Premium Dry Red and dull Waimanu Premium Dry White from New Zealand, the estery Daunia Trebbiano and Sangiovese wines, the tedious Beaujolais Blanc from Duboeuf) and concentrating on the nuggets of gold (some of which are listed below). If you need – sorry, I mean 'can justify the purchase of' – cases of Champagne there's a fine range and loadsadeals on them here; other very strong areas are California, Australia and French country wines. I've already mentioned the beers in passing, but the range is hugely improved in recent years; indeed you don't even have to like wine to come home overloaded from Majestic. Special deals are worth looking out for, especially if the bottles concerned have been opened on the tasting bench and you can get a sip of them first (there was a mouthwatering '95 Touraine Sauvignon from Delaunay at £4.99 in spring '96, for example, though you wouldn't have given it the time of day to look at). The fine wine range is enterprising and expanding; pick your way carefully through the off-vintages to find the good stuff. There was a toe-in-the-water for '95 Bordeaux *en primeur* this year: many of the châteaux featured didn't really need buying *en primeur*, convenience aside, since their price won't have risen much before they are bottled; the top wines, though, were competitively priced (especially the Mouton at £520:

Hours
Mon-Sat 10.00am-8.00pm; Sun 10.00am-6.00pm

Minimum sale
I case (mixed)

Credit cards
Access/Mastercard, Visa, AmEx, Diners, Switch

Discounts
Champagne/sparkling wines 15% per case; many other discounted lines

Delivery
Free locally

Mail order
Tel 01727 847912; Fax 01727 810884

Glass hire
£9.60 deposit per 12

Tasting facilities
Themed weekends; private tastings; supplier-supported tastings; tasting bottles always open

Storage facilities
No

how many of you got any?). Majestic's staff are, in my experience, an exceptionally pleasant group of people, no doubt all over-qualified and under-paid as is the wine-trade way.

Worth a punt

White: 1994 Chardonnay Altesino £3.99 (17/25); 1993 Château Haut-Mazières £4.99 (15/25); 1993 Muscat-Gewürztraminer, Andante £5.49 (14/25); 1994 Chardonnay del Salento Barrique £5.99 (15/25); 1995 Reuilly, Beurdin £5.99 (14/25); 1994 Fumé Blanc Beringer £5.99 (16/25); 1995 Riesling Domdechant Hochheimer £6.49 (16/25); 1994 Meritage White, Beringer £7.49 (20/25); 1995 Chablis, Vocoret £8.49 (15/25); 1989 Riesling Oberemmeler Rosenberg Auslese, von Kesselstatt £9.99 (18/25); 1991 Hermitage Blanc, Chave £19.99.

Red: 1994 Negroamaro del Salento £3.99 (16/25); 1994 Minervois Domaine des Murettes £3.99 (15/25); 1994 Montepulciano d'Abruzzo Barone Cornacchia £4.29 (18/25); 1988 Notapanaro Taurino £4.99 (15/25); 1994 Rioja Marqués de Griñon £4.99 (16/25); 1994 Côtes du Rhône Domaine de la Baranière £4.99 (14/25); 1993 Shiraz Bin 50 Lindemans £5.49 (17/25); 1994 Mas de Bressades Costières de Nîmes £6.99 (16/25); 1994 Montepulciano d'Abruzzo Vigna Le Coste, Barone Cornacchia £6.99 (21/25); 1993 Zinfandel Ridge Lytton Springs (half-bottle) £7.49; 1993 Shiraz Bin 28 Penfolds £7.99; Meritage Beringer £10.99 (17/25); 1993 Côte Rôtie Jamet £17.99 (16/25); 1992 Cabernet Sauvignon Penfolds Bin 707 £19.99 (21/25).

Sparkling: Yaldara Rosé £5.99 (15/25); Bouvet Saumur £7.99 (15/25); Quartet Roederer £13.99 (18/25); Devaux Grande Réserve Champagne £14.99 (16/25); 1988 Bollinger Grande Année £35.49 (21/25).

Fortified: Hidalgo Manzanilla La Gitana £5.99 (20/25); Fino San Patricio Garvey £5.99 (16/25); 1984 Quinta do Bomfim Vintage Port £17.99 (20/25).

Marco's Wines

13 Ferrier Street, London SW18 1SN   Tel: **0181 871 3233**
Fax: **0181 871 2265**

Weekend wonder

Marco's has now slimmed itself down to one 'Wine Superstore' in London; expansion abroad, however, continues under the 'Wine and Beer Company' banner, with two stores in Calais, one in Le Havre and one in Cherbourg. The Wandsworth store trades on with a complex but fundamentally very appealing series of discounts: 20 per cent off everything on Friday, Saturday and Sunday, while during the week there is 10 per cent off

Hours
Mon-Sat 10.00am-
8.00pm; Sun
11.00am-5.00pm

Minimum sale
No

Credit cards
Access/Mastercard,
Visa, AmEx

Discounts
20% off all list prices
every Fri-Sun for
collected goods (excl.
promotional lines);
ring for details of
normal discounts
(Mon-Thurs)

mixed cases, 15 per cent off unmixed cases and 17.5% off some champagnes. Terry Horton, formerly of M&S, consults on purchases. The range as listed is sound but unexciting; it is, though, supplemented with other more unusual wines from time to time. There's a good range of sparkling wines and champagnes.

Worth a punt

White: 1995 Côtes de Gascogne, Marquis de Lassime £3.99; 1994 Chardonnay, Dominique Laurent, Vin de Pays d'Oc £4.49; 1994 Sauvignon Blanc Reserva Santa Rita, Chile £5.49.

Red: 1992 Cabernet Sauvignon Reserve, Santa Rita £5.49; 1993 Bourgogne Pinot Noir, Rodet £5.99; 1992 Rioja Vega £6.49; 1993 Château Sigognac, Médoc £7.49.

Sparkling: Seaview Pinot-Chardonnay £7.99; Joseph Perrier Champagne £15.99.

Marks & Spencer

Head Office: Michael House, 57 Baker St, London W1A 1DN
Tel: **0171 935 4422**   Fax: **0171 487 2679**

Everything in its place

Raunchy? Not really. Wild and unpredictable? Hardly. Boring, then? Not that either. Marks & Spencer's wine department, like the shop's underwear ranges, is in the main neat, tidy and conventional, spiced with occasional flurries of daring. Last year was a good year for wine at M&S: it achieved greater consistency across the range as well as hitting the spot with some really characterful individual wines at a time when other supermarkets were floundering in misguided attempts to hold or even lower price points. This year has consolidated those gains − though the fact that its rivals have also done a spot of sock-raising has meant that M&S has shone, relatively speaking, less brightly. The kind of wines which Chris Murphy and Jane Kay are good at tracking down include Chardonnays of all sorts, South American wines, Italian reds, sparkling wines and fairly well-behaved choices from Australia and regional France; M&S is good at sticking with suppliers, too, so if there's something you grow fond of you can be fairly sure it will still be there next year, in its new vintage guise. The range is bigger than you'd imagine from a visit to most branches; shelf plans, alas, put the emphasis on shifting large quantities of a small number of lines. Whenever I've tried the M&S versions of classics against those of its rivals, I have to say, St Michael usually emerges with a halo.

Worth a punt

White: 1995 Malvasia del Salento £3.99 (14/25); 1996 Chardonnay Casa Leona £3.99 (16/25); 1995 Frascati Superiore £4.49

Delivery
Free locally for
2 cases or more
(Mon-Thurs only)

Glass hire
Free with order

Tasting facilities
In-store tastings
daily; occasional
large tastings

Storage facilities
No

Nearest BR station
Wandsworth Town

Hours
Mon-Sat 9.00am-
6.00pm (varies from
store to store). Some
stores open Sundays
10.00am-4.00pm,
11.00am-5.00pm or
12.00pm-6.00pm

Minimum sale
No

Credit cards
M&S Chargecard,
Delta, Switch

Discounts
1 free bottle
per case

Delivery
No

Glass hire
No

Tasting facilities
In-store tastings

Storage facilities
No

(15/25); 1995 Chardonnay/Semillon, Carmen £4.99 (17/25); 1995 Semillon/Chardonnay Honey Tree £4.99 (15/25); 1993 Montagny Premier Cru £6.99 (14/25); 1995 Sancerre Les Ruettes £6.99 (15/25); 1993 Capel Vale Chardonnay £10.99 (16/25);.

Red: 1995 Syrah Domaine de Mandeville £3.99 (17/25); 1994 Minervois Domaine St Germain £3.99 (15/25); 1995 Cabernet Sauvignon/Malbec Trapiche £3.99 (15/25); 1994 Merlot Casa Leona £3.99 (14/25); 1994 Cabernet Sauvignon Central Valley £4.49 (16/25); 1994 Shiraz/Cabernet Bin 505 £4.49 (15/25); 1992 Malbec Oak Cask Reserve Trapiche £4.99 (16/25); 1994 Pinot Noir Gold Label £4.99 (14/25); 1991 Gran Calesa £5.50 (20/25); 1994 Shiraz Rosemount Estate £5.99 (16/25); 1993 St Emilion, Moueix £7.99 (14/25); 1990 Amarone della Valpolicella £9.99 (15/25).

Sparkling: 1992 Australian Chardonnay Blanc de Blancs £7.99 (14/25); Premier Cru Blanc de Blancs Champagne Chevalier de Melline £15.99 (17/25); 1990 Premier Cru Champagne de St Gall £18.99 (20/25).

Fortified: Fino Sherry £4.99 (21/25); 1988 Late-Bottled Vintage Port £7.99 (15/25); 10 Years Old Tawny Port £9.99 (18/25).

Mayor Sworder

See Davisons

Laurent Metge

Unit 20, Liverpool Street Station, London EC2M 7PY
Tel: 0171 377 9440   Fax: 0171 377 5928

Spit on

Hours
Mon-Fri 9.00am-
9.00pm

Minimum sale
None

Credit cards
Access/Mastercard,
Visa, Delta, Switch

Discounts
Negotiable on 12
bottles or more

Delivery
Free locally; Central
London £5; Greater
London £8

Glass hire
Free; £1 deposit
per glass

**Tasting
facilities**
Tutored and informal
tastings in store
around spittoon

This new wine merchant up beneath the glass-house roof of Liverpool Street's 'Shopportunity Knocks' concourse is owned by Beaujolais grower's son Laurent Metge and run with help from Caspar Auchterlonie, late of Harcourt Fine Wines. The aim is to have something for everyone – 60 everyday wines at £2.99 to £4.99, 60 Sunday-lunch wines between £4.99 and £8.99, and 60 knock-your-spots-off bottles at £8.99 plus; the emphasis is on the unusual. The shop is spacious and well-laid-out, with vines in pots to take advantage of the extravagant light (from which the bottles, of course, have to be protected); its centrepiece is a magnificent fountain-like spittoon, rescued from wine-trade receivership and said to have originally been a miners' communal urinal. Benches are arranged reverentially around it: pop in and put it to use sometime. You can see the clock from where you spit, so you won't miss the train home.

Worth a punt

White: 1994 Cortese, Alasia £4.99; 1994 Dessert Muscat (50cl), Yarden, Israel £6.49; 1994 Bourgogne Blanc Vieilles Vignes, Icarus £6.99; 1994 Gros Manseng, Domaine de Maubet, Vin de Pays des Côtes de Gascogne £6.99; 1995 Semillon/Sauvignon Blanc, Cape Mentelle, Western Australia £8.29; 1995 Sauvignon Blanc, Cairnbrae, Marlborough, New Zealand £9.99.

Red: 1995 Pinotage/Cinsault, Ruitersvlei £3.99; 1994 Cabernet Sauvignon, Vin de Pays d'Oc, Pellerin £4.99; 1994 Grenache, Saddle Mountain, Washington State £4.99; 1986 Pinot Noir, Cricova, Moldova £4.99; 1994 Valpolicella, Rizzardi £5.99; 1988 Château Musar, Lebanon £9.99.

Sparkling: Saumur, Caves de Grenelle £8.99; J.P. Séconde Champagne £12.99.

Fortified: Quinta do Noval L.B. £9.99; 1977 Vintage Port Presidential £16.99.

Moreno

2 Norfolk Place, London W2 1QN   Tel: **0171 706 3055**
Fax: **0171 724 3813**
11 Marylands Road, London W9 2DU   Tel: **0171 286 0678**
Fax: **0171 286 0513**

The history of Spain

Every wine-producing nation needs a good specialist retailer, and Moreno is Spain's. There are fine ranges from some of the country's key wine producers; more important is the excavatory work Manuel Moreno and Carlos Read get up to in unearthing wines from Spain's obscurer corners, like Galicia or Priorato. This is particularly important, as Spain is putting on a turn of speed unnoticed by many other retailers. There is a fine collection of Reserva and Gran Reserva wines going back to the '50s. Portugal, another greatly underappreciated actor on the world wine stage, contributes nearly two dozen lines. Spanish brandies are fun – dark, sweet-edged and rich; there's a big range here. For New World wines, Moreno has great bottles from the innovative Viña Casablanca and subtle Viña Porta in Chile.

Worth a punt

White: 1994 Navajas Blanco Sin Crianza £3.99; 1995 Chardonnay/Sauvignon Casablanca, Chile £5.99; 1995 Barrel-Fermented Chardonnay Casablanca, Chile £8.99; 1994 Scala Dei Blanc, Priorato £12.99.

Red: 1995 Granacha Marqués de Aragon £3.69; 1995 Guelbenzu 'Jardin', Navarra £4.99; 1994 Scala Dei Novell, Priorato £5.49; 1992 Viña Bajoz Crianza, Toro £5.49.

Storage facilities
No

Nearest tube/ BR station
Liverpool St

Hours
Norfolk Place:
Mon-Wed 12.00pm-7.00pm; Thurs 10.00am-10.00pm; Fri-Sat 10.00am-10.30pm; Sun 12.00pm-10.00pm

Minimum sale
No

Credit cards
Access/Mastercard, Visa, Delta, Switch

Discounts
5 per cent per case

Delivery
Free locally

Glass hire
Free with order: £1 deposit per glass

Tasting facilities
Monthly tastings

Storage facilities
No

Nearest tubes
Norfolk Place: Paddington
Marylands Place: Warwick Avenue

Sparkling: Cristalino Brut Cava £4.99; Raimat Chardonnay £7.69.
Fortified: Fino Inocente Valdespino (half bottle) £4.35; Oloroso Solera 1842 Valdespino £8.99.

NOT A SHOP

Hours
Mon-Fri 8.00am-6.00pm

Minimum sale
1 case (mixed)

Credit cards
None

Discounts
No

Delivery
Free in London

Internet site
100072.263@
compuserve.com

Glass hire
Free with order

Morris & Verdin

10 Leathermarket, Weston St, London SE1 3ER
Tel: **0171 357 8866**   Fax: **0171 357 8877**
The intellectual fringe

Jasper Morris MW is one of the most thoughtful wine merchants in the country. His lists and mailings are always worth reading for a clear-sighted overview, justified by acute and honest tasting, of exactly what is going on. Morris's specialisms are burgundy and California wine; clarets are well-bought; and interesting wines from the Loire and the South of France join growers whom Morris represents on an agency basis to make a well-balanced and well-argued list. Wines of this quality are not cheap, but they are fairly priced. Anyone who has been lucky enough to access the top wines in the '94 and '95 Bordeaux en primeur campaign has been well-treated by this merchant: '95 Eglise Clinet at £285 was the most generous piece of pricing I have come across in the whole of '96, and I understand that at least two customers as well as the proprietor benefitted.

Worth a punt

White: 1995 Malvasia Blanca Ca' del Solo £8; 1994 Vouvray Sec, Bourillon d'Orléans £8.30; 1994 Mâcon La Roche Vineuse, Merlin £10.50; 1994 Hautes Côtes de Nuits Blanc, Devevy £11; 1994 Chablis Montmain, Race £12.90; 1994 Chardonnay La Bouge, Au Bon Climat £20.

Red: 1994 Bourgogne Rouge Les Bons Batons, Rion £9.50; 1993 Château Paloumey, Haut-Médoc £10; 1994 Syrah, Qupé £11; 1993 Le Cigare Volant, Bonny Doon £15; 1994 Jade Mountain Les Jumeaux £16.

Sparkling: Champagne André Jacquart £18.

Fortified: Quinta de la Rosa Finest Reserve Port £9.99.

Hours
9.30am-5.00pm

Minimum sale
No

Credit cards
Access/Mastercard, Visa,
Delta, Switch

Discounts
Collection discount

Le Nez Rouge

12 Brewery Road, London N7 9NH   Tel: **0171 609 4711**
Fax: **0171 607 0018**

Drink out at home

A wine leaves France for Britain. It may end up in a retail store; it may end up in a restaurant. There is surprisingly little overlap between the two: widely retailed wines are generally not welcome in restaurants (odious price comparisons are too easy to make), while those selling to restaurants prefer to keep clear of the hard dealing imposed on them by retailers. It's a pity. The Red Nose belongs to restaurant specialist Joseph Berkmann: it's particularly good for burgundy and Beaujolais (Duboeuf), but Norton from Argentina, Morton from New Zealand, Beringer from California and Bruno Paillard's champagnes are all worth a close look.

Worth a punt

White: 1995 Viognier, Vins de Pays de l'Ardèche, Duboeuf £5.99; 1994 Riesling, Côte de Rouffach, René Muré £7.38; 1994 Chardonnay Reserve Black Label, Morton Estate £10.50.

Red: 1995 Regnié, Domaine des Buyats, Duboeuf £5.99; 1993 Privada, Bodega Norton £7.99; 1992 Cabernet Sauvignon, Beringer £9.99; 1993 Châteauneuf-du-Pape, Beaurenard £11.83; 1993 Santenay Premier Cru La Maladière, Girardin £12.49.

Sparkling: Bruno Paillard Première Cuvée Champagne £15.90.

Fortified: Pineau des Charentes Rouge Five-Year-Old £10.50.

Delivery
Free throughout mainland UK for 1 case or more

Glass hire
No

Tasting facilities
2-3 tastings per year

Storage facilities
£3 per case per year

Nearest tube
Caledonian Road

Nicolas

157 Great Portland Street, London W1N 5FB
Tel: **0171 436 9338**   Fax: **0171 637 1691** plus 8 other London branches (Fulham Road, Old Brompton Road, Holland Park Avenue, Kensington Church Street, St John's Wood High Street, New Row, Sheen Road Richmond, Kew Green).

For Francophiles

If *la France profonde* is your thing, then Nicolas should be one of the wine merchants you patronise. You'll need money, because the French notion of margins is more ambitious than its British counterpart. However the range of French country wines, wines from lesser-known appellations, and of French classics, too, is outstanding, and is backed up by other comforting crumbs of French gastro-culture, like Armagnac and Calvados, eaux-de-vie made from most things found in a hedge, and mineral water like the wonderfully salty Ste Yorre. There are a few wines from outside France's borders (including Musar's rival Kefraya from Lebanon). Historic stocks are particularly good: Nicolas lists nine clarets from 1975, six from 1970, seven from 1966 and so on back to two '53s, four '28s and one 1916. The lesser Bordeaux vintages of 1991, 1992 and 1993 are more widely stocked here than at any other London address. The 'petites récoltes' series of minimally labelled vins de pays at £3.95 is one way in which Nicolas tries to compete on value; another is through discounts on the labelled prices (especially for champagne).

Hours
Vary: generally midday to mid-evening seven days a week

Minimum sale
No

Credit cards
Access/Mastercard, Visa, AmEx, Switch

Discounts
10%-20% off selected wines and Champagnes at all times. Other regular discounts schemes include 3 bottles for the price of 2

Delivery
Free within Central London

Glass hire
Free with order (deposit required)

Tasting facilities
In-store tastings: contact local branch for details

Storage facilities
No

Worth a punt

White: 1995 Vins de Pays des Côtes de Thau, Petites Récoltes, £3.95; 1994 Bordeaux Blanc, Réserve Nicolas, Léon d'Aubert £4.99; 1995 Chardonnay, Coteaux de l'Ardèche £5.99; 1994 Jurançon Grain Sauvage, Cave des Producteurs £6.75; 1993 Chasselas Vieilles Vignes Réserve, Sparr £6.99; 1995 Château d'Epiré, Savennières £9.95; 1989 Savagnin d'Arbois, Fruitière Vinicole £14.95; 1992 Chablis Grand Cru Vaudesir, Bichot £28.

Red: 1994 Vins de Pays de la Vallée du Paradis, Petites Récoltes £3.95; 1994 Côtes du Saint-Mont, Producteurs Plaimont £4.99; 1991 Bordeaux Rouge, Réserve Nicolas, Léon d'Aubert £4.99; 1994 Lirac, Domaine de la Mordorée £9.95; 1993 Prieuré de St Jean de Bebian, Coteaux du Languedoc £12.50; 1992 Clos du Marquis, St Julien £18.50; 1992 Château Angélus, St Emilion £28.40; 1992 Château Léoville-Las-Cases, St Julien £29.

Sparkling: Champagne Georges Vesselle £15.80.

Fortified: Muscat de Rivesaltes, Domaine Cazes £9.95

EROS AWARD FOR HIGH-STREET
CHAIN OF THE YEAR

Oddbins

Head Office: 31-33 Weir Road, London SW19 8UG.
Tel: **0181 944 4400**   Fax: **0181 944 4411**

For sale: great wine chain

The news that Seagram is dangling Oddbins at potential purchasers was, in many ways, the worst any wine lover could hope to have heard during 1996. For a decade now, Oddbins has been the frontiersperson among wine retailers: it has pioneered sales of 'new wave' wines from Australia, Chile, California and the South of France while others were still trying to find these places on the map; it's slugged away remorselessly at the £3.99 to £6.99 zone which is where all the greatest value in wine drinking is to be found; above all it has given customers a huge range and variety of top-quality wines, and sold it to them with energy, enthusiasm and humour. It deserves a knighthood in the Queen's Birthday Honours list: arise Sir Oddbins. Instead, it may end up in the hands of ... who exactly? Greenalls (Wine Cellar), Tesco and Thresher have all been in the frame of rumour; at the time of writing, the price doesn't seem to be right. Long may that remain the case. Whoever took Oddbins over would doubtless protest that nothing would change. They would protest too much: the corporate culture

Hours
Mon-Sat 10.00am-
9.00pm; Sun
12.00pm-3.00pm
and 7.00pm-9.00pm
(varies according to
location)

Minimum sale
No

Credit cards
Access/Mastercard,
Visa, AmEx

Discounts
5% per case
(unmixed); Sat 10%
on tasting wines; 1
bottle free per 7 for
sparkling wines and
champagne at £5.99
or over

Delivery
Free local delivery

Glass hire
Free with order (£1
deposit per glass)

would inevitably evolve and almost inevitably decay, particularly if the new owner wanted to set about partial dismemberment of the estate; thus a great tradition would come to an end. I remember writing back in 1990, when I edited *Which? Wine Guide*, that 'Oddbins may not be the best for ever, even if it looks that way in 1990': it seemed so hard, then, to imagine any way in which the Oddbins tradition might be squandered. Now it's all too easy.

For the time being, anyway, business continues as normal: Oddbins has had another good year, with consolidation on all fronts despite short harvests, rising prices and a world wine shortage. Its strengths remain in the up-and-coming areas: the best from right around the New World, especially Australia and Chile, larded with try-harder producers in Languedoc, in Spain and in Italy. In tasting terms, Oddbins certainly has as many outstanding wines as any other retailer; this year it seems to stock fewer dull wines than the others. I don't like everything on the Oddbins shelves: the ungracious Oddbins White and thinnish Oddbins Red, at £3.99 and 10/25 each, seem to let the side down; the cheaper Californian whites – '93 Three Valleys, '94 Mariquita and '94 Château de Baun Symphony – are all rather sweet and flabby; the resinous '95 La Cata Blanca from Penedés seems a drab wine. Portugal could do with more work, too. These disappointments are exceptional: my general level of enthusiasm for what I have tasted of the current range is high. The Fine Wine Shops live up to their name: not only will you find the kind of classic stock which Farr Vintners trades in available by the single bottle, but they also include Californian and Australian rarities that no one else bothers to get hold of; I'm told the average spend there is £17 per bottle, which even Justerini & Brooks would envy. Cultivate your manager in November 1997 when the '95 Bordeaux 'en primeur on the shelf' offerings are released: Oddbins claims that it will be selling at original en primeur prices, which is extremely generous in the light of subsequent market rises in Bordeaux, particularly for the top growths. The staff remain on the ball, and ancilliaries (like beer and whisky) are brilliant. Tastings every Saturday, too. While stores last.

Tasting facilities
In-store tastings every Saturday; 2 consumer wine fairs per year

Storage facilities
No

Worth a punt

White: 1995 Marino White, Berberana £2.99 (16/25); 1995 Dry Muscat, Nagyrede, Hungary £3.29 (17/25); 1995 Terre Arnolfe, Colli Amerini £4.39 (15/25); 1995 Durius, Marqués de Griñon £4.49 (16/25); 1995 Chardonnay/Semillon, Santa Carolina, Chile £4.49 (14/25); 1994 Greco di Puglia £4.99 (14/25); 1994 La Dame Maucaillou, Bordeaux £4.99 (15/25); 1995 Pinot Blanc, Denbies, England £4.99 (16/25); 1995 Chardonnay White Label, Casablanca, Chile £4.99 (18/25); 1995 Chardonnay, Concha y Toro Casillero del Diablo £4.99 (16/25); 1995 Chardonnay, Viña

Porta, Chile £5.99 (17/25); 1995 Pinot Blanc, Mann £6.25 (15/25); 1994 Viñas de Gain, Rioja Alavesa £6.99 (15/25); 1995 Chardonnay Barrel-Fermented, Casablanca £8.49 (17/25); 1995 Chardonnay Reserva Familia, Santa Carolina £8.99 (16/25); 1995 Pinot Gris Vieilles Vignes, Mann £9.99 (20/25); 1990 Château de la Chartreuse, Sauternes (half-bottle, sweet) £9.99 (21/25); 1993 Chardonnay Santa Cruz, Ridge, California £14.99 (17/25); 1993 Pouilly-Fuissé, Tête de Cru, Ferret £18.99 (18/25); 1993 Chassagne-Montrachet, Fontaine Gagnard £18.99 (16/25); 1994 Condrieu Vieilles Vignes, 'Chaillets', Cuilleron £19.99 (21/25).

Red: 1995 Tierra Seca, La Mancha £3.99 (19/25); 1995 Malbec, Balbi Vineyard, Argentina £3.99 (18/25); 1995 Orobio Tempranillo, Rioja £4.49 (20/25); 1994 Castel del Monte, Puglia £4.49 (15/25); 1995 Artadi, Rioja Alavesa £4.99 (21/25); 1995 Cuvée Simone, James Herrick, Vin de Pays d'Oc £4.99 (21/25); 1994 Malbec, Norton, Argentina £4.99 (22/25); 1995 Pinotage, Beyerskloof, South Africa £4.99 (15/25); 1995 Grenache, Peter Lehmann, South Australia £4.99 (16/25); 1995 Torre del Falco, Puglia £5.49 (17/25); 1994 Syrah, McDowell, California £5.99 (16/25); 1993 Old Vine Shiraz, D'Arenberg, South Australia £5.99 (20/25); 1995 d'Arry's Original, D'Arenberg £6.49 (18/25); 1994 Syrah, Côtes du Rhône, Lionnet £7.99 (18/25); 1994 Zinfandel, Ravenswood, California £9.99 (20/25); 1994 Shiraz, Ironstone Pressings, D'Arenberg, South Australia £9.99 (21/25); 1994 Shiraz, Dead Arm, D'Arenberg, South Australia £9.99 (21/25); 1993 Château Clerc-Milon, Pauillac £14.99 (17/25); 1993 Cabernet Sauvignon, Santa Cruz, Ridge, California £14.99 (18/25).

Sparkling: Segura Viudas Brut Reserva Cava £5.99 (15/25); Champagne Bonnet £14.99 (14/25) £14.99; 1989 Champagne, Billecart-Salmon £29.99 (19/25).

Fortified: Valdespino Sherries; 1983 Vintage Port, Smith Woodhouse £16.99.

Panzer Delicatessen

13-19 Circus Road, London NW8 6PB   Tel: **0171 722 8596**
Fax: **0171 586 0209**

More salmon than in the Spey

Panzer steals into this Guide on the basis that it's one of the few delicatessens which takes its wine selection seriously. The time to drop in, I'm told, is on Sunday morning when fifty sides of smoked salmon are sliced up for stuffing into bagels; drop in in the winter and you might get a glass of mulled wine. The extensive Japanese clientele admires the wide selection of half bottles (as well as the fifteen ways with herring).

Hours
Mon-Fri 8.00am-7.00pm; Sat 8.00am-6.00pm; Sun 8.00am-2.00pm

Minimum sale
No

Credit cards
Access/Mastercard, Visa, Delta, Switch

Discounts
No

Delivery
£2 any delivery to selected London areas

Worth a punt

White: 1995 Panzer's Sauvignon £3.99; 1994 Sauvignon de Touraine, Domaine de la Presle £5.99; 1994 Pouilly-Fumé, André Dezat £9.95.

Red: 1995 Panzer's Merlot £3.99; 1995 Merlot-Cabernet Sauvignon, Domaine du Nouveau Monde, Vin de Pays d'Oc £6.75; 1989 Rioja Marqués de Murrieta £9.99; 1991 Rosso del Conte Regaleali, Sicily £14.99; 1993 Santenay 'Clos de la Confrère' Vincent Girardin £15.45.

Sparkling: Champagne Gallimard Père et Fils £13.99.

Glass hire
Free with order

Tasting facilities
Sunday morning tasting
3 times a year

Storage facilities
No

Nearest tube
St John's Wood

Pavilion Wine Company

Finsbury Circus Gardens, London EC2M 7AB   Tel: **0171 628 8224**, fax: **0171 628 6205**

Little gems

D avid Gilmour celebrates his silver jubilee as an importer for some of his growers and producers this year (among them Hidalgo in Sanlucar, Verret in Saint-Bris, Jaubert in Beaujolais, Brunier/Vieux Télégraphe in Châteauneuf and Soulez in Savennières). He tastes and selects wines well, writes a clear and succinct list, and supplements his own French purchases with good things from other agents and importers (like Adam Bancroft and Jasper Morris of Morris & Verdin, q.v.). For a taste of some of his purchases, visit the pretty Pavilion Wine Bar (see page 292).

Worth a punt

White: 1994 Pinot Blanc d'Alsace, Bernard Staehle £57.57 per case; 1993 Viognier, Domaine du Rieu Frais, Vin de Pays des Coteaux des Baronnies £88.13; 1993 Mâcon-Charnay, Domaine Manciat-Poncet £77.55 per case.

Red: 1994 Corbières, Christian Baillat £56.40 per case; 1993 Minervois, Château d'Argères £65.80 per case; 1994 Pinot Noir, Devil's Lair £138.65 per case.

Sparkling: Champagne Ailerons et Baie £164.50 per case.

Fortified: Manzanilla La Gitana, Hidalgo £7.56 per case of 24 halves.

NOT A SHOP

Hours
Mon-Fri
8.30am-8.30pm

Minimum sale
1 case (unmixed)

Credit cards
Access/Mastercard,
Visa, AmEx

Discounts
2% off 6-11 cases
(unmixed);
2.75% off 12-25
cases (unmixed)

Delivery
1 case £8;
2 cases £6;
3 cases £3;
4+ cases free
England and Wales

Glass hire
No

Tasting facilities
Tastings tailored to
customer
requirements

Storage facilities
£7.50 + VAT per case
per year

Philglas & Swiggot

21 Northcote Road, London SW11 1NG   Tel: **0171 924 4494**
Fax: **0171 223 8637**

Wired up to Down Under

K aren Rogers' enterprising SW11 shop features Australian wines as a clear speciality; several Australian wineries use

Hours
Mon 5pm-8.30pm;
Tues-Sat 11.00am-
9.00pm; Sun 12.00pm-
2.00pm, 6.00pm-8.30pm

Minimum sale
No

243

Credit cards
Access/Mastercard,
Visa, AmEx, Diners,
Switch

Discounts
5% per case

Delivery
Free in London; also
nationwide service
at cost

Glass hire
Free with order

Tasting facilities
Regular in-store
tastings and tutored
tastings on request

Storage facilities
No

Nearest BR station
Clapham Junction

Phil & Swig as their UK outlet via a sort of long-distance mail order, and UK customers can now return the favour by sending wine to family, friends and business contacts in Australia. Another innovation for this year is the subscription service: a mixed case to your door bi-monthly or quarterly. Strine wine provides much of the list's interest, but there's a good selection from France and other countries (like South Africa) too. Organic and dessert wines are further specialities.

Worth a punt

White: 1995 Chenin Blanc Stormy Cape, South Africa £5.10; 1995 Semillon/Chardonnay, Ironstone, Western Australia £6.29; 1993 Riesling, Mitchelton Blackwood Park, Victoria £6.99; 1994 Pouilly-Fumé, Theveneau £8.65; 1995 Semillon/Sauvignon Blanc, Cape Mentelle, Western Australia £8.99; 1990 Riesling, Freie Weingartner, Austria £11.55; 1993 Recioto di Soave Le Columbare, Pieropan (sweet; half-litre) £12.99; 1995 Chardonnay Tyrrells, New South Wales £12.99; 1992 De Bortoli Noble One (sweet; half-bottle) £12.99; 1995 Chardonnay, Moss Wood, Western Australia £13.99.

Red: 1994 Garnacha, Marqués de Aragon £3.99; 1993 Pinot Noir, Monterey Vineyard, California £5.69; 1993 Douro, Duas Quintas £5.99; 1994 Cabernet/Merlot Cassegrain Five Mile Hollow, New South Wales £6.29; 1993 Shiraz, Basedow, Barossa Valley £7.99; 1993 Grenache-Mourvèdre-Syrah, Mitchelton III, Victoria £7.99.

Sparkling: Montlouis Brut, Deletang £7.99; Wolf Blass Brut £8.69; Roederer Quartet £13.49.

Fortified: Liqueur Muscat, Stanton & Killeen, Victoria (half-bottle) £6.49.

Le Picoleur

See La Réserve

Hours
Mon-Sat 12.00pm-
8.30pm; Sun
12.00pm-7.00pm

Minimum sale
No

Credit cards
Access/Mastercard,
Visa, AmEx, Diners,
Switch

Discounts
5% per case

Pont de la Tour Wine Shop

The Butler's Wharf Building, 36D Shad Thames, London SE1 2YE
Tel: **0171 403 2403**   Fax: **0171 403 0267**

Gulp

Pont de la Tour (the restaurant) has a well-balanced and unusually wide-ranging wine list; you can buy it all at the attached wine shop, where prices are slightly cheaper (and there's no service charge). That makes it a kind of El Vino (q.v.) with bells on, for the seriously wealthy. There is a particularly good range of half-bottles.

Worth a punt

White: 1994 St Véran, Drouhin £7.85; 1995 Sauvignon Blanc, Jackson Estate £8.95; 1992 Gewürztraminer Princes Abbés, Schlumberger £9.15; 1993 Chardonnay Ronco del Gnemmiz £15.45; 1990 Chablis Premier Cru Côte de Lechets, Defaix £18.95; 1993 Puligny-Montrachet, Clerc £22; 1988 Château Les Justices, Sauternes (sweet) £22.50.

Red: 1993 Cabernet Reserva, Echeverria, Chile £5.75; 1993 St Nicolas de Bourgueil, Amirault £8.50; 1986 Château Musar, Lebanon £8.95; 1993 Santenay, Girardin; 1991 Coteaux d'Aix en Provence les Baux, Trévallon £15.25; 1992 Nebbiolo delle Langhe Il Favot, Conterno £16.25; 1989 Château de Marbuzet, St Estèphe £17.95.

Sparkling: Champagne Alexandre Bonnet £14.99; 1985 Champagne Alain Thiénot £29.95.

Delivery
Free with London postal districts for orders over £100

Glass hire
Free with order

Tasting facilities
Tutored tastings on request

Storage facilities
By arrangement

Nearest tube
Tower Hill/ London Bridge

La Réserve

56 Walton Street, London SW3 1RB   Tel: **0171 589 2020**
Fax: **0171 581 0250**

Le Picoleur, 47 Kendal Street, London W2 2BU   Tel: **0171 402 6920**
Fax: **0171 402 5066**

Le Sac à Vin, 203 Munster Road, London SW6 6DX   Tel: **0171 381 6930**   Fax: **0171 385 5513**

Heath Street Wine Company, 29 Heath Street, London NW3 6TR
Tel: **0171 435 6845**   Fax: **0171 431 9301**

Clapham Cellars (case sales only), 7 Grant Road, London SW11 2NU
Tel: **0171 978 5601**   Fax: **0171 978 4934**

Choice mouthfuls

La Réserve is a delightful shop full of good and great wines, with an atmosphere which encourages experiment and discussion. Mark Reynier has a knack of dreaming up enticing schemes and offers — not just the usual claret and burgundy, but 'blood tubs' full of whisky, some of the Italian classics from 1990 which seemed otherwise to have passed Britain by, English landed cognac, and casks of malt whisky as an investment (unlike much of the semi-criminal trading in this area, La Réserve's sale of Springbank seems likely to increase its value, and you can be sure that you're buying goods exactly as described). Beneath La Réserve is a tasting cellar where you can take your bottle and, for £10, drink it with a plate of cheeses, terrines and salads. The range of wines is wide; France may lead and Burgundy star, but the Italian, American and Australian sections are all first rate. The other shops, too, carry different ranges from La Réserve itself. Worldwide deliveries of anniversary bottles can be arranged; there's a regular tasting pro-

Hours
Mon-Sat 9.30am-9.00pm (may vary)

Minimum sale
No

Credit cards
Access/Mastercard, Visa, AmEx, Switch, JCB

Discounts
5% per case (cash payments only)

Delivery
Free over £200; otherwise £7

Glass hire
Free with order

Tasting facilities
Tastings throughout the year

Storage facilities
£6 per case per year

Internet address
Reynier@lareserve. netkonect.co.uk.

Nearest tube
Walton Street: South Kensington

gramme; even vineyard visits. Reynier's advice is generally good, with occasional lapses into madness (like describing Fonseca's extraordinarily weak 1980 as 'wine of the vintage').

Worth a punt

White: 1994 Montravel, Château Le Bondieu £5.95; La Réserve's Alsace £5.95; 1993 Bourgogne Blanc, Sauzet £13.95.

Red: 1991 Coteaux de la Cèze, Domaine Maby £4.75; 1992 Château Renjardière Cuvée Spéciale, Pierre Dupond £5.95; 1994 Bourgogne Passetoutgrains, Marquis d'Angerville £7.95; 1990 Brunello di Montalcino Baricci £16.50.

Sparkling: Carte Corail Brut Rosé, Jean Baumard £8.50; Champagne Charles Leprince Grande Réserve £13.95.

Fortified: Inocente Fino, Valdespino £8.75; Don Gonzalo Oloroso, Valdespino £10.50; 1933 Malmsey, Leacock £120.

Howard Ripley

35 Eversley Crescent, London N21 1EL   Tel/Fax: **0181 360 8904**

Burgundy blow-out

The amazing Howard Ripley continues to produce one of Britain's best burgundy lists, both in terms of its selection and the level of information it provides. The range of older vintages on offer is good, as is the price spectrum, from modest Mâcon to grandest Chambertin. Most of the wines are given tasting notes for which a pinch of salt is perhaps necessary – enthusiasm oscillates between unbridled and wild. Prices are modest, considering the quality of the wines, and there is representation from the very best of the region's producers.

Worth a punt

White: 1994 Mâcon-Verzé, Coteaux de la Croix Jarrier £6.29; 1994 Pouilly-Fuissé Les Vieux Murs, Pacquet £9.52; 1992 St Aubin Premier Cru La Chatenière, Thomas £12.69; 1992 Meursault, Pierre Morey £21.15; 1992 Chassagne-Montrachet Premier Cru Chenevottes, Marc Morey £23.50; 1989 Meursault Premier Cru Charmes, Michelot £30.55.

Red: 1993 Savigny-Lès-Beaune Les Bourgeots, £12.10; 1994 Nuits St Georges, Domaine de l'Arlot £13.40; 1994 Gevrey-Chambertin Premier Cru Lavaux St Jacques, Esmonin £14.10; Beaune Premier Cru Epenottes, Domaine André Mussy £15.28; 1992 Gevrey-Chambertin Vieilles Vignes, Bachelet £16.45; 1988 Pommard Premier Cru Les Saucilles, Boillot £22.33.

NOT A SHOP

Hours
Mon-Fri 9.00am-10.00pm; Sat 9.00am-1.00pm; Sun 9.00am-12.00pm

Minimum sale
1 mixed case

Credit cards
None

Discounts
No

Delivery
Free in London 5 cases or more; otherwise £8.50

Glass hire
Free with order

Tasting facilities
Group tastings on request

Storage facilities
No

Roberson

348 Kensington High Street, London W14 8NS
Tel: **0171 371 2121**   Fax: **0171 371 4010**

The wine stage

This good-looking, spacious, extravagantly stocked shop is the wine-drinker's equivalent of those showrooms stuffed with Rolls-Royces and Ferraris which Central London seems full of. New for this year is the walk-in fine-wine lock-up full of older vintages, rarities and large bottles; fine-wine sales are going particularly well. In general, the range remains exemplary, with claret and champagne outstanding; Cliff Roberson intends to beef up the burgundies. Roberson will hunt down particular wines on request.

Worth a punt

White: 1995 Semillon/Chardonnay, Stoney Vale, South Australia £4.95; 1995 Chardonnay, Castillo de Molina, Chile £4.95; 1992 Riesling, Dr Loosen £6.95; 1994 Sauvignon Blanc, Aotea, New Zealand £6.95; 1994 Chardonnay Chavant, Louisvale, South Africa £7.95; 1993 Sancerre Vigne Blanche, Bourgeois £10.50; 1992 Château Haut-Caplanc, Sauternes (sweet) £13.95; 1992 Puligny-Montrachet Premier Cru Pucelles, de Villamont £22.50.

Red: 1994 Cabernet Sauvignon Castillo de Molina, Chile £4.95; 1994 Five Mile Hollow Cabernet Sauvignon/Merlot/Cabernet Franc, New South Wales £6.75; 1990 Château Sergant, Lalande de Pomerol £9.95; 1993 Marsannay, Philippe Naddef £12.25; 1986 Château Musar, Lebanon £12.95; 1991 Brunello di Montalcino, Argiano £17.95; 1990 Fiefs de la Grange, St Julien £19.95.

Sparkling: Vin Sauvage, Monluc £6.95; Champagne Veuve Borodin £11.95.

Fortified: Muscat de Beaumes de Venise, Nativelle (half-bottle, sweet) £6.95.

Hours
Mon–Sat
10.00am-8.00pm

Minimum sale
No

Credit cards
Access/Mastercard, Visa, AmEx, Diners, Switch

Discounts
10% per unmixed case; 5% per mixed case

Delivery
Free in Central London (min. 1 mixed case)

Glass hire
Free with order (deposit required)

Tasting facilities
Saturday tastings; impromptu quarterly tastings planned

Storage facilities
By arrangement

Nearest tube
Kensington High Street

Sac-à-Vin

See **La Réserve**

Safeway

Head Office: 6 Millington Road, Hayes, Middlesex UB3 4AY
Tel: **0181 848 8744**   Fax: **0181 573 1865**

Bouncing back

After the bad-vintage and weak-currency disappointments of 1995, Safeway's wine department has been as competitive as any during 1996. Head buyer Liz Robertson M.W. is one of the

Hours
8.30am-8.00pm (some until 10.00pm); most stores Sun 10.00am-4.00pm

Minimum sale
No

Credit cards
Access/Mastercard, Visa, Delta, Switch

Discounts
5% per case (bottle price
£2.99 or over); special
offers

Delivery
No

Glass hire
Free with order

**Tasting
facilities**
Biannual wine fair

**Storage
facilities**
No

wine scene's best communicators, always anxious to explain the reason for this or that purchase, generally without the corporate spin that makes such communications slippery. It's a complex range, and if you like variety it changes more than most during the course of the year; Liz is a new-vintage fanatic (and this is the only supermarket whose entire range is now vintage-dated). Safeway has given its Wine Fairs more emphasis than most of its competitors, adding to the fun. Like all supermarkets, of course, Safeway stocks bad wines – wines bought to get a famous name onto the shelf at a 'bargain' price, like the half-litres of thin, fruitless Chablis Premier Cru (£4.99; 10/25), the dodgy, pongy 1994 Chapel Hill Rheinriesling (£2.79; 8/25) and the decidedly beery Cava in magnums (£7.99; 8/25), all in the May Wine Fair; or wines bought just to fill out the shelves in certain key zones even if quality doesn't match up, like the sour, sulphidey 1995 Tempranillo from Viña Albali (£3.49: 8/25), the hard, pickled 1995 Sauvignon Vin de Pays du Jardin de la France (£3.29; 9/25) and the coarse 1992 Berberana Viura (£4.29; 10/25). The 1995 Kirkwood Cabernet/Merlot (£3.49; 11/25) and the 1995 Brown Brothers Tarrango (£4.99; 11/25) both look increasingly weak. Most of Safeway's wines, of course, fall into the middle ground: some customers will like them; some won't; the price, either way, is fair. This is the bread-and-butter stock of all those selling wine. What most interests people like you and me, by contrast, is the number of 'headline' wines, wines which make the taster and drinker sit up and take notice. These are the real buying coups which all supermarket wine departments are after, and Safeway has had as many as any this year – the pick of the wines from Hungary's key Neszmely winery, for example; Wine Fair bullseyes like the Pinot Noir Rosé from Neszmely and a delicious organic Crozes-Hermitage; as well as some of the fine purchases from Australia, South Africa, Chile and Spain listed below. As this book is published, Safeway is promising a complete overhaul of the organisation and look of its drink shelves, as well as a revamp of the style categorisations for its wines; news of this next year, but Safeway customers should prepare for changes.

Worth a punt

White: 1995 Irsai Oliver River Duna £2.99 (16/25); 1995 Sauvignon Blanc/Rikat, Rousse £3.19 (14/25); 1995 Pinot Grigio, Nagyrede £3.49 (16/25); 1995 Chardonnay, Vin de Pays d'Oc £3.99 (15/25); 1995 Sauvignon Blanc River Duna Special Cuvée £3.99 (18/25); 1995 Safeway Chilean Chardonnay £3.99 (16/25); 1995 Chardonnay Somontano £3.99 (15/25); 1995 Chardonnay Nottage Hill £4.99 (15/25); 1995 Safeway Australian Marsanne £4.99 (14/25); 1994 Gewürztraminer d'Alsace, Turckheim £5.79

(17/25); 1994 Chardonnay Hunter Valley £5.99 (17/25); 1994 Chardonnay Hardy's Barossa Valley £5.99 (15/25).

Rosé: 1995 Grenache Rosé, Breakaway £4.99 (15/25).

Red: 1995 Cabernet Sauvignon Young Vatted, Haskovo £2.99 (18/25); 1994 Casa di Giovanni £3.99 (16/25); 1995 Merlot Domaine de Picheral Organic £3.99 (17/25); 1994 Barrique-Aged Montepulciano £4.49 (16/25); 1994 Merlot Glen Ellen £4.99 (15/25); 1991 Tinto da Anfora £5.25 (16/25); 1993 Salice Salentino Riserva £5.49 (17/25); 1993 Cabernet Sauvignon Hardy's Coonawarra £7.99 (18/25).

Sparkling: 1990 Safeway Albert Etienne Champagne £14.79 (16/25).

Fortified: 1988 Safeway Late Bottled Vintage Port £7.29 (15/25); Safeway 10-Year-Old Tawny Port £9.99 (14/25).

Joint winner
EROS AWARD FOR SUPERMARKET

WINE SELECTION OF THE YEAR

Sainsbury's

Head Office: Stamford House, Stamford Street, London SE1 9LL
Tel: **0171 921 6000**   Fax: **0171 921 6988**

Clearing the hurdles

The tasting organised by Sainsbury's in the spring of 1996 showed a dramatic improvement on the previous year's offerings. How, you might wonder, are these things measured? By making notes on each wine, of course, but also by assessing, over the three or four hours spent among the bottles, overall intent and achievement. The best bottles are re-tasted later for confirmation of their scores. What was evident on this occasion was that Sainsbury's, with the institution of its 'classic selection' range and the expansion of its fine wine range, was making a determined effort to escape the tyranny of price points (see page xx). Moreover those wines which did remain pegged at £2.99, £3.49, £3.99, £4.49 and £4.99 were, as often as not, better in quality than the previous year thanks to kinder harvests – and keener selection. Credit to the buyers: there were some very good wines on show. Not everything was successful, of course – wines to avoid include the raw Sicilian Nero d'Avola-Merlot (£3.99, 9/25), the dull Gaillac Blanc (£3.99, 11/25) and Domaine Rio-Magno Pinot Noir (£3.99, 10/25), the feeble Beaujolais Village Les Roches Grillées (£4.95, 8/25) and the acerbic Vin de Pays de l'Aude Rouge (£3.39, 8/25). Within the Classic Selection range,

Hours
Branch-specific,
including regular
late-night opening

Minimum sale
No

Credit cards
Access/Mastercard,
Visa, AmEx, Switch

Discounts
5% on six bottles
or more

Delivery
Mail-order service

Glass hire
Yes

Tasting facilities
No

Storage facilities
No

the Sauternes was a disappointment (£7.95, 10/25) – though if you're near the largest 38 stores there are the sumptuous half bottles of Château de la Chartreuse '90 (£9.95, 21/25) as consolation. The many more exciting wines are listed below; this is a far larger listing, relative to overall range, than last year, and it makes Sainsbury's a worthy joint winner of this year's Eros Award for Supermarket Wine Selection of the Year. Does it also mark a profounder change in supermarket wine culture? Is it the end of the line for the price point? I doubt it; price points are linked far too closely with perceived value for supermarkets to be able to abandon them. It might, though, herald the beginning of a return to quality for its own sake. It will all depend on sales – so I hope Sainsbury's gamble in raising its game pays off, and customers respond by spending their money on beautiful aromas and flavours rather than the needless clutter which most of us are herded, by marketing and advertising, into acquiring.

Worth a punt

White: 1995 Irsai Oliver Sainsbury's Hungarian £2.99 (14/25); 1993 Chardonnay Reserve, Khan Krum £3.69 (15/25); Bordeaux Blanc, Hardy £3.75 (17/25); 1995 Chenin Blanc, Vin de Pays du Jardin de la France £3.89 (15/25); 1993 Chardonnay Chapel Hill Barrique Aged £3.99 (18/25); 1995 Sauvignon Blanc Sainsbury's South African Reserve Selection £4.45 (15/25); 1995 Chardonnay Vin de Pays d'Oc £4.45 (16/25); 1994 Vouvray Couronne des Plantagenets £4.45 (14/25); ; 1995 Roussanne Barrique Réserve, Galet £4.99 (15/25); 1995 Semillon-Sauvignon, Sainsbury's Australian £4.99 (15/25); 1995 Semillon Saltram Classic £4.99 (16/25); 1995 Pouilly-Fumé Classic Selection £6.95 (20/25); 1994 Chardonnay Penfolds Barrel Fermented £6.95 (15/25); 1994 Chablis Classic Selection £7.45 (17/25); 1990 Riesling Piesporter Goldtropfchen Spätlese £7.75 (15/25); 1994 Chardonnay Lindeman's Padthaway £7.95 (17/25); 1990 Château de la Chartreuse (sweet, half-bottle) £9.95 (21/25); 1993 Chablis Premier Cru Montée de Tonnerre, Brocard £9.95 (18/25); 1994 Pouilly-Fuissé Classic Selection £9.95 (17/95); 1992 Puligny-Montrachet Premier Cru Les Chalumeaux £16.95 (16/25); 1993 Château Carbonnieux Blanc £16.95 (17/25).

Rosé: Bordeaux Clairet £3.99 (16/25); 1995 Merlot Rosé, Domaine de la Tuilerie £3.99 (14/25).

Red: Lambrusco Secco Rosso Vecchia Modena £3.29 (16/25); 1995 Sangiovese di Toscana Cecchi £3.69 (17/25); Squinzano Mottura £3.69 (15/25); Jumilla Sainsbury's £3.69 (20/25); 1992 Cabernet Sauvignon Reserve Iambol £3.69 (15/25); 1991 Cabernet Sauvignon Special Reserve Iambol £3.99 (16/25); 1995 Bush Vine Grenache, Coteaux du Languedoc £3.99 (18/25); 1995 Pinotage

Sainsbury's South African Reserve Selection £5.45 (18/25), 1994 Cabernet-Merlot Santara £4.79 (18/25); 1993 Merlot Domaine de la Baume £5.95 (15/25); 1994 Crozes-Hermitage Les Jalets £7.95 (16/25); 1993 St Emilion, Classic Selection £7.95 (14/25); 1993 Shiraz Penfolds Bin 28 £7.95 (18/25); 1991 Cabernet Sauvignon Wynns Coonawarra £7.95 (16/25); 1993 Cabernet Shiraz Penfolds Bin 389 £9.95 (21/25); 1990 Cornas les Serres £12.95 (15/25); 1992 Château Lagrange £13.95 (15/25); 1994 Côte Rôtie Brune et Blonde, Chapoutier £18.95 (20/25); 1991 Château Lynch-Bages £21.95 (19/25); 1991 Hermitage Monier de la Sizéranne, Chapoutier £19.95 (18/25).

Sparkling: Rosada Cava Sainsbury's £4.99 (18/25); Pinot Noir Chardonnay Seaview £7.95 (17/25); Extra Dry Champagne Sainsbury's (16/25); 1990 Champagne Sainsbury's £14.95 (15/25).

Fortified: Aged Amontillado Sainsbury's (half bottle) £3.29 (18/25); Old Oloroso Sainsbury's (half bottle) £3.29 (20/25); Palo Cortado Sainsbury's £3.29 (23/25); Fino Sainsbury's £4.69 (18/25); 1994 Moscato di Pantelleria (half bottle) £5.45 (16/25); 1989 LBV Port Sainsbury's £7.29 (14/25); 1982 Vintage Port Fonseca £17.95 (17/25).

Selfridges

400 Oxford Street, London W1A 1AB
Tel: **0171 629 1234**, fax: **0171 491 1880**

The richer mixture

Selfridges' wine department continued to improve since the last edition of this book, guided by wine buyer William Longstaff who, tragically, was killed in a road accident in June 1996. Let's hope Longstaff's successor keeps up the good work. Of all of the big department-store wine sections, this is the most catholically stocked, with a huge range of wines at all price levels as well as superb selections of beers, whiskies and other drinks. Champagne is a particular speciality (Selfridges has not only arranged a millenium offer, but has also organised a trip to Champagne for its customers); this is probably the best place in London to buy port (sales of which increased 45 per cent during 1995 for Selfridges); Bordeaux, California, Australia and New Zealand are all very well selected. Twice-yearly sales help bring prices down a little.

Worth a punt

White: 1994 Gewürztraminer Blanc de Blancs Boisviel St Pierre £5.95; 1995 Klein Constantia Chardonnay £7.25; 1994 Chablis Vieilles Vignes, Defaix £11.50; Muscat Vin de Glacière, Bonny

Hours
Mon-Sat
9.30am-7.00pm
(Thurs until 8.00pm).
Open five Sundays
before Christmas
11.00am-5.00pm

Minimum sale
No

Credit cards
All major cards plus
Selfridges Gold and
Sears

Discounts
8.5% per case (10%
for Gold Card
customers)

Delivery
Free nationwide on
orders of over £100
and for Gold Card
customers on orders
of over £50; £3.95
Greater London
(£6.95 elsewhere) on
orders of less than
£100

Glass hire
Free with order

**Tasting
facilities**
In-store, daily

Storage facilities
£5 per case per annum

Nearest tube
Bond Street

Doon £11.95; 1994 Viognier, Arrowood, California £19.95.

Red: 1994 Quinta do Crasto, Douro £5.50; 1993 Valpolicella Classico Superiore, Tedeschi £6.50; 1993 Vacquéyras, Le Couroulu £8.95; 1994 Pinot Noir Willamette Valley, Oregon £8.95; 1992 Crianza Bodegas Mauro £10.95; 1990 Reserva Bodegas Mauro £17.95.

Sparkling: Hostomme Blanc de Blancs Champagne £19.95; 1989 Jacquesson Signature Brut Rosé Champagne £45.

Fortified: 1985 Selfridges Vintage Port (Quinta do Crasto) £16.95.

Hours
Mon-Sat
8.30am-6.00pm
(may vary); Sun
10.00am-4.00pm
(main stores)

Minimum sale
No

Credit cards
All major cards

Discounts
No

Delivery
No

Glass hire
No

Tasting facilities
Monthly in-store tastings

Storage facilities
No

Somerfield

Head Office: Somerfield House, Hawkfield Business Park, Whitchurch Lane, Bristol BS14 0TJ
Tel: **0117 935 9359** Fax: **0117 978 0629**

The hit squad

Somerfield's *modus operandi* makes writing an entry in a guide of this sort difficult. This supermarket hits customers with a succession of special offers – lead wines discounted down to levels which must often be well below cost price. Having picked and nibbled the flesh off these cherries, the theory is that customers will stick with them when they return to their pre-offer price. More likely, I had thought, is that the canny ones move on to the next special offer a month later – but tuck a few extras into the trolley on each visit, thereby making the whole exercise worthwhile for the retailer. Buyer Angela Mount tells me, though, that customers do follow their discoveries. "In every case," she says, "sales of promoted wines have gone up after the promotion ends." Either way, the carousel tends to move round briskly here. I taste Somerfield samples regularly; some are good. The 1994 Chianti, for example, on special offer in June at £2.79, had the authentic green coffee-bean style the name promises and was simple, warm, fresh and full: 19/25. (At its normal £3.79 price it would merit 13/25.) The Castillo Imperial on offer during the same period was as near devoid of personality as it is possible for wine to be, though at £1.99 I had to give it 14/25 just for being drinkable. Bargain of the year was last year's Eros-winning Sweet Wine of the Year, the 1990 Château Bastor-Lamontagne in half-bottles, which for some reason ended up in Somerfield's January bin-end sale at £5.66. (This was a great sale: Penfolds Bin 389, Château Musar and Beringer Cabernet Sauvignon, all at £5.33; Penfolds Coonawarra Cabernet Sauvignon at £5.99; Lindeman's Limestone Ridge at £6.69. Take a look in Somerfield in January: Angela Mount is planning to repeat the exercise.) Other middling to good wines which have been through the promotions mill include the '94 white Hautes Côtes de Beaune, the Argentine Country White, the '93 I Grilli di Villa Thalia, the '93 Château Baron-Ségur and the '92 Château Latour-Ségur. Some promoted wines, though, have been poor: during 1996, I have rated at least half-a-dozen promotion lines at 10/25 or less, even at their promoted price. In more general terms, buyer Angela Mount offers interested consumers helpful background information via leaflets and the Somerfield magazine. The list seems to be in slow expansion, though the fact that most of Somerfield's stores are high-street rather than out-of-town means that shelf space, and hence complete range, is more limited than for its main rivals (the total range of 350 wines is in up to 150 stores, Kingston being the London flagship). The special offers have certainly proved their point and got Somerfield on the map, but don't stick with the special offers alone: as the list below shows, there are many other worthwhile wines of the Somerfield list which stay out of the promotions fray.

Worth a punt

White: Welschriesling & Misket Country White, Bulgaria £2.75 (15/25); 1995 Vin de Pays des Côtes de Gascogne £2.99 (14/25); Chardonnay, Vin de Pays du Jardin de la France £3.29 (15/25); 1996 Sauvignon Blanc, Gyöngyös, Hungary £3.69 (14/25);1996 Chardonnay, Gyöngyös, Hungary £3.69 (16/25); 1995 Entre-Deux-Mers, Mau £3.99 (15/25); 1994 Chardonnay, Vin de Pays d'Oc, Herrick £3.99 (16/25); 1995 Chardonnay, Caliterra, Chile £3.99 (17/25); 1995 Sauvignon Blanc, Bellingham £4.29 (15/25); 1995 Chardonnay Unwooded, Berri Estates, Australia £4.49 (16/25); Chardonnay, Redwood Trail, California £4.99 (16/25); 1995 Gewürztraminer, Turckheim £5.25 (18/25); 1995 Semillon, Rosemount, New South Wales £6.49 (16/25).

Rosé: 1995 Syrah, Vin de Pays d'Oc, Val d'Orbieu £3.25 (15/25); 1995 Château de la Bouletière, Coteaux de Cabrerisse £3.99 (16/25).

Red: Merlot & Pinot Noir Country Red, Sliven, Bulgaria £2.89 (14/25); 1993 I Grilli de Villa Thalia £3.65 (15/25); 1991 Copertino £3.99 (16/25); 1994 Château le Clairiot, Bordeaux £4.25 (16/25); 1993 Château Valoussière, Jeanjean, Coteaux du Languedoc £4.49 (18/25); 1993 Château Caraguilhes, Corbières £4.59 (15/25); 1994 Domaine La Tuque Bel Air, Côtes de Castillon £4.85 (17/25: December onwards); 1993 Crozes-Hermitage, Noblens £4.95 (17/25); 1994 Oak-Aged Claret, Peter Sichel £4.99 (15/25); 1995 Quinta de Pancas, Agricola Purio £4.99 (21/25); Redwood Trail Pinot Noir, California £4.99 (15/25); 1995 Chianti Classico, Conti Serristori £5.49 (15/25); 1992 Shiraz, Hardy's Bankside, Australia £5.99 (20/25); 1989 Château Musar, Lebanon £7.99

(19/25); 1994 Domaine de la Solitude, Châteauneuf-du-Pape £8.99 (18/25).

Sparkling: Chardonnay Cava, Codorníu Brut Premiere Cuvée £5.99 (18/25); Blanc de Blancs Champagne, Prince William £14.99 (16/25).

The South African Wine Centre

70 Wigmore Street, London W1H 9DL
Tel: **0171 224 1994**   Fax: **0171 224 1995**

The showcase

South Africa differs from Chile, that other newly respectable Southern Hemisphere wine producer, in that it has a remarkable network of well-resourced, individual wine estates each putting great efforts into producing wines they hope will compete with the best of Australia, California and Europe. A few of these make their way into our supermarkets and chains; the majority don't. Find them here, among the largest range of South African wines in Europe, enthusiastically assembled by Brian White and Warren Davies. The mustard-keen might like, for an annual fee of £15, to join the South African Wine Club — giving access to bi-monthly tastings, reserve wines not for public sale, bin-ends and 7.5% discount on purchases.

Worth a punt

White: 1995 Chardonnay Le Chardon, Avontuur £4.99; 1996 Colombard Goedverwacht £4.99; 1995 Sauvignon Von Orloff £5.99; 1995 Chardonnay, Vriesenhof £5.99; 1996 Sauvignon Blanc, Klein Constantia £6.99; 1995 Chardonnay Jordan £8.15; 1995 Chardonnay Claridge £8.99.

Red: 1993 Merlot Wellington £4.99; 1991 Cabernet Sauvignon Reserve Avontuur £5.99; 1993 Cabernet Sauvignon Clos Malverne £6.99; 1993 Cabernet-Merlot, Neil Ellis £6.99; 1995 Pinotage Warwick £7.99; 1994 Cabernet Sauvignon Plaisir de Merle £9.99; 1992 Cabernet Sauvignon Thelema £9.99; 1991 Rubicon Meerlust £9.99.

Sparkling: Blanc de Blancs Pierre Jourdain £10.30.

Fortified: 1989 Allesverloren Fine Old Ruby £13.99.

Hours
Mon-Fri 9.00am-
7.30pm; Sat
10.00am-7.30om
Minimum sale
No
Credit cards
All major cards
accepted
Discounts
7.5% for wine club
members
Delivery
Free in Central
London; also
nationwide service
Glass hire
Free with order
Tasting facilities
Tutored and in-
house tastings of
South African wine
**Storage
facilities**
No
Nearest tube
Bond St

Stones of Belgravia

6 Pont Street, London SW1X 9EL
Tel: **0171 235 1612**   Fax: **0171 235 7246**
Jeroboams, 24 Bute Street, London SW7 3EX
Tel: **0171 225 2232**

Hours
Mon-Fri
10.00am-8.00pm;
Sat 10.00am-7.00pm
Minimum sale
No

Jeroboams, 51 Elizabeth Street, London SW1W 9PP
Tel: **0171 823 5623**
Jeroboams, 6 Clarendon Road, London W11 3AA   Tel: **0171 727 9359**

The larger larder

Stones has a fine stock of clarets with an impressive historical dimension: 23 1982s at the time of writing, for example, as well as Mouton back to '45 and Yquem back to '21. Its selection from other parts of France is more modest but generally well-chosen (the burgundy selection is said to be in renovation during 1996). This merchanting is supplemented with a number of agencies, including those of Moss Wood and Alkoomi (both in Western Australia), as well as the champagnes of Georges Vesselle; there's a great wodge of vintage port, too. The branches of Jeroboams carry a lot less wine (but a lot more cheese).

Worth a punt

White: 1995 Sauvignon Blanc, Alkoomi, Western Australia £7.95; 1992 Gewürztraminer, Schlumberger £8.95; 1994 Château Talbot Blanc, St Julien £20; 1991 Chardonnay, Grgich Hills £21.

Red: 1992 Crozes-Hermitage, Bernard Chave £7.95; 1994 Pinot Noir Moss Wood, Western Australia £12.95; 1993 Cabernet Sauvignon Moss Wood £13.95.

Sparkling: 1988 Champagne Georges Vesselle £18.95.

Fortified: 1982 Vintage Port, Churchill £15.

Tesco

Head Office: Tesco House, PO Box 18, Delamare Road,
Cheshunt EN8 9SL   Tel: **01992 632222**   Fax: **01992 644235**

The route through the maze

Tesco as a whole may have had a glorious year routing the competition and charming its shareholders, but its wine department still trails some of its rivals for the number of exciting bottles per yard of shelving and consistency across the range. Quite why this should be I don't know, since Tesco's buyers are as skilled as those of their competitors, they work every bit as hard, and the resources needed to build a classy list should be available. There are many good wines stocked by Tesco, as the long list of puntables below suggests; the problem is that these top-quality purchases are let down by many other wines which are average or mediocre. Variety is only desirable once a certain quality threshhold has been assured, and I, for one, would be happier to see a slightly smaller but more consistent selection from Tesco.

But let's be fair: those who live near the largest 16 stores, like Australian red wine, and are prepared to shell out £5+ can enjoy

---

Credit cards
Access/Mastercard, Visa, AmEx, Switch

Discounts
5% per case

Delivery
Free on £50 order in Central London

Glass hire
Free with order

Tasting facilities
Monthly in-store tastings

Storage facilities
No

Nearest tube
Pont Street: Knightsbridge/Sloane Square
Bute Street: South Kensington
Elizabeth Street: Sloane Square
Clarendon Road: Holland Park

Hours
Mon-Sat 8.00am-10.00pm; Sunday 10am-4.00pm (may vary from store to store)

Minimum sale
No

Credit cards
Access/Mastercard, Visa, Switch

Discounts
5% discount on purchases of 6 or more bottles costing £2.99 or more

Delivery
Via Tesco Direct

---

one of the best specialist wine ranges in the country. Tesco has made some first-class purchases from South America, South Africa and Spain (the two Viña Mara Riojas are very fine, and Tesco did well to secure the lion's share of the stunning Valdepusa Syrah); its better quality French wines are in general impressive. (The cheaper French wines are patchy – avoid the coarse, rustic Domaine Saubagnère Côtes de Gascogne, £3.99, 8/25.) There's an exciting choice of sweet wines at larger Tesco stores. The company adopted a brave strategy for its 1996 spring tasting: it showed its entire range from Australia and Italy. Australia demonstrated Tesco at its best, with a very fair range of own-label wines (only the hard, unlovely Chardonnay, £4.29, 9/25, and the coarse, appley Sauvignon Blanc, £3.99, 8/25, were a disappointment), and some first-rate purchases from both leading and small-scale Australian producers. Italy, by contrast, showed the weaker side of Tesco: another big range of wines, but this time much of the variety was illusory, a mere collection of names and labels, since the wines in the glass repeated the same flavours time and time again. There are good selections (see below), but wines like the thin, acidic Chardonnay del Veneto (£3.49, 10/25), the bony Valpolicella (£3.29, 8/25), the raw, bitter Rosso del Lazio (£3.49, 10/25) and sweetish, confected Sicilian Red (£2.89, 8/25) do neither retailer nor consumer any favours. Many other bottles in this section are merely average (I marked no less than 17 wines from the Italian range at 11/25, including names which one might hope would deliver exciting flavours like Barolo or regional Merlot and Pinot Noir selections). It may be that price points and harvest difficulties are to blame, but the job of the retailer is to find strategies for overcoming these difficulties. The Spring Wine Festival provided a few good wines at keen prices (the full-fruited Picajuan Peak Chardonnay at £3.49, 19/25; or the salty, earthy Santa Ines Cabernet/Merlot at £3.79, 16/25) while attractive reduced prices on standard lines included Nottage Hill Chardonnay at £3.99 and Tesco's bright Crozes-Hermitage at £4.99; other wines were poor value at any price (like the Catalan White and Red, £2.99 each, 8/25 and 10/25 respectively). The good wines prove that Tesco can do it; now let's see Tesco do it more often.

Worth a punt

White: Chiara Villa Pigna £2.99 (14/25); 1995 Tesco Verdicchio Classico £3.59 (17/25); Chardonnay, Picajuan Peak, Argentina £3.79 (19/25); Rhine Riesling Tesco Australian £3.99 (15/25); 1994 Chardonnay del Salento, Le Trulle £3.99 (16/25); Chilean Sauvignon Blanc £3.99 (18/25); 1994 Moscato di Pantelleria (half-bottle, sweet) £4.99 (17/25); 1994 Old Penola Botrytis Gewürztraminer (half-bottle, sweet) £4.99 (15/25); 1995

Chardonnay Nottage Hill £4.99 (15/25); 1995 Chardonnay, Errazuriz, Chile £4.99 (16/25); 1994 Californian Chardonnay £4.99 (16/25); 1994 Riesling Tesco Clare Valley £4.99 (14/25); 1995 Chardonnay Casablanca, Caliterra, Chile £5.49 (18/25); 1995 Chardonnay Schoone Gevel, South Africa £5.99 (15/25); 1995 Chardonnay Rosemount £6.49 (16/25); 1992 Semillon Tesco Noble (half bottle, sweet) £6.99 (14/25); 1994 Chardonnay Chapel Hill Unwooded, South Australia £7.99 (16/25); 1993 Chardonnay Lindemans Padthaway £7.99 (17/25).

Red: Rosso Piceno Villa Pigna £2.99 (14/25); Bonarda Picajuan Peak, Argentina £3.29 (18/25); Sangiovese, Picajuan Peak, Argentina £3.49 (18/25); 1992 Copertino £3.49 (17/25); 1995 Cabernet/Merlot, Santa Ines, Argentina £3.79 (16/25); 1994 Blauer Zweigelt Lenz Moser £3.79 (17/25); 1994 Corbières, Domaine Sansoure £3.99 (16/25); 1994 Tesco Chianti Rufina £4.29 (15/25); Petit Verdot Casale Giglio £4.49 (20/25); 1994 Primitivo del Salento le Trulle £4.49 (15/25); 1993 Tesco les Domaines Château St Louis La Perdrix £4.49 (16/25); 1994 Tesco Chianti Classico £4.69 (14/25); Rioja Alavesa, Viña Mara £4.89 (20/25); 1994 Côtes du Rhône La Vieille Ferme £4.99 (18/25); 1993 Bordeaux Château Léon £4.99 (16/25) 1990 Salice Salentino £4.99 (16/25); 1994 Penfolds Rawsons Retreat Bin 35 £4.99 (15/25); 1994 Rioja Marqués de Griñon £4.99 (16/25); 1994 Merlot, Schoone Gevel, South Africa £4.99 (16/25); 1995 Shiraz/Cabernet Rosemount £5.29 (15/25); 1988 Rioja Reserva Viña Mara £5.49 (19/25); 1993 Shiraz Lindemans Bin 50 £5.49 (17/25); 1994 Cabernet Sauvignon Coonawarra Tesco £5.99 (17/25); 1992 Merlot Tesco Barossa £5.99 (15/25); 1993 Tesco Rosso di Montalcino £6.29 (15/25); 1994 Grenache Temple Bruer Cornucopia £6.49 (17/25); 1994 Shiraz Tesco McLaren Vale £6.99 (16/25); 1992 Shiraz Barossa Cranswick Estate £6.99 (16/25); 1993 Shiraz McLaren Vale Maglieri £6.99 (17/25); 1993 Cabernet/Merlot Château Reynella £6.99 (20/25); 1990 Valpolicella Amarone Villa Cerro £7.49 (19/25); 1993 Shiraz Bin 28 Kalimna Penfolds £7.99 (18/25); 1991 Cabernet Sauvignon Coonawarra Old Penola £7.99 (16/25); 1993 Shiraz Chapel Hill £7.99 (17/25); 1993 Syrah, Marqués de Griñon £8.49 (22/25); 1991 Durif Mick Morris £9.99 (20/25); 1993 Shiraz St Hallets Old Block £9.99 (21/25); 1992 Château Cantemerle, Macau £10.99 (16/25); 1992 Wynns John Riddoch £15.99 (19/25); 1993 Cabernet Sauvignon Bin 707 Penfolds £16.99 (22/25).

Sparkling: Zonin Pinot Brut Sparkling £4.59 (15/25); 1991 Seppelts Sparkling Shiraz £7.99 (20/25); Cabernet Sauvignon Sparkling Yalumba £8.49 (16/24); Pinot Noir-Chardonnay Yalumba £8.49 (14/25); 1993 Green Point £10.49 (16/25).

Fortified: Muscat Liqueur Mick Morris (half-bottles) £4.95 (21/25); Tesco Australian Oak Aged Tawny Liqueur Wine £6.99 (16/25).

Hours
Mon-Sat
10.00am-10.00pm;
Sun: Bottoms Up
and Wine Rack:
10.00am-10.00pm;
others 10.00am-
4.00pm, 7.00pm-
10.00pm

Minimum sale
No

Credit cards
Access/Mastercard,
Visa, AmEx, Delta

Discounts
Thresher Wine Shops
and Wine Rack 5%
per case or 10% per
case over £120, plus
10% per case for
champagne (and
Wine Rack 7 for 6 on
sparkling wine and
champagne).
Bottoms Up 10% on
all cases and 15% on
cases of champagne.
Further discounts are
available for club
members.

Delivery
Locally free and
nationally through
Drinks Direct (0800
232221).

Glass hire
Free with order

**Tasting
facilities**
Wine Rack and
Bottoms Up every
Friday and Saturday;
Threshers Wine
Shops at regular
intervals.

**Storage
facilities**
No

Internet site
Bottoms Up:
http://www.bottoms
up.co.uk/bottomsup.

Thresher Wine Shops, Bottoms Up, Wine Rack, Drinks Cabin, Huttons

Head Office: Sefton House, 42 Church Road, Welwyn Garden City, Herts AL8 6PJ

Tel: **01707 328244**, fax: **01707 371398**

Getting across

Whitbread-owned Thresher is constantly refining its offering to the public, with the result that you now need the mind of a medieval theologian to understand its hierarchies, dominions, principalities and powers. But here goes: Wine Rack and Bottoms Up jointly occupy archangelic spot, with Wine Rack being a high-class, up-market browsing shop which spreads over the core-range cake a generous icing of expensive and recherché wines (Alsace, New Zealand and South Africa all specialities), while Bottoms Up has more of a warehouse style with tasting facilities, special parcels, the biggest discounts in the group, an Internet presence, a stylish and beautifully illustrated list (worth getting, so you can learn what the full range is and order what your local branch doesn't stock), plus buccaneering managers. Thresher Wine Shops offer the basic Thresher package: most of the wine list, plus the four-packs, the Hooch and the fags. This is also the home of the 'Wine Buyers Guarantee': if you don't like it, you can swap it for something else. Wine Shops have a Wine With Food Club, the idea also being to expand customer experiment. Drinks Cabin is yer classic offie, with an emphasis on promotions and offers; while Huttons is a convenience store. In general, the company has had a good to very sound year in '96, and featured on a regular basis as a potential purchaser in the rumours surrounding the possible sales of Oddbins (by Seagram) and Victoria Wines (by Allied Domecq). Were either of these to happen it would doubtless lead to a further proliferation of shop sub-groups, so let's hope it doesn't: I won't be able to cope. The company has ample buying power, and has done a great job with some of its specialities during the last year – the South African range, in its full Wine Rack guise, is the best on the high street.

Worth a punt

White: 1995 Chenin Blanc, Winelands, South Africa £3.89 (15/25); 1995 Bush Vine Chenin, Winelands £4.49 (15/25); 1995 Sauvignon Blanc, Bellingham £4.79 (15/25); 1994 Pinot Blanc Reserve, Turckheim £4.99 (16/25); 1994 Barrel-Fermented Chardonnay, Cool Ridge, Hungary £4.99 (17/25); 1995 Chenin Blanc, Villiera, South Africa £4.99 (17/25); 1994 Scheurebe Niersteiner Pettenthal, Rappenhoff £5.49 (15/25); 1994 Pinot Gris Reserve, Turckheim £5.59 (20/25); 1994 Gewürztraminer Reserve,

Turckheim £5.99 (18/25); 1995 Blanc Fumé, Villiera, South Africa £5.99 (16/25); 1994 Riesling Kabinett, Forster Pechstein, Von Bühl £7.99 (22/25); 1995 Chardonnay d'Honneur, Wetshof £7.99 (17/25); 1994 Chablis Vieilles Vignes, Defaix £9.99 (18/25); 1994 Chardonnay, Ormond Estate, Montana, New Zealand £10.99 (16/25).

Red: 1992 Cabernet Sauvignon Reserve, Iambol, Bulgaria £3.49 (15/25); Oak-Aged Cabernet Sauvignon, Twin Peaks, Rousse, Bulgaria £3.99 (15/25); 1990 Cabernet Sauvignon Special Reserve, Iambol £3.99 (16/25); 1995 Cinsaut/Tinta Barroca, Winelands, South Africa £3.99 (17/25); 1995 Cabernet Sauvignon/Cabernet Franc, Winelands, South Africa £4.49 (18/25); 1994 Estremadura, Bright Brothers £4.59 (16/25); Boschendal Red, South Africa £4.59 (15/25); 1995 Montevelho, Reguengos, Alentejo £4.79 (14/25); 1995 Douro, Bright Brothers £4.99 (15/25); 1994 Rioja, Marqués de Griñon £4.99 (16/25); 1992 Cabernet Sauvignon Crianza, Remonte, Navarra £4.99 (16/25); 1995 Premium Shiraz/Cabernet, Winelands £4.99 (20/25); 1995 Pinotage, Beyerskloof, South Africa £5.49 (17/25); 1992 Valduero, Ribera del Duero £6.99 (19/25); 1994 Cabernet Sauvignon/Merlot, Church Road, Montana £7.99 (15/25); 1995 Pinotage, Warwick, South Africa (19/25); 1993 Cabernet Sauvignon Dominio de Valdepusa £9.49;

Sparkling: 1993 Pinot-Chardonnay Seaview, Australia £7.99; 1993 Gren Point, Victoria £10.49; Champagne Jean de Praisac £12.99.

Fortified: Molmsey 10-year-old Madeira, Blandy £14.79; 1984 Quinte do Panascal Vintage Port £16.00; plus 1994 vintage ports (order by December 1st).

Uncorked

15 Exchange Arcade, Broadgate, London EC2M 3WA
Tel: **0171 638 5998**   Fax: **0171 638 6028**

Unbridled

This tidy little shop tucked away in the back passages of Broadgate has sussed the needs of its locals fairly exactly: a core of classy European wines (especially the Parker-picked, with surges from burgundy, champagne, Bordeaux and Rhône) complemented by clever selections from the Southern Hemisphere and California. Advice (from Jim Griffen and Andrew Rae) is good; the list is in slow expansion; there are bin-end sales to help move stock along from time to time. Cognac Frapin, vintage port and Riedel glasses lend further texture and tone: leave the screen, take a look, have a chat.

Hours
Mon-Fri
10.00am-6.30pm

Minimum sale
No

Credit cards
All major cards

Discounts
5% per case table wines; 10% on 6 or more bottles of champagne

Delivery
Free throughout UK mainland for 1 case or more

Glass hire
Free with order

Tasting facilities
Via wine club
Storage facilities
Warehouse terms
Nearest tube
Liverpool St

Worth a punt

White: 1995 Sauvignon Blanc, Echeverria, Chile £4.95; 1994 Sauvignon Blanc, Matua Valley, New Zealand £6.95; 1993 Chardonnay Columbia Winery, Washington State £7.95; 1994 Chardonnay Au Bon Climat, California £12.95; 1991 Bourgogne Blanc, Leflaive £13.95.

Red: 1994 Merlot Reserva, Mont Gras, Chile £6.95; 1994 Don Pietro, Sicily £7.95; 1994 Pinot Noir Au Bon Climat, California £14.95; 1993 Maranges 'Clos des Loyères' Premier Cru, Girardin £12.95; 1990 Rosso del Gnemiz, Friuli £15.95.

Sparkling: Gallimard Cuvée de Reserve Champagne £12.95; Vilmart Grande Reserve Champagne £18.95; Gosset Grande Reserve Champagne £26.95.

Hours
Majority of shops
Mon-Sun 10.00am–
10.00pm
Minimum sale
No
Credit cards
Access/Mastercard,
Visa, AmEx, Diners,
Delta, Switch
Discounts
5% on 6 bottles,
10% on 12 bottles;
12.5% on orders
over £200
Delivery
Free locally
Glass hire
Free with order
Tasting facilities
In-store tastings;
others by
arrangement
Storage facilities
No

Unwins

Head Office: Birchwood House, Victoria Road, Dartford, Kent DA1 5AJ   Tel: **01322 272711**   Fax: **01322 294469**

The right place at the right time

Unwin's 310 branches, most of them in *Standard* country, makes it the largest independent wine merchant in Britain. One bustling branch I visited in June '96 led me to the realisation that, no matter how much wine writers spout on about this or that wine or this or that chain, what really makes the success or failure of a drink shop is being in the right location, at the hub of a community and with a bit of parking at the front; opening at the right times; stocking all the basic wines, beers, snacks and tobacco; and being run by friendly, locally familiar characters. Unwins generally gets most of this right. It does not begin to compete in terms of range or buying effort with the Oddbins and Bottoms Ups of this world, and its list is mildly aggravating in that it still does not specify all the producers' names. The listed selection is at best moderately adventurous; it is supplemented, though, by what the company calls 'parcels' and 'undiscovered wines' from time to time. Areas of recent expansion include Australian wines and South African wines; Champagne, too, is taking off at Unwin's, with everything from Veuve Clicquot providing fun for the well-funded.

Worth a punt

White: 1994 Grüner Veltliner, Wienviertel, Austria £3.99; 1994 Dão Grão Vasco £4.59; 1994 Mâcon-Igé La Berthelotte £5.99; 1995 Chardonnay, Rosemount £6.79; 1994 Chardonnay, Klein Constantia £6.99; 1995 Sancerre Les Roches, Vacheron £9.99.

Red: 1994 Pedras do Monte £3.79; 1995 Cabernet Sauvignon Canepa, Chile £4.99; 1987 Garrafeira Reserva Particular, Bernardino £5.99; 1994 Quinta do Vale da Raposa, Douro £5.99; 1990 Cabernet Sauvignon, Wakefield £5.99; 1993 Madiran Château de Crouseilles £6.39; 1991 Amarone Recioto della Valpolicella Classico £9.99; 1992 Château des Fines Roches, Barrot £11.49; 1989 Château Gruaud-Larose, St Julien £29.

Sparkling: 1992 Seaview Pinot Noir/Chardonnay £7.99; 1989 Veuve Clicquot La Grande Dame £59.95.

Victoria Wine

Head Office: Dukes Court, Duke Street, Woking, Surrey GU21 5XL
Tel: **01483 715 066**   Fax: **01483 755234**

Teamwork

Victoria Wines is, together with Oddbins, one of the large chains about which sale rumours ebb and flow as I write. For the time being, it remains part of Allied Domecq, and follows a quiet and steady path of range consolidation and shop upgrades. With 1550 stores, it is a major player, and one can only hope for competition's sake that it never falls into the hands of one of its major rivals. VW divides its estate into two strands – the smarter, larger Victoria Wine Cellars; and the more modestly sized Victoria Wine Shops, slowly working their way through a general refit. A third strand is, apparently, imminent at present: Firkin Wine & Beer Shops, the Firkin name being that of a pub chain (some of which brew their own beer) from elsewhere in the Allied portfolio. It's a good idea – no retailing chain has yet fully explored the potential of selling beer with the same depth of buying research and communicative effort which goes into wine sales. A warehouse is also said to be in the pipeline. On the buying front, Victoria Wine has had a steady year, with lots of good purchases from the South of France, Chile, Argentina and South Africa. The wines made by VW's own back-room boy Hugh Suter M.W. (affectionately known as 'Mr Detail-Bar-Nothing' to his colleagues) were justifiably acclaimed for their subtlety and depth; let's hope there's lots more to come.

Worth a punt

White: 1995 Sauvignon, Bordeaux, Calvet £3.65 (16/25); Côtes de Duras Blanc, Bois de Lamothe £3.99 (15/25); 1995 Muscadet de Sèvre et Maine (Hugh Suter) £3.99 (17/25); 1995 Gewürztraminer Cono Sur, Chile £3.99 (17/25); 1995 Coteaux du Layon, Domaine du Plessis (half-bottle; sweet) £4.29 (17/25); 1995 Sauvignon Blanc, Mohr-Fry Ranch, California (Hugh Suter) £4.49 (16/25); 1995 Chardonnay, Carmen, Chile £4.49 (15/25);

Hours
10.00am-10.00pm (may vary)

Minimum sale
No

Credit cards
Access/Mastercard, AmEx, Visa

Discounts
5% per case; Victoria Wine Cellars 7 bottles for 6 sparkling wines over £5.99, + 10% case discount

Delivery
Locally free; Post Haste system for national delivery: charges vary

Glass hire
Free with larger orders

Tasting facilities
Occasional in-store tastings

Storage facilities
No

Internet site
http://www.ltl.net/go/to/victoria wine

1995 Muscadet de Sèvre et Maine, Domaine de la Roulerie (Hugh Suter) £4.99 (19/25); 1995 Oaked Chardonnay, La Langue, Domaine Ste Madelaine, Vin de Pays d'Oc £4.99 (15/25); 1995 Chardonnay, Ranch Series, California (Hugh Suter) £4.99 (18/25); 1995 Chardonnay, Caliterra, Casablanca Valley, Chile £5.49 (15/25); 1994 Chardonnay Corbans Private Bin, Gisborne £9.99 (17/25); 1994 Chablis Premier Cru Vaudevey, Moreau £10.49 (17/25).

Red: Chilean Cabernet Sauvignon, Altura £3.59 (19/25); 1995 Grenache/Syrah, La Baume, Vin de Pays d'Oc £3.99 (17/25); 1995 Merlot, La Langue, Vin de Pays d'Oc £3.99 (16/25); 1995 Merlot/Malbec, Concha y Toro, Chile £3.99 (16/25); 1995 Malbec, Balbi Vineyards, Argentina £3.99 (16/25); 1994 Domaine St Benoit, La Langue, Vins de Pays d'Oc £4.29 (17/25); Syrah, Domaine Ste Madelaine, La Langue, Vins de Pays d'Oc £4.49 (18/25); 1995 Merlot, Carmen £4.49 (18/25); 1995 Cabernet Sauvignon, Balbi, Argentina £4.99 (17/25); 1995 Cuvée Simone, James Herrick, Vins de Pays d'Oc £4.99 (21/25); 1994 Cabernet Sauvignon Caliterra Reserva £6.49 (19/25); 1993 Vieux Château Gaubert, Graves £10.99 (17/25); 1992 Vieux Château Certan, Pomerol £24.95 (19/25).

Sparkling: 1990 Seppelt Sparkling Shiraz £7.99 (19/25); 1991 Green Point £10.49 (17/25); 1990 Millenium Cuvée Champagne £21.99.

Fortified: Palo Cortado (half-bottle) £3.99 (16/25); 1976 Quinta do Noval Colheita Port (half-bottle) £9.99 (21/25); Dow's Crusted Port bottled 1990 £11.99; Oloroso Matusalem £19.89 (23/25).

La Vigneronne

105 Old Brompton Road, London SW7 3LE
Tel: **0171 589 6113**   Fax: **0171 581 2983**

Browse awhile

This unassuming shop on the Old Brompton Road continues its long-established tradition of rooting out and importing all manner of delicious curiosities. Most are French, though these are seasoned by choice selections from beyond France. Fine older vintages are generously stocked, too. There is no list; pop in and have a look.

Worth a punt

White: 1994 Menetou-Salon, Clément £7.95; 1990 Riesling Cuvée Frédéric Emile, Trimbach £18.95; 1994 Meursault Goutte d'Or, Latour.

Red: 1994 Nine Popes, Charlie Melton £12.50; 1989 Bouscassé

Hours
Mon-Fri 10.00am-8.00pm; Sat 10.00am-6.00pm

Minimum sale
No

Credit cards
Access/Mastercard, Visa, AmEx, Diners

Discounts
5% off shop sales by the case

Delivery
Free nationwide on orders of £200 or over

Glass hire
No

Tasting facilities
Tastings held every week

Vieilles Vignes, Madiran £13.95; 1986 Château de la Rivière, Fronsac £14.95; 1982 Château Musar, Lebanon £15.95; 1993 Pinot Noir, Cuvaison £15.95; 1994 Côte-Rôtie, Rostaing £21.95.

Sparkling: Champagne Ruinart £19.95; 1988 Champagne Ruinart £27.50.

The Vintage House

42 Old Compton Street, London W1V 6LR
Tel: **0171 437 2592**   Fax: **0171 734 1174**

Get 'em down

The Vintage House occupies something of a mid-point, both geographically and alcoholically, between the pile-it-high mentality of Gerry's (q.v.) and the exhaustive whisky selection of Milroy's round on Greek St. Whisky, of course, is not the concern of this Guide, but let us note in passing that the Vintage House, too, has one of the best selections in Britain – over 500 malts. Wines are well-chosen and diverse; the speciality is 'vertical' swathes of grand Bordeaux châteaux like Mouton (20 vintages), Latour, Batailley and Palmer, though there are lots of bottles that are cheaper as well (including Silver Birch Wine from Scotland). Cuban cigars are extensively stocked, to put the seal on that good time you're having.

Worth a punt

White: 1995 Colombard Aston Vale, South Africa £3.99; 1993 Rully, Château de Rully £9.78; 1993 Chassagne-Montrachet, Rodet £13.75; 1983 Riesling Beerenauslese Binger Scharlachberg £24.99.

Red: 1994 Melnik Reserve, Bulgaria £2.99; 1988 Château Batailley, Pauillac £16.99; 1990 Château Cantenac-Brown, Margaux £27.60.

Sparkling: Pongracz £8.99; 1989 Champagne Lanson £18.99.

Waitrose

Head Office: Doncastle Road, Southern Industrial Area, Bracknell, Berks, RG12 8YA   Tel: **01344 424680**

Steady as she goes

Waitrose, last year's Eros winner for Supermarket Wine Selection of the Year, has justified that award with a strong performance since the publication of the 1996 Guide. This remains the most reliable and consistent of all supermarkets for its wine selection – the supermarket, in my opinion, where the consumer runs fewest risks in experimenting with a wide range of wines. And its girth is expanding: there are now over 500 different wines to chose from, taking both Waitrose and its mail-order operation, Waitrose Direct (formerly Findlater Mackie Todd)

Storage facilities
No

Nearest tube
South Kensington

Hours
Mon-Sat
9.00am-11.00pm;
Sun 12.00pm-
10.00pm

Minimum sale
No

Credit cards
All major cards

Discounts
5% per case
(cash/cheque
payment only)

Delivery
Free in London
postal area

Glass hire
Free with orde

Tasting facilities
Monthly in store
tastings

Storage facilities
No

Nearest tube
Tottenham Court
Road, Leicester
Squarer

Hours
Mon, Tues, Sat
8.30am-6.00pm;
Weds-Fri 8.30am-
9.00pm; about half
the stores open for 6
hours on Sunday

Minimum sale
No

Credit cards
Access/Mastercard,
Visa, Eurocard

Discounts
Wine of the month:
1 bottle free per
case; 5% per case
(unmixed)

Mail order
Through Waitrose
Direct: 0181 543
0966 or Freepost,
London SW19 3YY

Glass hire
Free with order

Tasting facilities
Occasional in-store
tastings

**Storage
facilities**
No

into account. Unlike other supermarkets, most wines go into most stores, making the task of following up recommendations relatively straightforward. The marketing is still on the plain side, as John Lewis tradition dictates, though subtle profile-raising modifications are said to be on the way. (Since most marketing is deceit, I appreciate and admire this modest, shy silhouette.) It's hard to pick out areas where Waitrose is particularly strong, since that implies weaknesses which this department doesn't really have; if you're looking for pure value, though, Waitrose has made excellent white-wine selections from Hungary (Deer Leap) and red-wine selections from Chile (Isla Negra, Cono Sur, Valdivieso), accurately reflecting those parts of the wine world where general value is best at present. I'm even impressed by the wines I don't like at Waitrose, since my dislike of them is generally positive (there is some characteristic which doesn't appeal to me, but may well appeal to someone else) rather than negative (empty, dreary, over-filtered, over-sterile, nothing-of-a-nothingness wines). So few genuinely bad bottles here; those that appeal least include the over-slender 1992 red Hautes Côtes de Beaune (£6.99; 9/25); the sweetish, confected 1995 Cabernet Sauvignon/Shiraz from Du Toitskloof (£3.99; 10/25); the weak-flavoured 1995 Tarrango from Brown Brothers (£4.75; 10/25); the coarse 1995 Le Pujalet (£3.15; 10/25); and the cardboardy-resiny 1995 Ridgewood Trebbiano (£3.49; 10/25). For the stars of the list, see below.

Worth a punt

White: 1995 Hárslevelü Deer Leap £2.99 (18/25); 1995 Pinot Gris Deer Leap £3.65 (14/25); 1995 Gewürztraminer Deer Leap £3.85 (15/25); 1995 Sauvignon Blanc Deer Leap £3.85 (16/25); 1995 Sauvignon Blanc BRL Hardy £3.99 (15/25); 1995 Chardonnay Santa Julia £3.99 (15/25); 1995 Sauvignon Blanc Bellingham £4.49 (17/25); 1995 Viognier Cuckoo Hill £4.99 (17/25); 1995 Chardonnay Avontuur £5.49 (15/25); 1993 Gewürztraminer d'Alsace £5.79 (16/25); 1995 Sancerre La Vraignonette £6.99 (19/25); 1994 Chardonnay Saltram Mamre Brook £6.99 (16/25); 1994 Organic Chardonnay/Sauvignon Penfolds £6.99 (15/25); 1995 Mâcon-Solutré £6.99 (15/25); 1995 Pouilly-Fumé Masson-Blondelet £7.49 (17/25); 1994 Gewürztraminer Spätlese Ungsteiner Honigsäckel £7.99 (15/25); 1995 Sauvignon Blanc Katnook Estate £7.99 (14/25); 1995 Chardonnay Ninth Island £7.99 (15/25); 1994 Chardonnay Rosemount Show Reserve £8.95 (15/25); 1989 Château de la Chartreuse Sauternes (sweet; half-bottle) £9.75 (20/25); 1993 Chablis Premier Cru Beauroy £9.95 (16/25).

Red: 1994 Syrah/Cabernet Sauvignon Domaine Fontaine de Cathala (half-bottle) £2.49 (16/25); 1995 Cabernet Sauvignon/Merlot Iambol £2.99 (16/25); 1995 Winter Hill Red

£3.29 (15/25); 1995 Côtes du Ventoux £3.35 (15/25); 1994 Sangiovese Fiordaliso £3.75 (18/25); 1994 Isla Negra Red £3.99 (18/25); 1994 Malbec Santa Carolina £3.99 15/25); 1995 Coteaux du Languedoc Pic St Loup £3.99 (18/25); 1994 Special Reserve Claret £4.49 (14/25); 1995 Graves £4.75 (17/25); 1992 Agramont Navarra £4.75 (15/25); 1993 Château St Auriol Corbières £4.99 (16/25); 1994 Cabernet/Merlot Barrel-Fermented Valdivieso £4.99 (16/25); 1990 Vale do Bomfim Reserva £5.35 (15/25); 1994 Château La Favière £5.35 (17/25); 1995 Grenache Yaldara Reserve Whitmore Old Vineyard £5.75 (15/25); 1994 Cabernet Sauvignon Tatachilla £5.99 (17/25); 1992 Crozes-Hermitage Cave des Clairmonts £6.45 (17/25); 1995 Pinot Noir Reserve Cono Sur £6.45 (15/25); 1994 Gigondas Domaine Ste Lucie £6.95 (16/25); 1994 Shiraz Browns of Padthaway £6.99 (16/25); 1993 St Aubin Premier Cru Les Combes Prunier £9.95 (16/25); 1985 Campillo Rioja Gran Reserva £9.95 (15/25); 1994 Clos St Michelle Châteauneuf-du-Pape £9.95 (15/25); 1987 Le Pergole Torte £9.95 (18/25).

Sparkling: Blanquette de Limoux £5.99 (17/25); Chapel Down Century English £6.45 (14/25); Clairette de Die Tradition (sweet) £6.45 (15/25); 1992 Krone Borealis Brut £6.99 (18/25); Waitrose Blanc de Blancs Champagne £13.95 (15/25).

Fortified: Fino Sherry Waitrose (half-bottle) £2.85 (20/25); Manzanilla La Gitana £5.99 (18/20); 1979 White Jerepigo £6.99 (15/25); Dry White Port, Churchill £8.99 (16/25); 10-Year-Old Tawny Port £10.45 (16/25).

Waterloo Wine Company

59-61 Lant Street, London SE1 1QL
Tel: **0171 403 7967**   Fax: **0171 357 6976**

Freshen up

This company, whose business address is actually in Vine Yard (though the shop and warehouse are in Lant Street), makes something of a speciality of fresh-flavoured wines from the Loire valley and from New Zealand; indeed owner Paul Tutton now has his own vine yard in New Zealand – Waipara West. The balance of the list is made up with a fair selection of wines from other parts of France and from Italy, with one or two other items present on an agency basis.

Worth a punt

White: 1995 Azay-le-Rideau Blanc Sec, Pibaleau £5.49; 1995 Sauvignon Blanc, Waipara West, New Zealand £7.99; 1993 Pinot Gris Grand Cru Zotzenberg £8.75; 1995 Chardonnay, Waipara West, New Zealand £8.99; 1990 Savennières Coulée de Serrant, Joly £21.99.

Hours
Mon-Fri 10.00am-6.30pm; Sat 10.00am-5.00pm

Minimum sale
None

Credit cards
Access/Mastercard, Visa, Switch, Connect

Discounts
Special offers only

Delivery
Free to SE1; free within M25 on 5 cases or more; also nationwide service

Glass hire
Free with order

Tasting facilities
Monthly tastings

Storage facilities
No

Nearest tube
Borough

Red: 1993 St Nicolas de Bourgeuil Clos Corioux, Mabileau £6.69; 1994 Cabernet Sauvignon/Cabernet Franc, Waipara Springs, New Zealand £7.25; 1992 Corbières, Cuvée Hélène de Troie, Château Hélène £8.39; 1995 Pinot Noir, Stonier, Victoria £8.99; 1989 Barolo Vigneti Rocche, Settimo £9.49.

Hours
Mon-Sat 9.00am-10.30pm; Sun 10.00am-10.00pm

Minimum sale
No

Credit cards
Access/Mastercard, Visa, AmEx, Switch

Discounts
Variable

Delivery
Free locally; also nationwide service

Glass hire
Free with order

Tasting facilities
Weekend in-store tastings

Storage facilities
No

Internet site
http://www.winecellar.co.uk

Nearest tube
Turnham Green, Chiswick Park

Wine Cellar

294 Chiswick High Road, London W6
Tel: **0181 987 9502**

Hang on to your hats

Wine Cellar's presence in Standard country is discreet as yet (in addition to the Chiswick branch, there are shops in Epsom and Welwyn Garden City). This could change dramatically should any of the rumours about parent company Greenalls' purchase of Oddbins or even Victoria Wines come to fruition. What is certain is that the team behind Wine Cellar is ambitious and full of ideas — this year has brought food and videos to the shops, in-store cafés and an internet site, and the company is said to be looking at the possibility of taking the café theme further, enabling customers to try the wines and beers they buy in the shop with food. (Ironically this would put it on a footing with arch-traditionalists El Vino, the Reynier Wine Libraries and La Reserve, qqv., but you can't keep a good idea down.) The list is magazine-like, full of discursive introductions, tips on wine-and-food matching — and adverts. The wine buyers, you might think, get to occupy a back seat compared with all of this marketing frenzy, yet you'd be wrong: Kevin Wilson and David Vaughan have pulled in some cracking wines this year. There's a big, bright New World emphasis (12 from Washington State, for example), but the European wines stocked are generally chosen for quality and not price, keeping standards up. We just need a few more branches.

Worth a punt

White: 1995 Chardonnay, Cordillera Estate £4.49; 1994 Chardonnay, Welmoed Estate, South Africa £4.99; 1994 Bourgogne Aligoté, Pillot £7.49.

Red: 1995 Red Balbi Vineyards, Argentina £3.69;1995 Cabernet Sauvignon Apalta, Montes, Chile £4.99; 1995 Cinsault, Ruitersvlei, South Africa £4.99; 1994 Teroldego Rotaliano, Concilio £4.99; 1994 Reds from Laurel Glen, California £5.99; 1994 Cabernet/Merlot, Hedges, Washington State £6.99.

Sparkling: Seaview Brut £5.99; Roederer Quartet £13.99.

Fortified: 1985 Vintage Port, Quinta do Crasto £14.49.

The Wine House

10 Stafford Road, Wallington, Surrey SM6 9AD
Tel: 0181 669 6661   Fax: 0181 401 0039

Plums and cherries

This smallish shop has a fine and varied stock: Morvin Rodker tastes and buys intelligently, and value for money is good. The wines are divided, on the list, into three broad categories, depending on price and use; most regions get a look in. Top-quality independent local merchants like The Wine House are rarer and rarer nowadays: make the most of it, Wallingtonians.

Worth a punt

White: 1995 Vin de Pays des Côtes de Gascogne, Domaine de Pomes £4.50; 1994 Pinot Blanc Dopff & Irion £5.60; 1993 Menetou-Salon, Chavet £7.95; 1992 Vacquéyras Blanc Château des Roques £8.75; 1988 Riesling Brauneberger Juffer Auslese, Fehres £9.45; 1993 Savennières Clos du Papillon, Baumard £9.50; 1992 Pouilly-Fuissé Vieilles Vignes, Guyot £12.55.

Red: 1994 Montepulciano d'Abruzzo, Citra £3.99; 1988 Viña Vermeta Reserva, Alicante £4.99; 1994 Maître d'Estournel, Bruno Prats £6.85; 1992 Tempranillo Ochoa £6.85; 1993 Zinfandel Foppiano £6.85; 1992 Petite Syrah, Foppiano £8.25; 1989 Château Cabannieux, Graves £8.50; 1989 Château Roudier, Montagne St Emilion £8.95; 1987 Agamium, Anticchi Vigneti di Cantalupo £8.95; 1993 Shiraz Grant Burge, Old Vine £9.75; 1990 Château Tailhas, Pomerol £13.75.

Sparkling: 1990 Seppelt Salinger £10.99; Perrier-Jouët, Blason de France £28.50.

Fortified: Manzanilla La Gitana £6.75; Amontillado 51-1A, Domecq £13.99; 1987 Quinta da Eira Velha Port £16.85.

Hours
Tues-Sat 10.00am-6.00pm; Sun 12.00pm-2.00pm

Minimum sale
No

Credit cards
Access/Mastercard, Visa, AmEx

Discounts
10% per case cash/cheque/ Delta payments; 7% per case card payments

Delivery
Free locally over £50; mail-order service in preparation

Glass hire
Free with order

Tasting facilities
Bi-annual tastings; in-store tastings; private tastings by arrangement

Storage facilities
No

Nearest BR station
Wallington

Wine on the Green

35 Fortune Green Road, West Hampstead NW6 1DU.
Tel: 0181 794 1143

Supercellar

First of all, note the strange opening times. Why? This is the wine library of the man who owns the tyre company next door. Alan Pollock wanted, after 30 years of tyres, something more personally satisfying; he enjoyed and collected wine; so he opened his cellar on Fridays and Saturdays and became a wine merchant. The selection is eclectic but based purely on quality: 'I don't want to sell wines I don't like,' says Pollock. What will you

Hours
Fri 11.00am-5.30pm; Sat 9.30am-1.00pm

Minimum sale
No

Credit cards
Access/Mastercard, Visa

Discounts
5% on mixed cases for cash or cheque

Delivery
No

Glass hire
Free with order

find? A huge selection of Rhône valley wines, with a particular emphasis on Châteauneuf-du-Pape; lots of Bordeaux, 'all good vintages'; a wide choice of Zinfandel; carefully picked burgundies; a huge variety of sweet wines; plenty of half-bottles. And willingly shared enthusiasm.

Worth a punt

Stocks change all the time, and particular lines may be in short supply: discuss your needs with Alan Pollock.

Wine Rack

See **Bottoms Up**

Zachys

206 Haverstock Hill, London NW3 2AG
Tel: **0171 431 4412**   Fax: **0171 431 2360**

The last word

Zachys is a clean, neat and tidy wine merchant with a medium-sized range. Particular strengths include Australian wines, Californian wines and clarets; there's a good selection of half-bottles too. Service is pleasant and helpful, and the range is said to change frequently according to the devices and desires of customers. Indeed if customers take the trouble to register they become 'preferred', and will be invited to tastings and sent details of special purchases. The music is quiet but jolly; prices are in line with local property values.

Worth a punt

White: 1995 Riesling, Alan Scott, New Zealand £7.29; 1995 Sauvignon Blanc, Hill-Smith, South Australia £8.49; 1994 Chardonnay, Goldwater Estate, New Zealand £9.49; 1995 Sancerre, Pascal Jolivet £10.49; 1989 Riesling Kiterlé, Schlumberger £19.99.

Red: 1994 Zinfandel, Monteviña, California £5.99; 1991 Cabernet Sauvignon, Beaulieu Vineyard, California £8.69; 1991 Mishac, Grant Burge, South Australia £15.99; 1989 Clos de la Maréchale, Faiveley £23.69; 1993 Château Canon, St Emilion £28.99; 1992 Shiraz, Hill of Grace, Henschke £34.99.

Sparkling: Pongracz, South Africa £8.99; Deutz Marlborough Cuvée £10.99; Roederer Quartet £13.99; Champagne Jacques Selosse £22.99.

Fortified: Muscat Show Reserve Yalumba (half-bottle) £7.99.

Tasting facilities
No

Storage facilities
No

Nearest tube
West Hampstead

Hours
Mon-Fri 10.00am-9.00pm; Sat 10.30am-10.30pm; Sun 12.00pm-19.30pm

Minimum sale
No

Credit cards
Access/Mastercard, Visa, AmEx, Switch

Discounts
5% off mixed cases (certain wines only)

Delivery
Free within local area. Other areas by negotiation

Glass hire
Free with order

Tasting facilities
Regular tastings throughout the year

Storage facilities
No

Nearest tube
Belsize Park

National Mail-Order Specialists & Other Merchants

Wine is heavy. The great advantage of buying wine by mail order is that no physical exertion is necessary, other than leafing through a wine list, grasping a pen sufficiently firmly to fill out an order form, licking a stamp and sauntering through the late afternoon sunshine to a bright red post box. Many of the London merchants listed on the previous pages offer mail-order facilities, as do some supermarkets, but there are also some first rate wine merchants outside London from whom (thanks to quality of wine list, range of wines and standards of service) it is a pleasure to buy.

Adnams Wine Merchants The Crown, High Street, Southwold, Suffolk IP18 6DP. Tel 01502 727220, Fax 01502 727223. A beautifully written and illustrated list; wines of character and singularity.

The Australian Wine Club Freepost (WC5500), Slough, Berks SL3 9BH. Tel 01753 544546, Fax 01753 591369. Gets you into the outback of the Australian wine scene (no membership fee).

Philip Eyres Wine Merchant The Cellars, Coleshill, Amersham, Bucks HP7 0LS. Tel 01494 433823, Fax 01494 431349. Astute claret and German wine selections. Working in tandem with S.H. Jones of Banbury.

Halves Wood Yard, off Corve Street, Ludlow, Shropshire SY8 2PX. Tel 01584 877866, Fax 01584 877677. Lovely things, half-bottles: get them here.

Roger Harris Loke Farm, Weston Longville, Norfolk NR9 5LG. Tel 01603 880171, Fax 01603 880291. Beaujolais and nothing but. Fine, informative list.

Lay & Wheeler 6 Culver Street West, Colchester, Essex CO1 1JA. Tel 01206 764446, Fax 01206 560002. A reference list for every serious wine enthusiast: superb stocks, strong in every area, plus first-class standards of service. The head boy among British mail-order merchants.

Laymont & Shaw The Old Chapel, Millpool, Truro, Cornwall TR1 1EX. Tel 01872 70545, Fax 01872 223005. Spanish specialities sold with knowledge and humour.

The Nobody Inn Doddiscombsleigh, near Exeter, Devon EX6 7PS. Tel 01647 252394, Fax 01647 252978. Crazed enthusiasm sees this delicious country pub moonlighting as a wine merchant with a varied and opinionated list.

Peatlings Direct Westgate House, Westgate Street, Bury St Edmonds, Suffolk IP33 1QS. 01284 714545, Fax 01284 70575. Extensive stocks, particularly of 'little' clarets.

Raeburn Fine Wines The Vaults, 4 Giles Street, Leith, Edinburgh EH6 6DJ. 0131 554 2652, Fax 0131 554 2652. Skilled buying from Scottish virtuoso Zubair Mohammed.

Reid Wines The Mill, Marsh Lane, Hallatrow, Bristol, Avon BS18 5EB. Tel 01761 452645, Fax 01761 453642. Expanding list of well-chosen wine drinker's wines; also old and curious bottles, annotated with humiliating frankness.

T & W Wines 51 King Street, Thetford, Norfolk IP24 2AU. Tel 01842 765646, Fax 01842 766407. Leading winefinder with an extensive fine-wine list supplemented by mid-market purchases. Big range of halves, too.

Tanners 26 Wyle Cop, Shrewsbury, Shropshire SY1 1XD. Tel 01743 232400, Fax 01743 344401. Sound all-rounders with a well-balanced range, an informative list and a reputation for service second to none.

The Vine Trail 5 Surrey Road, Bishopston, Bristol BS7 9DJ. Tel/Fax 0117 942 3946. Well-selected wines from deepest France.

Frank Ward Ltd Forrest House, 193 Beach Street, Deal CT14 6LY. Tel 01304 369317, Fax 01304 366381. Hand-picked fine French wines (especially burgundy).

The Wine Society Gunnels Wood Road, Stevenage, Herts SG1 2BG. Tel 01438 741177, Fax 01438 741392. An extensive French range, together with astute selections from elsewhere summed up in one of the intelligent and discursive of all wine lists. The one-off membership fee of £20 is refundable (plus dividends) on death.

Yapp Brothers The Old Brewery, Mere, Wilts BA12 6DY. Tel 01747 860423, Fax 01747 860929. Rhône, Loire, Provence: get them here.

Noel Young Wines 56 High Street, Trumpington, Cambs CB2 2LS. Tel 01223 844744, Fax 01223 844736. Well-selected specialities from Austria and elsewhere.

Wine Bars

EROS WINE BAR OF THE YEAR

Albertine

1 Wood Lane, W12   Tel: **0181 743 9593**

The Real Thing

Albertine, this year's Eros award-winning Wine Bar of the Year, defines the genre: "We continue to be resolutely a bar and not a restaurant with the emphasis on good-value wine over a large range, substantially reflecting my own enthusiasms," says proprietor Giles Phillips. The key to the appeal of this place is that Phillips' enthusiasms are sound ones, based, so far as I can ascertain, on fine-honed tasting ability rather than friendship with a single agent (the droppings of at least five different ones are detectable) and consequent quality-compromising trade-offs and deals. The list is not only wide-ranging and full of sapid and occasionally beautiful wines, but it is also exceptionally good value: this is one of the few bars in this Guide to offer an extensive selection at under £10. The choice of wines by the glass (21) and by the half bottle (24) is exemplary; a fine-wine selection complements the main list. It's clearly organised, with accurate and well-phrased descriptions of the wines, making this the easiest of places to slide into for an evening's entertaining drinking. The food, like the wine, offers quality and keen pricing: there's a wholegrain style to it, and it's generous and successful, most of the main-course dishes costing between £4.50 and £6.50 (whereas many pubs now charge £7.50 or £8 for horribly misconceived plates of food). The appropriate euphemism for the decor is functional; some might label it scruffy (the upstairs room is more soigné). Regulars consider this lightly ragged edge part of the charm. Albertine redeems Shepherd's Bush.

Worth a punt

White: 1995 Chardonnay, Canepa £8.80 (£2.20 per 175-ml glass); 1994 Chardonnay, Two Mile Creek, Australia £9.70; 1995 Viognier, Chais Cuxac, Vins de Pays d'Oc £9.75; 1994 Bourgogne Aligoté, Goisot £12.50; 1994 Chenin Blanc, Coriole, South Australia £12.95; 1994 Sauvignon Blanc, Shaw & Smith £14.95; 1994 Chablis Vieilles Vignes, Hamelin £18.40.

Red: 1995 Merlot, MontGras £8.90 (£2.15 per 175-ml glass); 1994 Coteaux du Languedoc, Mas de Bruguière £10.30; 1991 Malbec, Norton, Argentina £10.50; 1994 Morgon, Jean Descombes £12.30; 1993 Bourgogne Pinot Noir, Chopin-Groffier £13.95; 1993 Pinot

Hours
Mon-Fri
11.00am-11.00pm;
Sat 7.00-11.00pm;
Sat 7.00pm-11.00pm

Annual closure
24 Dec-2 Jan

Credit cards
Access/Mastercard,
Visa

Seats
40 ground floor,
30 upstairs

Nearest tube
Shepherd's Bush

Noir, Firesteed, Knudson-Erath, Oregon £14.25; 1994 Grenache, Tim Gamp £15.75; 1990 Savigny-lès-Beaune, Pavelot £21.50.

Sparkling: Champagne Hostomme Blanc de Blancs £24; Champagne Vilmart Grand Cru £28.40.

Fortified/dessert: 1991 Rhine Riesling Redwood, New Zealand half-bottle £8.95 (glass £2.95); 10 Year Old Tawny Port, Quinta da Ervamoira, Ramos-Pinto glass £3.75; 1983 Château Coutet, Barsac half-bottle £16.50.

The Archduke

Concert Hall Approach, SE1   Tel: **0171 928 9370**

Underneath the arches

The good things about The Archduke are its position (very handy for the South Bank); its ingenious use of space (the original conversion of 17 years ago was clever and appealing, though it's beginning to look in need of a makeover now; time to say goodbye to those tablecloths, too); its jazz; and parts of its wine list, especially now that Paul Chadwick has returned to brush it up. The food is poor, though, and dispensed at times grudgingly and gracelessly.

Worth a punt

White: 1995 Chenin/Chardonnay Parral, Trapiche, Argentina £10.50; 1995 Chenin Blanc Azay-le-Rideau £14.95 (£3.75 per 175-ml glass); 1995 Riesling, Waipara Springs £15.95.

Red: 1995 Malbec/Sangiovese Parral, Traphiche, Argentina £10.50; 1994 Ochoa Tinto £11.50 (£2.95 per 175-ml glass); 1992 Capello di Prete £13.55.

Sparkling: 1990 Cava, Freixenet £15.95.

Fortified/dessert: Palo Cortado, Garvey £1.50 per 125-ml glass; 1992 Muscat de Rivesaltes half-bottle £8.50 (£2.75 per glass).

Bacchanalia

1a Bedford Street, Covent Garden, WC2 Tel: **0171 836 3033, 0171 240 3945**

Boogie on down

This is a spacious, friendly and relaxed wine bar in a handy location run with style by ex-City man and self-proclaimed eccentric Leon Kramer. Both wines and food are adequate but unexceptional; the wine list (with its paucity of producer names and vintages) is inadequate. The Friday-night disco ensures Bacchanalia local notoriety; even Leon Kramer admits it is 'not for

Hours
Mon-Fri
11.00am-11.00pm;
Sat 5.00pm-11.00pm

Annual closure
Christmas

Credit cards
Access/Mastercard,
Visa, AmEx, Switch

Seats
150

Nearest tube
Waterloo

Hours
Mon-Fri
11.00am-11.00pm;
Sat 5.00pm-
11.00pm

Annual closure
Bank holidays

Credit cards
All major cards

Seats
115

Nearest tube
Charing Cross,
Covent Garden

the faint-hearted'. The contrast with Café Baroque could not be greater – but that's what an area needs, after all.

Worth a punt

White: 1994 Semillon-Chardonnay, Denham Estate £10.25 (£2.60 per 175-ml glass); 1995 Sauvignon Blanc, Santa Helena £11.65; 1994 Chardonnay, Grant Burge, South Australia £16.95.

Red: 1995 Shiraz-Cabernet Sauvignon Pearl Springs, South Africa £10.25 (£2.60 per 175-ml glass); 1993 Cabernet Sauvignon, Grant Burge, South Australia £16.95.

Sparkling: Champagne Krayer £20.95 (£4.50 per flute).

Fortified/dessert: 1987 Late-Bottled Vintage Port, Delaforce half-bottle £9.95.

Balls Brothers

Head Office: 313 Cambridge Heath Rd E2   Tel: **0171 739 6466**
Gows Restaurant, 81-82 Old Broad St EC2   Tel: **0171 920 9645**
Carey Lane (off Gutter Lane), EC2   Tel: **0171 600 2720**
Bucklersbury House, Cannon St EC4   Tel: **0171 248 7557**
St Mary at Hill EC3   Tel: **0171 626 0321**
Hay's Galleria, Tooley St SE1   Tel: **0171 407 4301**
The Hop Cellars, 24 Southwark St SE1   Tel: **0171 403 6851**
20 St James's St (entrance Ryder St) SW1   Tel: **0171 321 0882**
Moor House, London Wall EC2   Tel: **0171 628 3944**
6/8 Cheapside EC2   Tel: **0171 248 2708**
42 Threadneedle St EC2   Tel: **0171 628 3850**
Great Eastern Hotel, Liverpool St EC2   Tel: **0171 626 7919**
Great Eastern Hotel Champagne Bar   Tel: **0171 626 7919**
Kings Arms Yard EC2   Tel: **0171 796 3049**
Mark Lane EC3   Tel: **0171 623 2923**
11 Bloomfield St EC2   Tel: **0171 588 4643**

Hours
Vary:
mainly Mon-Fri
11.00am-9.00pm

Annual closure
Christmas, Easter,
Bank Holidays

Credit cards
Access/Mastercard,
Visa, AmEx, Diners,
Switch

Seats
80-350

Job done

The Balls Brothers' chain is one of several to get the City lunched and then lubricated before the journey home. These bars always seem to be clean, tidy and well-run. Stylistically the aim is 'charm, intimacy and the traditional "English" atmosphere'; the props are high quality; value is good. The core wine list (which fails to cite all producers' names) is mostly European, with an increasingly prominent New World presence, reinforced with monthly wine promotions which bring in half-a-dozen or so 'specials'. There are usually about a dozen wines by the 175-ml glass chalked up on blackboards, the exact selection varying from moment to moment; 15 half-bottles, too. In general, wine standards are high (the Grand Moulas '95 offers fine value for a tenner and half-bottles of La Gitana outstanding value for a fiver), though some wines are dull (the '93 Roc de Monpézat, or

Fairview's Pinot Gris). The bar food (some have restaurants) is straightforward; sandwiches are freshly made and juicily filled. All you can really reproach these bars for, perhaps, is a lack of personality; yet given the tripartite purpose for which wine-bars are mostly used (commerce, conversation and seduction), personality is not always a desideratum – whereas efficiency always is. I'm a fan.

Worth a punt

White: 1994 Marsanne, Domaines Virginie £11.75; 1995 Sauvignon Blanc, West Peak, South Africa £12.35; 1994 Pinot Gris Patergarten, Blanck £13.75; 1994 Sancerre Chavignol, Delaporte £16.75; 1990 Meursault, Domaine Matrot £23.

Red: 1995 Côtes du Rhône Château du Grand Moulas £10.20; 1992 Ochoa Tempranillo £12; 1992 Faugères Les Bastides, Alquier £12.50; 1993 Crozes-Hermitage, Remizières £14; 1989 Château Beaumont, Haut-Médoc £21.

Sparkling: Champagne Joseph Perrier £25.

Fortified/dessert: La Gitana Manzanilla (half-bottle) £4.90; 20-Year-Old Tawny Port, Gold Cap 125-ml glass £4.20.

Blackfriars Pavilion

242 Blackfriars Road SE1   Tel: **0171 928 8689**

Discretion is all

This discreet little basement winebar, reached by a stroll over some particularly unpromising Railtrack cobblestones, is quiet and relaxed. The rather hard benches and maroon stools which provide the seating under the arch remind me, though I'm not sure why, of a nineteenth-century railway worker's carriage — perhaps it's the lace curtains at the end. You can sit outside in the summer sun, though the view is one of London's less sublime prospects. The food at lunchtime is good – close in quality to what is served in the adjacent restaurant area; wines, too, are well-chosen (the owner is wine agent Peter McKinley), though storage of open bottles under corks rather than by a wine-preservation system does not always do the quality of what's inside justice, and the list is neither a long nor wide-ranging one.

Worth a punt

White: 1995 Pinot Grigio, Ca Donini £11.95; 1994 Mâcon-Loché, Perraton £13.95 (half-bottle £7.95); 1995 Sauvignon Blanc, Jackson Estate, New Zealand £15.95.

Red: 1993 Merlot Torreon de Parades, Chile £10.95; 1994 Morgon, Marcel Jonchet £14.95; 1991 Cabernet Sauvignon,

Hours
Mon-Fri 11.00am-
9.00pm
Annual closure
Christmas, Easter,
Bank Holidays
Credit cards
Access/Mastercard,
Visa, AmEx, Diners
Seats
60, plus 20 outside
Nearest tube
Blackfriars,
Waterloo

Longridge, South Africa £16.95.

Sparkling: Champagne Gosset £23.50 (half bottle £14.50).

Fortified/dessert: Churchill's Crusting Port bottled 1987 £19.45 (175-ml glass £4.85).

EROS AWARD RUNNER-UP

Bleeding Heart

Bleeding Heart Yard, Hatton Garden EC1 **Tel: 0171 242 8238**

The wine cavern

The old cliché about 'location, location and location' being all that matters in the hospitality biz is neatly disproved by the success of the Bleeding Heart, which in some ways occupies an infernal location (so subterranean the owners scarcely need bother with central heating; so far off the tourist track that sherpas are required to locate it). Once you're there, though, you'll enjoy the Marshalsea theme to the decor, the hyper-efficient and poutingly chic French staff, the superb wine list ('55 wines under £15', including 30 by the glass – bravo) and the generally successful food. In the summer there are tables in the yard for those desperate for a view of the sky. The strengths of this list are manifold – particularly good New World wines, but well selected European options, too. At lunchtime the Heart becomes more of a bistro, in that it is assumed that almost all patrons want to sit and eat; in the evening, though, it is a true wine bar, where you can down bottles galore without so much as a mouthful of solid stuff. For the formally hungry, there is an adjacent restaurant with an even better wine list (one of London's finest – a great place for a wine treat).

Worth a punt

White: 1994 Muscadet Les Ormeaux, Sauvion £10.95 (£2.25 per 175-ml glass); 1994 Chardonnay, Monterey, California £11.95 (£2.50 per glass); 1994 Sablet Côtes du Rhône-Villages, Domaine du Terme £12.95 (£2.75 per glass); 1993 Fumé Blanc, Beringer, California £14.25 (£3.25 per glass); 1994 Chardonnay, Kumeu River, New Zealand £14.95 (£3.50 per glass); 1994 Bleeding Heart White Burgundy £14.95 (£3.50 per glass).

Red: 1995 Malbec, La Fortuna £10.45 (£2.25 per glass); 1993 Petite Syrah, L.A. Cetto, Mexico £12.95 (£2.95 per glass); 1988 Rioja Reserva, Coto de Imaz £13.95 (£3.20 per glass); 1992 Zinfandel, Beringer £14.95 (£3.50 per glass); 1994 Rosso di Montepulciano, La Casalte £14.95 (£3.50 per glass).

Fortified/dessert: 1992 Muscat de Beaumes de Venise, Domaine Coyaux £3.95 per glass.

Hours
Mon-Fri
12.00-11.00pm

Annual closure
24 Dec–2 Jan

Credit cards
Access/Mastercard,
Visa, AmEx, Diners,
Switch

Seats
65

Nearest tube
Farringdon

Hours
Mon-Thurs
12.00-11.00pm;
Fri-Sat
12.00-11.30pm;
Sun 12.00-10.30pm

Annual closure
3 days at Christmas

Credit cards
Access/Mastercard,
Visa, AmEx, Diners,
Switch

Seats
40

**Nearest BR
station**
Clapham Junction

La Bouffe

11-13 Battersea Rise SW11   Tel: **0171 228 3384**

Get wined

La Bouffe, on the sunset strip of Battersea Rise, continues to prove that there's life in the old wine-bar concept yet, and that being cool doesn't preclude drinking well. Those here for the blow-out are generally young and slender. The sketches on the wall last year have now turned into a fully-fledged mural of slender technique but ample gusto. The bar list contains about 30 wines, most of them available by the glass, with 'specials' parachuting in from time to time; I'm told you can also choose from the more ambitious restaurant list if you want, though this is not obvious in situ. Both lists are well-balanced: Cloudy Bay (even the Sauvignon, at least until it runs out) rubs capsules with Cheverny. The food is intelligently diverse (Toulouse sausages, Thai green chicken curry, imam bayaldi, ratatouille, four types of Croques), appealingly priced (none of the aforementioned costs more than a fiver) and carefully prepared. There's a terrace for stargazing or pierced-navel-gazing on beautiful Battersea nights. This seems to be the home of the Battersea Rise Temperance Cricket Club, and adventure holidays to Ecuador are advertised.

Worth a punt

White: 1994 Chardonnay, Canepa, Chile £10.95 (£2.75 per 175-ml glass); 1994 Sauvignon Blanc, Uitkyk, South Africa £13.50 (£3.40 per glass); 1992 Pinot Blanc, Schlumberger £15.95.

Red: 1994 Cabernet Sauvignon, Canepa, Chile £10.95 (£2.75 per glass); 1993 Cabernet-Shiraz, Ironstone, Western Australia £11.95 (£2.95 per glass); 1993 Côtes du Rhône, Coudoulet de Beaucastel £19.95.

Sparkling: 1991 Pelorus, Cloudy Bay £21.95.

Hours
Mon-Sat 11.00am-
11.00pm; Sun
12.00pm-10.30pm

Annual closure
Christmas Day

Credit cards
Access/Mastercard,
Visa, AmEx, Diners,
Switch

Seats
80

Nearest tube
Tower Hill

Butler's Wharf Wine Bar

The Cardamon Building, 31 Shad Thames SE1 Tel: **0171 403 2089**

Style station

This is still the best-looking wine bar in town, with its plants, canopies and caparisons; this whole district, indeed, becomes prettier by the month, probably because cars are kept at bay and people (for once) take priority. Manager Jason Howard-Ady points out that this is one of only two establishments in the area to serve hot and cold food all day, which is worth knowing since the main point of Shad Thames nowadays is to tittilate the palate. The wine list is still not as interesting as I'd like, despite a modest internationalization of the previously all-Spanish range; the cocktails, by contrast, seem prodigiously creative, and the spirit range is diverse. The tapas-style food is well-conceived though variable in quality (cordero la chilindron is meltingly good, yet the Nepalese potatoes would only work if — and we all know how difficult this is — you can purchase or grow some good potatoes to start with). The wines by the glass now number 12, and you can sit outside when the isobars allow.

Worth a punt

White: 1994 Viña Irache £9.95 (£2.65 by the 175-ml glass); 1994 Palacio de Bornos, Rueda £12.25; 1996 Chardonnay, MontGras, Chile £12.95; 1991 Rioja Monopole, Cune £14.50.

Rose: 1994 Viña Irache £9.95 (glass £2.65).

Red: 1992 Rioja Berceo Crianza £13.50; 1992 Pago de Carraovejas, Ribera del Duero £17.90; 1986 Rioja Gran Reserva Viña Real £20.50.

Sparkling: Cava Cristalino £14.95 (glass £4.50); House Champagne (H. Blin) £19.95 (glass £5.50).

Fortified/dessert: 1983 Vintage Port, Dow's glass £5.10; Puerto Fino (half-bottle) £8.95.

EROS AWARD RUNNER-UP

Café Baroque

33 Southampton Street, London WC2   Tel: **0171 379 7585**

Restauration drama

Upstairs there's a restaurant; the small zone of passage downstairs functions as a wine bar. There are none of the customary trappings and jollyisms of wine barhood; instead, just half a dozen tables covered with tablecloths, the wine list and menu, and an enquiring waiter or waitress to supply you with whatever you order. So much the better. So much decidedly the better when the wine list is as interesting as this one is, with a fine claret and burgundy range as well as wines plucked cleverly from the great beyond (white Château Musar; red Sparkling Shiraz; creative Californians). There is no shortage of options in half-bottles, by the glass or even by the sample glass (a 25-ml affair which arrives, complete with tasting notes, for as little as 30p); you are under no pressure, either, to eat if all you want to do is get quietly and stimulatedly sozzled while Handel wafts around you (live on Wednesdays). All the same, the food is good for those with an

Hours
Mon-Sat midday to midnight

Annual closure
between Christmas Day and New Year

Credit cards
Access/Mastercard, Visa, AmEx, Diners, Switch

Seats
24

Nearest tube
Covent Garden, Charing Cross

appetite: domestic familiars (sausages, haddocks, ducks, root veg-
etables) are given sympathetic roastings and grillings. All in all,
proprietor Hilary Marsh has created a most civilized and congenial spot for wine lovers to play in.

Worth a punt

White: 1992 Château Musar Blanc £17.95 (12.5cl glass £3.60;
2.5cl sample glass 85p); 1993 Pouilly-Fumé, Blanchet £19.95
(12.5cl glass £3.95; 2.5cl sample 90p); 1994 Chardonnay Au Bon
Climat £29 (12.5cl glass £4.95; 2.5cl sample glass 99p); 1993
Chassagne-Montrachet Premier Cru Jean Pillot £39.

Red: 1995 Gamay de Touraine Jacky Marteau £12.95 (12.5cl glass
£2.60; 2.5cl sample glass 60p); 1992 Crozes-Hermitage Cave des
Clairmonts £16.95 (12.5cl glass £3.40; 2.5cl sample glass 80p);
1995 Grenache Bonny Doon Clos de Gilroy £18.50 (12.5cl glass
£3.70; 2.5cl sample glass 85p); 1979 Château de Canterrane Côtes
du Roussillon £18.95.

Sparkling: 1990 Sparkling Shiraz £19.95 (12.5cl glass £3.95); André
Jacquart Grand Cru Champagne £28.50 (half-bottle £15.95).

Café Fish

Hours
Mon-Sat
11.30am-11.00pm
Annual closure
Christmas
Credit cards
Access/Mastercard,
Visa, AmEx, Diners,
Switch
Seats
35
Nearest tube
Piccadilly Circus

Basement wine bar, 39 Panton St SW1   Tel: **0171 930 3999**

Fish in crannies

This basement wine bar (underneath the ground-floor restaurant)
is small but well-nooked, an ideal place in which to plan indis-
cretions over a bivalve or two by the light of a flickery little can-
dle. (Indeed some of the clientele get beyond the planning stage.)
The wine list is short but cleverly selected and white-heavy to
partner the broadly piscatorial menu. The ingredients seem fresh,
as they should be; the cooking is artless. A little cheeseboard waits
by the fish tank; the orange juice, I overhear, is freshly squeezed
each morning – which is why it has run out. There are around
eight wines by the glass (on the blackboard) and four half-bottles.
Value is fair, and the service promises '*amour et attention*' (sic). The
latter is evident; the former a question, perhaps, of interpretation.

Worth a punt

White: 1995 Monferrato Bianco £10.50; 1995 Chenin Blanc,
Tharakkoma, South Africa £11.50; 1995 Sauvignon de Touraine,
Chapelle de Gray £11.95; 1995 Sauvignon Blanc, Casa Lapostolle
£12.95.

Red: 1994 Côtes du Roussillon, Mas de la Garrigue £12.25; 1992
Raimat Abadia £14.75.

Sparkling: Lonsdale Ridge, South Australia £15.50.

Corney and Barrow

19 Broadgate Circle EC2   Tel: **0171 628 1251**
9 Cabot Square, Canary Wharf E14   Tel: 0171 512 0397
1 Leadenhall Place EC3   Tel: 0171 621 9201
2B Eastcheap EC2   Tel: 0171 929 3220
3 Fleet Place EC4   Tel: 0171 329 3141
5 Exchange Square, Broadgate EC2   Tel: **0171 628 4367**
44 Cannon St EC4   Tel: 0171 248 1700
16 Royal Exchange EC3   Tel: 0171 929 3131

Hours
Mon–Fri
11.00am–10.30pm

Annual closure
Bank holidays

Credit cards
Access/Mastercard,
Visa, AmEx

Seats
30-350

Back to the future

The C&B entry in this Guide last year provoked a feisty response from the admirably committed managing director Sarah Heward, the gist of which was that a) far from being 'ultra-male', these were female-friendly wine bars; b) all the City stuff (clocks, currency rates, market info) was 'reassuring'; and c) no one in City wine bars wanted a wine list of any depth or variety. Since then, I've been back at least three times on separate occasions to different C&B wine bars, both alone and with female companions, in a spirit of sympathy-extending flexibility. In the end, though, my views remain broadly unchanged: these are style bars rather than wine bars. The furnishings are striking but uncomfortable; loud music bonks away in the foreground rather than the background; there are video screens with adverts for chocolate bars and petrol sandwiching endless dreary sport – indeed one bar had two sports on two screens simultaneously; there are cards promoting vodka; most of the clientele seems to drink beer or cocktails or house white; the full wine list is relatively short and relatively expensive, with a disappointingly meagre selection by the glass; there is far too much deep-fried food on the menu (served with ketchup), and little which is genuinely nourishing. I do, however, like the mugs of tea. In a last attempt at fairness, I should point out that the bars are, at key times, hugely popular – though I suspect for their style and buzz rather than the classic wine-bar virtues of good bottles in civilized and congenial surroundings. I await the post with trepidation.

Worth a punt

White: 1995 Muscadet Coteaux de la Loire, Clarac et Terrien £9.95 (£2.80 for a 175-ml glass); 1994 Fumé Blanc Staton Hills, Washington £12.50; 1995 Pouilly-Fumé Chaumiennes, Figeat £17.95; 1994 Montagny Premier Cru Les Cloux, Olivier Leflaive £21.95.

Red: 1995 Syrah, Domaine de la Jonction, Vin de Pays d'Oc £10.75; 1990 Château Bel Air, Bordeaux Superieure £12.75; 1987 Pata Negra Gran Reserva Rioja £15.95; 1990 Château des Moines, Lalande de Pomerol £18.50.

Sparkling: Champagne Delamotte £19.95 (glass £4.95).

Fortified/dessert: Corney & Barrow 10 Year Old Tawny glass £4.

EROS AWARD RUNNER-UP

The Crescent

99 Fulham Road SW3   Tel: 0171 225 2244

The mammoth

Hours
8.30am-11.00pm
Mon-Sat; 10.00am-
10.30pm Sun

Annual closure
Christmas

Credit cards
Access/Mastercard,
Visa, Switch

Seats
60

Nearest tube
South Kensington

The Crescent is, in at least one vital respect, London's leading wine bar: nowhere else has a list like this. It covers two tightly spaced A3-sized sheets and then runs on into a separate fine-wine list – over 150 different wines, all bar the fine wines fully annotated with a tasting note. In charge of selection is Matthew Jukes, the same man who puts together the wine list for Conran's Bibendum restaurant, just a door or two up the Fulham Road. All of the wine world is here, beginning with a fair-minded trawl through France's country wines, continuing with a romp through the best of the New World, cruising back through Italy and Spain's over-achievers to end with a flurry of top Bordeaux and burgundy. It's a serious attempt to bridge the gap between London's internationally renowned restaurants and its often underachieving, hand-me-down winebars. Like most new operations, of course, there are improvements to be made. The layout of the bar is unfortunate, since there is too little space upstairs (where everyone wants at present to be) and too much downstairs; the look is rather austere; the food is still finding its way. Prices by wine-bar standards are high, and the selection by the glass could usefully be broadened from eight to twenty or so (though note this selection changes regularly); the red wines served by the glass, too, need to be cooler than they were in the summer of '96. This is, though, an essential station on every wine lover's tour of London, and its heroic opening hours (breakfast onwards) means that none of us have an excuse not to visit.

Worth a punt

White: 1994 Cheverny, Domaine du Salvard £15.25; 1994 Abbaye de Valmagne Blanc, Coteaux du Languedoc £17.50; 1992 Villa Bel Air, Graves £20.95; 1994 Chardonnay, Thelema £21.95; 1986 Riesling, Clos Sainte-Hune, Trimbach (half-bottle) £23.50; 1993 Viognier, Vernay £31.50; 1993 Pouilly-Fuissé Cuvée Première, Vincent £33.95.

Red: 1994 Côtes de Roussillon Cuvée des Rocailles, Gauby £16.50; 1994 Château Mourgues de Gres, Terre d'Argence, Costières de Nîmes £17.50; 1994 Coteaux du Languedoc, Domaine de l'Hortus £19.95; 1991 Parrina Rosso Riserva £19.95; 1993 Shiraz, Primo Estate, South Australia £19.95; 1990 Carrascal, Weinert, Argentina £20.95; 1992 Valpolicella Classico La

Grola, Allegrini £26.50; 1991 Coteaux d'Aix en Provence les Baux, Domaine de Trevallon £35.

Sparkling: Champagne Billecart-Salmon £29.95.

Cork and Bottle
see **Hanover Square Wine Bar**

Davys
Bottlescrue, Bath House, 53/60 Holborn Viaduct EC1 Tel: 0171 248 2157
Burgundy Ben's, 102/108 Clerkenwell Road EC1 Tel: 0171 251 3783
City Pipe, Foster Lane, off Cheapside EC1 Tel: 0171 606 2110
City Vaults, 2 St Martin's le Grand EC1 Tel: 0171 606 8721
Colonel Jaspers, 190 City Road EC1 Tel: 0171 608 0925
Davys, 15/17 Long Lane EC1 Tel: 0171 726 8858
Bangers, 12 Wilson St EC2 Tel: 0171 377 6326
Bishop of Norwich and Bishops Parlour, 91/93 Moorgate EC2 Tel: 0171 920 0857, Parlour Tel: 0171 588 2581
City Boot, 7 Moorfields High Walk EC2 Tel: 0171 588 4766
The Pulpit, 63 Worship St EC2 Tel: 0171 377 1574
Udder Place and Udder Place Wine Rooms, Russia Court, Russia Row, 1/6 Milk St EC2 Tel: 0171 606 7252, Wine Rooms Tel: 0171 600 2165
Bangers Too, 1 St Mary at Hill EC3 Tel: 0171 283 4443
City Flogger, Fenn Court, 120 Fenchurch St EC3 Tel: 0171 623 3251
City F.O.B., below London Bridge, Lower Thames St EC3 Tel: 0171 621 0619
The Habit, Friary Court, 65 Crutched Friars EC3 Tel: 0171 481 1131
Davys, 10 Creed Lane EC4 Tel: 0171 236 5317
Shotberries, 167 Queen Victoria St EC4 Tel: 0171 329 4759
Docks Bar & Grill, 66a Royal Mint St E1 Tel: 0171 488 4144
Grapeshots, 23 Artillery Passage E1 Tel: 0171 247 8215
The Vineyard and Vineyard Coffee House Tel: 0171 480 6680
International House, Coffee House, 1 St Katharine's Way E1 Tel: 0171 480 5088
Boot and Flogger, 10/20 Redcross Way SE1 Tel: 0171 407 1184
The Cooperage, 48-50 Tooley St SE1, Tel: 0171 403 5775
Guinea Butt, Chaucer House, Tel: 0171 407 2829
White Hart Yard, Borough High St SE1
The Mug House, 1-3 Tooley St SE1 Tel: 0171 403 8343
Skinkers, 42 Tooley St SE1 Tel: 0171 407 9189
Crown Passage Vaults, 20 King St, St James, SW1 Tel: 0171 839 8831
Tapster, 3 Brewers Green, Buckingham Gate SW1 Tel: 0171 222 0561
Davys at Canary Wharf, 31/35 Fisherman's Wharf E14 Tel: 0171 363 6633
Bung Hole, 57 High Holborn WC1 Tel: 0171 242 4318
Bung Hole Cellars, Hand Court, 57 High Holborn WC1 Tel: 0171 831 8365
Truckles of Pied Bull Yard, Off Bury Place WC1 Tel: 0171 404 5338, Wine Rooms Tel: 0171 404 5334
Champagne Charlies, 17 The Arches, off Villiers St WC2 Tel: 0171 930 7737
Crusting Pipe, 27 The Market, Covent Garden WC2 Tel: 0171 836 1415
Tappit Hen, 5 William IV St WC2 Tel: 0171 836 9839

Hours
Various

Annual closures
Christmas, bank holidays

Credit cards
Access/Mastercard, Visa, AmEx, Diners, Switch

Seats
Various

The Chiv, 90/92 Wigmore St W1   Tel: **0171 224 0170**
Chopper Lump, 10c Hanover Square W1   Tel: **0171 499 7569**
Dock Blida, 50/54 Blandford St W1   Tel: **0171 486 3590**
Lees Bag, 4 Great Portland St W1   Tel: **0171 636 5287**
Gyngleboy, 27 Spring St W2   Tel: **0171 723 3351**
Colonel Jaspers, 161 Greenwich High Road SE10   Tel: **0181 853 0585**
Davys Wine Vaults, 65 Greenwich High Road SE10   Tel: **0181 858 7204**
The Wine Vaults, 122 North End, Croydon   Tel: **0181 680 2419**

The old familiar

Anyone who regularly drinks at wine bars in London will be familiar with this extensive chain. To many overseas visitors they must seem the epitome of London, with their queer names, their sawdust, their darkness, their candles, their juicy ham, their ports, their battered tankards of Old Wallop. One might turn to find the Elephant Man one's slurpy neighbour; one might imagine Jack the Ripper pacing a nearby alley in silent rage; one might half-hear Holmes playing drug-fuelled sonatas in the rooms above. For all of this, much thanks; one Davys is worth one hundred formula pubs. Davys does not offer huge choice in terms of wines or food, but what it does offer is sound and reliable, and often (a bottle of Manzanilla, a jug of 'Ordnary' Port) fine value. Better ten well-selected wines than a motley fifty, and all of the Davys' own-label wines I've tried have been good to very good; the small range makes for desirably fast turnover at this level. During the last year the list has expanded, bringing new Southern Hemisphere whites and a revised collection of clarets. For those capable of planning ahead, there is a fine-wine leaflet of grand bottles to be ordered in advance: 21 ancient Latours and some truly seigneurial port (including four '45s and three '63s). The food is very English, very straight.

Worth a punt

White: Best Bordeaux Sauvignon £9.95 (£2.50 per 175-ml glass); Davy's Muscadet sur lie £10.95 (£2.75 per glass); Chardonnay, Carmen, Chile £11.95 (£3 per glass); Chardonnay, Astonvale, South Africa £12.50 (£3.20 per glass); Davy's White Burgundy (Montagny Premier Cru) £16.50 (£4.25 per glass).

Red: Davy's Claret £9.80 (£2.50 per glass); Davy's Rioja £10.65 (£2.70 per glass); 1986 Château La Roche Beaulieu, Côtes de Castillon £13.50; Davy's Celebration Margaux £14.95.

Sparkling: Davy's Sparkling Savoie £13.95 (flute £2.50; tankard £3.95); Davy's Celebration Champagne £19.95 (flute £3.50).

Fortified/dessert: Finest Manzanilla £10.50 (£1.75 per 125-ml glass); 'Ordnary' Tawny Port £13.75 (£2.30 per glass, £11.95 per tankard); 1980 Vintage Port, Quarles Harris £34 (£5.75 per glass); 1970 Vintage Port, Graham £55 (order in advance).

Ebury Wine Bar

139 Ebury St SW1   Tel: **0171 730 5447**

Carriages, 43 Buckingham Palace Road, SW1   Tel: **0171 834 0119**

Hoults, 20 Bellevue Road, Wandsworth Common, SW17   Tel: **0181 767 1858**

Joe's Brasserie, 130 Wandsworth Bridge Road, SW6   Tel: **0171 731 7835**

West-side story

The Ebury Wine Bar is a familiar West London landmark, known as much for good food (of challenging diversity) as for its shortish but well-annotated wine list; in some ways, Carriages and Hoults are truer wine bars, in that the onus on eating isn't so evident. The selection of ten or so wines by the glass is fair; prices, with little under £10, are fairly expensive. The wine selection does go where the value is, though (hence the present emphasis on good wines from the Midi and Chile). The Ebury is cheerfully decorated, with droll little messages painted on the walls. It has saved the lives of those serving time in Victoria Coach Station before now.

Worth a punt

White: 1994 Bianco di Custoza Tereza Rizzi £10.50 (£2.80 for 175-ml glass); 1995 Chardonnay, MontGras, Chile £12.50; 1994 Menetou-Salon, Domaine du Catenoy £17.50 (half bottle £9.90); 1994 Sauvignon Blanc, Shaw & Smith, South Australia £19.50.

Red: 1993 Teroldego Rotaliano Ca Donini £12.50 (glass £3.30); 1994 Château Mourgues du Gres '94, Costières de Nîmes £15; 1994 Merlot Reserva, MontGras, Chile £18; 1993 Pinot Noir, Firesteed, Oregon £19.50.

Fortified/dessert: 1992 Morsi di Luce, Pantelleria (half-bottle) £12.50 (£4.20 for 120-ml glass).

Hours
Mon-Sat
11.00am-11.00pm

Annual closure
Christmas, Boxing,
New Years Day

Credit cards
Access/Mastercard,
Visa, AmEx, Switch,
Diners, Transmedia

Seats
76

Nearest tube
Sloane Square

El Vino

Head Office: 1-2 Hare Place, Fleet St EC4   Tel: **0171 353 5384**

47 Fleet St EC4   Tel: **0171 353 6786/7541**

6 Martin Lane, Cannon St EC4   Tel: **0171 626 6876/6303**

30 New Bridge St EC4   Tel: **0171 236 4534/5548**

Alban Gate, 3 Bastion Highwalk, 125 London Wall EC2   Tel: **0171 600 6377**

Softly, softly

"There is no danger of 'infanticide' here!" proclaims Graham Mitchell in the spring 1996 edition of *El Vino News*. Indeed not. Those who thirst after time-rounded, age-softened, maturely gentle wines will find plenty of them at El Vino: they make up the core of the list. Such infants as are offered for sacrificial purposes are generally those intended to be taken young – like La Fortuna's

Hours
Mon-Fri
11.30am-8.00pm

Annual closure
Christmas

Credit cards
Access/Mastercard,
Visa, AmEx

Seats
Around 100

Chilean Sauvignon Blanc, which Mitchell endearingly describes as "a real 'Tigger' of a wine". During the last year, a fourth tasting house has been added to the El Vino estate, situated at a tranquil station of the Alban Highwalk: its spaciousness redeems its modernity (though the 'horsebox' design, and instantly smoke-yellowed wallpaper, contrives to make it feel older than it really is). No one, as I've said before, can really call themselves a Londoner until they've drunk in the Olde Wine Shades: the authentic relic among capital wine bars. The El Vino Advantage, as I'm sure they wouldn't call it, is range: the full list can be drunk (and purchased on a retail basis) at all four branches. The food is as soft and rounded as the wines: sandwiches, salmon, pies and puds.

Worth a punt

White: 1995 Sauvignon Blanc, La Fortuna, Chile £9.90; 1994 Pinot Blanc, Alsace £10.70; 1994 Chardonnay, Château Reynella, Australia £14.95; 1993 Rully £15.20; 1993 Mercurey Les Mauvarennes, Faiveley £19.00.

Red: 1993 Côtes du Rhône, Domaine des Romarins £10.20; 1992 Côtes de Beaune-Villages £14.00; 1990 Château Monlot-Capet, St Emilion Grand Cru £16.70 (half bottle £9.15); 1986 Crozes-Hermitage, Domaine de Thalabert, Jaboulet £19.95; 1989 Château Beau-Site, St Estèphe £20.15; 1990 Morey St Denis £19.20.

Sparkling: Champagne Louis Boyier £19.90 (half-bottle £10.75, glass £4.40, magnums £41.80).

Fortified/dessert: No.1 Manzanilla per 125-ml glass £1.80; 1982 Vintage Port, Offley Boa Vista per 125-ml glass £5.80.

Hours
Mon-Fri 11.00am-11.00pm

Annual closure
Christmas, public holidays

Credit cards
Access/Mastercard, Visa, Access, Diners

Seats
110 (70 in garden)

Nearest tube
Farringdon

The Fence

67-69 Cowcross Street EC1   Tel: **0171 250 3414**

Right side of the tracks

The Fence is a newish wine bar opened by Neil Tyler, who used to work at Vat's. It looks good: lots of pale wood and space, with more space outside in the plantless garden, fenced off from the Metropolitan and Circle lines, for summer evenings. The wine list has made a good start, with a wide, well-selected spread encompassing everything from Western Australia's Leeuwin to Sussex's Breaky Bottom via Durup in Chablis and Trimbach in Alsace; 13 by the glass. How much these delights are appreciated by the locals I don't know, since Red Stripe seemed to be the favoured tipple when I dropped in, but perhaps that was my fault for choosing a Thursday night (party time: live jazz with associated jiving and japes). The bar menu is straightforward and unambitious; the full menu tries harder. Prices are high (nothing worthwhile under £10).

Worth a punt

White: 1995 Long Flat White, Tyrrells £10.95 (£2.75 per 175-ml glass); 1992 Seyval Blanc, Breaky Bottom £13.50; 1995 Sancerre, Saget £17.95 (glass £4.50); 1992 Gewürztraminer, Trimbach £18.95.

Red: 1994 Cabernet Sauvignon, Montes, Chile £12.50; 1994 Pinot Noir Redwood Trail, California £12.50 (glass £3.25); 1992 Tempranillo, Ochoa £14.75; 1993 Gevrey-Cambertin, Rodet £35.

Sparkling: Mumm Cuvée Napa Rosé £17.50.

Fortified/dessert: 1977 Vintage Port, Smith Woodhouse £48.50 (£9.50 per 125-ml glass).

Gascogne

12 Blenheim Terrace NW8   Tel: **0171 625 7036/7034**

A turn on the terrace

Gascogne is a friendly neighbourhood wine bar in a neighbourhood which can sometimes seem low on friendliness. The upstairs section is small and largely dominated by the handsome, mirror-backed bar, but there is a large terrace for when the weather allows and a downstairs, too. It isn't a great wine list, but there's enough to have fun with. The food, on my visits this year, seemed to have improved – the vegetable flan is particularly good; and peeled, seeded cucumber in the salad suggested efforts beyond the norm. The clean and tidy look is encouraging.

Hours
11.00am-11.00pm

Annual closure
25th-27th December

Credit cards
Access/Mastercard, Visa, AmEx

Seats
40

Nearest tube
St John's Wood

Worth a punt

White: 1995 Chenin Blanc, Paarl Heights, South Africa £10.95 (£2.50 for a 175ml glass); 1995 Chardonnay, Stellenryk, South Africa £15.15; 1993 Rully, Domaine de la Bressande £23.50.

Red: Cuvée Jean-Paul £8.50 (£2.25 per glass); 1994 Shiraz, Aston Vale, South Africa 13.50 (£3.25 per glass); 1993 Cabernet Sauvignon Reserva, Caliterra £17.35; 1990 Mercurey, Domaine du Château de Mercy £27.

Sparkling: Laurent Perrier Rosé Champagne £40.

EROS AWARD RUNNER-UP

La Grande Marque

47 Ludgate Hill EC4   Tel: **0171 329 6709**

Bank check

Lay & Wheeler, the Colchester wine merchant which is a part-owner in La Grande Marque, is impressively efficient and

Hours
Mon-Fri
11.30am-9.30pm

Annual closure
Christmas, Easter, Public holidays

Credit cards
Access/Mastercard,
Visa, AmEx, Switch
Seats
70
Nearest tube
St Pauls, Blackfriars

thorough; it's no surprise, then, that this former bank on Ludgate Hill should now be one of the best of the City's wine bars. The conversion is superb: varnished wooden tables separated by screens with grape motifs; uplighters illuminating an elegant patterned wallpaper and a fine plaster ceiling; a pretty tiled floor and a marbled central service aisle. The list is much improved on last year; indeed for my money it is model in every respect: ample choice (100 wines, with 13 half-bottles and 25 wines by the glass), high quality, options for most occasions (including Yquem and foie gras for two, with one hour's notice, for when your proposal is accepted – a mere £175; or if you're on a budget two glasses of the superbly tangy Ostra Manzanilla for under a fiver). The glassware is elegant, in contrast to most; the food stretches beyond the basic sandwich portfolio to a small selection of imaginative hot dishes; the place usually looks spotless; for the time being there is no building next door so one can admire the setting sun as the wine takes hold. Admirable.

Worth a punt

White: 1994 Sauvignon Blanc, Château Nicot, Bordeaux £12.75 (£2.50 per 175-ml glass); 1995 Muscadet du Sèvre-et-Maine sur lie, Chereau Carré £11.95; 1995 Chardonnay Reserve, Santa Rita, Chile £13.75 (£2.90 per glass); 1994 Sauvignon Blanc, Frog's Leap, California £18.50 (£4.10 per glass).

Red: Lay & Wheeler Claret £12.95 (half-bottle £6.50, glass £2.50); 1992 Salice Salentino Reserva, Candido £14.50; 1991 Lirac, Domaine Les Queyrades £17.50; 1994 Pinotage, Uiterwyk £22.50.

Sparkling: Gobillard Brut Grande Réserve Champagne £20.95 (glass £4.50).

Fortified/dessert: Ostra Manzanilla glass £2.30; Oloroso Especial, Hidalgo glass £2.80; Lay & Wheeler 10 Year Old Tawny glass £2.75.

Hours
Mon-Fri
11.00am-11.00pm

Cork & Bottle:
Mon-Sat 11.00am-
12.00am; Sun
12.00pm-10.30pm
Annual closures
Public holidays
Credit cards
Access/Mastercard,
Visa, AmEx, Diners
Seats
130

Hanover Square Wine Bar

25 Hanover Square W1   Tel: **0171 408 0935**

Cork & Bottle, 44-46 Cranbourne St WC2   Tel: **0171 734 7807**

Domain of the Don

There can't be many Londoners who haven't been into the Cork and Bottle at one time or another; I remember it as being uncomfortably crowded twelve years ago, and on my inspection visits this year it still was uncomfortably crowded, but customers obviously like what they find there. Indeed faced with the stinking, fast-food wasteland of Leicester Square, I like what I find there, despite the heaving masses. The newer Hanover Square

Wine Bar is more spacious, calmer. The Installation of satellite televisions in both of them seems an intrusive and distracting move, detracting from what wine bars should offer: good wine and good conversation. Nonetheless the Hewitson package – whatever you want to eat or drink at any time during opening hours – remains central to the wine bar ideal, and Don does buy some extremely good wines. Just as importantly, he writes them up in his list with infectious if swollen-headed enthusiasm, and it is this communication of excitement which is the key to Hewitson's success. Not all the wines are brilliant – Don's apparent inability to follow the grammar of this entry last year led to my being misquoted in the list about the far-from-perplexing Wolf Blass wines (see page xx Wolf Blass Sth Australia if you want to know my real opinion, Don); while at the other stylistic extreme I still find the Listel rosé a fruitless and dreary wine, despite Don's protestations. The Champagnes remain patchy, something that (since there is a Hewitson book on Champagne) is genuinely perplexing. Hewitson is at his best in his French red selections, with antipodean small producers, and with Chardonnay in general. Prices are high for both wines (almost nothing under £10) and food – dishes of the day on my last visit were £10.95 and £12.95. The sausages, though, have improved. Service is generally efficient. Wines by the glass are not listed, but chalked on blackboards; ditto for fortified and dessert wines. Hanover Square has a wine club which organises tutored tasting evenings with food – both fun and good value.

Worth a punt

White: 1994 St Véran les Plantes £14.95; 1994 Chardonnay, Rothesay, Collards, New Zealand £22.50; 1993 Chardonnay, Russian River Ranches, Sonoma-Cutrer £22.50; 1993 Chassagne-Montrachet Premier Cru Clos St Jean £29.50.

Red: 1991 Coteaux du Tricastin Domaine du Vieux Micocoulier £11.95; 1993 Château Belregard-Figeac, St Emilion Grand Cru £18.95; 1991 Cabernet Sauvignon, Coonawarra, Mildara £18.95; 1988 Gran Reserva '125 Anniversario' Chivite, Navarra £18.95.

Sparkling: Mumm Cuvée Napa Rosé £16.95; Blanc de Blancs Chardonnay, Henriot £32.50.

Hours
12.00pm-1.00am
Annual closure
Christmas and
Easter: 4 days each
Credit cards
All major cards
Seats
100
Nearest tube
Holland Park

Julie's Bar

137 Portland Rd W11   Tel: **0171 727 7985**

Where squirrels dine and butterflies fret

Julie's Bar is a beautifully strange place. Press on through the parlour-like front room into the fern-hung bar/restaurant, pass the butterflies frozen fretfully for eternity in their glass case, carry on up the stairs where squirrels are taking dinner in another glass case, find a seat among the ecclesiastical woodwork, gaze at the light-warming stained glass, listen to the curious Aboriginal music filling the air. Who needs wine? For those that do, the list is modest in length and, until recently, only modestly inventive. However it took a marked turn for the better in the summer of 1996, and further improvements are promised before publication with the 'revamping' of the bar (which I hope doesn't lead to the eviction of the squirrels). The food has always been inventive (Stilton, watercress and walnut terrine; grilled West Indian spiced chicken with banana) and, generally speaking, skilfully prepared, an advantage of those bars which, like this one, are serviced by a restaurant kitchen. The staff dress with gratifying inventivity, too.

Worth a punt

White: 1995 Muscadet Carte d'Or sur lie £9.95 (half-bottle £6); Chardonnay, Domaine Leasingham, South Australia £14.95; 1994 Mâcon Lugny, Cuvée Etienne Chevalier £15.25; 1993 Château Millet, Graves £16.95.

Red: 1995 Château du Grand-Moulas, Côtes du Rhône £9.95; 1994 Merlot Reserva, Montgras, Chile £11.95; 1992 Shiraz, Botolobar, New South Wales £13.50; 1987 Château Duhart-Milon-Rothschild, Pauillac £25.95.

Sparkling: Champagne Ellner £27 (half-bottle £13.50; glass £5).

Fortified/dessert: 1989 Late-Bottled Vintage Port, Graham half-bottle £10.85 (glass £2.75).

Hours
Mon-Sat 7.30am-
11.00pm
Annual closure
Christmas
Credit cards
Access/Mastercard,
Visa, AmEx, Diners
Seats
50
Nearest tube
Knightsbridge

Le Metro

28 Basil St SW3   Tel: **0171 591 1213**

In a glass of its own

Le Metro, last year's Wine Bar of the Year, continues to offer exceptionally good food and a well-chosen range of wines, many of them served by the glass. The location (a basement within staggering distance of Harrods) remains useful; the decor agreeably neutral; the service efficient. What it lacks in personality it more than makes up for in quality – to be able to eat pan-fried halibut on butter beans and leeks, pork loin with prunes and lentils or deep-fried tiger prawns with saffron mash and wash it down with glasses of Langi's Ghiran Shiraz, Louis Jadot's Rully La Fontaine or Shaw and Smith's Sauvignon Blanc, pursue a conversation in relative tranquility, and emerge into the Knightsbridge air with change from thirty pounds is extraordinarily meritorious. The word is out, though, and you may need to book, especially at lunch time.

Worth a punt

White: 1994 Gewürztraminer Réserve, Turckheim £13 (£3.25 per 175-ml glass); 1993 Riesling, Schloss Johannisberger £15.95 (£3.95 per glass); 1994 Sauvignon Blanc, Shaw and Smith, South Australia £17.00 (£4.25 per glass); 1993 Rully La Fontaine, Jadot £18.00 (£4.50 per glass); 1993 Chardonnay, Hess Collection, California £24.50 (£5.85 per glass).

Red: 1992 Crozes-Hermitage, Cave de Tain £11.50 (£2.90 per glass); 1991 Corbières, Château Lastours £13.50 (£3.30 per glass); 1992 Shiraz, Mount Langi Ghiran, Australia £19.50 (£4.75 per glass); 1990 Merlot, Weinert, Argentina £19.95 (£4.80 per glass).

Sparkling: Bollinger Champagne £45 (£9.25 per glass).

Fortified/dessert: 1991 Recioto di Soave 'Le Columbare', Pieropan £22 (£5.75 per 125-ml glass); 1981 Warre's Traditional Late Bottled Vintage Port £33 (£4.25 per glass).

EROS AWARD RUNNER-UP

Morgan's

4-6 Ganton St W1   Tel: **0171 734 7581**

First things first

This always gives the impression of being a high-effort wine bar, and quality and standards of both food and wine seem to improve yearly. 4-6 Ganton St, while convenient for both the shopping and nightlife zones of town, isn't an easy set of premises – every bit of the bar seems to be tiny, and those venturing downstairs into the mirrored blue lagoon in search of intimacy will certainly find it. There are so many nooks and crannies I wouldn't be surprised to come across a minotaur enjoying a glass of Chardonnay here (the clientele is, as it happens, particularly diverse). The full menu is, admirably, available at any time between midday and 10.45 at night, with tapas from 3.30pm onwards: there is lots of variety, prices are reasonable and thoughtful touches (little dishes of soured cream with the vegetable chilli, for example) suggest care in the kitchen.

Hours
Mon-Sat
11.00am-11.00pm

Annual closures
Bank holidays

Credit cards
Access/Mastercard,
Visa, AmEx, Diners

Seats
70

Nearest tube
Oxford
Circus/Piccadilly
Circus

The wine list, likewise, is one of laudable diversity and keen pricing (the vast majority of the list costs less than £15). All the wines are given tasting descriptions, and no less than 38 are available by the glass; there's a classy beer list, too. Service can at times be slow, largely I suspect because of the difficulty of locating customers in a popular bar built like a Swiss cheese. John Morgan deserves success and with it, perhaps, a further bar or two.

Worth a punt

White: 1995 Muscaté Sec, Alasia £10.90 (£2.65 per 175-ml glass); 1995 Chardonnay, Carlyle Estate, Victoria £11.90 (£2.90 per glass); 1988 Riesling Kabinett Hallgartner Schönhell, Matuschka-Greiffenclau £12.90; 1995 Sancerre les Roches, Vacheron £16.50 (£3.95 per glass); 1994 Chardonnay, Poole's Rock, New South Wales £16.90 (£4.05 per glass).

Red: 1993 Cahors, Château Eugénie, Couture £11.90; 1993 Vigneto San Lorenzo, Rosso Conero, Umani Ronchi £11.90 (£2.90 per glass); 1994 Cabernet Sauvignon, Carlyle Estate, Victoria £11.90 (£2.90 per glass); 1989 Château Haut-Logat, Haut-Médoc £15.90 (£3.80); 1991 Barolo di Serralunga d'Alba, Fontanafredda £16.90 (£4.05 per glass); 1994 Shiraz, Mount Langhi Ghiran £16.90 (£4.05 per glass).

Sparkling: House Cava £13.50 (£3 per glass).

Fortified/dessert: Muscat de Saint-Jean de Minervois £13.50 (£2.20 per glass).

Odette's

130 Regents Park Road, NW1   Tel: **0171 722 5388**

Down you go

Hours
Mon-Fri
12.30pm-2.30pm,
5.30pm-11.00pm;
Sat 12.30-3.00pm,
5.30-11.00pm;
Sun 12.30-3.00pm.

Annual closure
Christmas

Credit cards
Access/Mastercard,
Visa, AmEx, Diners,
Switch, JCB

Seats
45

Nearest tube
Chalk Farm

Odette's wine bar (downstairs, beneath the multi-mirrored restaurant) was exiled to the limbo of the now-defunct 'In Contention' section last year because it is in truth more bistro than wine bar. Arrive at 7:30 in the evening and you will find tables laid for dinner and a waitress asking you if you've booked; whereas the true wine bar, it seems to me, is a place where those who merely want to sit and drink can do so at any time. Odette's Wine Bar doesn't seem quite laid-back enough to feel like a wine bar. The quality of the wine list, however, is excellent – selected, organised and annotated with great intelligence and offering a superb selection by the glass; the food, too, is innovative, stimulating and offers good value (especially the £10 Sunday lunch). Service is brisk and efficient. You can prop up the ferociously neat and tidy bar if you wish, and if there's space you can sit and drink and slob about to your heart's content, even if those around you are 'out for dinner'. The photographs of naked locals are diverting. Odette's merits, in other words, make my fastidiousness about genre seem footling: tuck in.

Worth a punt

White: Riesling, Moenchhof £12.50 (£4 per 175-ml glass); 1994 Viognier, Domaine Etang de Colombes £15.75 (£4.25 per glass); 1994 Pouilly-Fumé Les Berthiers, Claude Michot £19.95 (half-bottle £10.90, £5.65 per glass); 1991 Gewürztraminer, Rolly Gassmann £21.50 (1993 half bottle £15.50).

Red: 1991 Rioja Crianza, Viña Real £14.25 (half-bottle 1992 £8.70; glass £4.25); 1994 Bonny Doon Big House Red £16.95 (glass £4.50); 1990 Cahors, Domaine de Paillas half-bottle £10.90 (glass £5.25); 1985 Château Bon Pasteur, Pomerol £62.50.

Sparkling: Champagne Drappier Carte d'Or £32.50 (half-bottle £17.95).

Fortified/dessert: Manzanilla La Gitana, Hidalgo £3.50 per 75-ml glass; White Port, Niepoort £3.95 per glass; 1991 Recioto di Soave, Suavia half-bottle £21.95.

Over the Hill

96 Alexandra Park Road, Muswell Hill N10   Tel: **0181 444 2524**

Drop in for a chat

This friendly, slightly chaotic Muswell Hill bar makes a pleasant resting spot for an hour or two; it's one of those rare places in London where everyone seems to know everyone else, and if they don't you'd have to be determinedly monosyllabic to remain incognito after a visit or two. The wine list is short but contains one or two good bottles (though vintages and producers need to be listed for all wines rather than at random); there's a large if mixed bag of beers, too. Inexpert touches (grubby glasses, badly stored bottles, grilled cheese "which if it saw the grill did so from a great distance", Virgin Radio) can let the side down, even though everyone may be having fun.

Worth a punt

White: 1994 Riesling, Stoneleigh, New Zealand £12.50 (£2.50 per 175-ml glass).

Red: 1994 Rioja, Marqués de Griñon £10 (£2.10 per glass); 1993 Chinon, Domaine du Puy Rigault £14.

Sparkling: Cava, Freixenet £12 (£2 per glass).

Hours
11am 11pm
daily

Annual closure
25-26 December

Credit cards
Access/Mastercard,
Visa

Seats
40

Nearest tube
East Finchley,
then bus

The Pavilion

Finsbury Circus Gardens, Finsbury Circus EC2   Tel: **0171 628 8224**

Hours
Mon-Fri
11.30am-8.30pm
Annual closure
Christmas
Credit cards
Access/Mastercard,
Visa, AmEx
Seats
30
Nearest tube
Moorgate/Liverpool St

Rus in urbe

The Pavilion, a small wooden building gazing out onto the manicured verdure of the City of London Bowling Club greens, makes a fine wine bar – and a calming contrast to the officescapes in which most of the clientele have passed their morning. David Gilmour's wine list is exceptionally well-organized and annotated, and the wines he buys (on personal buying visits in the case of the French selections) are to a high standard. The food is simple (three hot dishes and a range of cold options) in recognition of the one real drawback of The Pavilion: it's too small. If you want to have a table for lunch, you'll need to arrive at 12:15 or so; all the food is designed to be eaten standing if necessary. The list contains so many interesting wines (and is so well annotated, too) that it's worth returning after work to discuss a further bottle or two. Wines by the glass (either 125ml or 175ml; flutes 170ml) and pichet (600ml) vary: they are those stationed on the bar with little labels round their necks like wartime evacuees. The closed front door (a regulatory requirement) adds to the clubby feel.

Worth a punt

White: 1994 Pinot Blanc, Staehlé £11.50; 1993 Jasnières, Gigou £15; 1994 Rioja Conde de Valdemar £15.50; 1993 Hautes Côtes de Nuits Blanc, Jayer-Gilles £20; 1993 Chardonnay, Swanson Vineyards, California £22.

Red: 1992 Minervois, Château d'Argères £12.50; 1993 Shiraz, Capel Vale, Western Australia £14; 1994 Pinot Noir, Devil's Lair, Western Australia £18.50; 1993 Maranges Premier Cru Clos des Loyères, Girardin £19; 1995 Château d'Issan, Margaux £30.

Sparkling: Champagne Ailerons et Baie £24 (flute £4.80).

Fortified/dessert: Manzanilla La Gitana, Hidalgo £11.50 (half bottle £5.75; large glass £2.80l; small glass £1.90); Ten Year Old Tawny Port, Fonseca £20 (large glass £4.90, small glass £3.40).

Pimlico Wine Vaults

12/22 Upper Tachbrook St SW1   Tel: **0171 834 7429**

St Paul's Wine Vaults, 29-33 Knightrider St EC4   Tel: **0171 236 1013**

The bottle dungeon

This pleasant SW1 wine bar has one of the strangest vestibules in London: you take the stairs down into a long corridor on either side of which bottles lurk in cells like felons. The passage is said to run under an undertaker's — thus (for a change) the living pass beneath the dead. The bar itself is quite spacious, the fabrics and furnishings making it seem like a living room, the evening candlelight softening it, the once-weekly live jazz galvanising it; there are popular, good-value monthly wine tastings, too. The list, Eldridge Pope's, is well-selected and helpfully annotated, and there are now 25 wines by the glass to chose from as well as a separate fine wine list for when you're flush. The menu isn't large, but is imaginatively conceived, and hot dishes are available in the evenings as well as at lunchtimes, something which is by no means the wine-bar norm. Prices are reasonable throughout. See also **Reynier Wine Library**.

Worth a punt

White: 1994 Costières de Nîmes, Château Lamargue £8.95 (£2.30 per 175-ml glass); 1993 Chairman's White Burgundy, Rodet £13.50 (glass £3.40); 1994 Sancerre, Clos de la Crêle £16.95 (half bottle £8.95); 1993 Savennières Clos du Papillon £16.95.

Red: 1993 Coteaux du Languedoc, Abbaye de Valmagne £10.50 (glass £2.70); 1994 Barbera del Piemonte, Giordano £10.95 (glass £2.75); 1993 Black Shiraz, Andrew Garrett, South Australia £13.95; 1993 Cabernet Sauvignon, Gundlach-Bundschu, California £16.95.

Sparkling: 1990 Chairman's Champagne £26.95.

Fortified/dessert: La Gitana Manzanilla, Hidalgo half-bottle £6.50 (£2.35 per 125-ml glass); Chairman's Late Bottled Port £16.95 (half-bottle £8.50; glass £2.85).

Hours
Mon-Fri 11.00am-11.00pm

Annual closure
Bank holidays, Christmas and New Year

Credit cards
Access/Mastercard, Visa, AmEx, Delta, Switch

Seats
140

Nearest tube/ BR station
Victoria/Pimlico

Pissarro's

1,3 and 5 Kew Green, Kew, Richmond   Tel: **0181 948 2049**

Gardener's delight

The biggish, rangy wine bar within sniffing distance of Kew Gardens looks, with its farmhouse wooden furniture, sienna walls, hop festoons, old beams and horseshoes, like a country pub, though the remorseless traffic on the red route outside soon disabuses those leaving of any pastoral idyll they might have

Hours
Mon-Sat 11.30am-11.00pm; Sunday 12.00pm-10.30pm

Annual closure
Christmas

Credit cards
Access/Mastercard, Visa

293

Seats
80
**Nearest tube/
BR station**
Kew Gardens/
Kew Bridge

slipped into. The Green has changed since Pissarro painted his *Fête à Kew*, a reproduction of which hangs in the bar. It's a relaxed, good-time kind of place ('slightly raffish' is the owner's description) with a wide cross-section of customers – men in blazers with floozies, the mobile-phone set, the odd quiet botanist; both food and wine are appealingly priced. The wine list is mid-length, not particularly ambitious or original but usefully annotated and with something for most tastes; the food (fish pie, shepherd's pie, chicken curry) ditto; the muzak ditto. The big wine press occupies the space of at least two tables, a generous concession to atmosphere.

Worth a punt

White: 1995 Bianco di Custoza, Rizzi, £9.80 (175-ml glass £2.30); 1995 Marsanne, Domaine Montmarin, Vin de Pays des Côtes de Thongue £11.20; 1994 Mâcon-Azé, Georges Blanc £14.70.

Red: Richmond Ridge Red, Australia £9.20 (£2.20 per glass); 1994 Château Lasfons, Côtes du Roussillon £10; 1994 Grenache-Shiraz, Owens Estate, Austalia £12.90.

Sparkling: Vauban Frères Champagne £24.10 (half-bottle £15.60)

Fortified/dessert: 1994 Muscat de Rivesaltes, Cazes £21 (half-bottle £11.85, 50-ml glass £2.80).

Hours
Mon-Fri 11.30am-
2.00pm
Annual closures
Bank Holidays,
Christmas and New
Year
Credit cards
Access/Mastercard,
Visa, AmEx, Switch
Seats
Upper Tachbrook St:
32
Trinity Square: 45
**Nearest tube/
BR station**
Victoria/Pimlico

Reynier Wine Library

16 Upper Tachbrook St, SW1   Tel: **0171 828 0039**
The Basement, 43 Trinity Square, London EC3. Tel: **0171 481 0415**

The choice is yours

The deal here is that, for £8.95 (£9.75 in The Basement) you can eat as much buffet food as you want and drink anything stocked by the adjacent wine shop for the shop-shelf price plus £1 corkage. As with the Pimlico Wine Bar (q.v.), the selection is that of Eldridge Pope; there's well over 100 wines to chose from. Obviously it makes most sense to chose something special: two of you could share a bottle of Grand-Puy-Ducasse '90 or Vincent's Pouilly-Fuissé Vieilles Vignes '93 and eat lunch for under £20 each. It's popular: get there early. (Note La Réserve in Walton Street, listed in the merchant section, also offers the same facility.)

Worth a punt

White: 1995 Gewürztraminer, Dopff & Irion £7.57 (half-bottle £4.72); 1993 Savennières Clos de Papillon, Baumard £9.35; 1993 Chablis Premier Cru Montée de Tonnerre, Durup £11.23 (half-bottle £6.56); 1993 Pouilly-Fuissé Vieilles Vignes, Vincent £22.08 (half-bottle £12.32).

Red: 1989 Toro Gran Colegiata Reserva, Fariña £6.93; 1993 Châteauneuf-du-Pape Cuvée Classique, Domaine de Monpertuis £11.56 (half-bottle £6.84); 1989 Château Potensac, Medoc £15.05; 1990 Château Grand-Puy-Ducasse, Pauillac £19.55.

Sparkling: Carte Corail Sparkling Rosé, Baumard £7.91; 1990 Chairman's Blanc de Blancs Champagne £21.49; Moët & Chandon Brut Impériale £22.13 (half-bottle £12.10, quarter bottle £7.30).

Fortified/dessert: 1989 Chairman's Dessert Wine (Château de Berbec) £7.79 (half-bottle £5.05); 1975 Anjou, Moulin Touchais £22.52.

St Paul's Wine Vaults

See **Pimlico Wine Vaults**

Vats

51 Lamb's Conduit St WC1   Tel: **0171 242 8963**

Staging post

This old-established wine bar looks its age — the bare floor boards and bare tables make few concessions to charm, and the bare bar in the back room looks like something in a village hall used for a bring-and-buy sale. Sitting out on the pedestrian precinct in the summer provides most decorative diversion. The wine books on display are old and very tatty; the pictures on the wall are framed promotional wine posters of ancient date. The wine list has kept up with the times a little better: mid-length, mid-priced, with a number of more expensive French bottles for the mobile-phone-wielding middle-aged men who hang out here, emitting roars of spivvy laughter from time to time. The menu is quite imaginative by wine-bar standards, yet expensive, too: you'd get much better value, for example, at La Bouffe or Morgans. Still there's no other options at all around here — the secret, I suspect, of Vat's perennial success.

Worth a punt

White: 1993 Seyval Blanc, Breaky Bottom £12.95; 1994 St Véran Domaine des Deux Roches £16.95; 1992 Gewürztraminer, Trimbach £17.95 (half-bottle 1991 £10.50).

Red: 1993 Château de Cabriac, Corbières £10.95; 1987 Rioja Reserva, Cune £14.95; 1994 Crozes-Hermitage La Petite Ruche, Chapoutier £15.50; 1991 Cabernet Sauvignon, Montes Alpha, Chile £17.95.

Sparkling: Mumm Cuvée Napa Rosé £16.95.

Hours
Mon-Fri
12pm-11pm

Annual closure
Christmas (2 weeks),
public holidays

Credit cards
Access/Mastercard,
Visa, AmEx

Seats
75

Nearest tube
Holborn

Index

Index

Index

Index

Index

Index